Elephants and Kings

THOMAS R. TRAUTMANN

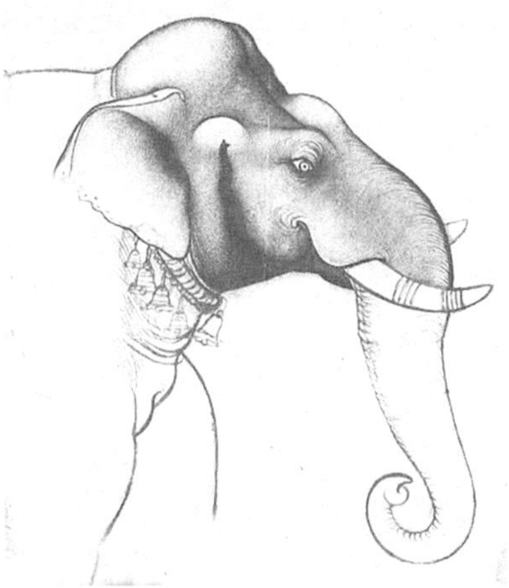

Elephants and Kings

An Environmental History

THE UNIVERSITY OF CHICAGO PRESS
Chicago and London

THOMAS R. TRAUTMANN is professor emeritus of history and anthropology at the University of Michigan. He is the author of many books, including *Dravidian Kinship, Lewis Henry Morgan and the Invention of Kinship, Aryans and British India*, and *India: Brief History of a Civilization.*

The University of Chicago Press, Chicago 60637

Printed in the United States of America

24 23 22 21 20 19 18 17 16 15   1 2 3 4 5

ISBN-13: 978-0-226-26422-6 (cloth)
ISBN-13: 978-0-226-26436-3 (paper)
ISBN-13: 978-0-226-26453-0 (e-book)
DOI: 10.7208/chicago/9780226264530.001.0001

LIBRARY OF CONGRESS CATALOGING-IN-PUBLICATION DATA
Trautmann, Thomas R., author.
Elephants and kings : an environmental history / Thomas R. Trautmann.
pages : maps ; cm
Includes bibliographical references.
ISBN 978-0-226-26422-6 (cloth : alk. paper) — ISBN 978-0-226-26436-3 (pbk. : alk. paper) — ISBN 978-0-226-26453-0 (e-book) 1. Elephants—War use—India—History. 2. Asiatic elephant—India—History. 3. India—History, Military. 4. India—Kings and rulers—History. 5. Asiatic elephant—Ecology—India—History. 6. Forest conservation—India—History. I. Title.
UH100.5.E44T73 2015
355.4'24—dc23

2014035716

Published for the world, excluding South Asia, by arrangement with Permanent Black, Ranikhet and New Delhi.

♾ This paper meets the requirements of ANSI/NISO Z39.48-1992 (Permanence of Paper).

Contents

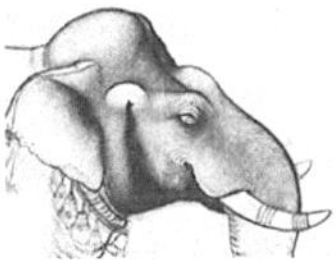

Illustrations

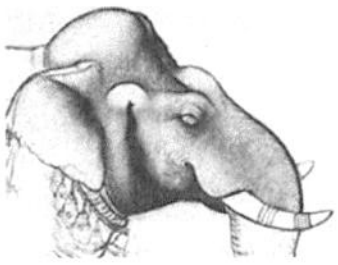

Chapter 1

Chapter 2

Chapter 7

Chapter 8

Sources and credits

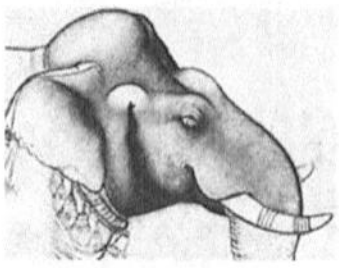

1.1 After Wen Huanran 1995: 213. Map Nicole Scholtz, Elisabeth Paymal.

1.2 After Wen Huanran 1995: 214. Map Nicole Scholtz, Elisabeth Paymal.

1.3 After Sukumar 2011: 318. Map Elisabeth Paymal.

1.4 After Trautmann 1982: 265, Map 2. Map Elisabeth Paymal.

1.5 Data from EFT Report 2005: 158–61. Map Nicole Scholtz, Elisabeth Paymal.

1.6 Data from Habib 1982. Map Nicole Scholtz, Elisabeth Paymal.

1.7 Data from Habib 1982. Map Nicole Scholtz, Elisabeth Paymal.

1.8 Mayer 1885, 5: 509. Digitization Wikipedia.

1.9 MacPhee ed. 1999: 258. Drawing Patricia J. Wynne. With kind permission from Springer Science and Business Media.

1.10 After Spate and Learmonth 1967: 47, Fig. 2.1. Map Elisabeth Paymal.

2.1 Marshall 1951, vol. 3, pl. 170, u, v. Reprinted with the permission of Cambridge University Press.

2.2 After Chowta 2010: 116, pl. 2. Drawing Elisabeth Paymal.

2.3 Davies 1973 vol. 2, pl. XXIII. Courtesy Art Resource/ Metropolitan Museum of Art.

2.4 Maspero 1903: 137. Drawing Faucher-Gudin.
2.5 Wooley and Mallowan 1976. Photo University of Pennsylvania. Courtesy University of Pennsylvania.
2.6 Frankfort 1936: 95, Fig. 73. Courtesy of the Oriental Institute of the University of Chicago.
2.7 Laufer 1925, Figs. 1–7.
2.8 Hunan Provincial Museum. © Asian Art & Archaeology, Inc./CORBIS.
2.9 Courtesy Harappa.com.
2.10 Courtesy Harappa.com.
2.11 Kenoyer 1998: 166. Photo Richard H. Meadow/Harappa.com. Courtesy Dept. of Archaeology and Museums, Govt of Pakistan.
3.1 Soar 2007: 180, Fig. 22.1.
3.2 © Trustees of the British Museum.
3.3 Smith 1924: 276 (facing).
4.1 Akbarnama. © Victoria and Albert Museum, London.
4.2 Akbarnama. © Victoria and Albert Museum, London.
4.3 Akbarnama. © Victoria and Albert Museum, London.
5.1 Drawing Rebecca Grapevine.
5.2 After Davies 1959: 6. Map Elisabeth Paymal.
5.3 After Davies 1959: 13. Map Elisabeth Paymal.
6.1 Data from Scullard 1974: 207, Fig. 19, Rance 2003, and Bosworth 1973 . Map Rebecca Grapevine, Nicole Scholtz, Elisabeth Paymal.
6.2 Svoronos 1904: 2, pl. V, no. 9.
6.3 Budge 1907, 2: 150.
6.4 Fukai et al. 1983, pl. XI. Permission of the Institute for Advanced Studies on Asia, The University of Tokyo.
6.5 Canepa 2009: 97, Fig. 17. Photo Matthew P. Canepa. Copyright © 2010, The Regents of the University of California.
6.6 The Louvre, OA 9063. Photo Chuzeville, Louvre. © RMN-Grand Palais/Art Resource, NY.

7.1 Taylor and Aragon 1991: 64. Drawing Marcia Bakry. Courtesy the Smithsonian Institution.
7.2 Taylor and Aragon 1991: 65. Drawing Marcia Bakry. Courtesy the Smithsonian Institution.
7.3 Poncar and Maxwell 2006: 29. Photo Jaroslav Poncar. Courtesy Jaroslav Poncar.
7.4 Poncar and Maxwell 2006: 28. Photo Jaroslav Poncar. Courtesy Jaroslav Poncar.
7.5 Poncar and Maxwell 2006: 12. Photo Jaroslav Poncar. Courtesy Jaroslav Poncar.
7.6 Jacq-Hergoualc'h 2007: 62. © Presses Universitaires de France.
7.7 Raffles 1817: 296 (facing).
7.8 Quaritch Wales 1952: 201–2. Courtesy Bernard Quaritch Ltd.
8.1 Russell 1877: 282 (following). Engraving Sydney P. Hall.

Preface

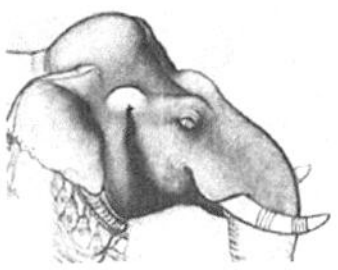

SIMON DIGBY'S *WAR-HORSE AND ELEPHANT in the Dehli Sultanate: a study of military supplies* (1971) is a great favorite of mine. It was a favorite of my students too, who loved it so much they would forget to return it after taking away my copy to read. And who can blame them? The power it holds over those who get it in their hands is such that they cannot bear to part with it.

This immortal work shows that the power of the Delhi Sultanate lay in its strategic location between the Ganga and the Indus valleys, and on the ability of its kings to control the eastward flow of horses and the westward flow of elephants—to the disadvantage of other North Indian kingdoms. It introduced me to the long-term structure of military supply for Indian kings that stretched back two thousand years from the time-horizon of Digby's book, and forward for the better part of a thousand. Digby helped me grasp, for a period much before the one of which he wrote, the significance of Megasthenes' testimony that the Mauryan emperor held a *monopoly* of horses, elephants, and arms. This condition was starkly different from that of the Vedic period, which shows a warrior class definable by its *ownership* of horses, elephants, and arms. The contrast points to the novelty and power of the Mauryan army over all other Indian states of the day and accounts for its success in creating the first Indian empire. It also supplies the key to unlock a statement of Strabo. The Greek writers on India, said Strabo, were liars because they contradicted one another. Megasthenes' account of the Mauryans opposed that of Nearchus, who described an India in which horses and elephants were privately owned, and everyone went about on some sort of animal mount or in an animal-drawn conveyance. I showed that the contradiction disappeared when one understood, as Strabo had not, that Megasthenes was describing the newly growing eastern power of the Mauryas, with its novel policy of a royal monopoly of the sinews of war, centered upon the Ganga valley. Nearchus on the other hand was describing an old-style late-Vedic regime of private ownership in the valley of the Indus, to the northwest. This idea got published as "Elephants and the Mauryas" (1982).

I believed the article had "legs," and that there was very much more to be said about elephants and horses—but especially elephants, and in relation to Indian kingship. I collected materials as I came across them, such as the Sanskrit texts on elephant science and the British-Indian literature on elephant management and care; the early work of Armandi, *Histoire militaire des éléphants* (1843), and Scullard's admirably thorough account, *The elephant in the Greek and Roman world* (1974). I was fortunate to attend a one-day seminar by a great elephant biologist, the late Jeheskel Shoshani, who was then at Wayne State University; I joined the Elephant Interest Group of the American Society of Mammalogy to get the journal he edited. My idea was to write a book about elephants in relation to kingship, and as a problem of military supply. It would be framed in a long time period and provide the kind of deep history perspective that has always appealed to me.

After many years filled with other projects, the elephant book finally came to the front of the queue. At that very moment, I came upon the work of Wen Huanran on the distribution of wild elephants and other animals in China, and the stages of their retreat or demise as documented in Chinese sources from ancient times to the present. I first learned of the book by Wen when reading another, by Mark Elvin, *The retreat of the elephants* (2004). This builds a masterful environmental history of China around the idea that the range of elephants shrank as the Chinese sphere of kingship and agriculture expanded. Both books showed me that while my topic was one of military supply, it had a profoundly environmental-history dimension. From Elvin and Wen I got the direction of this book: the relation of Indian kings to the forest and its inhabitants; above all, to forest people and elephants. It became evident that a comparison of Indian and Chinese land-use and animal domestication could bring out the special features of the relation of kingship to forest in India.

These were the formative influences. The execution was greatly assisted by the works of Raman Sukumar, whose lifelong dedication to the physiology, environment, and behavior of Asian elephants has made him the leading expert. His first book, *The Asian elephant: ecology and management* (1989) is a monograph based on fieldwork in South India which greatly improves upon the knowledge of wild elephants purveyed by writings of the colonial period. His most recent one, *The story of Asia's elephants* (2011), is a wide-ranging overview of the Asian elephant in human history. The former is my rod and my staff for the physiology and behavior of wild elephants. The comprehensiveness of the latter allows a more specialized work such as the present one to focus upon its core questions without having to deal with issues secondary to it.

The book was made possible by help from many friends.

Robbins Burling, my first reader, believes as I do that merciless critique of a piece before its publication is the sincerest form of friendship.

As the topic took me far afield of my own skills I had the pleasure of learning from the special knowledge of those I know and admire: on ancient Egypt, John Baines, Janet Richards, and Salima Ikram; on Assyria and Mesopotamia, Piotr Michalowsky; on China, Michael Hathaway (who introduced me to Elvin's book) and Charles Sanft; on Alexander and Hellenistic history, Ian Moyer and Pat Wheatley; on Southeast Asia, Robbins Burling, John Whitmore, Victor Lieberman, and Robert McKinley; on environment and ecology, Raman Sukumar, Surendra Varma, Kathleen Morrison, and Sumit Guha; on captive elephants and mahouts, Surendra Varma; on elephant history, Daniel Fisher. For help during fieldwork in India and Cambodia I am grateful to

Upinder Singh, Valmik Thapar, Divyabhanusinh Chavda, Vibodh Parthasarathi, Iqbal Khan, Kushlav and Tara, Kenneth Hall, and Gene Trautmann. I am deeply grateful to them all, more than I can say. As ever, my good friends Theodore Baskaran and Thilaka were generous with hospitality and encouragement.

Aspects of the book were first tried out as talks at the Centre for Ecological Sciences, Indian Institute of Science, Bangalore; Environmental History Group, Jawaharlal Nehru University; Department of History, Delhi University; the Center for South Asian Studies, University of Michigan; the University of Otago; the Symposium on Human–Elephant Relations, University of Canterbury, Christchurch NZ; and the South Asia Conference, University of Wisconsin. I am grateful to these institutions and to Raman Sukumar, R. D'Souza, Upinder Singh, Farina Mir, Will Sweetman, and Piers Locke for invitations to speak.

I am profoundly grateful to Rebecca Grapevine for her splendid work as my research assistant and electronics mentor. I especially appreciate her work on forming the database for the "battles and sieges" map (Fig. 6.1), itself a tough battle and a long siege. Nicole Scholtz was unfailingly generous of her time and expertise in generating digital versions of four of the maps (Figs 1.5–7, 6.1). Elisabeth Paymal drew the final versions of all the maps.

The research was funded by the Mellon Foundation through a Mellon Emeritus Fellowship, with matching funds from the College of Literature, Sciences and the Arts, University of Michigan, for which I am deeply grateful. The Department of History, its staff and its then chair, Geoff Eley, were especially helpful. My thanks to them all.

I am among the lucky many upon whom Rukun Advani of Permanent Black has conferred the inestimable benefit of his editorial mastery and friendly good sense. My luck was doubled when the project came also under the care of David Brent at the University of Chicago Press.

Translations from ancient sources are as indicated in the bibliography, though I have sometimes altered passages I quote to better bring out my sense of the original.

1

The retreat and persistence of elephants

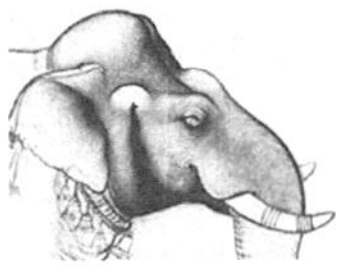

IN THE LAST TWO CENTURIES, THE NUMBERS of wild elephants in the world have crashed. Their very survival is a cause for concern.

Population counts of wild animals are inherently difficult, even for animals as large as elephants, and the results are subject to a large element of uncertainty. But the information we have is clear enough: there are still ten times as many African elephants as Asian ones, with population estimates in the order of 500,000 and 50,000, respectively. However, although the African elephant population far outnumbers the Asian, it is declining more rapidly because of poaching for the international ivory market, with very strong demand from East Asia. While the Asian elephant population is better protected by national governments and is even increasing in some places, it too is endangered by the high price of ivory. The future of African and Asian elephants depends upon uninterrupted institutional effort to protect them from the variety of human forces making for their destruction. The survival of wild elephants is uncertain and requires continuous, determined, and effective measures from governments; wild elephants have become wards of the state.

Given the threat, it is helpful to learn everything we can about the causes of elephant *retreat*. It may be even more helpful to understand the causes of their *persistence* in face of forces pushing them toward extinction. This book is devoted to the elephant and its relation to humans in India. It focuses on kingship in India and on the places influenced by Indian royal elephant use—from North Africa and Spain to Indonesia—as well as on the environmental entailments of such use. It takes a long view of how the present situation came about over the past five thousand years.

India and China

Because the focus is on India, the Asian elephant will be at the forefront of the book, although the African elephant will feature during discussions of when Indian elephant culture spread to North Africa. An overview of the Asian elephant population in recent times, therefore, is a good place to begin.[1] I give the figures in descending order of the higher numbers of the range.

India	30,770	–	26,390
Myanmar	5,000	–	4,000
Sri Lanka	4,000	–	2,500
Indonesia	3,400	–	2,400
Thailand	3,200	–	2,500
Malaysia	3,100	–	2,100
Laos	1,000	–	500
Cambodia	600	–	250
Bhutan	500	–	250
Bangladesh	250	–	150
China	250	–	200
Vietnam	150	–	70
Nepal	125	–	100
Total	**52,345**	–	**41,410**

India has the greatest number by far, about 30,000 of the total of some 50,000. Of these the largest population is in South India, in the forests of the Western Ghats where the borders of the states of Tamilnadu, Karnataka, and Kerala come together. The second largest is in the states of the North East—Assam, Meghalaya, and Arunachal. Tame elephants make up about 3,500 of India's elephant population.[2] The neighboring countries in South Asia also have

[1] Sukumar 2011: 319.

[2] Varma 2014; surveyed in Varma, *et al.* 2008, 2009.

elephant populations, Sri Lanka containing the largest, with small numbers in Bhutan, Bangladesh, and Nepal. There is no report for Pakistan, whose elephant population today is insignificant. Wild elephants do not recognize international boundaries, of course, and there is considerable movement of elephants back and forth where the terrain allows.

The countries of Southeast Asia also have substantial numbers of elephants, namely those of the peninsula: Myanmar, Thailand, Malaysia, Laos (once a kingdom called Lan Xang, land of a million elephants), Cambodia, and Vietnam. In Indonesia wild elephants are found in the island of Sumatra, but whether Java had wild elephants in historic times is uncertain. Wild elephants are also found in the Indonesian province of Kalimantan and the Malaysian state of Sabah on the island of Borneo. We know that to supply the rulers of Southeast Asia's "Indianizing" kingdoms there was a considerable maritime trade in tamed elephants in medieval and early modern times, and that the essentially Indian-style use of elephants by kings in Southeast Asia continued after the coming of Islam. In particular, the raja of Sulu was supplied with elephants by the East India Company in 1750, which may be the source of the current wild population. However, it is difficult to distinguish feral elephants that came from the maritime trade from remnant populations of a deeper past: the case of Borneo is still disputed.[3] It is however agreed that the elephants in the forests of the Andaman Islands in the Bay of Bengal, belonging to India, are feral descendants of tamed elephants imported for work in the industry abandoned as recently as 1962.[4]

China is also on the list, near the bottom, with 250–200 wild elephants. All of them are in the mountainous province of Yunnan in the southwest, adjoining Myanmar: in other words, in habitat resembling that of Southeast Asia. Their number is so small that China could be left out of the story. But that would be a mistake, for in historic times wild elephants were found more or less

[3] Sukumar 2011: 217–18.
[4] Ibid.: 278.

throughout China. Moreover, Yunnan has become a center of environmentalism in China, with the protection of elephants at its forefront.[5]

Wen Huanran documented the existence of wild elephants in China over the last 7,000 years, and their retreat to the Yunnan area.[6] Mark Elvin made use of Wen's studies in his magisterial work on the long-term environmental history of China, *The retreat of the elephants* (2004). Both these are important to the present study in that they establish a point of comparison with India.

Wen's work on elephants was part of a larger project tracking the changing distribution of certain species of plants and animals in the historical record. He says that when elephant remains were found in the Yin (Shang) ruins at Anyang, Henan Province, in the 1930s, they were interpreted as those of imported tamed elephants from Southeast Asia, it being unknown at the time that wild elephants were once distributed throughout China. Several gifts of tamed elephants from kings of Southeast Asia to the Chinese emperor have been recorded in historical texts of the Ming period, which was perhaps the basis of the 1930s conjecture.[7] Only later was the former wide distribution of elephants in China established by paleontology and an examination of the written sources of ancient Chinese history. It then came to be understood that, by stages over the last several thousand years, wild elephants had been killed off or driven away from all the provinces of China except Yunnan, a fact well established yet not widely known outside the country.

Wen's map of elephant distribution in China was developed out of ninety data points from many regions, representing the finds of elephant remains or written references to live elephants or both (Fig. 1.1). From the chronological patterning of these data points Wen interpolated boundary lines representing the northernmost

[5] Hathaway 2013.

[6] I am grateful to Charles Sanft for translating the relevant chapters (15, 16, 17) of the book for me. See Bibliography, s.v. Wen Huanran 1995, for the details.

[7] Details of this are in Chapter 8.

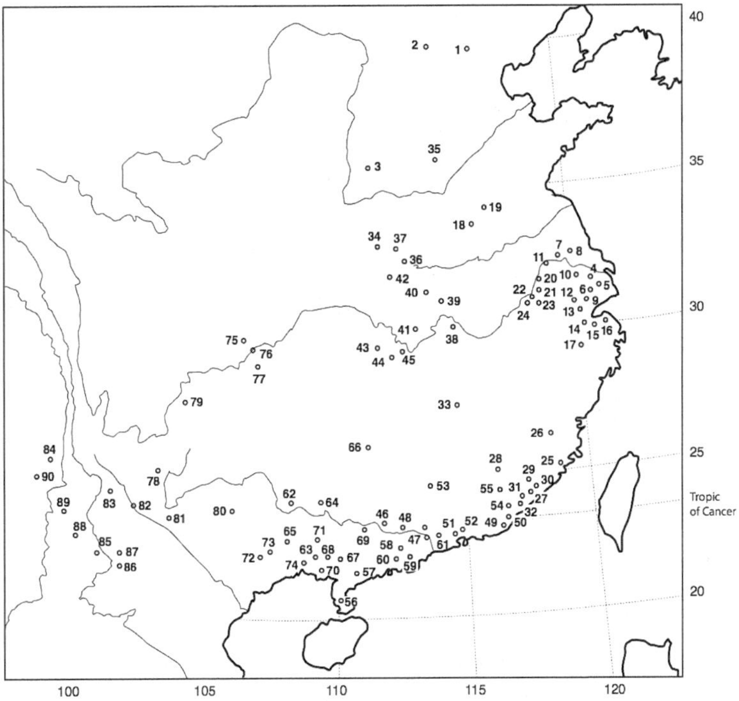

Fig. 1.1: Map of data points for elephants in China

Beijing: 1. Guohui Avenue (Beijing).
Hebei: 2. Yangyuan.
Shanxi: 3. Xiangfen.
Shanghai: 4. Jiading 5. Maqiao (part of Shanghai) 6. Hongjiang.
Jiangsu: 7. Yangzhou 8. Taizhou 9. Wujiang 10. Suzhou 11. Nanjing.
Zhejiang: 12. Huzhou 13. Tongxiang 14. Xiao Mtn. 15. Shaoxing 16. Yuyao 17. Dongyang.
Anhui: 18. Bo pref. 19. Dang 20. Dangtu 21. Wuhu 22. Fanchang 23. Nanling 24. Tongling.
Fujian: 25. Hui'an 26. Minhou 27. Zhangpu 28. Wuping 29. Zhangzhou 30. Longhai 31. Yunxiao 32. Zhao'an.
Jiangxi: 33. Anfu.
Henan: 34. Xichuan 35. Anyang 36. Tanghe 37. Nanyang.
Hubei: 38. Ezhou 39. Huangpi 40. Anlu 41. Mianyang 42. Xiangfan.
Hunan: 43. Li pref. 44. Anxiang 45. Huarong.

Guangdong: 46. Fengkai 47. Nanhai 48. Gaoyao 49. Huyang 50. Shantou 51. Huizhou 52. Huiyang 53. Shaoguan 54. Huzhou 55. Mei pref. 56. Haikang 57. Huazhou 58. Xinxing 59. Enping 60. Yangjiang 61. Dongwan.

Guangxi: 62. Du'an 63. Ling Mtn. 64. Liujiang 65. Nanning 66. Quanzhou 67. Bobai 68. Pubei 69. Teng pref. 70. Hepu 71. Heng pref. 72. Ningming 73. Chongzuo 74. Qinzhou.

Sichuan: 75. Tongliang 76. Chongqing 77. Qijiang.

Yunnan: 78. Kunming 79. Zhaotong 80. Guangnan 81. Gejiu 82. Yuanjiang 83. Jingdong 84. Tengchong 85. Mengyang (part of Jinghong) 86. Mengla 87. Yiwu (part of Mengla) 88. Ximeng 89. Cangyuang 90. Yingjiang.

limit of wild elephant distribution at a given time. The lines on the map give snapshots of the distribution at different periods. Taken together they give a picture of the consistent southwestward retreat of wild elephants over the whole course of Chinese civilization till today, when but a few hundreds are left in pockets of Yunnan (Fig. 1.2). Wild elephants once roamed China from about 40° to 19° north latitude, but now the northernmost limit is about 25°.

How to interpret the retreat of elephants in China? Wen argues that climate was the prime cause, reinforced by human action—forest clearance for agriculture, and ivory hunting. In his view the evolution of the Asian elephant has given it attributes that make it an especially sensitive indicator of changes in its environment: principally its large size and consequent need for large quantities of food and water, but also the slowness of its reproductive cycle (two-year gestation, single birth, long interval between births) and its vulnerability to cold. Being highly specialized by its size, the elongation of its trunk, and the structure of its teeth (development of tusks from incisors, reduction of teeth numbers to four massive molars at a time), its requirements of warmth, sunlight, water, and food are high and its ability to adapt to changes in its environment relatively low. The overall direction of climate change in China over the past 7,000 years or more, according to Wen, has been from warmer to colder, although within that trend there have been shorter periods of reversal. The climate pattern matches the

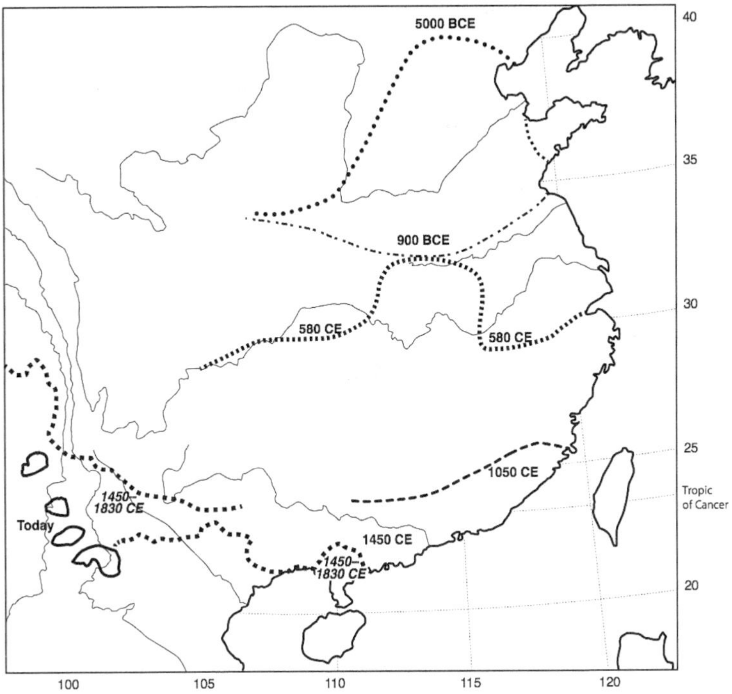

Fig. 1.2: Map of the northern limit of elephant range in China at different periods

southward shift of the northern limit of the wild elephant range, which at times went up or down on account of minor reversals in the overall trend. Writing from a natural history perspective over a fairly long period of time, Wen puts climate at the fore among the causes of elephant retreat in China. But human activities, a close second to climate change, caused ecological damage that put the elephant in its present endangered condition. The wanton capture and killing of elephants in the historical period—that is, the span of Chinese civilization—has been calamitous for them, Wen argues.[8]

Elvin accepts this argument and the special status of the wild elephant as the equivalent of the miner's canary for environmental

[8] Wen 1995: 185–201.

history. He reproduces Wen's map early in his book to set the stage.[9] He pays due respect to climate change but gives greater weight to the human causes of environmental degradation. While Wen's orientation is in the direction of natural history, Elvin's is more toward human history.

Elvin focuses on deforestation and the expansion of cultivation, which he tracks in great, indeed extraordinary, detail through a wide range of Chinese sources, both literary and governmental. In his analysis humans waged a 3,000-year war upon elephants, and the elephants lost. Right from the beginning, in the culture of the Zhou dynasty, from which classical Chinese civilization emerged, there was a "war against wild animals generally."[10] Is this put too strongly? Charles Sanft analyzes imperial statutes from the Qin and Western Han periods which decree seasonal limits on the taking of wildlife, prohibiting it during seasons of growth (especially spring and summer) and permitting it in times of fallow.[11] The proscriptions are against the taking of pregnant animals, foals and fetuses, eggs and nests of birds and fish, the felling of timber, and hunting by setting fire to grasslands. The regulations, he argues, show the existence of a conservationist intent, although it was not effective in preventing the environmental degradation that Elvin makes so evident. This finding alters the story insofar as Elvin's formulation of the "war" concerns human, especially royal, intentions. But it does not alter his book's general argument about the results of human action on the environment.

Elephants function in Elvin's narrative as bellwether and symptom of a general environmental degradation. This he emphasizes at the outset to establish the prime fact of elephant retreat. Elephants serve as a leading example of his more general object of study: the environment as a whole in its decline before the forces of Chinese civilization. Once elephant retreat has been placed in evidence, the book goes on to identify the human agents and processes responsible for the general distress of wildlife in

[9] Elvin 2004: 10.
[10] Ibid.: 11.
[11] Sanft 2010.

China, of which the elephant is taken to be the emblematic species. The war against elephants was fought on three fronts: first, the clearing of forests for farming; second, the defense of farmers' crops through the extermination or capture of elephants; and third, the hunting of elephants for their ivory and trunks (considered a delicacy by gourmets), for war, transport, and ceremonial uses.[12] In my reading of the evidence on the relation of king to elephant in China, the use of elephants for war was rare and seems to have been practised only by non-Han peoples. Unlike India's well-developed culture of the war elephant, in China the war elephant never became an institution.

Elvin surveys the rich written record of the environment in Chinese history, philosophy, literature, and religion, and indeed devotes three long chapters to ideas of nature and the emergence of a proto-environmentalist attitude in these writings. He concludes that though the vast written record of China's past is hugely informative for environmental history, attitudes of reverence for nature were largely ineffective as conservation measures. This is an important point with wide implications, worth quoting at length:

> Finally, the history of values and ideas as outlined here presents a problem. A problem not just for our understanding of China's past but for environmental history generally. The religious, philosophical, literary and historical texts surveyed and translated in the foregoing pages have been rich sources of description, insight, and even, perhaps, inspiration. But the dominant ideas and ideologies, which were often to some degree in contradiction with each other, appear to have little explanatory power in determining why what seems actually to have happened to the Chinese environment happened the way it did. Occasionally, yes. Buddhism helped to safeguard trees around monasteries. The law-enforced mystique shrouding Qing imperial tombs kept their surroundings untouched by more than minimal economic exploitation. But in general, no. There seems no case for thinking that, some details apart, the Chinese anthropogenic environment was developed and maintained in the way it was over

[12] Elvin 2004: 9–18.

> the long run of more than three millennia because of particular characteristically Chinese beliefs or perceptions. Or, at least, not in comparison with the massive effects of the pursuit of power and profit in the arena provided by the possibilities and limitations of the Chinese natural world, and the technologies that grew from interactions with them.[13]

So, characteristic beliefs and perceptions of nature have very little effective play in the environmental history of China. The real motor, Elvin persuasively shows, is the pursuit of power and profit, a finding with profound implications for historians of India, whose written sources are mainly generated by religious specialists. That said, when China's land-use pattern is compared to that of France, as in Elvin's book, or with that of India, as in this one, the Chinese pattern seems more than a simple effect of the pursuit of power and profit. It appears to be a fundamental choice or preference about how land should be partitioned among its uses: what I shall call a *land ethic*—a dominant ideology in its own right, however much the texts may propound its opposite.

The striking difference between India and China in this matter, I propose, lies not in literary, philosophical, or religious ideas, but in the relation of kings to elephants. To come right to the point, Indian kingdoms and the Indianizing kingdoms of Southeast Asia are states in which wild elephants were captured and trained for war, whereas the use of the war elephant never took root in China. Indeed, we may say that though Chinese kings were exposed to warfare using elephants, they refused to adopt it as a battle technique. An India–China comparison on this matter will involve examining many differences, including the garden-style agriculture of China and its intensive reliance on human labor, as against Indian agriculture with its reliance on domesticated animals and the pasturing of grazing animals. We can use the history of the war elephant to shed further light on the subject: it helps explain the contrast between on the one hand China where elephants have largely retreated, and on the other India and

[13] Ibid.: 471.

Southeast Asia where wild elephants, though largely in retreat over recent times, have persisted.

Elephants and horses

The distribution of Asian elephants today, and the former range from which they have retreated, is shown in Fig. 1.3. In it we see that the former distribution of Asian elephants includes the larger part of China, as Wen has documented. It also includes large territories of India and Pakistan, making up the western half of the Indian subcontinent, and a slender territory westward, reaching Syria.

The retreat of elephants, then, shows a dramatic shrinkage at the eastern and western extremities of the range, so that they are now restricted to the countries in the middle, i.e. those of South and Southeast Asia, and the province of Yunnan in China. Within these the present distribution is highly partitioned into isolated islands of elephant habitat within an ocean of human habitation. The retreat mapped here occurred in historic times, which is to say it happened during the period of those early civilizations

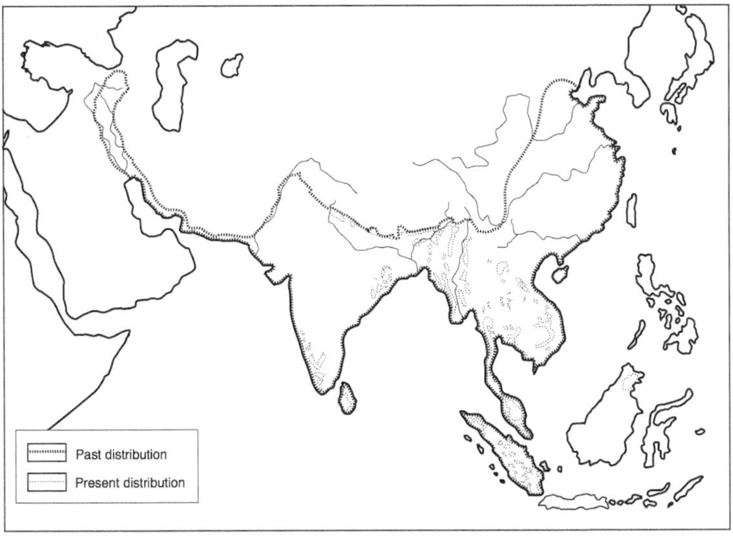

Fig. 1.3: Map of current and earlier distribution of Asian elephants

that have left written documents. From this archive we can, to some extent, trace the causes and tempo of their decline, which coincided with the expansion of the earliest literate civilizations that record it.[14]

Within the large history of an Asia-wide *retreat* of wild elephants to their present greatly reduced range there is also a history of the *persistence* of elephants in parts of India and those of its neighbors. To get a more detailed picture of the range of wild elephants in ancient India, we can look to the eight elephant forests (*gaja-vanas*) mentioned in Sanskrit texts (Fig. 1.4). The list appears in the *Arthaśāstra* of Kauṭilya, a Sanskrit treatise on kingship that will figure large in this book; it names the eight forests and grades their elephants for overall quality. The *Arthaśāstra* is the earliest known text the list appears in; the date of the treatise is debated but most would agree it was written two thousand years ago or earlier.[15] Four later texts give the same list of eight elephant forests: it had obviously become a stock list. The later texts also specify the boundaries of the forests, allowing us to draw a map of them.[16]

The boundaries of the eight elephant forests in this map are approximations. There will of course have been settled areas within these forests. There will also have been afforested areas which probably had elephants but are not shown with separate boundaries in our sources.[17] The list was fashioned from a northern

[14] The interactions of these early civilizations with elephants is examined in Chapter 2.

[15] See Chapter 5 for the debate on the date.

[16] The sources on the eight elephant forests: a commentary on the *Arthaśāstra*, the *Nītinirṇīti* of Yogamma also known as *Mudgavilāsa*, date unknown, from a twelfth-century manuscript; the *Hariharacaturaṅga* of Godāvaramiśra, minister to the sixteenth-century king Pratāparudradeva of Orissa, titled Gajapati or "Lord of Elephants"; two manuscripts called *Gajaśāstra*, one from the Saraswati Mahal Library in Tamilnadu and the other from the library of the Raja of Aundh in Maharashtra, attributed to Pālakāpya Muni, legendary transmitter of the elephant science to mankind (but perhaps late; see Chapter 5); and the *Mānasollāsa* of king Someśvara III Cālukya, composed in 1131 CE.

[17] Specifications of boundaries in the source texts are analyzed in Trautmann 1982.

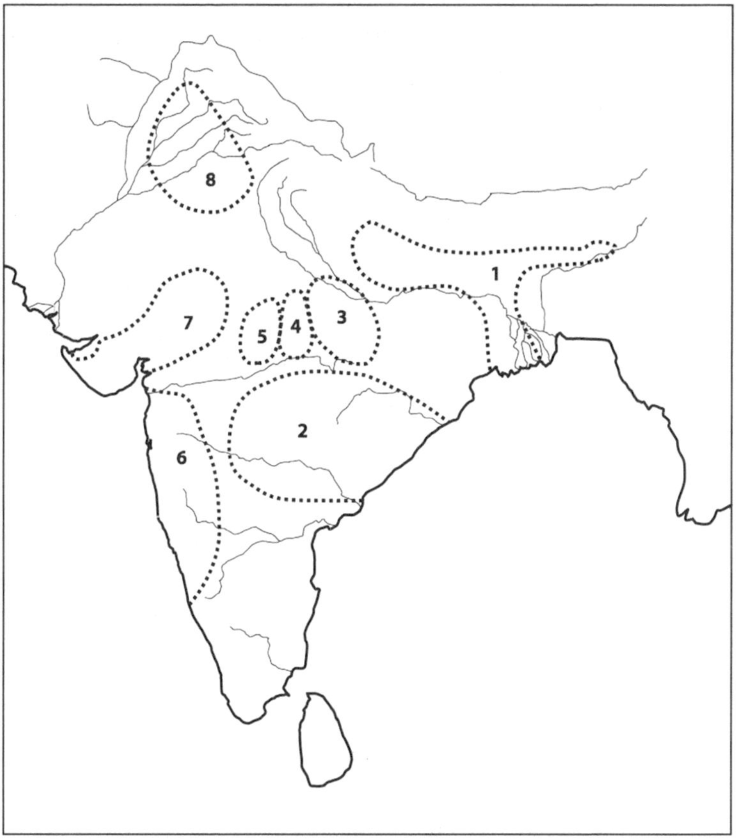

Fig. 1.4: Map of the eight elephant forests of ancient India

1. Prācya forest 2. Kāliṅga forest 3. Cedikarūṣa forest 4. Dāśārṇa forest 5. Āṅgareya forest 6. Aparānta forest 7. Saurāṣṭra forest 8. Pāñcanada forest.

Indian point of view, for it does not include the elephant forests of the Western Ghats in South India that, as we have seen, have the largest populations of Asian elephants in the world today. The exception to the northern perspective is the *Mānasollāsa* (1131 CE), a text from the Deccan peninsula, which says that the Aparānta forest extends southward to the Western Ghats of Kerala, and the Kaliṅga forest extends south to the Tamil country

(Drāviḍa), both being details which the other sources do not support. It is evident that the *Mānasollāsa* reinterprets the list of elephant forests by extending the boundaries southward.

The doubtful case of South India apart, what the list of the eight *gaja-vanas* tells us is that Central and East India were well stocked with wild elephants, and that two thousand years ago the Indus valley (probably only the Punjab portion of it) and the western coast, where they are no longer found, also had some wild elephants. Since the historic trend on the Indian subcontinent has been for the western side of the elephant range to contract, the overall distribution of wild elephants can hardly have been smaller prior to the first extant listing in the *Arthaśāstra* of the forests containing them.

Our sources for the eight forests do not directly speak of the densities of their elephant populations. But if we compare the list with the map (Fig. 1.3) showing that the range has over time shrunk in the west, it is reasonable to infer that though wild elephants did exist in the forests of the Indus region and the west coast in ancient times, their numbers would have been smaller than of those in the elephant forests of Central India and the Ganga valley. And although the Sanskrit sources do not indicate densities, they do rank the eight forests for the quality of their elephants. There are some differences among the texts in their rankings, but points of agreement emerge by comparing them. The ancient authorities are unanimous that elephants of the worst sort are those in the Indus basin (the Pāñcanada forest) and the Kathiawar peninsula (the Saurāṣṭra forest). These are the very regions where wild elephants are now extinct and in which, we may infer, they were in the ancient past less abundant than in other forests. The middling and best varieties were said to be found in the forests of East and Central India. In respect of the quantity and quality of the elephants to which they had access, then, the North Indian kings of the Gangetic region, such as the Mauryas, were at a great advantage over the kings of the Indus region.

Taking the eight elephant forests map as our best information about the situation two thousand years ago, a recent report of the

Elephant Task Force to the Government of India supplies data for a map of the current distribution.[18] Here I map the official elephant reserves as they stood in 2005, numbering thirty-one in all (Fig. 1.5). These reserves are represented on the map by points, not as areas. Not all of India's 30,000 or so elephants are contained in them, but most are, so the map gives a picture of the whole range within the Republic of India. Many reserves are quite small, and all are separated by intervening territory, but some of them are connected by corridors allowing elephant migration. Reserves are grouped into "landscapes," as indicated in the map's legend. The drastic shrinkage of range from west to east that has taken place in the last two millennia—since the time of the *Arthaśāstra*—can be seen by comparing this map with that of the eight elephant forests. One also sees how small and fragmented the forest habitats for elephants have become. Their alleviation, in the shape of corridors through which elephants can travel between forests, is infrequent; it is also insufficient since the existence of these passages always holds the potential for clashes between elephants and humans. The isolation of elephant populations is, in short, a huge problem in an age of shrinking habitat.

How did we get from there to here, from the eight elephant forests across large areas of ancient India to the thirty-one elephant reserves of the present? It is useful to find an intermediate point between these two, a third period after the *Arthaśāstra* and before the Republic of India, to get a sense of the tempo of the retreat of elephants here. The Mughal period offers such a prospect because of the long history of the Mughal empire, its voluminous records, and the love of elephants among their kings. Akbar is the supreme example of this predilection, and Abu'l Fazl's description of the emperor and his empire, the *Ā'īn-i Akbarī* (1598),[19] has a great deal to say about elephants, wild and tamed. Many other Mughal sources as well as European travellers' accounts can be drawn upon to get a fairly detailed picture of the elephant range. Fortunately

[18] ETF Report 2010.

[19] Examined along with the *Arthaśāstra* in Chapter 5.

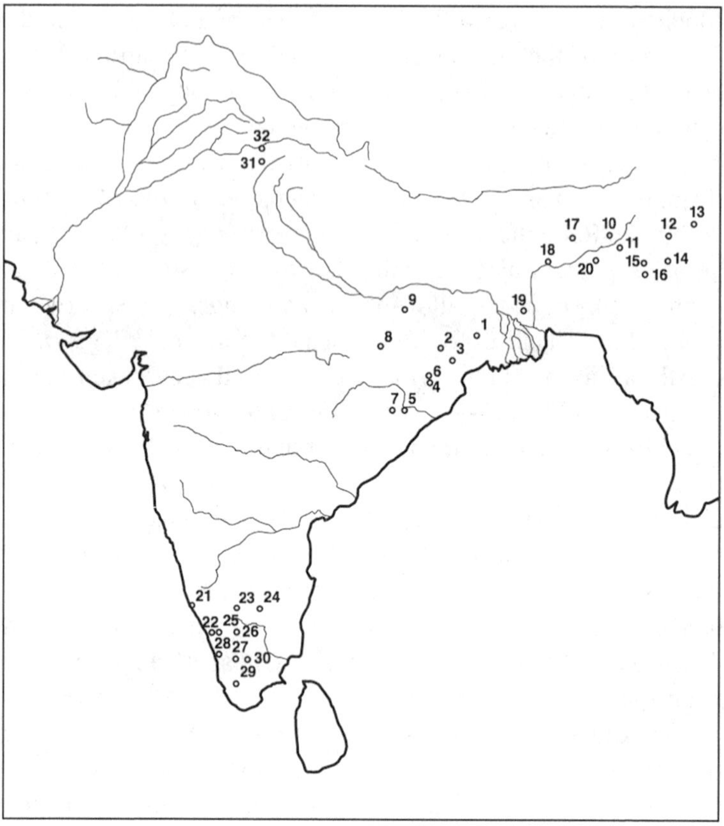

Fig. 1.5: Map of elephant reserves in contemporary India

East-Central Landscape: 1. Mayurjharna 2. Singhbhum 3. Mayurbhanj 4. Mahanadi 5. Sambalpur 6. Baitarni 7. South Orissa 8. Lemru 9. Badalkhol-Tamorpingala.

Kameng-Sonitpur Landscape: 10. Kameng 11. Sonitpur.

Eastern South Bank Landscape: 12. Dihing-Patkai 13. South Arunachal.

Kaziranga-Karbi Angalong-Intanki Landscape: 14. Kaziranga-Karbi Angalong 15. Dhansiri-Lungding 16. Intanki.

North Bengal-Greater Manas Landscape: 17. Chirang-Ripu 18. Eastern Dooars.

Meghalaya Landscape: 19. Garo Hills 20. Khasi Hills.

Brahmagiri-Nilgiri-Eastern Ghat Landscape: 21. Mysore 22. Wayanad 23. Nilgiri 24. Rayala 25. Nilambur 26. Coimbatore.

Anamalai-Nelliampathy-High Range Landscape: 27. Anamalai 28. Anamudi.

Periyar-Agasthyamalai Landscape: 29. Periyar 30. Srivilliputtur.

North-Western Landscape: 31. Shivalik 32. Uttar Pradesh.

this material has been sifted and mapped by the eminent Mughal historian Irfan Habib in *An atlas of the Mughal Empire* (1982). Wild elephants form only one item in Habib's atlas, which I have abstracted and plotted from to arrive at Fig. 1.6. The period of its coverage is about 1600–1800 CE, which is to say toward the recent end of the two-thousand-year interval between the *Arthaśāstra* and the report of the Elephant Task Force.

Comparing the Mughal period distribution of wild elephants with the eight elephant forests of the *Arthaśāstra*, we see that elephants have retreated from the Indus valley and the upper Deccan but are very well represented across Central India; indeed the great Central Indian forest, now so fragmented and degraded, was a continuous range for wild elephants, from sea to sea. In addition, the Mughal sources register the great South Indian wild elephant range, and that of Sri Lanka. Looking back in time to the *Arthaśāstra* and excluding the Indus valley and upper Deccan, the range is virtually unchanged well over a thousand years later. So what we see by looking backward is a thousand-plus years of kings capturing wild elephants for warfare without visible reduction in their number. Looking forward in time, however, to the Elephant Task Force Report of the present, it becomes clear that the drastic shrinkage of habitat (and, presumably, the crash in numbers) happens over the colonial and the national periods of India's history. This tells us that the sharp drop in number began not in the era of the war elephant but very recently, since about 1800. The tempo of elephant decline, then, was slow for a very long time, perhaps keeping pace with the incremental but relatively slow growth in human population, and increased rapidly over the last two centuries.

The Habib atlas also maps the distribution of horse pastures, mostly of cavalry horses but also "country breeds" called Gunt

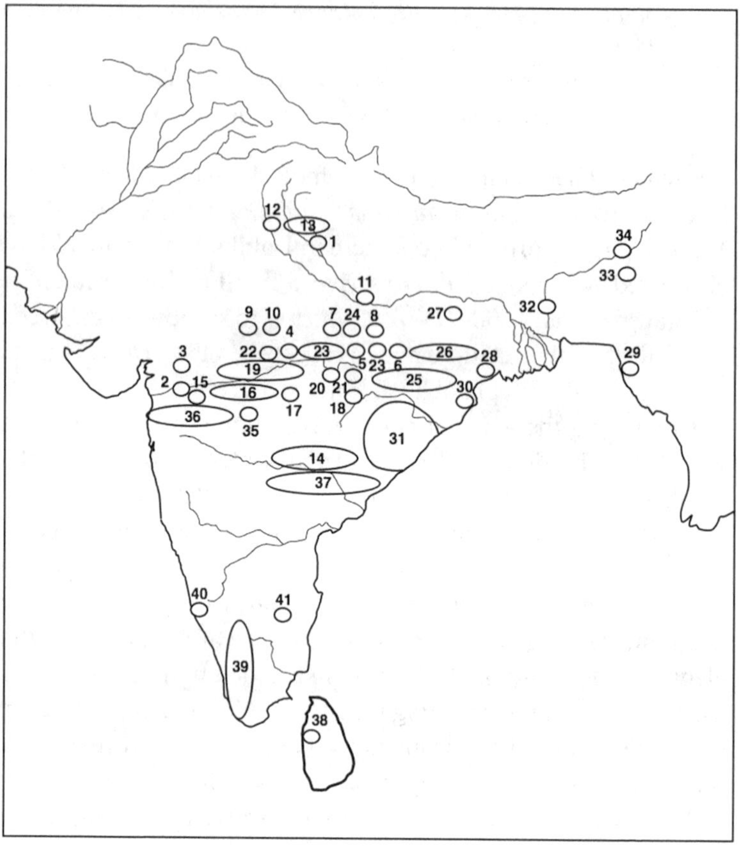

Fig. 1.6: Map of wild elephants in Mughal India

Punjab: 1. Haridwar & Kumaun.

Gujarat: 2. Dohad 3. Bindhachal Range.

Uttar Pradesh: 4. Chanderi 5. Son 6. Rhotas 7. Gahora 8. Kantit & Chunar 9. Narwar & Shivpuri 10. Payanwan 11. Gorakhpur 12. Haridwar 13. Nihtaur.

Central India: 14. Bhairagarh 15. Bijagarh & Sandhwa 16. Handia & Hoshangabad 17. Deogarh 18. Ratanpur & Madanpur 19. Unchod, Satwas & Raisen 20. Garh 21. Battha & Surguja 22. Chanderi & Kalinjar 23. Kalinjar & Gahora 24. Gahora, Kantit & Chunar.

Bihar: 25. Jharkhand 26. Southern Mountains 27. Murung.

Bengal: 28. Mahmudabad & Khilafatabad 29. Arakan 30. Satgaon.

Orissa: 31. Orissa & Jharkhand.

Assam: 32. Kajliban 33. Sadiq 34. Mishmi.
Deccan West: 35. Deogarh 36. Sultanpur & Rajpipla.
Deccan East: 37. Bastar.
South India and Ceylon: 38. Ceylon 39. Malabar 40. Kanara 41. Tirupati.

and Tangan. This information is most valuable because, as Digby (1971) shows in relation to war horse and elephant under the Delhi sultanate, these made up the main animal power of Indian armies. In addition, draft oxen were needed in large numbers for the supply train, and at times camels and donkeys as well. The capture and use of elephants being part of a broad array of animal power for the military, it is helpful to know something about the geography of supply. By plotting the information for horses from Habib's atlas (Fig. 1.7) we see that this animal came mostly from either the Indus valley and regions to the west in present-day Afghanistan, or from the foot of the Himalayas. The former were cavalry horse pastures, the latter were of the lower-valued country breeds. Multan was the major mart for foreign horses, especially Arabians, and for horses from Central Asia and Iran. In the peninsula horses were often imported, brought in by sea.

There is very little overlap between these horse pastures (not of wild horses, of course, which are native to Central Asia) and the forests that show wild elephants in the Mughal period, or indeed two thousand years ago. This complementarity of elephant and horse ranges has to do with the frontier between forest and grassland, the wet and dry landscapes. It has profound structuring consequences for human life under the regime of kings and armies relying heavily upon animal power. It means, on the one hand, that any given kingdom, on any given point of the map, was advantaged in respect of one or the other of these two sinews of war, horses and elephants, and disadvantaged in the other. It made the problem of supply, and considerations of battlefield tactics, complex in ways which followed fairly straightforwardly from the distributions. It also means that, given the way the frontier between horse and elephant habitat runs through India, armies here had access to *both*, whereas those of other countries may

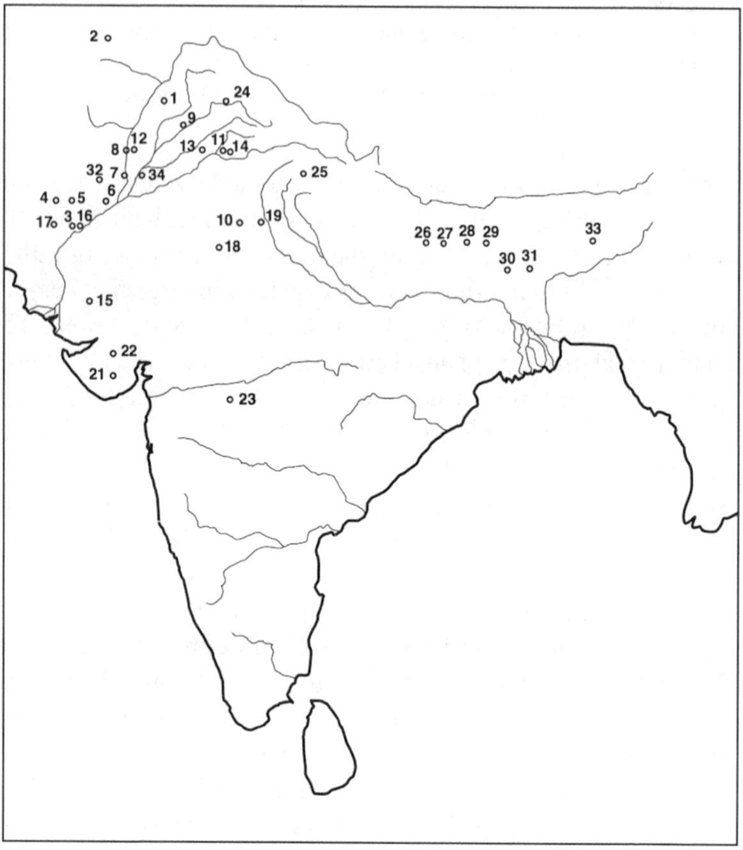

Fig. 1.7: Map of horse pastures in Mughal India

Cavalry horses

N. Afghanistan: 1. Ghakkar country 2. Badakhshan.

S. Afghanistan: 3. Kirthar Range 4. Qalat-i Nichara 5. Siwi 6. Barkhan 7. Duki 8. Dera Ismail Khan.

Kashmir: 9. Wazirabad.

Punjab: 10. Bamnikhera 11. Firozpur 12. Daira Ismail Khan 13. Patti Haibatpur 14. Bajwara.

Sind: 15. Soz 16. Kirthar Range 17. Kohinaz.

Rajasthan: 18. Suba Ajmer 19. Mewat.

Gujarat: 20. Junagarh 21. Bhadar R. 22. Navangar 23. Cutch.

Central India: 24. Bhihangaon.

Country breeds
Kashmir: 25. Khanpur.
Uttar Pradesh: 26. Kumaun.
Bihar: 27. Murus Hills.
Bengal: 28. Kuch & Ghoraghat 29. Bhutant Range 30. Murung Hills.
Assam: 31. Dafla Hills.

Mart for imported Arabian horses
32. Multan.

have had access to one or neither but not both. That horses and wild elephants were in complementary pastures in India was a long-term structuring factor of Indian history. The fact that this region straddled the separate yet reasonably contiguous habitats of elephants and horses meant that Indian kings could have both animals in their cavalries. Countries further west, including Afghanistan and Persia and the Middle East, had horses but no wild elephants. Southeast Asia had wild elephants but few horses. India's rulers had both.

The Asian elephant

The Linnean classification of the Asian elephant is as follows:

Mammalia (class)
Proboscidea (order)
Elephantidea (family)
Elephas (genus)
Maximus (species)

Elephants and their near relatives once ranged over Africa, Eurasia, and North America, but now only Africa and parts of Asia have wild elephants. Asian and African elephants differ on many points. The most immediately recognizable is the larger, triangular ear of the African, and the two bosses on the head of Asian elephants, called *kumbha* (literally, pots) in Sanskrit. The slope of the back, and the carriage and shape of the head, are different (Fig. 1.8). The Asian elephant holds its head higher. The back of the African elephant is concave, that of the Asian elephant convex.

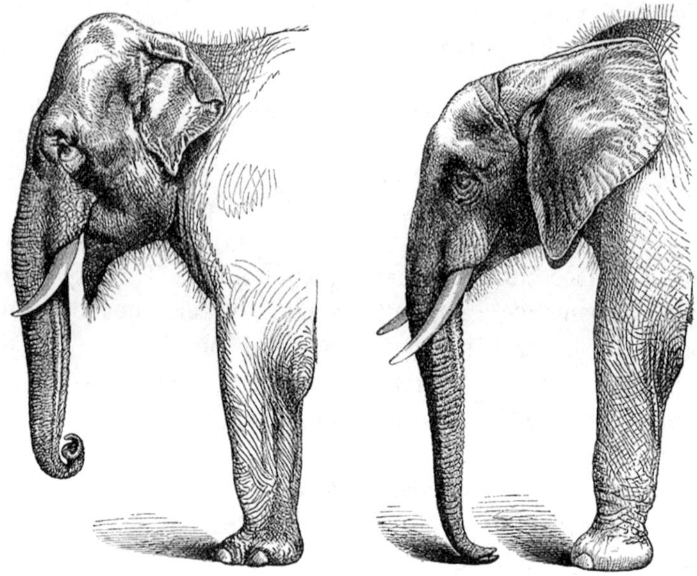

Fig. 1.8: Asian and African elephants

The African elephant is of another genus, called Loxodonta, "slant-toothed," referring to the patterning of ridges on its molar teeth. It has two main variants, the forest elephant and the bush or savanna elephant. These had been considered separate races of a single African species, but zoologists now consider them two distinct species, *L. cyclotis* and *L. africana*, respectively. The difference between the two varieties has a bearing on the history we are trying to trace. The savanna elephant is distinctly larger and heavier than the Asian elephant, but the forest elephant is smaller than the Asian; and, as we shall see, when the Hellenistic rulers of Egypt applied Indian techniques to the capture and training of wild elephants in their vicinity, they applied them to the smaller variety, which placed them at a disadvantage when confronting the larger Asian elephants in battle.[20]

Elephants belong to the order Proboscidea, whose closest relatives, from whom they separated millions of years ago, are

[20] The details of this are in Chapter 6.

the dugongs and manatees (*Sirenensis*) on the one hand, and the hyraxes, small burrowing animals, on the other. The great radiation of the Proboscidea, of which over 300 species have been recognized,[21] occurred after the extinction of the dinosaurs. Elephants, as the largest living land animals, took the place once occupied by massive herbivorous sauropods among the dinosaurs.

The age of the dinosaurs is the Cretaceous period, followed by the Tertiary, beginning about 65 million years ago. The two periods are very different because of a massive dying off of plant and animal species, notably of the dinosaurs, but extending to many others on both land and sea. A proposal that these multiple extinctions were caused by the collision of a massive asteroid with the earth has become the consensus view among scientists concerned with these matters.[22] Dense clouds of dust darkened the skies for years; effective sunlight reaching the earth was greatly reduced; plants died, temperatures plunged; and large animals, both herbivores and predators, went extinct within what in geological time seems an instant. The reptiles that survived are few (crocodiles; tortoises and turtles; lizards; snakes), while birds, descendants of flying dinosaurs, not only survived but flourished, radiating into many different species. With the age of the dinosaurs over for good, the age of mammals was about to begin. The large animals of the next age, both herbivores and their predators, were mammals. The great extinction of the dinosaurs was a catastrophe that gave mammals their chance over the ensuing 65 million years, including the two that figure in our story: humans and elephants.

After the great extinctions, the mammalian order Proboscidea proliferated lineages of new species. The family Elephantidea within this order developed about 6 million years ago, producing its three genera of well-known elephants, the Asian, the African, and the Mammoth (*Mammuthus*); its close relative, the Mastodon (*Mammut*), had branched off somewhat earlier. All four lineages

[21] Carrington 1959: 23, citing Osborne.
[22] Alvarez and Alvarez, *et al.* 1980.

persisted to recent times, though mammoths and mastodons are now extinct.[23]

The physiology of the Asian elephant was specialized in the course of its evolution in ways immediately obvious. The first is the elephant's trunk, really a nose and upper lip grown into a remarkable organ, used for conveying food and water to the mouth, communicating, breathing (and snorkeling when under water), and other purposes. The trunk has a finger-like extension at the tip, useful for grasping small objects; African elephants have two such "fingers," upper and lower. The trunk gives the elephant its early name in Sanskrit, *mṛga hastin*, the animal with a hand: *hāthi* in Hindi. The specialization of the teeth is equally remarkable. Two incisors have elongated into tusks, which, in males, can be enormous and very heavy, used both for the work of feeding but also for fighting. Females have only short tusks, which may not protrude far enough to be visible, and many males have short tusks or even very short non-visible ones in comparison with those of females; such elephants are called *makhna* in India. Earlier elephant species and their relatives also had two short tusks on the lower jaw, but mandibular tusks and other fancy forms of the incisors have disappeared and are known only from fossils. The molars are the other highly specialized component of the elephant's teeth. There are only four of them, one above and one below on each side of the mouth, massive things which grind up huge amounts of vegetable matter all day long and over part of the night. These molars wear out from such heavy use, and, fortunately, are replaced by a new set that emerges from behind the existing molars, pushing the latter forward and out, as if on a conveyor belt. Six sets of molars appear in an elephant's lifetime. By the time it is sixty an Asian elephant is on its last set and cannot live much longer than seventy before its molars wear out. Very old wild elephants may die of gradual starvation.[24]

The obvious distinction of the elephant is its great size, serviced by the specialized eating apparatus of trunk and molars. Size is

[23] Sukumar 2011: 17–20.

[24] Shoshani and Eisenberg 1982; Nowak 1999, 2: 993–8; Sukumar 1989.

an advantage in that the adult elephant has no fear of predators. It is a convention of Sanskrit poetry that in a contest between the lion and the elephant, the lion would win; so the poets would often liken their royal patron to a lion and the enemy king to an elephant. But it would in fact take many real lions to bring down a healthy adult elephant. A pack of lions has been filmed taking down an elephant in Africa, but in truth an adult elephant in good health is virtually immune from predators. Baby elephants, on the other hand, though they can walk shortly after birth, are prey for lions and tigers and must be protected by the bigness of their mothers and foster-mothers or "aunties." These charge and trumpet with ears flared to scare off a predator who gets too close.

In addition to the trunk and molars, the rest of the digestive machinery consists of throat, stomach, and a very long intestinal tract, over 30 meters (110 feet) in length. It is not very efficient, as some 44 per cent of what is eaten passes through and out. The Elephant Task Force Report conveys the information, useful in estimating wild elephant populations in forests, that elephants leave an average of 16.3 dung piles per day.[25] Unlike deer, antelope, and cattle, they do not have a second stomach with which to extract a higher amount of energy from their food. Their diet is not very high in energy to begin with: mainly browse (the leaves and twigs of trees and bushes, and of bamboo) and grass. Sukumar has established that in the wild 70 per cent of the diet is browse and grass only 30 per cent, which is one of several traits that tie the Asian elephant to forests and not open grassland.[26] Due to the energy demands of its large body, and the nature of its digestive tract, the wild elephant must spend most of its waking hours, twelve to sixteen hours per day, eating and moving in search of food.

It is useful at this point to pause and consider the very different digestive pattern of humans, as the difference between elephants and humans will become germane when we look at humans starting to capture elephants and becoming responsible

[25] ETF 2010: 39.
[26] Sukumar 1989.

for supplying their food. As we see from the admirable book by Richard Wrangham, *Catching fire: how cooking made us human* (2009), human evolution took us down the road of a large, high-energy and food-demanding brain. This in turn led to an ever higher degree of food processing outside the body and prior to eating: cutting, grinding, pounding; the domestication of plants and the selection of strains with high-energy characteristics; and above all, cooking with fire. Accompanying these developments in culture were changes in the human body. These took us further from our chimpanzee cousins, toward smaller jaws and teeth, weaker jaw muscles, and shorter and smaller intestines, giving in all a very much shorter time spent eating and digesting, and freeing up time for diverse activities. Several animal species love crops raised by humans and processed food, including cooked food, because of its higher available energy. Wrangham does not discuss the domestication of animals, but we shall see that the raising of foodcrops and the processing of food are crucial to the holding of tamed elephants.[27] They shorten the time that the animal would otherwise spend foraging and increase the time it can work for human ends.

The elephant's daily food requirements, then, are great and pressing, and its size is the maximum its metabolism can maintain. It also needs a large amount of water to drink, and a river or lake in which to bathe. Cooling in hot weather is a problem, for which the large, thin ears, with many blood vessels, are the main solution. Elephants do not have sweat glands all over to enable cooling; they have only a few, on the feet. So Asian elephants do not tolerate the full sunlight of the savanna well.[28] They need at least partial shade in hot weather, a second attribute tying them to the forest.

[27] The details of this are in Chapter 2.

[28] Actually, it is humans who are unusual among mammals in having sweat glands all over as a rapid cooling system. Some think this is an evolutionary adaptation connected with ancient hunting techniques, such as running down other mammals that, on account of their fur and comparatively few sweat glands, cannot survive a long pursuit.

Asian elephants, like African, move about in groups formed of a matriarch, her daughters and younger sons, and other relatives; such formations contain adult females, while adult males are solitary or in groups of young males. Adult males combine with adult females in herds temporarily, for love-making. This is triggered by the female becoming sexually receptive, indicated by bodily signs detectable by smell and behavior indicating interest. A tender courtship ensues, involving much use of the trunk, body, head, and the production of rumbling sounds. Eventually the male approaches the female from behind, sinks on his back legs, and raises his front legs onto the female's back, his body almost vertical, and the connection is made. Such bouts of love-making are repeated several times, sometimes over a few days; but finally the two part ways and return to their former social condition. Pregnancy lasts eighteen to twenty-two months and almost always results in a single birth. Twins occur but rarely.

Male elephants generally go into a condition called "musth" once a year, which may last for days or weeks, sometimes months. A surge of testosterone and other complex hormonal changes bring on a puffiness of the temples, followed by a flow of fluid—sticky, pungent, and bitter—from temporal glands in front of the ear-hole. A dark vertical streak of musth fluid is a visual sign of the condition. The elephant is aggressive and combative, often irritable; the penis drips urine for extended periods. Musth has to do with sexuality, but not in a simple way. It is usually called "rut" in English translations from Indian languages, which is a reasonable approximation, but inexact. Deer and other ungulates have a rutting *season*, in which hormonal inducements to sexuality affect males and females at the same time, bringing about fights among males and the mating of males and females. As regards elephants, however, musth among males is not synchronized, and males not in musth generally give way to a musth elephant; it establishes the latter's dominance, at least temporarily. And estrous in females is not seasonal or coordinated with the onset of musth in males, but has a periodicity of about three times a year (for those who are not pregnant or suckling their babies), with sexual receptivity lasting a few days. All in all, musth in males does not coincide with female sexual readiness; it only provokes male–male competition to establish dominance and brings on a heightened interest in sex.[29] So there is no such thing as a rutting or mating season among elephants. Musth is a sign of robust health and of the dominant male, and was highly valued as such in the Indian war elephant. Males who do not come into musth are perceived as non-dominant or in poor condition.

Turning from Asian elephant evolution and physiology, I now need to say something about the question of elephant–human relations in prehistory. It would be a great benefit to an understanding of the relation of elephants to kingship if we were clear at the outset about what came before the rise of kingship. A point of contrast between pre-kingship and kingship periods is helpful in assessing the difference that kingship made to the relationship of humans and elephants. It is also the context out of which king–elephant relations emerged. Unfortunately, the issue is highly debated.

Elephants and their near relatives formed several lineages, some of which died out long before humans came into the picture, for reasons difficult to ascertain. Others, especially mammoths and mastodons, went extinct in geologically recent times, after modern humans had spread out of Africa and around the world. Some of their remains have cut marks on the bones, which seem to show they were butchered by humans using stone tools; signs of a forced disarticulation of joints using wedges of some kind also suggest butchery. This is evidence that some humans were eating mammoths and mastodons; it is more difficult to find evidence that the animals were hunted and killed rather than scavenged after having died from causes other than human hunting.

Intriguing circumstantial evidence has come out of North America. The view that mammoths and mastodons, along with a whole array of large mammals, became extinct more or less simultaneously with the arrival of humans in North America

[29] Eisenberg, *et al.* 1971; Poole 1987.

about 13,000 years ago, has a leading proponent in Paul Martin. The more general phenomenon of large animal extinctions in geologically near time, called Late Quaternary megafaunal extinctions, coincided with the arrival of modern humans in many parts of the world—North America, South America, Europe, Australia, New Zealand—and were, according to Martin, the result of "overkill." The simultaneity of human arrival and the extinction of large animal species is good circumstantial evidence for human hunting as the cause of the extinction, though simultaneity is hard to establish within tolerably narrow limits, and the time of human arrival in the Americas continues to be controversial. The difficulties of establishing simultaneity seem trivial when comparing the extreme cases, Australia and New Zealand. Though next door to one another, Australia was reached by modern humans at least 50,000 years ago while New Zealand was reached little more than a thousand years ago. In both places large animals (giant kangaroos in Australia; giant flightless birds called moas in New Zealand) became extinct when humans appeared, conforming with the "overkill" hypothesis.[30] A worldwide study specific to elephants and their kin shows a close correlation of sites of human use of hunted or scavenged proboscideans with the frontiers of human (i.e. genus Homo) expansion over the last 1.8 million years, but it uses a very small sample of forty-one cases.[31]

While the pattern of Late Quaternary extinctions is well established, the experts are divided over Martin's overkill theory which attributes extinctions to human hunters; their skepticism deepens in relation to Martin's related hypothesis that it happened very rapidly, as a kind of blitzkrieg. There are, however, several possible alternative, non-human, causes of the extinctions. Among these, climate change is now established as the motor for so many extinctions that it is to be expected that it will be one of the first examined. In this regard Daniel Fisher and his associates have developed the study of the tusks of mammoths and mastodons.

[30] Martin 2005; Martin and Klein eds 1984.
[31] Surovell, *et al.* 2005.

Tusks grow throughout an elephant's life, and in cross-section tusks show bands of annual growth which are subdivisible into fortnightly and even daily bands. These growth bands on tusks can provide information about an elephant's nutrition and time of death. Fisher has been able to establish that the remains of mastodons which show signs of the animal having been butchered are, first, generally those of large adult males (therefore probably solitary); second, the season of their death appears to be the late fall; and third, their tusks show a history of good nutrition—all of which tends to confirm that they were deliberately hunted and their meat cached for winter retrieval. Sites without signs of butchery show a balanced sex ratio, with the season of death clustering at the boundary between winter and spring, this being the time when animals are in their poorest condition from the scarcity of food in winter, indicating death by natural causes. The overall tendency of these findings favors the hunting hypothesis and disfavors climate as a cause; everything goes to show that, except during winter, the habitat was favorable and the nutrition good. The analysis of tusks does however go against the blitzkrieg that Martin proposes, in part because the evidence for hunting-to-extinction in the Great Lakes region is spread over two thousand to three thousand years.[32]

The conclusion of the debate is not yet in sight, though it seems proven that human hunting played a role in the worldwide retreat of elephants and their kin. For our purposes, while we cannot gauge the strength of the human role, we can at least conclude that to some extent the retreat of elephants did not begin with the rise of the early literate civilizations a few thousand years ago, but was preceded by a dying off of large species, including the mammoth and mastodon. This has its own history, one that is only beginning to emerge. The evidence also establishes that prior to the rise of kingship there was no capture and training of elephants, let alone their use in war.

[32] Fisher 1987, 2001, 2008, 2009. The richness of the information that can be derived from analysis of tusks in this way cannot be overstated. Uno, *et al.* 2013 show that the year of death from recently taken ivory can be determined with great accuracy, making such analysis a forensic tool for combating the trade in illegal (recently taken) ivory.

Though the phenomenon of Late Quaternary megafaunal extinctions is well established, and while the experts are working out the causes, one of the virtues of the debate is that it has thrown into relief the countervailing pattern, namely the persistence of elephants and other large animals in Africa, India (South Asia), and Southeast Asia, running against the overall trend, as shown in Fig. 1.9. The persistence of large animals from the Late Quaternary to the present in these regions of early human contact implies that rather different conditions prevailed. To the degree that the *retreat* of the mammoth and mastodon is attributable to human activity in prehistoric times, the *persistence* of African and Asian elephants along with other large animals in Africa, India, and Southeast Asia becomes a problem to solve.

Martin's theory of overkill obliges him to give reasons that megafaunal extinctions were rapid, that they were blitzkriegs. The reason he offers is the "naïveté" of the animals who, not having encountered humans earlier, had not learned to avoid them. It also requires him to explain the persistence of elephants and other large animals in Africa and Asia, which the logic of his blitzkrieg argument makes him attribute to the long association of large animals with humans here: he believes it was a slow, long co-evolution over which elephants, and other animals in the region of human origin and early spread, survived on account of having grown wary of human hunters.

But this is not very convincing. The rapid killing-off thesis, which requires blitzkriegs, does not hold up before the evidence of a two- or three-thousand-year decline in North America shown by analysis of mammoth and mastodon tusks. Over such a long time the animals would have learned perfectly well to steer clear of humans. Analyzing the same problem, Surovell, *et al.* propose that tropical forests have been refuges for elephants because of low human population densities.[33] This remains speculative and impressionistic; it is not examined against the evidence of human elephant hunting and consuming in Africa, and South and Southeast Asia. The overkill hypothesis has better evidence backing it, but

[33] Surovell, *et al.* 2005.

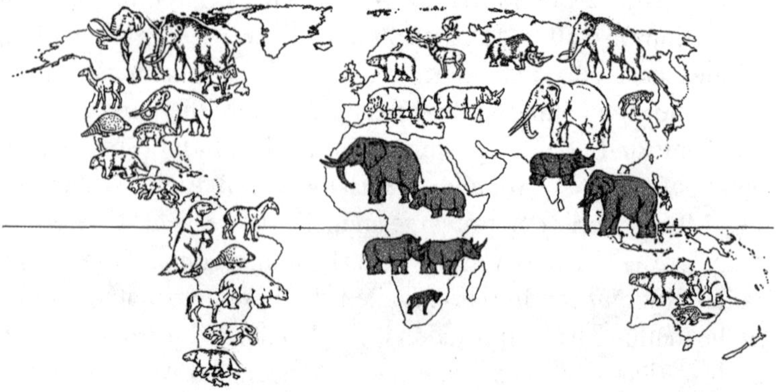

Fig. 1.9: Map of Late Quaternary megafaunal extinctions

by and large there is as yet no convincing explanation of the persistence of elephants over the very long haul.

The persistence of African and Asian elephants in prehistoric times is a problem that we must, at this point, leave to those who have the skills to assess the evidence. Ours is the problem of the persistence of Asian elephants in historic times. To that end we must now examine the forest.

The monsoon, a moist seaborne wind, blows landward from the southwest in summer, drawn by a low pressure zone along the Himalaya. The winds rise as they are heated by the land and drop their moisture as heavy rain. In winter, continental (and generally dry) air blows seaward from the northeast.

The southwest monsoon brings a distinct rainy season to the Indian subcontinent, the Southeast Asian mainland, and southern China, these together constituting the region named "monsoon Asia."[34] The concentration of rainfall in a single season and the comparative dryness the rest of the year combine with the variation between annually hotter and colder times to form a distinctive kind of seasonality in monsoon Asia. The seasons are essentially three: the rains, the cold, the hot. This structure is expressed in ancient Indian texts, in which the seasons are either

[34] In Dobby 1961.

three four-month periods or six two-month periods: the shining (spring, *vasanta*), the hot (*grīṣma*); the rains (*varṣāḥ*), autumn (*śarad*); the frost (*hemanta*), the cool (*śiśira*). The year, then, was subdivided into three or six periods—or even, for some purposes, two, for the northgoing and southgoing of the sun; it was not, as in temperate Europe and America, subdivided into four three-month seasons.

This structure of seasonality governed the ritual cycle of the year. For example, the religion of the Veda observed four-month rituals, *cāturmāsya*, marking the beginnings of the three seasons.[35] Poems about the seasons were similarly grouped; in poetry each season had its own attributes, characteristic love situations, and themes.[36]

For the monsoon forest, then, there is a pronounced rainy period, beginning June or July with the arrival of the southwest monsoon; a dry cold period beginning September or October; and a dry hot period beginning February, growing ever hotter and drier, and reaching a crescendo in April or May. Then the return of the rains causes temperatures suddenly to drop and the humidity to soar. During the hot period, when the trees are most stressed, the broadleaf varieties tend to drop most of their leaves and gradually begin new ones; the forest becomes more bare and transparent, and leaf litter piles up, replenishing the soil. The monsoon forest is *deciduous* because it has a hot dry season before the rains, unlike temperate regions where deciduous broadleaf trees drop their leaves in the stress of the *cold* season. Some forests in the region of this study, especially those near the sea, are wet throughout the year and have no pronounced dry season; in them, broadleaf trees are *evergreen*, replacing their leaves bit by bit throughout the year. With a closed leafy canopy year around, they admit little light for ground cover and shrubs to grow, locking most of the nutrients to themselves and leaving soils comparatively impoverished.[37] Of these two types, the monsoon deciduous forest is more conducive

[35] Vedic Index 1912: 259–60.
[36] Selby 2003.
[37] Reid 1995.

to grazing and browsing animals, including the elephant, as it has more openings and forest edges with grass and shrubs; the evergreen rain forest has fewer grazers.

The monsoon forest is especially suited to Asian elephants. However, its seasonality imposes upon them patterns of movement in addition to the need to find fresh grazing or browse when a patch has been depleted. Thus Sukumar, studying elephants in the Biligirirangan hills of the Western Ghats of South India, where there are two seasons of rain, found that the protein content of tall grasses declined in the dry season and was greatest in the new growth after the rains. Considerations such as these lead elephants to move between short grass, long grass, and browsing environments. They also vary the manner of grazing, eating the tops of new grass, but plucking up tufts of older grass and knocking off the dirt from the roots to eat the bottom half, discarding the less palatable and more siliceous top part.[38]

This picture of the monsoon and the vegetation pattern it produces is over-simple, for there are many variations. First, there is a retreating northeast monsoon blowing seaward from the Asian land mass in the winter, which generally has a drying effect but also brings a second season of lighter rains to certain regions near the sea. Second, there are arid regions the monsoon does not reach. Third, there are variations due to altitude, from the seashore to the Himalaya.

Forests in India show a good deal of variety, and their classification is accordingly complex. But, setting aside the specialized forests at higher altitudes and along the coast, Spate and Learmonth recognize four broad divisions of vegetation on the basis of annual rainfall:

over 80 in / ~2000 mm	evergreen (rain) forest
40–80 in / ~1000–2000 mm	deciduous (monsoon) forest
20–40 in / ~500–1000 mm	drier deciduous forest grading into open thorny scrub
under 20 in / under ~500 mm	thorny scrub and low open bush merging into semi-desert

[38] Sukumar 1989: 67–8, 71–4; Varma 2013.

The table posits an equivalence between rainfall (as a proxy for climate) and vegetation, such that the one stands for the other. When we analyze the posited equivalence, however, we find that it rests upon certain assumptions of what is natural.

Let us, as an experiment, take Spate and Learmonth literally, and plot the four vegetation types on their map of annual rainfall to generate a hypothetical vegetation map (Fig. 1.10). It will be seen that forests cover much of the Indian subcontinent, except for Baluchistan and the Thar Desert of Rajasthan and Sind. But

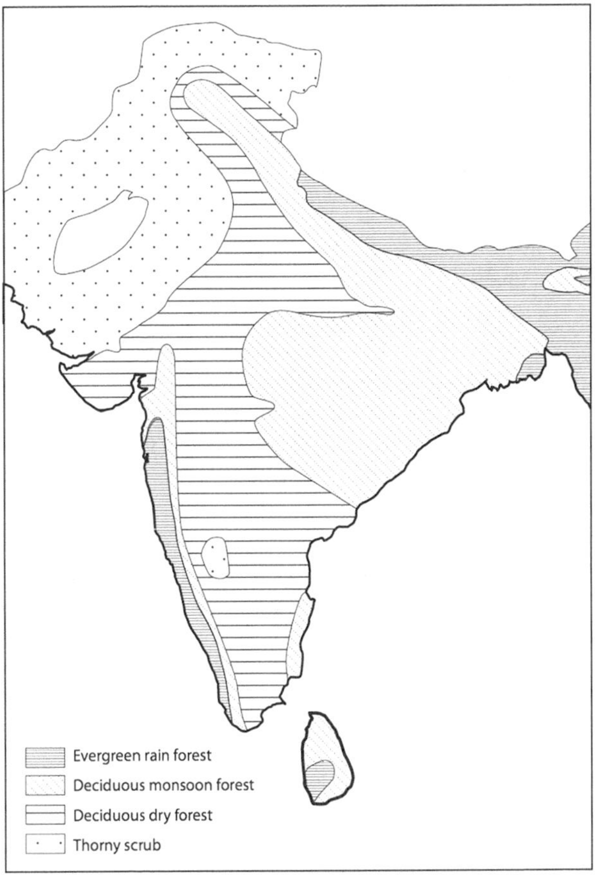

Fig. 1.10: Forest types of the Indian subcontinent plotted on the rainfall map of Spate and Learmonth

this is far from true today: the discrepancy between the map of India and on-the-ground vegetation is so very large that it needs no demonstration. What is the cause of the discrepancy? We must take the map to be in some sense ideal—a representation of the *past*, of vegetation *history*. We begin to suspect that the posited equivalence of rainfall and vegetation refers to a state of nature in the absence of humans and their works.

The Spate and Learmonth view is the summation of a well-established literature of scientific forestry in India, with well-settled views about forests and forest history.[39] The overall argument is that the natural vegetation of India is forest; but that this has been much degraded over the ages by clearing, agriculture, and overgrazing by domestic animals, that is, by human causes (*anthropogenic* ones, in the jargon). Spate and Learmonth express the central argument of that literature so very well that it is worth quoting them at length:

> The natural vegetation of the Indian sub-continent, except on the higher mountains and the more arid parts of Baluchistan and the Thar, is essentially arboreal. It has, however, been cleared, exploited and degraded to such an extent that this statement has little practical significance today. Something like a fifth of India is officially regarded as forest, against a notional optimum of a third; but of this area of 277,000 sq. miles (717,000 km^2), nearly 100,000 sq. miles are 'unclassed' and most of this is forest only by courtesy, and this also applies to a good deal of nominally 'Protected' forest. 'Reserved' forests are under half of the total forest area, and many of these, especially in the drier areas, are more subject than they should be to grazing and even illicit exploitation under cover of vague rights to minor forest produce. In any case, many of the best and least degenerated forests are in largely inaccessible Himalayan areas, there is very little forest of any sort in the Indo-Gangetic Plains, and much of the forest area of the Peninsula is really only scrub-jungle, very open

[39] The standard works are Stebbing 1922; Champion and Seth 1968; and Puri 1960. Quite different, and beginning much more recently, is the literature on the social history of the forest, of which leading works include Guha and Gadgil 1989; Gadgil and Guha 1993; the collection edited by Grove, *et al.* 1998; and the papers of Tucker 2011. A forthcoming collection edited by S.B. Hecht, K.D. Morrison, and C. Padoch is called *The social lives of forests*.

or stunted. Pakistan is an even worse case, with only 13,500 sq. miles (35,000 km^2, 3.7% of area) under forest. Yet there is good historical evidence for large forests even in the central Punjab in Alexander the Great's day, on the Yamuna in the time of Mahmud of Ghazni (11th century); and the Gangetic Plain was probably originally covered with vast forests, mainly of sal. Today, as Legris points out, it is only very rarely that one can travel as much as 186 miles (300 km) through even secondary forest that looks like forest, and then only by avoiding main routes, even on the Madhya Pradesh/Orissa borderland.[40]

One can see from this that the map in Fig. 1.10 represents not the actual vegetation of India but an inference about its natural vegetation in the past, minus the degradation caused by human activity. The leading form of this degradation is overgrazing. Speaking of the present state of the Gangetic plain, Mukherjee, in a much-quoted passage, says on the matter of overgrazing by domestic animals:

> On the plains the vegetation is rather delicately balanced against man at about the dry grass-land or the thorn-scrub stage. The soil over most of the Indo-Gangetic Plain seems to be supporting all of the human and bovine life that is possible under existing methods of exploitation. Increase in intensity of exploitation results in further destruction of natural vegetation and the amount and the character of vegetation sets a limit to the amount of animal life. Relaxation of pressure immediately results in a movement of vegetation towards the climax. But no relaxation is possible under present conditions. Dry grass-land and thorn-scrub formations remain practically stationary.[41]

[40] Spate and Learmonth 1967: 73. The same view of an adjacent region of monsoon Asia is expressed by Fisher (1964: 43–4): "In its primeval state almost the whole of South-east Asia must have been forested, and even today, in contrast to India and China proper, only a relatively small proportion of its area, mainly in Java, west-central Luzon, western Malaya and the better riverine and coastal lowlands of the Indo-Pacific peninsula, has been permanently cleared for cultivation. On the other hand, the natural vegetation of much of the remainder has in varying degree been modified by human activity, particularly in the extensive areas in both the mainland and the islands where the activities of shifting cultivators have led to the replacement of virgin forest by *belukar* or secondary jungle."

[41] Mukherjee 1938: 103.

Thus humans and their domestic animals, in this conception, are sources of disturbance from without, and the resulting dry grassland equilibrium state is a non-natural one, the result of overgrazing by domestic animals.

But is it correct to infer that the forest is the natural state prior to human settlement? For it is not a fact, but an inference based upon a theory—the theory of a natural succession of plant life ending in an equilibrium state called a "climax."[42] The concept of a climax is open to two serious objections. It rules out the effects of wild animals (biotic) and humans (anthropogenic) from its conception of the natural state, attributing such a state largely to climate and soil; so that, in this theory, the actions of animal life must be, oddly, judged non-natural. As a steady-state concept, this notion is also at odds with history, which knows only ceaseless change. The idea of the natural equilibrium state toward which the succession of plants tend was responsible for the dubious doctrine of the forest being the form of natural vegetation in the greater part of the Indian subcontinent—this being a projection backward in time of the idea of a natural equilibrium.[43] Being highly uncongenial to any kind of history, such analysis has largely been dropped in ecological science now.[44] We should start afresh, using other kinds of evidence. Doing so greatly enhances the prospect of forest history being a productive site of collaboration between ecologists, archaeologists, and historians.

[42] Woodbury (1954: 8), in the opening pages of a textbook of ecology, says, "This principle [of interacting agencies] assumes that a biotic community is in *dynamic equilibrium*, in which the organization is held intact because of the agencies involved approximately balance one another. If the potency of one agency is changed, the composition of the biota in the community will continue to change, until a new balance is reached. Such changes are known as *succession*. When an equilibrium is reached, in which the main biotic components are not overthrown by new invaders, a stage is reached that is known as *climax*."

[43] Much the same kind of "misreading of the landscape" has been demonstrated for the West African republic of Guinea and the French colony from which it came, by Fairhead and Leach 1996. Nikolas Sweet drew my attention to this work.

[44] Morrison forthcoming. A recent textbook of ecology (Smith and Smith 2009: 256–62) devotes several pages to *succession*, but none to *climax*, in contrast to the 1954 textbook of Woodbury.

Skepticism of this kind can help free us of the corollary position of the older forest science literature in India, which doubted that there was any true savanna in the region—that is, as a "climax" formation. To say there is no true grassland in India is a dark saying for a country that has large numbers and many types of wild grazing animals. Of deer there are some nine species, including sambar, swamp deer, muntjac, cheetal or spotted deer, hog deer, and mouse deer, of different sizes and specialized habitats; of antelopes six species, including the nilgai or blue bull, the blackbuck or black antelope, and the chinkara; and of cattle three or four species, including the wild buffalo and gaur.[45] George Schaller's classic study of the fauna of Kanha Park in Central India demonstrates the complementarity and niche specialization of several of these grazing species, living cheek by jowl in the same location.[46] Domestic sheep, goats, and cattle today descend from wild species found in South Asia itself, which is continuous with the region of the Middle East where these domestications were first accomplished.[47] So, for a very long time, grazing and browsing animals have been sculpting the Indian landscape with their teeth, maintaining grassy openings and meadows against encroachment or recolonization by trees. This is not to deny that overgrazing by domestic animals has been hugely destructive. But it is simply to register the fact that grazing animals have been in the picture for as far back as we can see, and that it is paradoxical to treat them as disturbances external to a hypothetical natural equilibrium. Humans too have been a part of Indian environments since the climate changes of the Holocene; one might argue that they emerged together. And wild grazing animals have been there forever.

With the purpose of starting afresh, then, and setting aside the conception of natural vegetation in the absence of grazing animals and human acitivity, I will review the archaeology of settlement and its evidentiary base, and its relation to recently adduced evidence of pollen analysis.

[45] Menon 2009: 38–51, 60–3.

[46] Schaller 1967.

[47] Possehl 2002: 23–4, 27–8.

I begin with the archaeology and settlement history of the Ganga plain. The archaeology of settlement and of what has been called the second urbanization of India—second, that is, to the cities of the Indus civilization centuries before—is viewed in terms of its effect on the environment; it is an archaeology of deforestation and environmental change. The historian D.D. Kosambi and the archaeologist D.P. Agrawal advanced the view that the Ganga valley had been heavily forested, and the second urbanization was accomplished when the iron deposits of Bihar were exploited: the iron was used to make the tools by which the forest was cleared and agricultural fields created in its place.[48] This version of forest history was greatly modified by the work of Makkhan Lal and George Erdosy.[49]

Looking at the plain of the Ganga, Makkhan Lal focussed upon the upper stretch, the Doab—the region between the two (*do*) rivers (*āb*), the Ganga and the Yamuna, right down to the point where they join at Prayaga (literally, "the confluence"), which is the old name of Allahabad. The Doab, and the Ganga valley generally, is a plain formed of a very deep bed of alluvium, as much as 4,000–6,000 meters.[50] Texts confirm its former afforestation. The *Śatapatha Brāhmaṇa* attests that from the Sarasvatī river to the Sadāṇīra (modern Gandak river) there was dense forest and settlement was only possible after it had been cleared by fire.[51] According to the *Mahābhārata* the capital city of the Kurus, Hastināpura, was located in a forest, and their exiled cousins, the Pāṇḍavas, founded their own capital, Indraprastha (modern Delhi), only after clearing dense forests. The country of the Pañcālas, a people allied with the Kurus, in the upper Doab, was founded in the Kuru forest. (Although the *Mahābhārata* in the form we have it today was composed much later than the Vedic times of which it speaks, it is likely that the information about forests would have been traditional knowledge and not later invention.) Later

[48] Kosambi 1956, 1965; Agrawal 1971.

[49] Lal 1984; Erdosy 1988.

[50] Lal 1984: 9.

[51] Expressed in ritual terms: it was made land fit for sacrifice after it had been tasted by Agni, fire. *Śatapatha Brāhmaṇa* 1.4, 14, 15, 16.

texts, the *Purāṇas*, speak of sacred forests, including three in the Doab: the Kuru, the Naimiśāraṇya, and the Utpālāraṇya,[52] the last of which is identified with the *Rāmāyaṇa* as the place where the sage Valmīki lived and Sītā gave birth to Kuśa and Lava.[53] From the older alluvium, fossils of ancient species of elephants (*Elephas antiquus*) have been found with those of the horse, the rhinoceros, and the hippopotamus. For early historic times there is textual evidence of the existence of the elephant, lion, tiger, rhinoceros, wild ass, and blackbuck. As late as the sixteenth and seventeenth centuries Abu'l Fazl records the hunting of lions, tigers, and elephants in the Doab.[54] Pollen records show the pine, sissoo, teak, deodar (cedar), babul, and Himalayan cypress, along with bamboo and acacia. When railways were introduced in the nineteenth century, the forest was abundant enough to be drawn upon both for fuel and for railway sleepers or ties, especially of sal.[55]

As a sample for reconstructing the settlement history of the Doab, Lal did a close survey of ancient settlements in an entire district, Kanpur. He sorted the settlements into periods by using a kind of ceramic clock consisting of the successive types of ware that had emerged: Black and Red Ware (BR), Painted Gray Ware (PGW), and Northern Black Polished Ware (NBPW). These were followed by the early historic period, which was indicated by coins and other kinds of objects. The number of settlements shows a continuous increase in numbers (9, 46, 99, 141) across the four periods. But most sites are on the banks of rivers and inland lakes, which would have required little or no clearing of forests. Moverover, the average distance between villages was nine kilometers, while the area of cleared land calculated to sustain villages was a radius of about one kilometer. Lal concluded from the evidence that there remained a great deal of uncleared forest between villages down to the nineteenth century, and that the greater part of the virtually complete deforestation of the

[52] *Devīpurāṇa* 74.
[53] Lal 1984: 14.
[54] Ibid.: 16.
[55] Ibid.: 14–15.

Doab occurred in the last two centuries. Erdosy, reviewing this work, believes that the overall effect of settlement history was the gradual and irreversible retreat of forests; but he concedes that the textual evidence of Mughal-era hunting of wild forest animals shows that deforestation was far from complete till recent times.[56] Lal uses Erdosy's study to refute earlier archaeological theories which argued that the settlement of the Ganga valley was accomplished by the heavy clearing of forests with the new types of iron tools made available via access to the superior iron deposits of Bihar. According to Lal, "extensive use of iron tools and the large scale forest clearing for human settlements and agricultural land is nothing but a myth."[57]

Turning to the Punjab, the land between the five (*pañc*) rivers (*āb*), Erdosy reviewed the evidence of pollen analysis (palynology) and archaeology, and concluded against widely held views which suggested that the climate was once much wetter, and that human settlement had caused large-scale deforestation in ancient times.[58] Possibly surface water had been more abundant, but the climate had been much as it is now, and the range of plants—including species that had been used in the past to argue for a formerly wetter climate—are all still found locally. Whether the Indus valley was forested, however, remains a mystery, though many parts of it would have been grassland. The settlement pattern there is similar to that in the Ganga valley, that is, along river banks where, according to Possehl, regular inundation would have drowned tree seedlings and preserved a grassy strip 100 meters wide. So there would have been no need to clear the forest, even if the region was generally forested. The impact of settlement on the environment, he argues, was not great.

Returning to the Ganga, we have seen that the notion of forest cover early in the historic period is attested by textual sources which refer to that period. In the meantime another kind of

[56] Erdosy 1988.
[57] Lal 1984: 83.
[58] Erdosy 1988.

evidence, that of pollen analysis, has been brought forward by S. Sharma and his team,[59] through study of lake-fill deposits in the central Ganga plain (Lake Sanai) covering the last 15,000 years. The second of the articles addresses the archaeological literature glancingly: "The pollen diagram shows the dominance of grasses throughout the lake's depositional history. Contributions of trees and shrubs is low, suggesting that throughout the last 15,000 years of the lake, the Ganga Plain was essentially a Savannah landscape with some forest thickets. This contradicts the existing conjectures that until the late Holocene, the Ganga Plain was covered by dense forest inhibiting humans to settle in this region."[60] Morrison puts it even more strongly: she believes this study, among others, shows *definitively* that many parts of the Gangetic plain were never *densely* forested.[61]

Thus from the older forest science literature to the more recent palynological contribution on the Ganga plain we have come right about, from dense forest to savanna. Should we accept the new view? The difficulty is that the evidence for forest cover in the Gangetic region is partly anchored in Sanskrit and Pali sources of the kind adduced by Lal, which do not go away, and which are not addressed by Sharma, *et al.* Should pollen trump texts? Perhaps, but one would like to see the two kinds of evidence brought together in discussion to see how the contradiction between them may be understood. We are, as of today, left unsure what to conclude about the state of forests in the Ganga valley at the start of the second urbanization. For now, there is good evidence, textual and palynological, that it was forested. But the question is how densely, and what the temporal pattern of variation was. It would seem that the list of the eight elephant forests shows that the lower Ganga plain (the Prācya or eastern forest), at least, was especially well endowed with forests and elephants.

[59] Sharma, *et al.* 2004, 2006.

[60] Sharma, *et al.* 2006: 976.

[61] Morrison forthcoming.

Of the many kinds of wild grazing animals in India, each with its own preferred ecological niche, there is one most closely identified with the Aryan settlers of the early historic period in northern India: the blackbuck or black antelope. The special quality of the blackbuck, compared with other deer and antelopes, is that it tolerates grazing in full sunlight, even in the hottest season, and prefers open land to the forest.[62] It thrives in grassland. Ancient North Indians identified their land with that of the blackbuck. Manu states that the natural range of the blackbuck is the land "fit for sacrifice"; beyond it is the land of barbarians (*mleccha*).[63]

The kind of landscape through which the blackbuck roams is called *jāṅgala*, which also designated the proper kind of landscape for human habitation. The English word jungle, meaning a tropical moist forest, comes from the Sanskrit *jaṅgala* (of which the adjectival form is *jāṅgala*)—which however meant the very opposite. *Jaṅgala* denotes a dry, open, grassy, thorny landscape. In the ancient medical texts *jaṅgala* is opposed to the wet, marshy and afforested landscape of the elephant, called *anūpa*.[64] The Punjab of the Vedic period was more of the *jāṅgala* type, whereas the Doab, into which the Aryans later migrated, was more afforested and wetter, at least at first. And it contained more elephants. The trajectory of this movement in history was a movement from horse country to elephant country.

The problem

Armandi observes that in the kingdoms of India and Southeast Asia the number of elephants a king held was the measure of his wealth and power. He further says—and this is crucial—that only kings could undertake the capturing of wild elephants in their tens or hundreds at a time. This was the practice in his day, described by European travellers; and it was current practice in the Mauryan

[62] Schaller 1967.

[63] *kṛṣṇāsāras tu carati mṛgo yatra svabhāvataḥ* |
sajñeyo yajñiyo deśo mlecchadeśas tv ataḥ paraḥ || Manu 2.23.

[64] Zimmerman 1987.

empire of the fourth century BCE, as reported by Megasthenes. Parties of such capturing men sometimes numbered in thousands, and only kings could gather such large bodies.[65] Thus the capture, training, and deployment of elephants in warfare belongs to the age of kingship.

To understand the persistence of elephants as well as their retreat, it is essential to understand the relation of kingship to elephants, and specifically the Indian model of kingship within which elephant capture and use were essential components. This model spread to the Southeast Asian kingdoms that are called "Indianized," and it influenced the military practice of ancient peoples to the west, including the Persians, the Hellenistic kingdoms of Syria and Egypt, and Greeks, Carthaginians, Numidians, and Romans. Over thousands of years, from about 1000 BCE to the nineteenth century, this development took the Indian idea of the war elephant as far afield as Spain and Java. Equally telling, it was *not* taken up by the Chinese, who were fully aware of it, at least in later times when they were interacting with the Indianizing kingdoms of Southeast Asia, if not earlier. But they chose not to adopt it.

This complex spread largely through king-to-king relations, whether peacefully by diplomacy and gift exchanges, or militarily through war and tribute-taking, or indirectly by emulation; it spread from ally to ally, and from enemy to enemy, and at a distance through the effects of reputation and imitation. We will need therefore to be alert to the king-to-king circulation of ideas, assets, knowledge, and practices as the means by which the use of elephants came to be diffused, becoming a universal norm for kingship within India and spreading to kings beyond. At the same time, I want to consider political forms other than kingship in order to determine the varying relations of kingdoms, republics, and tribal polities to elephants.

Tracking the king–elephant relation could lead to military history, as in the great work of Armandi. A whole shelf of books

[65] Armandi 1843: 26–9.

on military history in India can help such inquiry: one might begin with Hopkins (1889), a classic study of the warrior class in the epics, and continue by following up the excellent works by Sarva Daman Singh on the Vedic period, Simon Digby on the Delhi Sultanate, and Gommans on the Mughals, among others.[66] Moreover, the king–elephant relation can be used as a means to compare kingship with other political forms, that is, to contribute to political history.

In this book, however, I will use the relation as a thread that connects kings not only to elephants but also to forests and forest people. If we follow the thread—such is the hope—we will gain insights into the environmental history of India. For, to put it simply, kings are drawn to elephants because of their size, which is useful to kings as a signifier of the superlative character of kingship. Because of their bigness, elephants must, as noted, consume huge amounts of fodder daily; and as they do not become fit for work until age twenty,[67] it is uneconomical to raise them in stables and collect food for them during the long years of their unproductive youth. It is only practical to capture them as wild adults. Elephants can and do reproduce in captivity, but not at a rate high enough to obviate the need for further capture, and in any case it is simply uneconomical, as a general rule, to rely on captive breeding. This being so, kings have a direct interest in protecting wild elephants in forests. Toward this end, and subsequently for elephant capture and training, they need the help of forest people. The relation of kings to elephants is, in fact, a four-cornered relation of kings, elephants, forests, and forest people—a rich and complex field of relations. Studying it holds out the promise of bringing the forest and its inhabitants

[66] Works on the military history of India include several listed in the Bibliography, including Date 1929, Chakravarti 1972 (1941), Dikshitar 1944, Singh 1965, Bhakari 1981, Deloche 1986, 1988, 1990, 2007, Digby 1971, Gommans and Kolff, eds, 2001, Gommans 2002, and Irvine 1903. For the Indian epics Hopkins 1889 remains indispensable. Sen 2005 connects the work of Hopkins with the critical edition of the larger epic. Two recent collections have been edited by Kaushik Roy (2010, 2011).

[67] *Arth.* 2.31.9.

into the history of kingdoms, instead of looking upon the forest as the antithesis of the kingdom, of farmers and farming, of villages and cities—in short, all that makes up what we call civilization. The story will not be the same everywhere: it is different in India from that in China, especially, and therefore holds the potential of clarifying environmental aspects of the difference.

I want to make it clear that I do not argue for ancient kingship in general, or Indian kingship specifically, being intrinsically "green." Indeed, the power of kingship to mobilize people and resources placed an increased stress on the environment, as we see from the luxury trade in pearls, coral, furs, and pelts, and the trade in animal parts for medicinal purposes.[68] My view is simply that the specific desire of kings for elephants in their army creates an interest in protecting live wild elephants and their habitats. I am asking whether that interest may not have been effective enough to account, in part, for the India–China difference.

If one walks through the National Museum in New Delhi, one is struck by the many fine sculptures of elephants—beautifully rendered by anonymous stone-carvers who must have closely observed live, probably tamed, elephants—and Mughal miniature paintings of elephants. The elephant holds an important place in the art, folklore, mythology, and religions of India, and its presence in representations and rituals has to do with the persistence of wild elephants in forests and tamed ones in human settlements. Elephants suffuse the life and imagination of Indians at all periods.

At the core of the many representations of elephants, and of the many functions elephants wild and tamed have now and have had in the past, is the war elephant. Accordingly, I will focus upon the war elephant and its functions virtually to the exclusion of all the many other functions elephants have had in India's human history. For the war elephant is at the heart of the king–elephant relation, and it is this function that gives the logic of all other

[68] Rangarajan 2001, on India's wildlife history, gives further evidence on this point. On colonial hunting culture in India see Hughes 2013, and on the luxury trade, Trautmann 2012.

functions. Battles and sieges in which war elephants are deployed are rare, intense moments; but in the long intervals between battles, elephants are displayed, ridden on in processions, given as diplomatic offerings, paid as tribute, and so forth. Elephants are large, publicly visible signs of military potential, of a substantial living force at the command of a king. Their public movement and circulation between kings thus become functions drawing meaning from the war elephant. Conversely, the attributes of the ideal war elephant govern the selection criteria of wild elephants suited to capture. They also influence consideration of the "points," i.e. desirable and undesirable features—marks considered auspicious or inauspicious, and so forth—that furnish an expanding edifice of classifications of tamed elephants for all the uses to which they are put in addition to warfare. Elephants are an appealing topic and it is tempting to follow them all wherever they lead; but it is better for present purposes to concentrate upon the war elephant and not diffuse our attention. War elephants take us right to the heart of the matter.

In following the logic of this view I refuse the false dichotomy of instrumental and ceremonial uses of elephants by kings. The display of elephants in royal processions was, after all, the display of war assets. It had effects upon other kings, who were always assessing the strength of the various assets of their neighbors. The *Arthaśāstra* shows the king at all times comparing the assets of his kingdom with those of an adversary. It advises him on how to capitalize upon his relative advantages and work around his relative disadvantages; and elephants are one of his most important assets.

There is a body of scholarly opinion coming from the West and originating in the age of the great European empires—after heavy artillery had put an end to the age of the war elephant—which argues that Indian kings were excessively enamored of elephants to their own detriment, that is, that they were essentially irrational in the matter of elephants. I do not hold this view; I believe that such a position makes it impossible to account for the long duration and wide reach of the institution of the war elephant.

Even so, it is essential to start from the recognition that the war elephant is only one form that the king–elephant relation has taken. To begin with, then, in the next chapter, I will specify the entire range of the relation in the earliest civilizations, for it was the repertoire upon which Indian kingship drew when it invented the war elephant.

In India the ancient written sources, including sources for the history of kingdoms, were largely generated by religious specialists. There is consequently a tendency for the region's ancient history, and our understanding of Indian kingship, to be drawn into a narrative of the history of religion. Focusing upon king-to-king flows of information and goods and practices puts one somewhat at odds with the direction of the sources, and makes one read them in ways their authors did not intend. Some benefit will flow from the tension between the study of the king–elephant relation and the purposes for which religious sources were composed. It will become apparent, for example, that some forms flow *from* kingship *to* religion, as when a god or a sacred relic or a newly published book is carried on elephant back, like a king. It may also serve to show that kings have roles and relations that are in some ways superior to religions and religious specialists, and that have their own logic, including the logic of arbitrating among competing religions. Kingship, of course, has greatly to do with religion, but the representation of kingship by religious specialists has its own priorities. These priorities may not coincide with the royal perspective I hope to capture by reading the sources somewhat against the grain, trying always to find the perspective of kingship itself.

2

War elephants

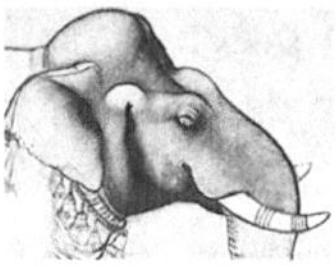

PRINCE RĀMA, HERO OF THE EPIC *RĀMĀYAṆA*, is in exile in the great forest of Central India. He has been sent there by his father, king Daśaratha of Ayodhyā, on account of a promise he made to Rāma's stepmother, queen Kaikeyī. Daśaratha having died, Kaikeyī's son Bhārata, one of Rāma's younger half-brothers, has reluctantly agreed to rule Ayodhyā as regent while Rāma completes his term in the forest. Early in the exile Bhārata journeys to see Rāma, who showers him with questions about the welfare of the kingdom. Taken together, these questions express a conception of perfect kingship. Some are lofty: "You have made brave men your counselors, I trust, dear brother, men you look upon as your very self—men who are learned, self-controlled, and highborn, and able to read a man's thoughts in his face."[1] Others are practical: "I trust you pay, when payment is due, the appropriate wages and rations to your army, and do not defer them." No surprises here, and many of these ideals of kingship could travel readily to other kingdoms in other countries. But there is one that is specifically and characteristically Indian:

kaccin nāga vanaṃ guptaṃ kuñjarāṇaṃ ca tṛpyasi |

You are protecting the elephant forests, I trust, and attending to the needs of the elephants.[2]

[1] *Rām.* 2.94.10.
[2] Ibid.: 2.94.43.

Indian kings need elephants and therefore need forests; the forests have to be protected and elephants' needs attended to. In this respect the forest is not the opposite of the kingdom—as a place of exile, to take the example at hand—or not only so; it is also an essential part of the kingdom. This expression of the duty of a good king connects the fortified royal capital to the elephant forest. It gives us a means of bringing the forest, forest people, and wild elephants into the history of the long era of kingship in India.

Understanding the logic and history of the Indian model of kingship as it involves the use of elephants is the task of the first part of this book. But this royal use of elephants was not only universal and normative for kingdoms *within* India, it was also powerfully influential *beyond*. From India the techniques of elephant use in battle spread both to the West: Persia, Hellenistic Syria and Egypt, Greece, Carthage, Rome, Ghazna; and to the East: the Indianizing kingdoms of Cambodia, Laos, Vietnam, Thailand, Burma, Malaysia on the mainland of Southeast Asia, and of Java and other regions of Indonesia. In the second part of the book I will show these developments as a connected whole, and, indeed, put Indian kingship and its elephant use in comparative perspective of the widest scope.

The ideal war elephant

Elephants served a variety of functions in Indian kingdoms—as the conveyances of kings, haulers of heavy materials for monumental architecture, perches from which to hunt game, leaders of temple processions, mythological guardians of the quarters, and even as the god Gaṇeśa. But war was their primary function. This firstness of the elephant's use in warfare was a logical priority, not a chronological one; as we shall shortly see, elephants were resources for ancient Indian kings long before the war elephant was invented. But, once invented, the war elephant served ever after as the standard, and all other functions became secondary and derivative. For this reason we need to examine the war elephant as the prototypical form which conditioned all other uses and representations.

This is an important principle of method for our inquiry. It is necessary to keep in mind that the war elephant disappeared from the picture some centuries ago. The ancient practices of elephant capture, training, and care have continued into the present, but the modern use of elephants has been dominated, rather, by timber extraction and other practices, and more recently by the critique of traditional practices by the animal welfare movement, each of which gives the human culture of elephant use a different centering and significance. This can have a distorting effect upon interpretations of the ancient scene, a problem of which we need to be aware.

To get to the ideal of the war elephant of ancient times we are well served by the fact that the Sanskrit poetics of kingship and warfare is preserved in an extensive archive. This comprises the epics—the *Rāmāyaṇa* and the *Mahābhārata*—and poems in praise (*praśasti*) of kings in inscriptions. Such texts do not give us the nuts and bolts of kingship—for those we will have to consult the science of kingship (*arthaśāstra*). They give instead ideal types, models of kingship in its perfected form, and as such are useful in showing us the logic of things.

Let us look, then, at how the war elephant appears in the poetry of kingship. This passage, taken from the *Mahābhārata*, is a particularly good one, not because it expresses a rare insight but on the contrary because it is perfectly typical of the representation of war elephants in poetry relating to Indian kingship. The terms of this verse (with one exception) recur in countless iterations of the type of the ideal war elephant.

bhīmāś ca mattamātaṅgāḥ *prabhinnakaraṭāmukhāḥ* |
kṣaranta iva jīmūtāḥ *sudantāḥ ṣaṣṭihāyanāḥ* ||
svārūḍhā yuddhakuśalaiḥ *śikṣitair hastisādibhiḥ* |
rājānam anvayuḥ paścāc *calanta iva parvatāḥ* ||

Terrifying rutting elephants with riven temples, well-tusked sixty-year-olds like gliding clouds, well-mounted by trained elephant-riders skilled in fighting, followed behind the king like moving mountains.[3]

[3] *Mbh.* 4.30.26–7.

Thus the ideal war elephant is a male, with large tusks, terrifying in appearance, at the height of its powers at age sixty, and in the state of elevated sexual ardor and combativeness called musth. Above all it is massive and stately, like a cloud or a living mountain. It is mounted by skilled fighter-riders. Let us examine each of these terms in greater detail.

First, its age. It is surprising, and perhaps for readers of a certain age pleasing to find, that sixty years is considered the ideal age of a war elephant. This is not frequently mentioned but is confirmed by another passage which likens two wrestlers to fighting elephants:

> *tāv ubhau sumahotsāhāv* *ubhau tīvraparākramau* |
> *mattāv iva mahākāyau* *vāraṇau ṣaṣṭihāyanau* ||

> They both had extraordinary staying power, both had ruthless strength and stood as large as two rutting sixty-year-old elephants.[4]

In another passage, a sixty-year-old elephant is among the rich gifts brought by royal guests to the anointment of Yudhiṣṭhira as king, from which we infer it is thought to be the ideal age on such a momentous occasion.[5] When we consult the "elephant science" literature in Sanskrit, we regularly find a discussion of the elephant at different ages, decade by decade, up to 120 years, with six decades of increasing powers, and six decades of declining powers.[6] As we saw, elephants at age sixty are on their last set of molars and cannot live a great deal longer. The sixty-year ideal age posited in the *Mahābhārata* is probably based on an observation of their increasing powers over the six decades, while the six decades of decline must be a later theoretical elaboration.[7]

[4] Ibid.: 4.14.20.

[5] *Gajendraṁ ṣaṣṭihāyanam, Mbh.* 2.49.7.

[6] *ML* 5.

[7] Aristotle, whose description of elephant physiology is quite good, also greatly overestimated elephant lifespan; 120 years is one of the numbers he gives (Scullard 1974: 45–6, citing *Hist. animal.* 9.46). See the discussion of Edgerton in the introduction to his translation of the *Mātaṅgalīlā*, p. 23. The *Ā'īn-i Akbarī* (1.41, 126) says the elephant is fully grown at sixty, drawing on the older texts of elephant science. Sanderson (1893: 56) says, "The general

The ideal war elephant, then, is a fully mature male. Possibly the sixty-year ideal has to do with it having very long tusks by that age, for tusks, as noted in the previous chapter, grow throughout the animal's life. But sixty is the age when elephants are nearing their end. The *Arthaśāstra* holds that forty is the age at which a war elephant is at its prime, which seems more realistic.[8]

The criterion of large tusks excludes the female elephant, though females were certainly captured and trained for other functions, including luring wild male elephants for capture. It is possible that the preference for capturing well-tusked (*sudanta*) elephants has acted as a selective pressure, increasing the proportion of *makhnas* among wild elephant populations in India over the last two thousand years and more.[9]

Most of the attributes are connected with the single quality of massiveness of body, likened to clouds and mountains. As the largest living land animals, elephants inspire awe (*bhīma*, terror) in people, this being part of their usefulness to kings. This central quality, their fearsome bulk, results in heavy demands upon kingdoms deploying war elephants. As high-maintenance assets, elephants require kings to devote considerable resources toward acquiring and holding them. We must assume that such kings weighed costs against benefits when deciding the animal was well worth the expense.

Among the huge costs involved, the first is food, in excess of 150 kilos daily, for in the wild, as I have noted, the animal feeds every waking hour.[10] Capture, taming, and being put to work alters that regime drastically; in particular, time devoted to work is time subtracted from feeding and seeking food. Not only must the captive elephant be fed, it must be fed rations of higher-energy food to enable the heavier workload.

---

opinion of the natives is that it attains 120 years in exceptional cases, but more generally to about 80 years."

[8] Details in Chapter 4.

[9] Sukumar 1989: 165–73.

[10] Ibid.: 79. Sukumar cites sources for a range of 12–19 hours per day.

G.H. Evans, a superintendent of the Civil Veterinary Department in colonial Burma at the beginning of the twentieth century, wrote a treatise on elephants and their diseases in which he put the matter succinctly: "If the animal in his natural condition, in which he develops a very small degree of energy, requires a whole day and the greater portion of the night to feed, whereby he may be able to replace that energy, then in the domesticated state when a greater consumption of energy is demanded and a reduced time prescribed for the repair of the loss, food must be supplied in a more concentrated form."[11] Underlying this passage is the conception of an energy budget, even if it is not quantified in calories. Work in captivity radically unbalances the energy budget, and the balance must be restored with high-energy food. Which is to say that elephants need crops raised by humans, crops dedicated to their energy requirements, and they need food that has been processed to enhance the available energy, as by cooking.

Indians in ancient times were well aware that the processed food supplied to a captive elephant was a departure from its natural diet, and that therefore the dietary change should be gradual so as not to upset the animal's digestion. According to a Sanskrit text on elephant science, the *Mātaṅgalīlā*,[12] a newly caught elephant should be given raw rice grits (*taṇḍula*) in the amount of one *kuḍuba*, mixed with grass, increased by one *kuḍuba* each day till it amounts to one *āḍhaka*; also boiled rice (*odana*) increased day by day in the same way, and other food preparations (*bhakṣaṇasādhanam*), which probably means cooked food.

The change in diet with captivity is the point at which the evolutionary paths of elephants and humans intersect, in somewhat contradictory ways. As noted in the previous chapter, elephant evolution has pursued the advantages of bigness coupled with a low-energy diet, at the expense of a large and inefficient digestive system. Humans on the other hand have developed large energy-demanding brains and short quick digestive tracts that require lots

[11] Evans 1910: 21.
[12] *ML* 11.11.

of external processing of food to pre-digest it, including pounding, grinding, cutting, and above all cooking—and raising crops especially suited to human tastes and energy requirements.[13] Such food appeals to many animals, including elephants. Sugarcane they find irresistible, and the massing of sugarcane in fields makes for an elephant food bonanza. The same can be said of many other crops, so that the elephant and the farmer are fated not to be friends. The raiding of crops by elephants is as old as agriculture itself, perhaps, and continues to this day. In India some 400 people are killed by elephants every year, and some 100 elephants are killed by people, many in retaliation, some in accidents.[14] Indeed, it is a paradox of our times that the more the measures to protect wild elephants succeed and the more their numbers increase, the greater the likelihood of conflict with human populations, which of course are growing at an even faster pace.[15]

This trajectory of elephant–human conflict over planted crops, which began ages ago, continues into the present and will, if wild populations are protected, continue into the future at an ever greater rate. Insofar as kingship depended upon agriculture and the appropriation of its surplus, it had a large stake in this conflict. Kings were called upon to protect farmers; but insofar as they needed elephants for war and had to cater to their diet, they had simultaneously to protect elephants from the wrath of the farmer.

Once humans began capturing and using elephants, the need to maintain them in good health created the need for medical care and specialized veterinary knowledge. The elephant physician was an early specialist among the attendants of captive elephants. A regime of treatment for internal ailments was worked out early on; it involved regulating the diet and the provision of special food and medicine to counter disease.

While war elephants were thought to reach their peak at the age of forty or sixty, it was at twenty that they were reckoned as

[13] Wrangham 2009.

[14] ETF Report 2010: 19, 78.

[15] This is a matter to which I will return in the last chapter.

having become fit for work.[16] This fact is fundamental and had huge consequences: to avoid the substantial dietary expenses of those first twenty years, young elephants were left in the wild and captured when they were ripe for work. A way of breeding elephants in captivity is to release them at night to fend for their food in the forest. But, as we shall see in the last chapter, records kept for large numbers of timber elephants in Burma/Myanmar show that under such a regime the birth rate is not sufficient to maintain the size of the herd. So, for all practical purposes, war elephants had to be captured as adults in the wild and then trained. It is this feature of the institution of war elephants that tied Indian kings to the forest: it ensured their practical interest in protecting forests and the wild elephants in them.

Capturing a wild adult male elephant who has the desired qualities is no easy task: it entails mobilizing lots of people and resources. For this reason the techniques of capture and training of these animals could only have been invented in the context of kingship, that being the only political form of ancient times with the capacity for projects of this magnitude. And these projects were additionally difficult because of the enormous resistance of wild elephants to being captured. Newly captured elephants do not cooperate with their trainers until they have been weakened by hunger to acquiesce in their restraints, and then mollified with food and kind words by their trainers. It is a difficult process in which elephants may perish or be badly injured, and in which humans put their lives at risk.

In ancient India it was frankly acknowledged that capture, and the transition from forest to village, was a severe hardship and indeed a life-threatening danger. The captive elephant always remembers his former freedom with longing and sorrow:

vanyās tatra sukhoṣitā vidhivaśād grāmāvatīrṇā gajā
baddhās tīkṣṇakaṭūgrāvāgbhir atiśugbhīmohabandhādibhiḥ |

[16] So *Arth.*, as we have seen; slightly different is *ML* 5.1: to the 12th year an elephant is of no worth; to the 24th year middling worth; to the 60th year of best worth.

udvignāś ca manaḥśarīrajanitair duḥkair atīvākṣamāḥ
prāṇān dhārayutuṃ ciraṃ naravaśaṃ prāptāḥ svayūthād atha ||

śailānāṃ kaṭukeṣu nirjharajale padmākare sindhuṣu
svacchandena kareṇukābhir aṭavīmadhyeṣu vikrīḍitam |
smāraṃ smāram anekadhāgranihitaṃ puṇḍrekṣukāṇḍādikaṃ
no kāṅkṣaty atidurmanā bahuvidhair duḥkhair upetaḥ karī ||

pūrvānubhūtam aṭavīṣu sukhaṃ vicintya
dhāyan muhuḥ stimitavāladhikarṇatāḷaḥ |
grāmavyathabhir adhikaṃ kṛṣatām upetya
kaiścid dinair mṛtim upaiti karī navīnaḥ ||

Forest elephants who dwelt there happily and by the power of fate have been brought to the village in bonds, afflicted by harsh, bitter, cruel words, by excessive grief, fear, bewilderment, bondage, etc., and by sufferings of mind and body, are quite unable for long to sustain life, when from their own herds they have come into the control of men.

On mountain ridges, in the water of the mountain torrents, in lotus pools and rivers, ever remembering how he played freely with female elephants in the midst of the forest, the elephant, dejected and beset with manifold troubles, is unwilling to eat stalks of white sugar cane, etc., though repeatedly placed before him.

Thinking on the pleasure he formerly experienced in the forests, constantly brooding, restraining the flapping of his ears and his tail, becoming very haggard from the hardships of the village, in a few days the newly caught elephant comes to death.[17]

We shall see in a moment the significance of mentioning forest (*vana*) and village (*grāma*) in the passage from wildness to captivity.

That the elephant retains memory of, and longing for, its former freedom is the underlying assumption of a striking simile in one of the many Sanskrit inscriptions from the Indianizing kingdoms of Cambodia:

dāsīn dāsāñ ca bhūmyādi- *dhanan tasyai pradāya saḥ* |
karīva vandhanirmmuktaś *śāntaye vanam āyayau* ||

[17] *ML* 11.1–3.

> Having given to the goddess (Prajñāpāramitā) a female and a male slave, land and other goods, like an elephant freed of its chains, he (Padmavairocana) has gone to search for peace in the forest.[18]

In the second line of the poem, a person slipping the bonds of everyday life to become a hermit monk in the forest (*āraṇyaka-bhikṣu*) is likened to a freed elephant returning to its original forest habitat. It is a lovely metaphor. The effect is somewhat spoiled for me, though, by the first line, which signals how very normal it was in the Southeast Asian kingdoms to include human slaves with rice fields, cattle, and buffaloes—and, rarely, even elephants—in a foundational gift to a religious institution such as a temple. The poet draws no connection between enslaved humans and the freed elephant, showing more understanding of the inwardness of the elephant than of human slaves who, in their bondage, may also have had memories of freedom.

In consequence of adult capture the elephant was tamed but not fully domesticated. The ancient Sanskrit texts recognize the essential wildness of elephants. In the *Mahābhārata* it is given as a teaching of the Veda that there are fourteen kinds of animals, seven of them forest-dwelling (*āraṇyavāsin*) or, simply, "of the forest" (*āraṇya*), namely lions, tigers, pigs, buffaloes, elephants, bears, and monkeys. Seven others are village-dwelling (*grāmavāsin*) or "of the village" (*grāmya*), namely cattle, goats, sheep, humans, horses, mules, and asses.[19] This contrast of forest and village animal species is elaborated in the medical literature called Āyurveda.[20] The British, by an entirely different route, namely common-law principles based on their own experiences of wild and domestic animals, came to a similar belief in the inherent wildness of elephants, applying it to disputes about ownership of straying animals in colonial India and Burma. In one case, a landowner (zamindar) had possessed a female elephant for six years when she fled to the forest and could not be found. A year

[18] IC 3: 67, verse 14, K 225.
[19] *Mbh.* 6.5.12–14.
[20] Zimmerman 1987: 101, 214.

later she was captured by the government, and the landowner sued for her return. The case went to the Supreme Court, which ruled for the government on the grounds that such animals, being *ferae naturae*, are a man's property only while in his keeping and cease to be so when they regain their natural liberty. This holds for animals that do not have *animus revertandi*, i.e. those known by their custom of returning.[21]

Elephants, then, are not domestic animals in quite the way that cattle, sheep, goats, and horses are. They remain wild even after capture and training, in the sense that they retain some memory of their former freedom and return to the forest if they slip their bonds. They are different from other domestic animals in other ways as well. They can be bred in captivity, and in modern times timber elephants which were released into the forest at night to feed and rested in forest camps during the hot season had opportunities to mate; and working mothers would often have a baby at heel as they worked. But, as we shall see,[22] under such conditions working elephants did not manage to replace themselves due to the stress of work further retarding their normally slow rate of reproduction. We must take it, then, that tamed elephant forces had always to be resupplied through wild elephants from the forest. This shows that the degree to which tame elephants have been modified by human selective action has been comparatively small, whereas other domestic species have been greatly modified—as were the East London pigeon fanciers whose work of artificial selection was so closely studied by Darwin in the development of the concept of natural selection.[23]

At the same time, if we follow biological criteria of genetic or behavioral modification of elephant populations by humans in deciding whether they are domestic animals, or if we follow the ancient Sanskrit texts which consider elephants to be of the forest

[21] Sanderson 1893: 77; cited in Evans 1910: 325, along with law cases from British Burma.

[22] Details in Chapter 8.

[23] Feeley-Harnik 1999. The weavers of East London were growing smaller while breeding their pigeons, being squeezed by enclosure into ever smaller quarters.

and not of the village, we may miss an important historical point. This point is that the capture and taming of wild elephants arose in the period of the great animal domestications, and the long history of domesticating animals was an important precondition for the taming of elephants. For historical analysis it is thus necessary to treat them as domestic animals of a certain kind, even if the domesticating was done individually, one by one, continually through the 3,000-year span of their human use. There is no settled terminology for this partial and piecemeal domestication. Some prefer the word "captive," others "tamed," but there is little to be gained in arguing definitions. The important thing is that, at some point after the first domestication of other large mammals, humans devised ways to organize the capture of elephants as wild adults and train them for war, and that the kingdom came in this way to be tied to the forest as the nursery of this most valuable asset.

We come, now, to the remaining feature of the ideal war elephant of the verse we have been examining—his being in rut, or musth. This is the most interesting and counterintuitive of the factors. As explained in the previous chapter, a male elephant at the start of musth has a surge of testosterone followed by a flow of fluid from the temporal gland before the ear that stains the temples with a dark vertical streak. He is in a state of heightened combativeness and may be irritable and difficult to control. This poses a problem for elephant handlers in zoos, circuses, and timber operations, and hence the current literature on musth treats it as a dangerous problem requiring management. As against this way of looking at musth, the quoted passage in the *Mahābhārata* makes it clear that in ancient times it was viewed very positively in respect of the war elephant, as a highly desirable attribute. This passage is not singular. Musth generally occurs once a year, yet it is something of a trope in poetry to describe war elephants as being in musth; that this is a literary convention is clear from the fact that it is unrealistic to suppose war elephants were in musth each time there was a battle. The desirability of musth in a war elephant is moreover carried to great lengths of hyperbole. In a passage of the *Rāmāyaṇa* describing the attributes of Ayodhyā as a perfect capital city, we are told it is filled with elephants large as mountains and always in musth.[24]

In relation to other domestic animals, male aggression deriving from heightened sexual energy is a decided inconvenience for owners, and measures have been devised to mitigate the problem. Given its size, a male elephant in musth is, to put it mildly, a very considerable inconvenience. But what makes the *war* elephant different from domesticated animals is that its function is to terrify by its huge proportions, and by the prospect of being gored or trampled or thrown by it. So musth at the time of battle is the ideal state for a war elephant to be in.

But as a war elephant will not actually be in musth every time it is brought to battle, a musth-like combativeness may be artificially induced. According to the *Ā'īn-i Akbarī*, "Elephant drivers have a drug which causes an artificial heat; but it often endangers the life of the beast. The noise of battle makes some superior elephants just as fierce as at the rutting season; even a sudden start may have such an effect. Thus His Majesty's elephant *Gajmuktah;* he gets brisk, as soon as he hears the sound of the Imperial drum, and gets the above mentioned [temporal] discharge."[25] Thus, musth-like excitement, and perhaps even a discharge from the temporal glands indicating actual musth, may be stimulated by the noise of battle preparations. War elephants were sometimes given wine before battles to promote the desired combativeness of musth by artificial means. According to *I Maccabees*, the Hellenistic rulers of Syria gave their elephants wine (the juice of grapes and mulberries) before battle, doubtless continuing Indian practice.[26] Aelian says the same,[27] but the wine is made of rice or cane, not grapes.[28] The Chinese Buddhist monk Xuanzang, who wrote a memoir of his visit to India to collect copies of the scriptures (629–45 CE), says that king Pulakeśin of Mahārāṣṭra had several hundred special warriors, and several hundred violent elephants

[24] *nityamattaiḥ sadā pūrṇā nāgair acalasaṃnibhaiḥ*: *Rām.* 1.6.23.

[25] *Ā'īn* 1.41, 128.

[26] *I Macc.* 6.34.

[27] Aelian 13.8.

[28] Scullard 1974: 187–8.

who were given wine as an intoxicant before battle, making them attack furiously.[29] The *Arthaśāstra* provides for a fortifying drink (*pratipāna*), containing liquor and sugar, for elephants, horses, and draft cattle when they are working; but in this case the purpose seems only to restore the energy deficit of work, not stimulate aggression.[30]

As we shall see, when elephants in opposing armies fight, they go head-to-head in a shoving match. This ends when one of them succeeds in turning the other while attempting to gore him in the flank. Polybius describes exactly this mode of fighting at the battle of Raphia.[31] What is striking about it is that this is the battlefield behavior of wild bull elephants when in musth.

The very terms of the *Mahābhārata* verse we have been examining—the words *matta* (in musth) and *prabhinnakaraṭa* (temples riven with musth fluid)—frequently recur as poetic tropes: the idealizing tendency of these poems, or one might say its very lack of realism, tells us how highly musth was valued despite the difficulty of managing the frenzy of the war elephant.

Musth is the Persian word *mast*, "drunken," adopted perhaps in Mughal times, a virtual translation of the Sanskrit *matta* of this passage. *Matta* as an adjective, or *mada* as the noun, indicates intoxication, joyousness, and madness, implying sexual desire. In erotic poems bees drawn to the temporal fluid of an elephant in musth are a mood-setting sign of human love through the association of bees and rutting elephants with flowers and springtime. Here is an example from Kalidāsa, a description of the god of love who shoots flowered arrows:

His choicest arrows
    beautiful clumps of mango blossoms,
his bow
    the best of flame trees
his bowstring
    a swarm of bees,

[29] Xuanzang 1996: 335–6.
[30] Details in Chapter 4.
[31] Details in Chapter 6.

his white parasol
    the white-rayed moon void of its spots
his rut-mad elephant
    the Malaya breeze
and his heralds cuckoos,
    may the World Conqueror
    the bodiless God of Love
    attended by spring
    grant you a wealth of luck![32]

In sum, the ancients took musth as a sign of health and vigor in a male elephant, and the concomitant surplus of aggression was thought valuable for warfare; more, it was the very essence of the war elephant. In the Sanskrit literature on elephants it is clear that musth is highly desirable, an elephant not achieving it being considered abnormal and in need of medical attention.

Finally, we must examine the people attached to the ideal war elephant of our passage, both those who are mentioned—the elephant riders—and one who is not, the driver.

The riders are the fighters. Skill in riding and fighting are both indicated in the epic as warlike virtues, both treated as separate kinds of skills. There is no mention in the epics of any howdah giving riders a secure platform from which to fight. This needs to be made clear, since much of the scholarship on the war elephant of India mistakenly assumes that the howdah was around from the start. Early sculptural representations and battle descriptions in the epics make it clear that over the earliest period warriors were essentially bareback riders, as were cavalrymen, holding on with their knees and with perhaps one hand gripping the harness—a kind of surcingle or girth. Both for horsemen and elephant warriors, riding was a skill by itself that had to be mastered, quite distinct from the art of using weapons. The kings too rode in this way, as we see exceptionally clearly in the sculptures at Sanchi,[33]

[32] *Ṛtusaṃhāra* 6.28 in Selby 2003: 154.

[33] The photographic survey of Sanchi by Morihiro Oki (Oki and Ito 1991), being exceptionally detailed and comprehensive, is ideal for the study of this question. Domesticated elephants regularly show the mahout and his *aṅkuśa*, and

and on a coin struck by the Greeks showing the Indian king Porus on elephant-back pursued by Alexander on his horse.[34] How and when howdahs came into existence is discussed later; here it suffices that there are "towers" in the Hellenistic kingdoms and proper howdahs in the twelfth-century reliefs at Angkor Wat.

The *aṅkuśa* or iron hook (Fig. 2.1) that the driver uses to control the war elephant is not mentioned either in the verse in question, where it is taken for granted, but we hear of it explicitly in other passages and see it often in sculpture. The fierceness of the *aṅkuśa*, with its two sharp points, stems from the need to control an animal whose boundless aggression is its most desired quality, the purpose

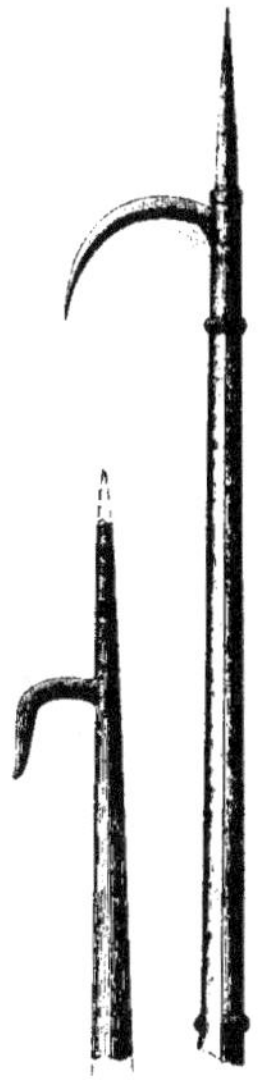

Fig. 2.1: *Aṅkuśas*, from excavations at Taxila

---

a rider, whether a common warrior or a king, or even a woman and child (ibid. pl. 39, "happy life in heaven"), riding astraddle, with no howdah. Examples are too numerous to specify. Other riders in the Sanchi sculptures also ride astraddle. Horses have bridles and saddle blankets but no saddle, notably in the scene of the Great Departure of the Buddha-to-be. Depictions of riders on unusual or fanciful animals—buffaloes, camels, goats, lions, composite beasts—show them riding bareback.

[34] Details in Chapter 6.

of the hook being to restrain it. To be sure, war elephants are not only curbed, they are also "urged on by hooks."[35] But it is consistent with the metaphor of this verse that, although the *aṅkuśa* may be used as a goad to impel the elephant *forward,* it is normally used to *restrain* a war elephant in the grip of musth.

The action of the hook is implied by the following verse:

> *bāhūyamānas tu sa tena saṁkhye*
> *mahāmanā dhṛtarāṣṭrasya putraḥ* |
> *nivartitas tasya girāṅkuśena*
> *gajo yathā matta ivāṅkuśena* ||

> Dhṛtarāṣṭra's son, now called to battle by the great-spirited warrior prince (Arjuna), was pulled back by the hook of his words, as a mad tusker by the hook of its driver.[36]

The restraining purpose of the *aṅkuśa* is indicated by the adjective *niraṅkuśa*, indicating a person who does not follow the rules, who is unrestrained, a bohemian perhaps. Poets, especially, are said to be rule breakers (*kavayaḥ niraṅkuśāḥ*), and there is a treatise on rules for wayward poets called *An elephant-curb for poets* (*Kavi-gajāṅkuśa*).[37]

The *aṅkuśa* is an iron hook with two points, one at the end of the shaft and the other at the end of the hook itself. It is the sign of a war elephant in ancient sculpture and of the poetry of Indian-style kingship all across the region to which the Indian technology of war elephants spread, extending to North Africa and southern Europe on the one hand, and to Southeast Asia on the other.[38] It is not the only instrument used by the mahout: we hear of less fearsome instruments—the *tottra* (prod), often paired with the *aṅkuśa*, and the *kaṅkaṭa* (perhaps a goad)—but the *aṅkuśa* is the most frequently used of these words and the only object depicted in ancient sculptural representations. The primacy of the *aṅkuśa*

[35] *aṅkuśair abhicoditān*: *Mbh.* 7.65.10.

[36] *Mbh.* 4.61.1.

[37] My thanks to Madhav Deshpande and Velcheru Narayana Rao for these examples.

[38] The Romans do not seem to have quite understood this; they called the hook *stimulus*, according to Armandi (1843).

in sculpture, however, does not mean that its use was universal, as we may see if we consult modern practice (with all due caution in view of the very different conditions which sustain it). Both in British Burma and in present-day South India a simpler, cheaper, and less dire iron hook is in use, attached to a wooden shaft with a rounded, not a pointed, end (Fig. 2.2); and a simple stick sometimes replaces it.[39] Of course we are not speaking here of war elephants. But I incline to think the *aṅkuśa* in ancient sculpture appears so regularly and exclusively not because it was always used, but because it signifies that the elephant under the driver wielding it is a war elephant. The *aṅkuśa* is a sign, then, in sculpture and poetry, of the tamed elephant in his highest function and most dangerous state.

From its realist perspective the *Arthaśāstra* partially confirms this interpretation of the poetics of the war elephant. It divides elephants according to their work into four categories: elephants under training (*damya*), the war elephant (*sāṃnāhya*), the riding elephant (*aupavāhya*), and the rogue elephant (*vyāla*, incorrigibly dangerous). Although it does not mention the *aṅkuśa* in connection with the war elephant, in relation to riding elephants it speaks of

Fig. 2.2: One-pointed elephant hook

[39] Evans 1910: 54; Chowta 2010: 61–2, 116.

one ridden with a stick (*yaṣṭi*) and one ridden with a goad (*tottra*), which shows that the aṅkuśa was not used for simple riding.[40]

So the hook is a sign of the war elephant and royalty. In peaceful processions it is for display. And what it points to is the idea of a boundlessly aggressive war elephant in full fighting fettle.

Kings and elephants

Elephants have attracted kings as valuable resources for royal projects virtually from the beginning of kingship. Where kings had access to elephants locally the attraction was magnetic. Part of the appeal was surely the elephant's awe-inspiring bigness and difficulty of control, which in turn had to do with the need for the king to establish a hierarchy of rank and secure his own place at its top. Through spectacular hunts, capture and display in menageries, tribute extraction, and the like, royal ownership of elephants symbolized the primacy of the king: only kingdoms and not republics or "forest people," for example—to take the main alternative political forms of ancient India—could mount the large and complex operations entailed.

The war elephant was not the first of these royal uses of the elephant; there was a long prehistory. The war elephant was invented *c.* 1000 BCE, and this was prepared by the invention of kingship itself; by the domestication of large animals, cattle, horses, sheep, goats; and by the various uses of elephants by the earliest kings of the first civilizations. It is my contention that the war elephant was invented in India, and by this I mean that the techniques of capturing wild adult male tuskers and training them for warfare were created here. It is probable that these techniques were invented under the auspices of kingship sometime in the late Vedic period and were then diffused within India, so that the war elephant quickly became a standard asset in Indian kingdoms. We cannot date this invention exactly, but I will give evidence to show that it did not exist at the beginning of the Vedic period (*c.* 1400 BCE). It arose in the late Vedic period and had become

[40] *Arth.* 2.32.1, 6.

normalized and virtually universal among kings of North India, as an ideal if not always as an actuality, possibly as early as 1000 BCE, and was normative in North India by 500 BCE at the latest.

To trace this prehistory we need to look at the relations of kings and elephants in the earliest literate civilizations: the Egyptians; the Assyrians and Mesopotamians; the Chinese; and, finally, the Indians of the Indus civilization. The Indus civilization (2500–1800 BCE) is the most important precursor of the invention of the war elephant in Vedic India, but the problem is that the Indus script has not yet been deciphered. So we do not have written documents through which to follow the king–elephant relation, nor do we have a clear understanding of Indus political organization. The kingdoms of early Egypt, Assyria, Mesopotamia, and China offer a more concrete sense of possible elephant uses in the early kingdoms, which may be a help when confronting the difficulties of interpreting elephant representations in the Indus civilization. Subsequently we will look at the invention of the war elephant in the late Vedic period.

The prevailing scholarly literature on the early civilizations, as it relates to our topic, is largely focused on the possible domestication of elephants on the basis of a quite small body of evidence. Archaeologists in site reports, and historians writing accounts of the early kingdoms of North Africa, the Near East, China, and India (that is, the Indus civilization), provide evidence of the possible domestication of elephants in very early times. Some are tentative; others believe that the domestication of elephants by ancient peoples, before the 500 BCE time horizon, is almost certain. Sarva Daman Singh, in his excellent study of warfare in the Vedic period, gives this view a strong form: "the docility, intelligence and easy obedience of the elephant must have quickly led to its domestication, once it was known and captured."[41] His belief is that elephants are readily domesticated; early domestications could have occurred in several places;

[41] Singh 1965: 72.

and the Aryans when they came to India had seen domesticated elephants among other peoples that will have inspired them to replicate the practice.

However, as explained, elephants are not domesticated like other animals by being raised in captivity from birth, so what we need is clear evidence of their capture in the wild followed by training. Having examined the evidence for elephant domestication prior to 500 BCE, my conclusion is that it shows the strong attraction of kings to elephants as resources, and a variety of ways in which kings used elephants including capture and display; but there is none showing war elephants or the techniques of producing them outside India. Even evidence for the riding of elephants before that date amounts to a single ambiguous instance. Let us review this evidence to see the range and nature of interaction between kings and elephants in the early days.

Egypt

African elephants were present in prehistoric and pre-dynastic Egypt, as shown by finds of bones, and were registered on cosmetic palettes, carved ivory, painted ceramics, and rock paintings.[42] Most spectacular are the finds in the earliest, pre-dynastic period of Egyptian civilization of two young elephants buried in graves at Hierakonpolis, near Edfu, in Upper Egypt.

Renée Friedman, the excavator of one of the elephants, tells us that the animal was buried whole, not dismembered, with grave goods including a cloth covering, pottery, and shell necklaces.[43] It was judged to be 10 to 11 years old and was found in a tomb—Tomb 24 of an elite cemetery—that had been plundered. A pelvis and a considerable number of bones and a large bit of the hide remained. Friedman infers the elephant was captured live and imported from the desert or from further south and held for a time before being sacrificed; stomach remains show it was fed on marsh grasses. Another elephant, judged to have been between 6 and 10 years old, was buried in Tomb 14 of the same cemetery.

[42] OEAE 2001, 1: 467.
[43] Friedman 2004.

She interprets the burials as sacrifices and considers them very significant for understanding "the embryonic conception of early kingship at the very dawn of Egyptian civilization."[44] She believes that the capture and import of live elephants may indicate local control of the source region and its sacrifice to have been part of the "association of kings with powerful beasts" in early documents, suggesting their "especially close relation with the elephant."[45] So we seem to have good evidence of the capture of young elephants and strong evidence of the connection of elephants with the beginnings of kingship in ancient Egypt.

In dynastic times, however, wild elephants disappeared from the valley of the Nile because of increasing aridity.[46] The expansion of farming and herding throughout the valley of the Nile precipitated a southward retreat of wild animals. While Egyptian religion, kingship, and art of later ages show a rich and highly developed interest in animal life, the elephant figures only rarely. It features in royal hunts and menageries but not in other uses, even though wild elephants lived just beyond Egyptian territory, in the savanna of central Sudan.[47] Only much later were elephants captured and trained, using Indian techniques, by the Hellenistic rulers of Egypt, the Ptolemies, who came in the wake of Alexander.[48]

Ivory was prized by Egyptian kings and they went far afield to acquire it. The material had become an item of the luxury trade, a signifier of wealth and status worked into objects of beauty by craftsmen well before the arrival of kingship. Kings in Egypt used their organizational power for complex projects to obtain ivory from distant places. Because ivory travels so well, however, it is not an indicator of elephant capture and training; besides, much Egyptian ivory came from hippos.

The most dramatic encounters of Egyptian kings with elephants occurred, then, not in Egypt itself, but during the New Kingdom

[44] Ibid.: 164.
[45] Ibid.: 163.
[46] OEAE 2001, 1: 467.
[47] Houlihan 1996.
[48] Details in Chapter 6.

campaigns beyond Egypt proper, into Syria, where a population of wild elephants of the Asian species existed at the time. The pharaohs Thutmose I and Thutmose III both hunted Syrian elephants in Niya, on the Orontes river in North Syria. The hunt of Thutmose III (r. 1504–1450 BCE) is exceptionally well documented by no less than three inscriptions. In an inscription on a stela at Gebel Barka in Sudan he modestly attributes his unprecedented success to God.[49]

> Now another occasion of victory that Re commanded to me
> redoubling for me (my) great valour at the water of Niya.
> He caused me to create an enclosure(?) of elephants;
> my Person fought them
> in a herd of 120.
> The like had never been done by a king
> since the gods who once received the White Crown.
> I have said this without boasting in the matter, there being no half-truths therein.[50]

The connection of the elephant hunt with kingship is taken to be evident in the inscription, needing no explanation. Its magnitude is asserted to be without precedent in the history of Egyptian kingship.

The hunt is confirmed by another inscribed stela of Thutmose III, at Armant. A biographical inscription of an official of the king, Amenamhab, adds the information that the elephants were hunted for their ivory. He claims to have saved the king's life on this occasion and been rewarded handsomely:

> Again I saw another effective deed which the Lord of the Two Lands achieved in Niya,
> when he hunted 120 elephants for their tusks.
> And then the great elephant which was among them raged near His Person.
> I it was who cut off his trunk while he was alive, before His Person, while I was standing in the water between two rocks.

[49] I am grateful to John Baines for the translation of this and the following passage, and for pointing me to the pre-dynastic material.

[50] Baines 2013.

And then my Lord rewarded me with gold,
[amount thereof: ;]
garments: 5 pieces.[51]

A fourth elephant-related document of the same time is a painting in the tomb of Rekhmire, vizier to the elephant-hunting king Thutmose III (Fig. 2.3). It shows tribute being brought to Egypt by the conquered Syrians, including (in this register of Rekhmire's tomb) an elephant on a leash, elephant ivory, a wild cat of some kind, and a pair of horses. The elephant is the size of a large dog relative to the human figures, the wild cat, and the horses, and one would be inclined to interpret it as young were it not for its tusks, though they are small ones. The proportions in Egyptian representations are seldom realistic, being often governed by the limits of the space available for composition. But when we see how small those tusks are, compared with the large tusks on the shoulder of the porter next to the elephant, it seems a young animal is intended. It jibes with the young age of the African elephants captured and buried much earlier at Hierakonpolis and, as we shall shortly see, the more nearly contemporary evidence from Assyria.

Assyria

There is a similar pattern—of royal hunts, and of live capture and display—a few centuries later, also concerning Syrian elephants, in the records of Assyrian kings.[52] The universe of published elephant references in cuneiform records of Assyria, a dozen in

[51] Baines forthcoming.

[52] Early Mesopotamians, using the Sumerian language, have left a small number of references to elephants but they are not very telling for our purposes. They did have a word for elephant, *amsi*, literally "toothed wild bull," which appears to be secondary. It reappears in the records of their successors, alongside the Akkadian word *pīru*. In a self-laudatory hymn in Sumerian, king Shulgi claims to have captured elephants, and here the term is *til(l)ug*, also known from a few other examples. An early Semitic loan word was *bi2-lam*, corresponding to Proto-Semitic **pīl*, related to later Akkadian *pīru*. I am indebted to Piotr Michalowski for this information.

Fig. 2.3: Egypt: elephant at the tomb of Rekhmire

all, are in the *Assyrian dictionary* (s.v. *pīru*). The main records are of the following rulers (all BCE):

Tiglath-pileser I	(1114–1076)
Aššur-bēl-kala	(1073-1056)
Aššur-dān II	(934–912)
Adad-nārārī II	(911–891)
Ashurnasirpal II	(883–859)
Shalmaneser III	(859–824)

Most of these records begin with a formula which is repeated verbatim from one king to another. The formula invokes the gods Ninurta and Nergal, and goes on to give the results of royal hunts and the capture of live animals for display:

> The gods Ninurta and Nergal, who love my priesthood, gave to me the wild beasts (and) commanded me to hunt.[53]

Unlike the records of the Egyptian Thutmose III and his vizier, in which the royal hunt and the display of captive animals are separate events, in some of these Assyrian cases hunting and capture are part of the same occasion.

The list begins with Tiglath-pileser I. A cylinder inscription records his conquests and his hunts. Of the latter it says that he killed four wild bulls in the country of Mitanni; he killed ten strong bull elephants in the country of Harran, in the district of the river Habur, a Syrian tributary of the Euphrates, and caught four alive, taking hides, tusks, and live specimens to his capital city of Aššur; he killed 120 lions hunting on foot, and 800 lions hunting by chariot; and he "brought down every kind of wild beast and winged bird of the heavens whenever I have shot an arrow."[54] Here we see very clearly the context in which elephants served as resources, symbolic and substantial, for kingship. Elephants are a prominent item, along with wild cattle and lions, in spectacular hunting. This is doubtless because of their size and the difficulty of killing them, making them signs of the king's superlative

[53] Stela of Ashurnasirpal II, RIMA 2: 226, A.O. 101.2.

[54] RIMA 2: 25–6, lines 59–84, A.O. 87.1.

courage and skill. These attributes then become part of the *res gestae* of the king, recorded in writing and through writing made public and present, and in the process exaggerated. We also see that captive elephants are byproducts of hunting. They are taken live, along with the hides and tusks of the elephants killed, to the capital, doubtless for public display in a royal menagerie. The reasonable inference is that the captives are immature elephants orphaned by the hunt. Finally, we see that elephants take their place among other wild animals—wild beasts and winged birds of the heavens—and figure in the emerging display practices of early kings. Exotic wild animals appear as signs of the king's reach and power, their pelts and teeth being items of conspicuous consumption.

Five successors of Tiglath-pileser I have left cuneiform records of elephants which confirm this pattern and add to it. This record takes us close to the time-horizon of the invention of the war elephant in India. Aššur-bēl-kala killed elephants with his bow and, capturing others, took them to his city of Aššur. Aššur-dān II killed 56 elephants, along with lions and wild bulls. Adad-nārārī II killed 6; Shalmaneser III killed 23 or 29 elephants.[55]

An inscription of Ashurnasirpal II shows especially clearly the way elephants circulated through tribute, collection, display, and hunting. The king undertook a military expedition to the Mediterranean and levied tribute on the peoples inhabiting that region. The tribute was taken as silver, gold, tin, bronze, linen cloth, and the ivory of sea creatures; also monkeys, great and small, which the king brought to his capital city, Calah, "and displayed (them) to all the people of my land." Through his courage and strength of arms he captured 15 lions and 50 lion cubs and caged them in his palace; he captured herds of wild oxen, elephants, lions, ostriches, monkeys, wild asses, deer, bears, panthers and others, "beasts of mountain (and) plain, all of them in my city

[55] Aššur-bēl-kala: RIMA 2: 103, ll. 6–7, A.O. 89.7 (not in the *Assyrian dictionary* list); Annals of Aššur-dān II: 161, rev. l. 27; RIMA 2: 135, ll. 68–72, A.O. 98.1; Adad-nārārī II: KAH 2 84: 125; RIMA 2: 154, ll. 122–7, A.O. 99.2; Shalmaneser III: Ernst 1952: 473; RIMA 2: 41, A.O. 102.6.

of Calah. I displayed (them) to all the people of my land." In the hunt he killed 30 elephants, 257 wild oxen, and 370 lions: so he says.[56] Live exotic animals, including elephants, are now levied as tribute from distant subordinate kings or governors. For example, a record of Shalmaneser says, "I received tribute from Egypt: two-humped camels, a water buffalo, a rhinoceros, an antelope, female elephants, female monkeys."[57] This record is inscribed on the famous Black Obelisk in the British Museum, which includes reliefs showing the tribute of conquered peoples. One of the panels (Fig. 2.4) depicts the elephants and monkeys or apes of this passage. Another, of Ashurnasirpal, says he received five live elephants as tribute from the governor of Suhi (Syria) and the governor of Lubda.[58] The overall context is the same. Wiseman says: "In common with the boasts of his predecessors the king lays much emphasis on his personal prowess in the hunt, which he also depicts on his throne-room walls. In addition to a bag of 450 lions and 390 wild bulls, the king collected herds of live bulls, lions, ostriches and apes and at least five elephants for his zoological gardens and for breeding purposes."[59]

After these kings we no longer hear of elephant hunts in the surviving record, and it appears that the Syrian elephant population soon went extinct. We do read in later cuneiform records of *war* elephants, but they date to the time of the Hellenistic rulers, the Seleucids, who got the elephants and the techniques of deploying them from India.[60] Thus in cuneiform astronomical daybooks from Seleucid Babylonia we find entries for 273 BCE of "20 elephants, which the satrap of Bactria had sent to the king"; and in 149 BCE of an army of king Demetrius containing 25 elephants.[61]

[56] RIMA 2: 226, ll. 25b–42, A.O. 101.2.
[57] RIMA 2: 150, A.O. 102.89.
[58] Wiseman 1952: 31.
[59] Ibid.: 28.
[60] As we shall see in Chapter 5.
[61] Sachs-Hunger 1996, 1: 345; 3: 87.

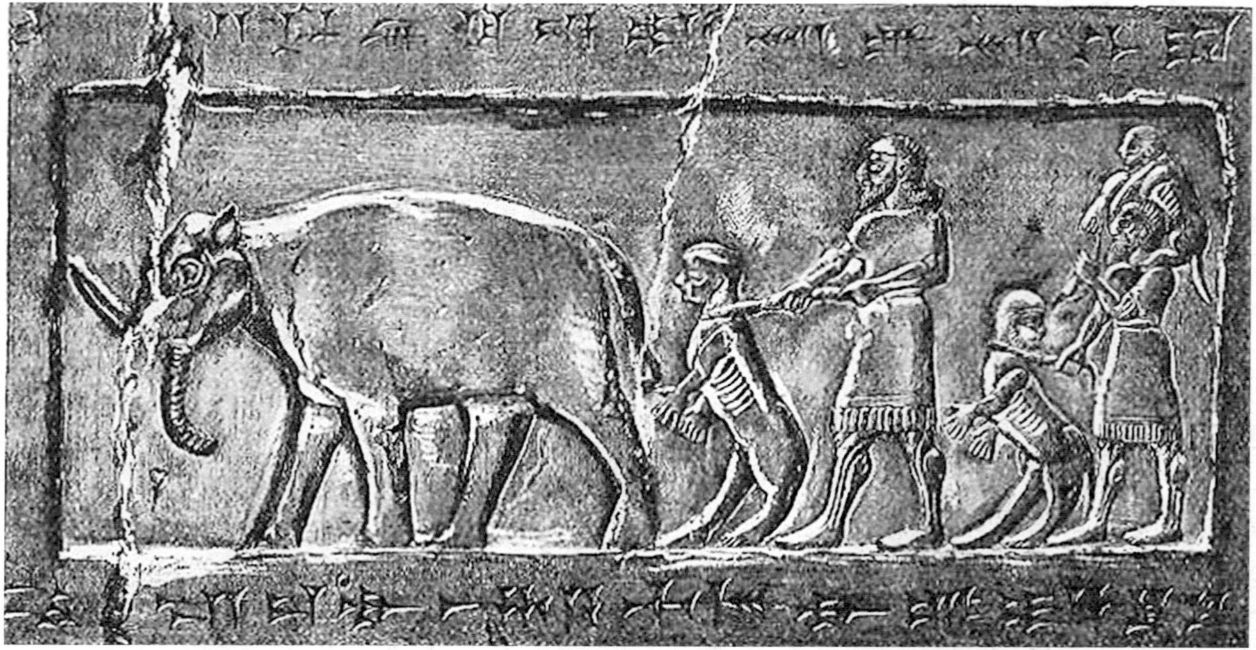

Fig. 2.4: Assyria: elephant and lions on the Black Obelisk of Shalmaneser III

Elephants also make an appearance in a few Assyrian omen texts, in the form of rare and monstrous hypothetical events, such as the unexpected coming of a comet. Suppose an elephant appears before the city gate, what does it portend? Or suppose a dog barks in front of my city's sanctuaries and an elephant answers?[62] These are the higher and more theoretical reaches of omen hermeneutics, which imagines possible if unlikely events and interprets their meaning.[63] Omens have to do with events that are out of the ordinary, so the appearance of elephants in omen texts implies their rarity, not their familiarity. Elephants were a part of the Assyrian imaginary, but they figure as wild, exotic, interesting animals, not as part of the daily scene.

The largeness of elephants, and the complexity and scale of operations implied by their capture and display, make them a sign of royalty that needs little explanation for viewers; the animal is virtually a natural symbol. That captive elephants were meant for public display is made perfectly explicit in the record of Ashurnasirpal II. He displayed elephants and other animals in his capital to convey his own magnificence. Kings were drawn to elephants as iron to a magnet.

Mesopotamia

Out of Assyria, in nearby Mesopotamia, a terracotta image of an elephant from the city of Ur is labeled "A man riding an elephant" in a site report by Leonard Woolley and Max Mallowan.[64] If the interpretation is correct it would be the one and only direct evidence of the riding of tamed elephants at so early a time—the second millennium BCE—anywhere among the early civilizations. The object is shown in Fig. 2.5, which should be compared with a similar scene of a man riding a humped bull, Fig. 2.6. Does the interpretation hold?

[62] *Assyrian dictionary* 2005: 419.

[63] I owe this interpretation to Piotr Michalowski. I am grateful for his help with these passages, and indeed the entirety of the material on Assyria and Mesopotamia.

[64] Woolley and Mallowan 1976: 182.

Fig. 2.5: Mesopotamia (Ur): elephant and rider (?)

Fig. 2.6: Mesopotamia (Ischali): humped bull and rider

The report quotes the notes of Leon Legrain of the University of Pennsylvania Museum, where this object is held:

> This is a rare but curious witness to the influence of Indian trade and models in the Larsa period. The animal is represented as walking. Its straight back, small ears and thick legs belong to the Indian type (Komooria Dhundia, *v.* E.J.H Mackay, *Further Excavations at Mohenjo-Daro*, Delhi, 1938, p. 329). Like those portrayed on Indian seals it shows no traces of tusks and may be a female. On our relief the tail is somewhat long and the trunk is rolled up as if collecting fodder; the marks around the neck may be folds of skin, or necklaces? The mode of riding is still more curious. A broad woven strap, as used today in India to fix the howdah, is tied round the body of the animal. The driver is sitting neither on the head nor on the back, but is represented at mid flank in an almost impossible position, with his right knee stuck below the strap. This is exactly the position of the man riding on the back of an Indian humped bull on a relief plaque from Ischali (H. Frankfort, Oriental Institute Communications 20, Chicago, 1936, fig. 73c), here transformed into an elephant rider. On both reliefs bust and arms are shown full-face, the left hand resting on the hump or shoulders of the animal, the right holding a slightly curved driving stick; both riders are nude except for a light loincloth and girdle.[65]

It should be said at once that there is no question of a howdah since, as we shall see, the howdah is a late invention. The reference to the Komooria Dhundia type will be examined shortly.

In another publication Legrain says the object "is evidently the work of an artist not familiar with elephants, or the proper way of driving them."[66] He considers the rendering of the elephant true to the Indian type mentioned, but the driver, "the Indian mahout—is here represented in an impossible position, sitting neither on the head nor on the neck, but hanging mid-flank on one side, his left hand resting on the shoulders, his right, armed with a short curved stick, simply hanging motionless."[67] The overall interpretation directs its criticism at the artist but does not doubt the reality of

[65] Ibid.
[66] Legrain 1946: 29.
[67] Ibid.

Indian elephant riding at that early period. One would wish this had been demonstrated rather than assumed.

A unique object is inherently difficult to interpret, especially when it represents a mode of riding that is impossible and impractical for controlling the movements of so large an animal. Legrain claims Indian influence upon a local artist, which, because of the parallel with the man riding an Indian humped bull, may well be correct, though Syrian elephants were nearer at hand and should have been considered. While the man riding the humped bull appears to be riding astraddle, it is impossible to interpret the man on the elephant riding so, unless we presume a U-shaped dip in the elephant's back not found in nature. I conclude that the position of the man is impossible, as Legrain has said. One does not know how to read this evidence, and what it is evidence of. Just possibly it is a distant echo of elephant riding in the Indus civilization, whose trade with Mesopotamia in this age is well attested; but if so one needs confirmation from the Indus remains, which, as we shall shortly see, do not supply it.

China

In China the elephant (*xiang*) appeared at the beginning of writing itself, on oracle bones and in inscriptions, with a symbol of its own (Fig 2.7).[68] These "bones" were the shoulder blades of oxen or the shells of turtles, heated with a hot poker till they cracked. A diviner would read the patterning of cracks to yield the answers to the questions posed, such questions being written on the object, whether before or after the fact. The jaw of an elephant, along with the scapula of a whale and the bones of many wild animals, was found at Anyang, capital of the Shan dynasty, dating to *c.* 1400 BCE, together with inscribed oracle bones and bronze weapons.[69] Anyang today is a city of five million in the north of Henan province. As we have seen, these elephant remains were first thought to be imports from the south, but it has since been

[68] Laufer 1925: 3.
[69] Li 1977: 70–1; Zheng 1982:101.

Fig. 2.7: China: early elephant representations

Top row: Archaic forms of the written symbol for the elephant.

Second row: Elephant from a bell of the Shang period, about 1500 BCE.

Third row: Symbols of the elephant from inscriptions on bronzes of the Chou period.

Fourth row, left: Elephant from a bronze beaker of the Zhou period; *right*: elephant from a bronze of the Shang period, applied to a seal of later date.

Bottom row: Elephant head in the pictographic writing of the Moso.

shown that wild elephants were once common in northern China. It is apparent that elephants had a significant role in the Chinese imaginary right from the outset of its civilization.

There is a delightful story about the mythical emperor Shun, known for his rustic simplicity, modesty, and hard work on the family farm when he was a boy. He is held up before children as a model in a work called *Twenty-four stories of filial piety* assembled by Guo Jujing of a much later time—that of the Yuan Dynasty (thirteenth–fourteenth century); in fact it is the very first story of the collection. Because Shun's parents and elder brother abused him, the filial piety with which he invariably acted toward them was so much the greater. His virtue was so transcendent that elephants plowed his fields and birds weeded the grain; we could say that his virtue turned the farmer's enemies into his collaborators.

In the previous chapter I introduced Wen Huanran's survey of evidence for elephants in Chinese history. Here I will examine the handful of early mentions in Wen's study for the period prior to 500 BCE—those that speak of the possible capture and keeping of live elephants with some degree of plausibility.[70]

From the Shang period (1600–1046 BCE) we have, besides the mention of elephants in early writing, the magnificent bronze ritual vessel shown in Fig. 2.8. Although its surface decoration is highly mannered, the overall shape is quite true to life. Of this period there is testimony in two texts about human–elephant relations. However, the texts which report these incidents belong to a time much later than the events of which they purport to speak.

The first of these comes from *Master Lü's annals* (*Lüshi chunqiu*, *c.* 239 BCE), a compendium of philosophical pieces on

[70] The period after 500 BCE will be examined in Chapter 8. In addition to the instances discussed here, Wen's survey refers to arguments of other scholars in the form of inferences drawn from written characters, including the character for elephant. For example, one scholar (Wang Guowei) believes the character *wei* comes from characters for *claw* and *elephant* and may have derived from the sense of "tame the elephant." Such claims are so tenuous and vulnerable to alternative interpretations that they require corroborating evidence and cannot stand on their own.

Fig. 2.8: Bronze ritual vessel in the shape of an elephant, late Shang period

good government compiled by a college of scholars brought together for the purpose by Lü Buwei, a prime minster of the state of Qin shortly before it formed its empire. One of the chapters, about the virtues of music in government, with examples from ancient times, has this to say about elephants: "When King Cheng was established, the Yin populace revolted. The king ordered the Duke of Zhou to crush the rebellion. The men of Shang had trained elephants, with which they maltreated the Eastern Yi. The Duke of Zhou consequently chased them with his armies to the area south of the Yangzi [River] where he composed the 'Three elephants' [song] in order to commemorate his power."[71]

It appears that elephants were used militarily, though in what way we are not told, and there appear to have been only three. They belonged to rebel remnants of the previous regime and

[71] *Lüshi chunqiu* 5/5.14, p. 151.

were driven south of the Yangzi, the proper place for elephants. The source dates to several centuries after the event of which it speaks, and we may reasonably wonder if its testimony is reliable. Even if it is a genuine tradition from the Shang period, we would have to say that the military use of elephants in China began and ended with the song celebrating their defeat, because Chinese (i.e. Han) armies did not incorporate trained elephants as a regular practice.

The second text, a passage in the writings of the great philosopher Mencius (372–289 BCE), tends in the same direction. He says that the (Shang period) Duke of Zhou performed a number of services to king Wu, among them that "He hunted the tiger and the leopard, the rhinoceros and the elephant, and drove them far away. There was great gladness below heaven."[72] Here again the text was written some centuries after the event of which it speaks. In this case the king is shown clearing wild animals from the forests, to make land habitable and cultivable. Evidently we have a different conception of virtuous rule than in the story about emperor Shun, and one that proved more influential.

One other bit of testimony concerns the war of 506 BCE, during which the kingdom of Chu was attacked by the forces of the kingdom of Wu and defeated. The armies of Chu, besieged in their capital, tied burning torches to the tails of elephants in their possession and directed them against the enemy, but without success.[73] Obviously, this was an act of desperation, not regular practice; and it did not impress Sun Tzu, who was present in the attacking force, as elephants get no mention in his classic work on the art of war. But it does imply the keeping of captive elephants in the city, in the non-Han kingdom of Chu, for reasons unknown.[74]

Thus, there are two possible instances of the capture of elephants and their use in war; but if true they were experiments without

[72] Mencius 1932: Book 6, 96.
[73] *Zuo zhuan* 1991: 756.
[74] Cf. Bishop 1921, who suggests religious purposes.

lasting effects. On the whole, kings in China seem to have used elephants for display and for their ivory, and to have taken credit for clearing the forests of wild animals and making them safe for farming. They did not institutionalize the use of elephants in war and were not in later times receptive to the eastward spread of the Indian war elephant.[75]

The Indus civilization

Finally, we come to the Indus civilization (2500–1900 BCE), the most important of the early civilizations for understanding the emergence of the war elephant in later Vedic times because it preceded the Vedic period and existed in close proximity with it.

The people of the Indus civilization are often said to have first domesticated the elephant, and indeed this has become the prevailing view in the scholarly literature; alternatively that the domestication began even earlier among their precursors. But this is the result of the hopeful reading of material remains that are ambiguous at best. I believe it is important to hold that scholarly consensus in suspension and review the materials to see whether, and if so for what uses, the elephants of the time of the Indus civilization were captured and trained.

While being the most important of the early civilizations for our purposes, the Indus civilization is also the most enigmatic, presenting several difficulties of interpretation. Like the others, it had a writing system, and we have many short inscriptions on seals, but unlike the others its script has so far eluded many attempts to decipher it. Thus we do not have a written record to go on as we do for Egypt, Assyria, Mesopotamia, and China; what we have is limited to visual representations of elephants. Further, we do not know what kind of political system the people of the Indus had, whether kingship or some other, although there are some signs of centralized functions in the remains of its great cities. We know very little about its military character, except for the defensive

[75] Details in Chapter 8.

walls of the citadel in the cities and some weapons of copper or bronze; in any case it does not resemble the horse-and-chariot-based military culture of the Vedic period. In sum, nearly a century after the discovery of the Indus civilization—which is to say the discovery that the remains of the cities belong to a bronze age prior to the composition of the texts of the Veda—we cannot make out clearly what was transmitted from the earlier civilization to the later. If the continuities were strong we could confidently use the Sanskrit records of the Vedic age to interpret the material remains of the Indus civilization; but we cannot confidently do so under the circumstances. In the matter of elephant use, the best way to proceed is to examine the evidence of other early civilizations as points of comparison for interpreting that of the Indus.

From the visual representations there is no mistaking the fact that the Indus people were familiar with elephants and that they played a large role in their thoughts. Using Mahadevan's concordance (1977) to get an overview of the evidence as a whole, we find 57 images of elephants in a corpus of over 4,000 inscribed seals and copper tablets. Most of them (44) are on steatite seals (one of them a sealing, that is, clay on which a seal has impressed the image), 13 on copper tablets that are thought to have been used as amulets. There is also an elephant with horns as well as tusks on a copper tablet, plus a few images of mythological, composite animals containing elephant trunks. Finally, there are a few toy elephants in clay. All of these are rather small objects; the seals are little more than 2.5 centimeters square, the copper tablets a bit larger. There are very few osteological remains of elephants—one find of bones, several of ivory being worked into beads, and a whole tusk. For the most part the question of elephant capture and training in the Indus civilization rests upon the seals, the amulets, and the toy elephants. Interpretation of these objects on this question is attended with lots of uncertainty. Nevertheless the images, small as they are, are executed well and realistically. They must have been made by craftsmen who had seen elephants in the flesh.

Of images in the seals and copper tablets, the greatest number is of the so-called unicorn, a bull-like animal with a single horn; and various kinds of cattle (all of them bulls), humped and unhumped, are by far the most frequent. But 57 elephant representations is a substantial number.

There are also a substantial number of very good images of the rhinoceros (40) and the tiger (21).[76] What is more, there are two seals on which the elephant, rhino, and tiger appear together, as a set. One of them is among animals surrounding a human figure in what looks like a yoga posture, which Marshall called Proto-Śiva, calling attention to Śiva's epithet Paśupati, "Lord of beasts" as well as Yogeśvara, "Lord of yogis" (Fig. 2.9). But Sanskrit *paśu* designates domestic animals generically, or specifically cattle; as opposed to *mṛga*, wild animals generically, specifically deer. In the case of this seal the animals as a set must be taken to be wild: elephant, rhino, tiger, deer. Again, on a copper tablet we find the elephant in a row of animals with the rhinoceros, urus bull, a gharial with a fish in its jaws, and a bird.[77] Today one may find wild elephants, rhinos, and tigers in the grasslands and forests along the Brahmaputra river at Kaziranga National Park in northeast India, and the same triad is in the wild animal set that the Duke

Fig. 2.9: Indus civilization: seal of "Proto-Śiva" with wild animals

[76] Mahadevan 1977: 793.
[77] Mackay 1937: 352, and pl. 90, no. 13.

of Zhou cleared from the forests of North China. They have long since disappeared from the Indus valley; indeed there are no wild elephants today in the entire region of the Indus civilization sites. But, as several archaeologists have suggested, the landscape may then have been more forested and therefore more hospitable to these wild species. However, this finding simply shows that in the Indus civilization the elephant was understood to be a wild animal, much as in classical India, thousands of years later, the elephant is of the forest, not of the village. It does not show domestication, but by the same token it does not preclude the possibility that the Indus people captured and trained wild elephants.

We can take it, then, that the people of the Indus cities and towns had wild elephants near at hand and that the images on seals and amulets are good ones because they are drawn by craftsmen who had seen them. Mackay, one of the civilization's excavators, says: "Great attention was paid on [four seals] to the representation of bristles along the outline of body and head, which is perhaps a mark of a younger animal, for adults generally lose this hair." We have already seen evidence of the live capture of young elephants in Egypt and Assyria. Mackay finds no trace of tusks on three seals and thinks females may have been intended. On the other hand, it is confounding that on some seals the end of the trunk distinctly shows two fingers, like an African elephant, rather than one, which is typical of the Asian elephant.[78]

Something else Mackay says on the topic is off the mark, in that he uses the thinking of his own day, the age of the timber elephant, to draw inferences about the Indus civilization:

> According to native lore, the elephant on seal 648 would be regarded as of very inferior breed, owing to the slope of its back and the length of its legs. There are two species of elephants in India, the better one for work being the Komooria Dhundia, with flat back, thick stout legs and square head. The Meergha is a poorer type which has a sloping back, long legs, less square head and is not so stocky. If the elephant was domesticated in the ancient Indus valley, it may have been used

[78] Mackay 1937: 290, 667.

only for state purposes and not as a hauler of materials, and its build would not have mattered much.[79]

The classification into the long-legged Meergha (Skt. *mṛga*) or "deer" type, and the superior Komooria Dhundia (Skt. *kumāra*) or "prince" type comes from the age of the war elephant; the latter is the ideal type for war. But these classes have a different application in the timber industry, in which the stronger Komooria type is better for hauling, the logic of which infuses Mackay's interpretation. He says that the "deer" type may not have been stigmatized in the Indus civilization if "used only for state purposes," by which I take him to mean riding and not hauling. The argument is doubly wrong, in that the riding elephant for an Indian king of later ages would have mattered a great deal and have been modeled upon the war elephant. This kind of muddled argument comes about from relying upon the British-Indian literature on elephants in the age of the timber elephant to interpret ancient evidence.

We come, then, to the big question, the matter of domestication and taming. The Indus people had a full range of domesticated animals drawn from local wild species, including humped Indian cattle (zebu), unhumped cattle, water buffaloes, goats and sheep, though not horses.[80] So they were skilled in the management of animals, and they had wild elephants nearby. The arguments that have been advanced to support some level of domestication rest upon certain features of the visual representations: (1) a "manger" placed before the elephant in some seals; (2) the representation of a vertical fold or line at the shoulder, interpreted as harness, or the edge of a blanket-like covering; and (3) decorative painting on a terracotta toy elephant. We need to look at each of these closely.

As for the manger, Marshall sees an association between it and *wild* animals, possibly in captivity:

Of the seven animals in question three are invariably shown on the seals feeding from what appear to be food troughs, viz. the Indian bison (Seals 310–26), the rhinoceros (Seals 341–7), and the tiger

[79] Ibid.: 290.
[80] Kenoyer 1998.

> (Seals 350–1); two, the elephant (Seal 369) and the buffalo (Seals 304–6), are sometimes feeding from these troughs, sometimes not; while the zebu (Seals 328–40) and the short-horned humpless bull (Seals 487 and 542) appear without them, though in the case of the latter there is a small object on the ground beneath its head, which is not clear enough to be distinguished. Is any significance to be attached to the presence of these troughs, or are they merely fortuitous? *Clearly they bear no relation to domestication*; for the two animals which alone we may safely assume to have been domesticated, namely the humped and short-horned humpless oxen, are without them; and, on the other hand, the tiger, rhinoceros, and bison, which have never been domesticated but might have been kept in captivity, are provided with them, while the buffalo and elephant, which might be either tame or wild, are sometimes provided with them, sometimes not.[81]

He thinks the manger represents food offerings showing the animal, whether captive or wild, to be an object of worship. This may be so; but these mangers in front of otherwise wild animals could represent a capture-and-display situation, as in Assyria. Mackay's suggestion that some at least of the images are of young elephants would fit that scenario for, as we have seen, captive elephants in Egypt and Assyria were young or can be inferred to have been so. Reading the evidence of Egypt, Assyria, and the Indus civilization together, it appears that the invention of the royal zoo, probably involving the capture of immature elephants among other exotic animals, preceded that of the war elephant.

Thus the evidence of the manger, which tends to support the possibility of capture and display. Now for the evidence of the supposed blanket or harness (Fig. 2.10), which has been used to suggest not just capture and display, but riding. On some seals we see a vertical line at the shoulder, from the back to just behind the front legs, which could be a bit of harness. In others there appears to be a covering such as a blanket; in one, vertical lines around the neck; in a "mythological" horned elephant image there is what appears to be a crupper under the tail, connecting with a harness or blanket. A toy elephant has painted geometric designs on the

[81] Marshall 1973: 70, emphasis added.

Fig. 2.10: Indus civilization: seal with elephant

body, again suggesting a blanket.[82] It is hard to know whether these suggestions are correct, and if correct whether they are sufficient as circumstantial evidence of riding. The difficulty of this line of reasoning is there is no representation of a human riding an elephant in the entire corpus of elephant images so far found in the Indus remains.

Finally, the archaeologist Mark Kenoyer,[83] who has unrivalled knowledge of Indus civilization craft productions, draws attention to a terracotta elephant head. Its ears flared dramatically to form a corona, this has red and white decorative painting on it (Fig. 2.11). Kenoyer connects this with the historic and current custom of decorative painting of tame elephants in India. If this

[82] Mackay 1943, pl. LVI, no. 9.
[83] Kenoyer 1998: 166.

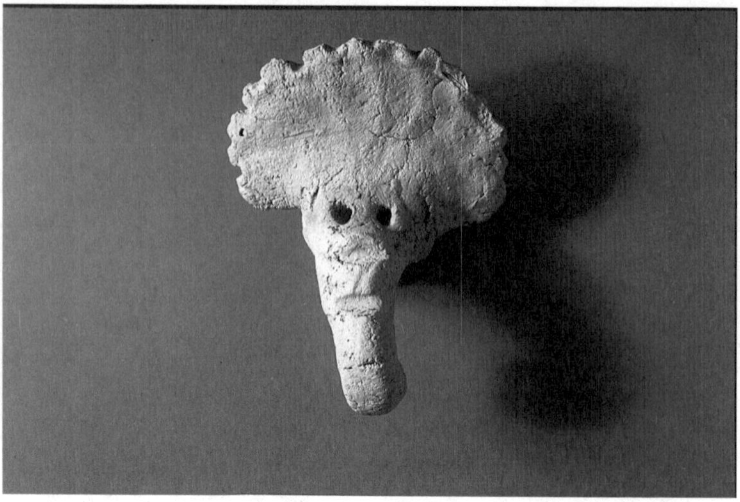

Fig. 2.11: Indus civilization: terracotta painted elephant head

object is intended as a realistic representation, the argument is a good one, for humans could hardly paint a live elephant if it were not somewhat tame. The object is not quite unique; we can join it with the toy elephant of Mackay (1943), previously mentioned. Both are painted. Are they evidence of the painting of live elephants? If it is a toy for children or a mythological creature for worship, the assumption of realism may not obtain.

This is the sum of the positive evidence for elements of elephant domestication among the first civilizations. The evidence of captivity and display in Egypt and Assyria is certain, and for the Indus civilization it seems good. When it comes to riding, however, there is zero evidence. Here we need also to weigh the significance of the negative evidence, namely, the complete absence of mahout and *aṅkuśa*, images which figure so regularly in visual representations of later times. As Sukumar says, "not a single elephant figure has a rider; this is rather surprising if the elephant had been tamed and put to some human use."[84] This is generally true of the written and visual evidence of elephants in ancient kingdoms across Asia in ancient times, before about the

[84] Sukumar 2011: 31.

middle of the first millennium BCE—Egypt, Assyria, Mesopotamia, India, China. The only exception is the terracotta representation of a man on an elephant from Mesopotamia, attributed by Legrain to a local and inexpert artist responding to influence of some kind from India, assuming that which is yet to be proved: the riding of elephants in that early period.

With so many elephant representations we may reasonably find it significant that there is no representation of a driver on the elephant's neck. We may thus reasonably conclude that the Indus people may have captured and displayed wild elephants, but we have no clear evidence—at best only one ambiguous item—that they or others of this time rode them. And even though elephants figure fairly prominently in the deeds and public performance of kingship in ancient Asia—and in ways that seem connected across a very large region—neither the Indus people nor any of its contemporary civilizations captured wild adult elephants and trained them for war.

The invention of the war elephant

The self-styled Aryans of the *Ṛg Veda*—the earliest extant text in the Sanskrit language (*c.* 1400 BCE)—had a culture of war based upon a warrior class, the kṣatriyas, who rode chariots drawn by two horses under yoke. Other forms of fighters, on horseback or on foot, accompanied the great chariot warriors but were of lower standing. This culture suffuses the text, which, however, consists of hymns to the gods. These deities resemble humans, but in exalted shapes, enabling them to appear at the sacrifice and be feasted. As described in the hymns, all the gods ride chariots; and their verses have kings giving chariots and chariot horses, among other things, to priests as sacrificial fees. These are also bestowed upon poets, to honor their creation of hymns deemed especially efficacious in inviting the gods to hitch up their chariots and descend to feast with the human offerer of a sacrifice.

Where did this culture of warfare come from, and what is its relation to the earlier Indus civilization? Some scholars think that the Aryans of the *Ṛg Veda* are the same as the people of the Indus civilization. But the great difficulty for this view is that while the material remains of the Indus civilization show solid-wheeled carts drawn by oxen, they do not show true chariots with spoked wheels, or even true horses, these not being indigenous to India. For this reason the majority of scholars believe, rather, that the Aryans came into India from the northwest at about 1400 BCE, after parting from their linguistic cousins, the Iranians—also chariot warriors. In recent decades archaeologists have begun to find, in the steppes of South Russia, southeast of the Urals, chariot-using peoples whose material finds seem to accord in place, time, and content with what philologists infer about the ancestral culture of the speakers of the Indo-Iranian language from which Sanskrit and the languages of Iran descend, the Sintashti culture.[85]

A text showing just how complex and technical was the knowledge required to manage chariots and chariot horses has been found in faraway Boghazkeui, in Turkey, from the cuneiform texts that make up the archive of the Hittites, whose empire depended upon skill in chariotry. The neighboring country of Mitanni, which fell under Hittite control, had a ruling class who spoke Hatti, the language of the people over whom they ruled, but who originally spoke an Indo-Aryan language close to Sanskrit. They retained words from that original language—mainly the names of gods and technical terminology to do with chariot warfare and chariot racing—which are very close to the Sanskrit of the *Ṛg Veda*. The Mitanni warrior class was not from India, it was a band from the South Russian steppe that split off and migrated toward the Mediterranean while another branch migrated to India. The text in question is the manual of a horse trainer named Kikkuli, of Mitanni, written around 1300 BCE in the Hittite language in the cuneiform script. It concerns the rigorous endurance training of chariot horses, extending over some seven months. Although written in Hittite, the text retains several technical terms pertaining to the management of chariot horses in the Indo-Aryan language.[86]

[85] Anthony 2008.

[86] An English translation by Peter Raulwing is available online. Gary Beckman kindly lent me his unpublished translation.

In brief, this evidence shows that the Aryans came into India from a grassy land of horses and chariots to the north. This was a land outside the range of elephants. India, however, was a land of elephants and forests into which horses had to be imported, and in which a horse-based warrior culture was maintained only at considerable effort and cost the further east and south the Aryans moved into the subcontinent.

The elephant, in one notable passage of the *Ṛg Veda*, is called *mṛga hastin*, the wild animal with a hand, that is, a trunk—recalling the inscription of the Egyptian Amenemhab, which also called the trunk a hand. This shows that the elephant was a novelty to the Vedic Aryans; having no word of their own they made up the descriptive word *hastin*—which, as we noted, survives to this day in Hindi, *hāthi*. *Mṛga*, "wild animal," is opposed to *paśu*, "domestic animal."[87] Of course, this says no more than do the Indus seals and copper tablets of earlier times, and the classical Sanskrit texts of later ages, that the elephant is fundamentally a wild animal, of the forest rather than of the village. It is not proof against domestication; it does not show that elephants were never captured in the wild and tamed. So, what is that proof?

The evidence against early Vedic capture and training is simply that the people of the *Ṛg Veda* and their gods did not use war elephants or even riding elephants: this we may see from the description of battles and warfare. The military consisted of chariots and foot soldiers, and perhaps some mounted warriors, but no elephants. The war elephant came later in the Vedic period.

The literature on military history in India also considers the war elephant a later development. However, Sarva Daman Singh, in his valuable book on warfare in the Vedic period, is singular in departing from the scholarly consensus that the Ṛgvedic Aryans did not use war elephants. He is very positive about the evidence for the taming of elephants in the Indus civilization prior to the Vedic period. He offers a handful of Ṛgvedic passages which may be interpreted to imply elephant capture and training, if not warfare; but even he concedes that the chariot was foremost and

[87] *Vedic Index* 2: 171–2; contra, Singh 1963, 1965: 74–6.

puts his claim about the war elephant tentatively: "we suggest that the use of the elephant [in warfare] was not impossible in the Ṛgvedic period as hitherto assumed."[88] But even "not impossible" is hard to sustain, for if war elephants were known the composers of Vedic hymns would hardly fail to speak of them in battle scenes.

The proof that the war elephant was invented only later in the Vedic period, and not at its beginning, has two sides. In the first place, the gods of the *Ṛg Veda* all ride chariots, and only later are the gods of Hinduism each connected with the riding of an animal particular to that god. The leading instance of this phenomenon is the god Indra, king of the gods, riding a chariot in the earliest texts but the celestial elephant Airāvata in later texts. In the second place, elephants never figure among royal gifts in the *Ṛg Veda*, but they do figure among royal gifts in later Vedic texts: indeed they become the supreme gift. More generally, elephants have only a marginal, and late, role in the royal sacrifices of the Veda.

As to the first point, the hymns of the *Ṛg Veda* are invitations to the gods to come to the sacrifice as honored guests. At its simplest, the sacrifice is a feast in which the gods are guests, the sacrificial offerings are the food, and the sacrificer is the host. Accepting the sacrifice puts the gods under obligation to reciprocate, and as they are such powerful beings they can reciprocate richly. The poet's skill lies in his ability to make the invitation irresistible. Here is one of the hymns to Indra, a short hymn given in its entirety, which is especially clear in the matter:

ā carṣaṇiprā vṛṣabho janānāṃ rājā kṛṣṭīnām puruhūta indraḥ |
stutaḥ śravasyann avasopa madrig yuktvā harī vṛṣaṇā
yāhy arvāṅ ‖ 1 ‖

ye te vṛṣaṇo vṛṣabhāsa indra brahmayujo vṛṣarathāso asyāḥ |
tām ā tiṣṭha tebhir ā yāhy arvāṅ havāmahe tvā suta indra some ‖ 2 ‖

ā tiṣṭha rathaṃ vṛṣaṇaṃ vṛṣā te sutaḥ somaḥ pariśiktā madhūni |
yuktvā vṛṣabhyāṃ vṛṣabha kṣitīnāṃ haribhyāṃ yāhi pravatopa
madrik ‖ 3 ‖

[88] Singh 1965: 76.

ayaṃ yajño davayā ayam miyedha imā brahmāṇy ayam indra somaḥ
stīrṇam barhir ā tu śakra pra yāhi pibā niṣadya vi mucā
harī iha ‖ 4 ‖

o suṣṭuta indra yāhy arvāṅ upa brahmāṇi mānyasya kāroḥ |
vidyāma vastor avasā gṛṇanto viyāmeṣaṃ vṛjanaṃ jīradānum ‖ 5 ‖

1. Indra, who cherishes the people, bull of the tribes, king of the races, called by many: praised, praise-loving, yoke thy pair of strong bay horses and come hither to me!
2. Thy mighty stallions, yoked by prayer, O Indra, thy swift horses yoked to the mighty chariot, ascend these and borne by them come hither; with soma pressed we call to thee.
3. Ascend the mighty chariot; mighty soma is pressed for thee, and sweets are sprinkled around. Yoke thy strong bay horses, bull of the human races, and come down to me.
4. Here is sacrifice reaching the gods; here the sacrificial victim; here, Indra, are the prayers, here the soma. Grass for a seat is strewn; come, Śakra, sit and drink; unyoke thy two bay horses.
5. Come here, O Indra, well-praised, to the prayers of the singer Māna. Singing, may we find early through thy help, may we find strengthening food in full abundance.[89]

Thus the poet calls to Indra to yoke his horses and drive his celestial chariot to the sacrifice, where the soma plant has been pressed to make an intoxicating drink for him, and an animal prepared for the sacrifice, which is to say, as food for the god. He is invited to unyoke his horses, sit on the soft grass strewn as a seat for him, and partake of the feast.

From invitations of this kind, which make up the majority of the hymns of the text, we find that the gods of the *Ṛg Veda* all ride chariots and neither elephants nor other animals, as do the gods of later Hinduism.[90] To be sure, as the gods have enhanced powers their chariots are enhanced too: they fly through the air. But the Vedic hymn regularly invites the gods to mount these chariots and direct the pair of horses that draw them to the sacrificial field where they will be feasted.

[89] *RV* 1966: 1.177.

[90] Gonda 1965; Sparreboom 1985.

The Hindu gods of a succeeding period each have a particular *vāhana* or animal mount, and this development constitutes an important difference of historic Hinduism from the Vedic religion from which it descended. Indra, in particular, the king of the gods and their leader in war, always and only rides a chariot in the *Ṛg Veda*, as in the hymn just given.[91] But in the later Vedic texts and ever after Indra is associated with his own *vāhana*, the celestial elephant Airāvata or Airāvaṇa. How exactly this development came about is far from clear, but Gonda is surely right to connect it with the rising dignity of riding horseback in the ancient chariot-using civilizations of western Asia and southern Europe generally.[92] The point to be made here is that horseback riding was known in Vedic India and was not first introduced in later times. The salient fact is that horseback riding was of low status in the warrior culture of Vedic times, while chariot riding was of the highest status. It is possible that the invention of the war elephant contributed to improving the status of riding on the back of an animal, relative to riding a chariot.

As for the second point, having to do with royal gifts and royal sacrifices: while a god is the person to whom the Vedic hymn is addressed, some verses of some hymns are addressed, rather, to a king, and serve to praise him for his generosity to the poet. Such hymns or parts of hymns are called *dānastuti*, "praise of gifts." These *dānastutis* specify the things given, which are almost always cattle, and often also gold, slaves, horses, and chariots with horses—but never elephants, at least not in the *dānastutis* of the earliest Vedic text, the *Ṛg Veda*.[93] But elephants soon figure in later Vedic texts as the gifts of kings to poets, or as fees to priests and others officiating at a sacrifice performed by a king. One of these later Vedic texts, the *Aitareya Brāhmaṇa*, celebrates the fantastically rich gift of king Aṅga to the priest who performed for him the "great anointing of Indra" (Aindramahābhiṣeka, the ritual consecration of a person as king): two thousand thousands

[91] Gonda 1989.

[92] Gonda 1965: 95–104. This is a subject to which I will shortly turn in the next section.

[93] Patel 1961.

of cows; 88,000 horses; 10,000 slave girls; 10,000 elephants.[94] The name Aṅga attaches to a country in eastern India where wild elephants abound, and we will meet a king of Aṅga later in this book, in connection with the literature of elephant science, *gajaśāstra*. Another such gift in the same text is that of king Bharata Dauḥṣanti, including 107,000 "beasts black with long tusks," clearly a poetic reference to elephants, surpassing the gifts of all kings before and after.[95] The *dānastuti* literature runs to hyperbole more or less from the start; early on we hear of a *śata-da*, the giver of a hundred (cows), then of a *sahasra-da*, the giver of a thousand.[96] But setting aside the exaggerated numbers and focusing on the objects of giving, elephants are simply absent from the early *dānastutis*, whereas, as noted for the later Vedic period and in the epics, they figure as a kind of pinnacle of gift-giving. They continued to play this role in Cambodia, judging from the Sanskrit inscriptions recording foundational gifts there. This role as the apex in the hierarchy of gifts follows the invention of the war elephant and its entry into a culture of war hitherto dominated by the chariot. This happened in the late Vedic period, *c.* 1000–500 BCE, by the end of which this new culture of war had become universal in North India.

It is significant that chariots figure in the royal sacrifices of the Vedic religion, but that elephants enter into such rituals only at the periphery, such as in the form of gifts or sacrificial fees given to officiating priests at the end, and not in the main business of the ritual. Thus in the sacrifice called the Vājapeya (drink of strength) there is a chariot race; and a chariot drive of some kind occurs in the Rājasūya (royal consecration), the Aśvamedha (horse sacrifice), and the Gavām ayana (a collective sacrifice marking the yearly turning points of the sun's journey).[97] The elephant comes to be deeply embedded in Indian kingship, but it is a latecomer. The chariot and its horses are present from the start.

The inventor of the techniques of capture and training of

[94] *Ait. Br.* 8.22; 1920: 337.
[95] *Ait. Br.* 8.23; 1920: 338.
[96] Patel 1961: 64–75.
[97] Heesterman 1957.

elephants is unknown, just as we do not know the first domesticator of other animals. As we shall see, the later Sanskrit texts of elephant science attribute the domestication of elephants to Romapāda, king of Aṅga, in a mythological tale of great charm. It is not an accident that the invention of the war elephant took place long after the domestication of other large animals, such as cattle, goats, sheep, and above all horses, by a people who had domesticated all these and were highly skilled in the management of horses. The idea of using animal power for war in the form of chariot horses had been in practice for a millennium by the time it was extended to elephants; and prior practices of capture and display had demonstrated the value of elephants for kingship. This leads to one other thing I can reassert about the circumstances of the invention of the techniques in question: the invention of the war elephant was in all likelihood an invention of kingship. Kingship had both the developed form of warfare into which elephants could be fitted to advantage, and the enormous resources required for the capture, training, maintenance, and deployment in war of elephants from the forest. In India, kingship also had the elephant-populated forests it needed for this purpose.

Consulting the *Arthaśāstra* for the universe of political forms available in the period of active use of war elephants, we find essentially three: kingship (*rājya*), the republic (*saṅgha* or, elsewhere, *gaṇa*), and "forest people" (*aṭavi*). The war elephant is everywhere associated with kings and kingdoms. There is some evidence that some of the republics had war elephants in significant numbers, but I think we must say that the institution diffused *from* kingdoms *to* republics. Forest people are certainly associated with the capture of wild elephants and appear as mahouts and riders—not as autonomous forest people but only in the service of kings, and under conditions that we will shortly explore. Thus, at some time before 500 BCE, by which time the use of the war elephant had become the norm—perhaps as early as 1000 BCE—North India is the scene of a conjuncture of kingship, elephant forests, and forest people, leading to the invention of the war elephant.

War elephants and forest people

I have tried to show thus far that the war elephant's appearance was the result of a long trajectory. This was a journey which took the people calling themselves "Arya" from a land of horses into a land of elephants, from the grassy steppe of Central Asia to the monsoon forest of the Ganga valley of North India.

In the *Mahābhārata*'s descriptions of battle, elephants are often ridden by unnamed elephant fighters, while the famous named warriors are all *mahārathas*, great chariot warriors. There are, however, several passages in which the names of elephant fighters are given, or the countries and locational origins of nameless warriors and mahouts are stated. If we collate these we can discern a pattern. Often, the riders of war elephants in battle are kings of certain countries; often, they are unnamed warriors or mahouts described as countrymen of particular places—significantly, all in the northeast, Central India, or the South. Sometimes they are tribal people, that is to say, forest people, such as Kirātas or Niṣādas; sometimes they are simply called barbarians (*mleccha*). One of the longer lists of warriors "skilled in elephant-fighting" (*gajayuddheṣu kuśalāḥ*) lists Easterners (Prācya), Southerners (Dākṣiṇātya), Aṅgas, Vaṅgas, Puṇḍras, Māgadhas, Tāmraliptakas, Mekalas, Kośalas, Madras, Daśārṇas, Niṣādas, and Kaliṅgas.[98] In addition to indicating Easterners and Southerners, the names of particular countries and tribes form an arc from north to south along the eastern side of the Indian subcontinent. Three of the country names in this passage are found in the list of the eight elephant forests: Prācya, Daśārṇa, Kaliṅga (Fig. 1.4). These forests, on the eastern side of the eight forests, are reputed to have had the best elephants.[99]

Other *Mahābhārata* passages confirm and elaborate upon this pattern. Bhagadatta, king of Prāgjyotiṣa in the northeast, is a prominent warrior on the Kaurava side of the war. He fights throughout from the shoulder of an elephant, unlike most of the

[98] *Mbh.* 8.17.1–4.

[99] Sources in Trautmann 2009: 254.

kings and named warriors, who fight on chariots; on one occasion he fights the king of Daśārṇa (whose country name attaches to one of the eight elephant forests), also on elephant-back.[100] In another passage, thousands of skilled elephant riders (*śikṣitā hastisādinaḥ*) from Aṅga are joined by many kings of the East, of the South, and of Kaliṅga (the name of another elephant forest) to surround one of the Pāṇḍava princes.[101] In another, a force of thousands of elephants is described as mounted by *mlecchas* delighting in battle and skilled in fighting.[102] The king of the Aṅgas and the elephant upon which he is fighting are both killed and fall together; he is called both barbarian (*mleccha*) and skilled in elephant lore (*hastiśikṣāviśārade*). The Aṅga elephant men (*mahāmātras*) turn upon Nakula for revenge; so also Mekalas, Utkalas and Kaliṅgas, Niṣādas and Tāmraliptakas.[103] *Mlecchas* or barbarians are again associated with elephant skill when a force of 1,300 attacks Arjuna on behalf of the Kauravas.[104] Finally, the Kulindas or Kuṇindras, a forest people, are added to the list of peoples named as skilled in elephant warfare.[105]

These passages taken together give us a set of associations: first, named countries from the entire eastern side of the Indian subcontinent from north to south, that is, the well-watered habitat of elephants. Second, barbarians or *mlecchas*, sometimes not further specified, sometimes identified with kings and fighters of some of these countries. And, third, tribal peoples, notably Kirāṭas and Niṣādas who, if they are to be understood as forest people (*vana-cāra* or *aṭavi*)—as they are in other texts—come from the same forests which produced the elephants. The kings and warriors of these named countries, named or unnamed barbarian peoples, and tribal people are the skilled elephant men in the *Mahābhārata*. They give an element of the exotic and distant,

[100] *Mbh*. 7.25.28.
[101] Ibid.: 7.68.31.
[102] Ibid.: 7.87.16–18.
[103] Ibid.: 8.17.17–18, 20.
[104] Ibid,: 8.59.10.
[105] Ibid.: 8.62.35–7.

lending magnificence to a scene of a war that is represented as having drawn armies from all parts of India.

We see this effect clearly when we also consider horses which, by contrast, are all associated with places far to the west, consistent with Habib's mapping of cavalry horse pastures in Mughal times (Fig. 1.7). This confirms the highly important fact that the habitats of horses and wild elephants in the Indian subcontinent are in complementary distribution. This is a matter with wide ramifications to which, therefore, we will frequently return.

The complementarity of (tame) horses and (wild) elephants is neatly captured in some verses of the *Rāmāyaṇa* that describes the magnificence of the royal city of Ayodhyā. Here is a passage describing warriors, horses and elephants, in other words, its whole fighting force:

yodhānām agnikalpānāṃ	*peśalānām amarṣiṇām* |
saṃpūrṇākṛtavidyānāṃ	*guhākesariṇām iva* ||
kāmbojaviṣaye jātair	*bāhlīkaś ca hayottamaiḥ* |
vanāyujair nadīś ca	*pūrṇāhayopamaiḥ* ||
vindhyaparvatajair mattaiḥ	*pūrṇā haimavatair api* |
madānvitair atibalair mātaṅgaiḥ	*parvatopamaiḥ* ||
bhadramandrair bhadramṛgair	*mṛgamandraiś ca sā purī* |
nityamattaiḥ sadā pūrṇā	*nāgair acalasaṃnibahaiḥ* ||

Like a cave filled with lions, it (the city Ayodhyā) was full of fiery warriors, skilled, unyielding, and accomplished in their art. It was full of the finest horses, bred in the region of Bāhlīka, Vanāyu, Kāmboja, and the great river (Indus), the equals of Hari's steed. It was filled with exceedingly powerful rutting elephants, like mountains, born in the Vindhya hills and the Himālaya. The city was always full of bull elephants, looking like mountains and always in rut; elephants of the *bhadramandra*, *bhadramṛga* and *mṛgamandra* breeds, descended from the cosmic elephants Añjana and Vāmana.[106]

Elephants are described in a pair of verses that are somewhat repetitive (in musth, "mountain-like"); they are from the mountains to

[106] *Rām.* 1.6.19–22.

the north (Himālaya) and south (Vindhya). Horses are associated with the Indus (Sindhu), Bactria (Bāhlīka) in Central Asia, Iran (Vanāyu), and the northwest (Kāmboja). Thus the perfection of Rāma's capital city is shown by its possession of the best and rarest horses and elephants, brought from the best and most distant sources, in opposite directions from one another.

The ancient Indian kingdom was tied to the forest by the institution of the war elephant, whether its own elephant forest—as in Rāma's question to his half-brother Bhārata quoted at the beginning of this chapter—or a distant source at the periphery of the sphere of Indian kingship, as in the epic passages above. The forests had human inhabitants as well as wild elephants. They had what the texts of Indian kingship call forest people, who had skills that were essential to the kingdom for the protection, capture, training, and deployment of war elephants. The Indian king had to have productive relations with barbarians (*mleccha*) and forest people (*aṭavi*) to maintain the kind of warfare that emerged with the invention of the war elephant.

3

Structures of use: *caturaṅga, vāhana, vyūha*

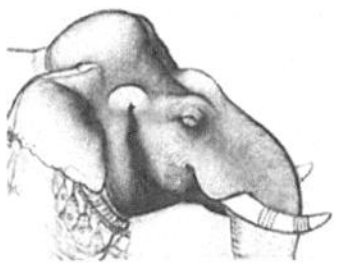

PRODUCING A WAR ELEPHANT REQUIRES THE coming together of a king, a forest, forest people, and a wild elephant, followed by a long period of elephant training. When the war elephant is put into action in the service of some human purpose it becomes part of the kingdom, an element within larger structures of which the kingdom is composed. The foremost of the *structures of use* for the war elephant is the army.

In this chapter I will examine three structures of use that are named and much discussed in ancient Indian texts. The first of these concerns the army as a whole. The army (*bala*) is conceived of as a beast with four (*catur*) legs (*aṅga*), whence it is a *caturaṅga-bala*, a fourfold army or an army of four parts or divisions, of which the war elephant is one, alongside the foot soldier, the horse, and the chariot. The second is *vāhana*, meaning a conveyance. Various kinds of *vāhana*s occupy varying positions in a hierarchy of esteem. At the apex is the elephant, the conveyance of the king, the ideal *raja-vāhana*, and every other conveyance holds its place in the scale in relation to it. The third is the most technical of the three: the battle array or *vyūha*. In this, elephants hold a certain place among other military forces that are drawn up in particular ways from a repertoire of arrays—when in camp, on the march, or on the field of battle. *Caturaṅga*, *vāhana*, and *vyūha*: these three are the most salient of the structures of use, the contexts in which war elephants, once produced, are set in motion. Understanding them will further illuminate the logic of the institution of the war elephant.

Caturaṅga

A full army, then, is like a beast with four legs, which signifies that it consists of foot, horse, chariot, and elephant divisions, combined and coordinated in certain ways. It is a *caturaṅga-bala*, using *caturaṅga*, "four-legged," adjectivally to qualify *bala*, "army," or simply *caturaṅga*, using the word by itself as a substantive, to mean "that which is four-legged," namely, the army.

This conception could only have arisen after the invention of the war elephant which, as we have seen, came about sometime in the late Vedic period, perhaps as early as 1000 BCE, and was normalized and universalized in Indian kingdoms of the North by 500 BCE. The army of the earliest Vedic period before the invention of the war elephant had only *three* forces: foot, horse, and, above all, chariots. The war elephant's insertion into the army changed military practice profoundly, turning a threefold structure into a fourfold one. This transformation took place in the course of an eastward expansion of the Vedic Aryans, from the Indus valley into the valley of the Ganga; for the geographic horizon of the earliest Vedic period (that of the *Ṛg Veda*) centers upon the Punjab or upper Indus valley, while in later Vedic texts and in the epics the scene shifts to the upper Ganga valley—and to the Kuru-Pañcāla rulers, who are set forth as the ideal of kingship in Vedic texts of royal consecration rituals. The concept of *caturaṅga* resulted from an eastward movement—from the land of horses toward the land of elephants, of a people who had long been skilled in the management and use of horses for warfare.

Accordingly, it is in the epics that we see the *caturaṅga* concept in its fullest flower. For the epics are centered upon the upper Ganga through their royal capitals, Hastināpura and Indraprastha of the *Mahābhārata*, and Ayodhyā of the *Rāmāyaṇa*. To be sure, some passages in the *Mahābhārata* have alternative conceptions, of a threefold, sixfold, or even eightfold army.[1] But the dominance of the *caturaṅga* concept is abundantly evident in the battlefield scenes of the *Mahābhārata*, and the word recurs often as a qualifier of "army" (*bala*, *sena*, *vāhinī*, *camū*), or by itself. It everywhere signifies a full-force army, a proper army of the highest form.

We also find the fourfold army in descriptions of processions and cities. In the *Rāmāyaṇa*, king Daśaratha orders his charioteer to muster "a fourfold army, provisioned with every luxury" (*ratnasusaṃpūrṇā caturvidhabalā camūḥ*) to accompany Rāma to his place of exile, while Ayodhyā, the perfect city (and a fortified one, like every royal capital) is described as filled with fiery warriors as well as the best horses and elephants, a kind of shorthand for the fourfold army.[2] Later, Vibhīṣaṇa gives a military report about the enemy city of Laṅkā, informing Rāma that it contains 1,000 elephants, 10,000 chariots, 20,000 horse, and more than ten million demons (*rākṣasas*, the foot soldiers)—a fourfold army of unimaginable size.[3] In the other epic the ideal military training of princes presumes the fourfold army model:

> *tato droṇo 'rjunaṁ bhūyo rathesu ca gajeṣu ca* |
> *aśveṣu bhūmāv api ca raṇaśikṣām aśikṣayat* ||
>
> Then Droṇa taught Arjuna the art of warfare, from chariots and elephants, from horses and on foot.[4]

The fourfold army saturates the epics. It is the image of repletion, of an army on the battlefield, of a royal capital, of a procession, of the military training of a prince.

While the *caturaṅga-bala* idea figures directly and positively in the many battle scenes of the *Mahābhārata*, it functions quite

[1] For a full discussion, see Hopkins 1889: 198n.

[2] *Rām.* 1.6.19–21. Shorthand or abbreviated reference to the four parts of the army is quite common, and can be misleading. Here, the animals of the fourfold army are named—men, horses, elephants; cavalry and chariots are not differentiated but are to be understood. This matter of shorthand reference will cause ambiguities about the date at which chariots ceased to be used on the battlefield.

[3] *Rām.* 6.28.4.

[4] *Mbh.* 1.123.7.

differently in the *Rāmāyaṇa*. Because the central feature of the narrative is Rāma's exile to the forest of Central India, it is largely a story of the loss and deprivation of this ideal of repletion, followed by its recovery. The fourfold army is among the things that Rāma leaves *behind* when he accepts exile. A fourfold army accompanies him to his place of exile, but there he abandons it, exchanging his princely clothing for bark cloth. He is a great chariot warrior (*mahāratha*) deprived of his chariot, reduced to the condition of a foot soldier. For much of the narrative he goes about on foot, armed with a bow.

Rāma's allies, too, the monkey army of Sugrīva, do not constitute a fourfold army, and their weapons are crude—although their power is superhuman and their rudimentary weapons consist of whole trunks of trees and large boulders. The king of the Niṣāda forest people, allied to him, is not intimidated by a fourfold army, which is to say, a more complex force than the simple body of foot soldiers he leads. He tells Rāma:

na hi me 'viditaṃ kiṃ cid *vane 'smiṃś carataḥ sadā* |
caturaṅgaṃ hy api balaṃ *prasahema vayaṃ yudhi* ||

> I have wandered the forest all my life, and nothing happens here without my knowing of it. Moreover, we are prepared to withstand in battle even an army of four divisions.[5]

In these circumstances, in Central Indian exile, Rāma engages several demons (*rākṣasas*) in fights in which the disadvantage he suffers—his not having a fourfold army, or even a chariot to fight from—serves to heighten the difficulty of, and magnify, the victories he achieves. The climactic battle against Rāvaṇa, the *rākṣasa* king who has abducted Rāma's wife Sītā, pits Rāma and his monkey allies against a full fourfold army of great size and strength, with enhanced powers and a monstrous look to it. But the heavenly forces—gods, *gandharvas*, and *dānavas*—declare it is not an even fight (*samam yuddham*).[6] What might

[5] *Rām*. 2.80.8.
[6] Ibid.: 6.90.4.

constitute an even fight is nicely expressed in this verse from the *Mahābhārata*:

rathā rathaiḥ samājagmuḥ pādātaiś ca padātayaḥ |
sādibhiḥ sādinaś caiva gajaiś cāpi mahāgajāḥ ||

Chariots engaged chariots, foot soldiers other foot soldiers, riders attacked riders, elephants elephants.[7]

The final face-off with Rāvaṇa in the *Rāmāyaṇa* is still very unequal by this standard, but the god Indra provides Rāma with his own chariot to make for a more even battle at least between the leaders, so that Rāma is able to fight as the great chariot warrior he is. After his victory Rāma returns to Ayodhyā to become a proper king with a proper fourfold army. Thus the idea of the fourfold army is present throughout the *Rāmāyaṇa*, even by loss or absence. Such loss or absence, in relation to the *caturaṅga-bala* idea and the concept of equal battle, is often made explicit.

The fourfold army that we find fully furled in the epics is not a poetic invention but the real frame of the ancient Indian military. The *Arthaśāstra* presumes a functioning fourfold army and gives a good deal of information about its maintenance and use. Buddhist and Jain sources jibe with brahmanical ones on this, and the kingdoms that appear in their canonical texts, especially those of Magadha in the lower-middle Ganga valley (eastward of the royal capitals of the epics), have full fourfold armies. The Greek and Latin historians of Alexander of Macedon corroborate this in their record of a report that the Nanda king of Magadha had an army of 200,000 foot, 20,000 horse, 2,000 chariots, and 4,000 elephants.[8] Megasthenes' memoir of his embassy, shortly after, to the court of the Mauryan king of Magadha, Candragupta, gives a description of military organization that includes the four *caturaṅga* divisions, plus two others connected with army supplies, oxcarts, and river boats. So we cannot doubt that the fourfold army was a living institution of actual armies.

[7] *Mbh.* 3.31.8.
[8] Details in Chapter 5.

The *caturaṅga* idea has a definite history, the broad outlines of which can be made out. It was created with the invention of the war elephant and its insertion into an army consisting of foot, horse, and chariot forces in the early Vedic period. It persisted until the chariot became obsolete on the battlefield, whereupon the Indian army became threefold again, but in a configuration different from that of the early Vedic period. Thus, we can distinguish three clear stages of the normative army force and date them roughly:

Early Vedic period	foot, horse, chariot
Late Vedic period	foot, horse, chariot, elephant (*caturaṅga*)
Classical period	foot, horse, elephant

I have dated the transition to the *caturaṅga* model to the period *c.* 1000–500 BCE. Once the transition was made, it could seem to have been in place forever. In the *Rāmāyaṇa*, for example, we find a passage which projects the *caturaṅga* structure backward in time, upon early Vedic-period armies which did not have war elephants. Thus Vasiṣṭha destroys the foot, elephants, horses, and chariots of Viśvāmitra's army in a famous rivalry that belongs to the period of the *Ṛg Veda*, before the invention of the war elephant.[9]

What about the transition *out* of the *caturaṅga* model, which follows the demise of chariot warfare? Because of ambiguities in the written record it is difficult to be sure when the chariot ceased to be a serious presence on the battlefield. Dikshitar drew attention to the vivid word picture of the decampment of the army given by the poet Bāṇa in the *Harṣacarita*, the biography of his patron king Harṣa of Kanauj (*r.* 606–47).[10] It contains no mention of chariots. This is an argument from silence, of course, which is the weakest kind of proof. But it gains strength from the fact that Bāṇa's description of the components of the army is highly detailed. The whole description is a tour de force, a single sentence containing a string of clauses made of compounds, which goes on for three pages of printed text. It is an outstanding example

[9] *tais tan niṣūditaṃ sainyaṃ* *viśvamitrasya tatkṣaṇāt* |
sapadātigajaṃ sāśvaṃ *sarathaṃ raghunandana*||: *Rām.* 1.54.4.

[10] Dikshitar 1987: 165–6; *Harṣacarita* 1897: 224–5.

of a "din and dust" picture, a trope of Sanskrit classical poetry in which bright images, energetic and confused motion, noise and dust combine to convey a sense of the energy of a great army on the move. The length and great detail of this description give the omission of chariots a heightened significance. Horses and elephants are mentioned repeatedly, so there is no question here of abbreviated reference to the fourfold army.

But this date is very late, long after civilizations of the time had ceased to use chariots on the battlefield. Indians seem to have been among the last to abandon the battlefield use of the chariot, but they must have done so well before this text by Bāṇa. We do not know how much earlier that happened because of the previously mentioned ambiguities of the record. When, for example, the early Gupta empire ruler Samudra Gupta (fl. *c.* 320 CE) is described by his poet in the Allahabad Stone Inscription as having no equal antagonist on earth, the expression used is "having no counter-chariot-warrior" (*apratiratha*).[11] Is the allusion to the chariot to be taken literally, or is it a metaphor drawn from the past? Again, the practice of abbreviated reference in poetic eulogies (*praśasti*) of kings at the beginnings of inscriptions can leave us uncertain about how we are to take some army descriptions, and whether they imply the presence of *all* four divisions of the army, including chariots.

The exact dating of the transition is elusive, then, but certain things point to the first century CE or so. The cause of the demise of the chariot is surely the rise of cavalry; and the rise of cavalry in India has surely to do with cavalry-based armies coming from the nomadic peoples of inner Asia, the habitat of wild horses and a region where domestic horses abound. These armies created conquest states in India. Inner Asian peoples periodically created formidable armies of this kind, mostly of mounted bowmen with short, powerful recurve bows, preying upon the settled civilizations around them, from China to Europe. In the history of

[11] *Gupta inscriptions* 1888: 6ff., Allahabad stone pillar inscription of Samudra Gupta, line 24.

India, the pattern shows a regular series of such invader cavalries at intervals of about 500 years:

- Scythians (Skt. Śaka), Parthians (Skt. Pahlava), and Kushans (Skt. Kuṣāṇas) from the first century BCE to the second century CE
- Hūṇas or Huns from the fifth century
- Turks from the tenth century
- Mughals from the sixteenth century

Each invasion series demonstrated anew the value of cavalry. It is likely that the rise of cavalry and the demise of the chariot force began with the first of these invasions, in the conquest states created by peoples the Indians called Śakas, Pahlavas, and Kushans.[12]

Having created new states in India and settling to stay, these horseback armies did not remain what they had been. They took up the use of war elephants and drew upon the limitless supply of foot soldiers in India. They formed vast, slower-moving threefold armies very different from the smaller, more rapid armies they had brought to India, but better suited to the task of governing than conquering. Thus, even when the army became cavalry-based, Indian kings—even those who had been Central Asian horsemen—perpetuated the use of the war elephant till just a few centuries ago.

On the other hand, although the chariot ceased to be used on the battlefield at some point prior to the reign of Harṣa in the seventh century, it lingered in other forms and had a lengthy afterlife—as among the Greeks and Romans. Long after the Romans ceased to use chariots in war they continued to grant the *triumphator* the right to be drawn by chariot in his triumph. In India, and in places where its culture of kingship was adopted, the *Mahābhārata* and *Rāmāyaṇa* kept alive the memory of chariots and the great chariot warrior in poetry and visual representations; and, like the Roman *triumphator*, Hindu gods continue to be drawn by temple cars called chariots (Hindi *rath*, Tamil *ter*) in public procession.

[12] I shall give evidence confirming this circumstantial account in the following section of the chapter.

Once the chariot ceased to appear on the battlefield, armies ceased to follow the *caturaṅga* ideal. Nevertheless the concept itself had a long and continuing afterlife in many forms of art. Everyone reading this book will have encountered a direct descendant of it, albeit in somewhat distorted form, in the international game of chess.

The Indian game of chess, from which the current international form derives, was called *caturaṅga*. It is a game of war, the perfect realization of the ideal of equal battle in which the numbers and kinds of forces are identical, and the terrain is perfectly level, so that the trial of strength is turned into a contest of pure intellect. Since chess has spread worldwide, a trace of the fourfold army has been perpetuated and universalized in a game of skill. *Caturaṅga* is a living presence in the world today, even if we do not know it. It is hidden in plain sight, so to say. It is worth sketching this development, drawing upon the large literature of chess history that serves the worldwide interest in chess.

It is a curious fact that the very text whose silence offers the best proof we have of the demise of the battlefield chariot, the *Harṣacarita* of Bāṇa, also contains the first datable allusion to the game of chess under the name *caturaṅga*, played on an 8 x 8 board called *aṣṭāpada*, similar to the board used today.[13] The board is attested long before the game of chess, in Patañjali's commentary of the first century BCE on the grammar of Pāṇini. It was used for many board games besides chess. We have sculpted representations of games using boards of this and other kinds in considerable number, as in Fig. 3.1 from Bharhut, and such boards were carved on stone in public places in Vijayanagara and other ancient sites, as may be seen in the admirable survey of Micaela Soar (2007). Andreas Bock-Raming's (1996) commentary and interpretation of the description of chess in the *Mānasollāsa*, the Sanskrit compendium of kingship we encountered in Chapter 1, is a major new contribution to the history of chess, establishing the moves of the pieces in the original Indian game. But chess has no clear trace prior to the time of Bāṇa in the seventh century.

[13] Macdonell 1898: 125; *Harṣacarita* 1897: 2.

Fig. 3.1: Players with board game, Bharhut

Once invented, chess developed several variant forms in India. The main Indian variant was four-handed chess, in which players each had armies of half the size of those for two-handed chess, arrayed in the right-hand side of the first two ranks on each of the four sides of the board. In this variant a throw of the dice governed the moves that could be made, thus adding an element of chance to what had been a game of pure intellect. In later times the name *caturaṅga* stuck to four-handed chess, while the two-handed original game acquired the new name *buddhi-bala*, "intellect-army," indicating that it depended solely upon mind, not chance.

The game spread westward to Persia and, soon after the Islamic conquests, to Arabia and thence to Spain and the rest of Europe; and eastward to Tibet, Southeast Asia, and China. The pattern of development was quite different in the two directions. To the east, Indian chess continued to develop new local varieties. But to the west, the two-handed game of skill evolved into a single standard that became universal, through a series of transformations that can be partly charted or inferred.[14]

Al-Adli of Baghdad (*c.* 840 CE), one of the early chess masters of the Arabic-speaking world, wrote a text on chess that is now lost but fragments of which are preserved in subsequent chess writers. He is quoted as having said: "It is universally acknowledged that three things were produced from India, in which no other anticipated it, and the like of which existed nowhere else, the book Kalila-wa-Dimna, the nine cyphers with which one can count to infinity, and chess."[15] These three things were the book of instruction for princes in worldly wisdom, called the *Pañcatantra* in India, and in Persia and the Arabic-speaking world *Kalila wa Dimna* (put in the form of a dialogue between two jackals called Kalila and Dimna); the place-notation of numbers using the nine symbols plus zero; and the game of chess; all of which had a wide diffusion beyond India, indeed through much of the world. They

[14] Murray 1913; Bock-Raming 1996; Mark 2007; for archaeological traces in Central Asia and Iran, Semenov 2007.

[15] Murray 1913: 171.

are all of them religiously neutral, so to say, and cross sectarian boundaries freely; and they are all the kinds of things that circulate especially well in king-to-king paths of communication, the same circuits through which the institution of the war elephant was diffused. The Sassanian kings of Persia were important conduits for their transmission westward. There is credible testimony that chess, which the Persians called *chatrang* and the Arabs *shatranj* after the Indian name, came to the Sassanian king Khosrau I Anushirvan (531–79) via the ambassador of a king of India, and he is also connected with the translation of the *Pañcatantra* into Pahlavi (in the Middle Persian *Čatrang nāmak*). As we shall see,[16] Sassanian kings also used Indian elephants in war, against the Romans among others, and for hunting, another reason for them to maintain good diplomatic connections with Indian kings.

Chess spread rapidly from Iran to the Arabs through the expansion of Islam, and the Arabs developed a literature of chess and chess problems soon after the introduction of chess, al-Adli being one of the first writers of such texts. Thence it reached Spain and Europe generally. In the course of this journey the opening distribution of pieces remained the same, but the names and moves of the pieces were changed at various points. By following the changes we can see how the fourfold army concept underlies them. The evolution, from the Indian to the international form devised in the West, can be summarized by indicating beginning and ending points, as follows:

Caturaṅga	Chess
foot	pawn
chariot	rook
horse	knight
elephant	bishop
king	king
minister	queen

The chariot and elephant were particularly subject to change. The Persians named the chariot *rukh*, the motive and meaning of which are obscure; in Europe rook or tower (*Turm*, in German).

[16] Details in Chapter 6.

The elephant remained an elephant in Persia, *pīl*, and in Arabic *al-fil*, which it remains in Spanish. But in English and other languages it became the bishop, in German the messenger (*Laüfer*), in French the jester (*fou*). The minister (Sanskrit *mantrin* or *amātya*) was, in Persian *wazir*, in Arabic *firzan*, but became the queen in Europe. The minister had been one of the weakest pieces, able to move only one square. In fifteenth-century Europe a change of rules made the queen the most powerful piece on the board. This and other changes at that time virtually fixed the modern form of the game. The fourfold army of India underlies its structure, but that structure has so changed it is no longer recognizable. Even the name has changed. *Chess* and *check* are reflexes of the Persian word for the king, *shāh*.

The Lewis chessmen in the British Museum, from the island of Lewis in the Outer Hebrides off the coast of Scotland, show the northern reach of chess by the twelfth century. The seventy-eight pieces that were found, originating from multiple sets, were made of walrus ivory. They are thought to be the cargo of a merchant ship, perhaps from Norway, on its way to Ireland. As one can see in Fig. 3.2, the transformation of elephant to bishop was already complete.

Meanwhile, in India, after the extinction of chariot warfare, the threefold nature of the army was institutionalized in the titles of the three powers who were the pillars of the new international order: the Turkish sultan of Delhi was called *aśva-pati*, lord of horses; the king of Orissa was called *gaja-pati*, lord of elephants; and the king of Vijayanagara was called *nara-pati*, lord of men. They even appeared in a game of cards in Mughal times.[17] Thus, the place of the war elephant continued for a good long time in the new structure of use.

Vāhana

The word *vāhana* indicates a means of conveyance, whether riding mounted on the back of an animal or in a vehicle drawn by animals. Conveyance is highly visible and highly differentiated, a sign of

[17] Described by Abu'l Fazl : *Ā'īn-i Akbarī* 2: 29.

Fig. 3.2: The Lewis chessmen

social status, a way of publicly displaying one's place in the social hierarchy. Elephants occupy the apex of the hierarchy of *vāhanas*, and accordingly are ridden by kings, for it is a necessity of kingship that the king be seen as the apex of the social structure.

Nearchus, one of the companions of Alexander, wrote a book about the expedition that has a remarkable passage on the hierarchy of conveyances—of *vāhana*—in the part of India he saw, the Indus valley, during the brief time Alexander's army was there over 327–4 BCE. The book Nearchus wrote is lost, but bits survive in quotations by later histories of Alexander that have been transmitted intact. Here is the passage of Nearchus as preserved in quotation by the later historian Arrian:

> They usually ride on camels, horses, and asses; the richer men on elephants. For the elephant in India is a royal mount; then next in dignity is a four-horse chariot, and camels come third; to ride on a single horse is low. Their women, such as are of great modesty, can be seduced by no other gift, but yield themselves to anyone who gives an elephant; and the Indians think it no disgrace to yield thus on the gift of an elephant, but rather it seems honourable for a woman that her beauty should be valued at an elephant.[18]

To this horse-riding military officer of Alexander the hierarchy of forms of conveyance of the Indians in the Indus valley had a logic all its own, very different from what he was used to. The hierarchy of *vāhanas* that the passage indicates is broadly consistent with what we find in Sanskrit texts. The elephant is explicitly the highest because it is the biggest, hence identified with royalty. Riding a chariot drawn by four horses is superior to being drawn by only one, and being drawn by a horse is superior to riding on the back of a horse (or camel, or ass). Even the matter of giving an elephant to a lover, though difficult to confirm from Indian texts, is consistent with what we have already seen, that the elephant is at the summit—of gift objects as well. Nearchus depicts a society so well provided with animals that everyone has a *vāhana*, and if anyone goes afoot we do not hear of it.

[18] Arrian, Indica (7) 17.2–4 (= Nearchus fragment 11).

Using this conception of a structured hierarchy of conveyances, which Nearchus captures so well, I should like to focus on one highly significant aspect of it, the greater dignity of riding a horse-drawn chariot than riding horseback.

I return to an issue raised in the previous chapter, about the antiquity of horseback riding in India. It used to be asked whether horseback riding was known in the earliest part of the Veda, with the idea that cavalry followed chariot riding in a developmental sequence. But it has long become clear that horseback riding *was* known in the *Ṛg Veda*.[19] Developmentalism was the wrong frame; the comparative prominence of the chariot in the Veda, and also in the epics, has to do with its greater dignity as a *vāhana* and instrument of war. The comparative obscurity of horseback riding is but the other side of this valuation. Under such circumstances cavalry does not develop fully as a division of the army, at least not at the start. We know, however, that in the long run the chariot ceased to be used on the battlefield, and that cavalry came to the fore, acquiring a dignity it formerly lacked. There is, then, an ages-long process in India by which horseback riding emerges from the shadows to become a sign of high status.

It is not difficult to demonstrate this higher dignity of the chariot—the gods themselves all ride chariots in the Veda, as we have seen. Gonda (1965) proposed that the increased importance of cavalry and growing prestige of riding horseback motivated the rise of the particular animal *vāhanas* associated with each Hindu god as its characteristic mount, abandoning the chariot for an animal conveyance specific to that god. The argument is convincing. Thus Śiva is associated with the bull Nandi; Viṣṇu's mount is the eagle Garuḍa; Indra's is the elephant Airāvata; and only Sūrya, the sun, continues to ride his chariot daily across the sky, like his Greek counterpart Helios.

Gonda's essay on the rise of the scheme of *vāhanas* for Hindu gods is valuable because he develops it from a reading of the literature on chariots and horseback riding concerning the

[19] Coomaraswamy 1942; Singh 1965: 58–62.

ancient civilizations of Egypt, Assyria, Mesopotamia, and Greece, viewing Indian developments with a much wider lens, as part of a larger pattern.[20] This region, plus Vedic India and indeed Shang China (which Gonda does not include in his survey), had chariot warfare and a strong association of chariots with kings and warrior aristocrats. Whether Gonda is right when he asserts that horseback riding came later than the chariot is doubtful; the salient point is that it has a lower status, connected with unnamed messengers and fighters acting in supporting roles to the chariot warriors. The subsequent improvement of status for horseback riding is, as noted, connected with horse-based fighting bands of inner Asia, and spread to the early agrarian civilizations, but at very different times. The armies of the Homeric epics privileged the chariot, for example, but Alexander's army consisted entirely of cavalry and infantry, with no chariots at all, when he encountered Indian armies, such as that of Porus. The latter were full fourfold armies, still using chariots as an important element of the whole. The high dignity of riding horseback among the Macedonians is evident in the coin of Alexander showing him mounted upon his horse Bucephelas, pursuing the Indian king Porus on an elephant.[21] It will have been striking to Nearchus, for whom riding on the back of a horse was a sign of high status, that in the Indian hierarchy of *vāhanas* riding a chariot was superior.

The status of horseback riding in India is difficult to track because it is so rarely mentioned. On the one hand, horseback fighting appears as one of the elements of the fourfold army. It is one of the four fighting arts that Arjuna is taught by Droṇa, as we have seen. Chariot, elephant, or cavalry divisions of the army can, in theory, be the lead element of a unit, combined with the other three as support units.[22] But in the narratives of battles in the epics we find no examples of units in which cavalry is the lead element, leaving the suspicion that it exists only in theory. (In the *Arthaśāstra*, on the other hand, cavalry clearly can be a lead

[20] Gonda 1965: 95–103.

[21] Goukowsky 1972; Scullard 1974: pl. XIII a, b.

[22] *Arth.* 10.5.

element of the army, and horsemen do not have only a supporting role.) In the epics we largely hear of horseback riding in connection with messengers who attend the king, in composite units led by chariots or elephants, and in episodes of chariot warriors resorting to horseback riding when they have lost their chariots in the course of battle.[23] Thus riding horseback is associated with the speed of anonymous messengers, secondary battlefield functions, and the emergencies to which chariot warriors are sometimes subject.

The received story of the Buddha's life offers the best example, not previously discussed in this connection as far as I know, of resorting to horseback to make a fast getaway, invoking the aforementioned elements of speed and emergency. The Śākya prince had to escape from the royal city quickly, under cover of darkness, lest his father and family detain him. He had set off to seek enlightenment in the forest, riding on the back of his horse Kaṇṭhaka. The scene is iconic and is given a name: it is called the great departure or *abhiniṣkramaṇa*. His desire to abandon the city for the forest had been awakened by the "rise of perturbation" (*samvegotpatti*). Driving about in a chariot, as befits the son of a rāja, the prince sees the signs of the sorrow and impermanence of the world from knowledge of which his father had hoped to keep him by surrounding him with pleasure. He sees a person suffering the pain of old age; a person wracked by illness; a dead person; and a world-renouncing mendicant. The sight of what he has been kept in ignorance of till this moment is deeply shocking—distinguishing the prince from ordinary people, for whom such things are commonplace. Conceiving the wish for an enlightenment that will resolve the problems of old age, disease, and death, he flees his father and family on horseback. Riding horseback, in sum, is for a prince something he is skilled at, but which he does in an emergency, when the greatest speed is needed; in normal circumstances he will go about by chariot.

The logic of this contrast between chariots and horseback as conveyances, which accords with the Nearchus passage, is clear

[23] Hopkins 1889: 264.

enough in the *Buddhacarita* or *Life of the Buddha* by Aśvaghoṣa, one of the early extant texts on the topic. But there are complications. Aśvaghoṣa is associated with the Kushans, inner Asian conquerors, and dated to the first or second century CE.[24] The text was written, therefore, many centuries after the events of the Buddha's life, which was lived around the fifth century BCE. So its historicity cannot be taken for granted. One obvious anachronism is that the father of the Buddha-to-be, Śuddhodhana, is portrayed as a single monarch of the Śākyas. But the Śākyas of that time had a republic, so that the father of the Buddha would have been one among many of the Śākya ruling warrior class, not a full-fledged king. This anachronism does not affect the point for us, however, which has to do with the relative prestige of chariot riding and riding horseback. But there is another anachronism which does affect this very point, muddying the clear contrast between chariot riding and horseback riding which gives the logic of the story, and it is likely due to the Kushans. For we get in Aśvaghoṣa's telling of the great departure a direct expression of the improved prestige of horse riding and cavalry action in battle. At the outset of the scene Aśvaghoṣa depicts the prince as speaking to his horse as if about to charge into battle (*dhvajinīmadhyam iva praveṣṭukāmaḥ*):

> *bahuśaḥ kila śatravo nirastāḥ*
> *samare tvām adhiruhya pārthivena* |
> *aham apy amṛtaṃ padaṃ yathāvat*
> *turagaśreṣṭha labheya tat kuruṣva* ||

> "Many a time did the king mount you, and vanquish his foes in battle; that is well known. So act in such a way, O best of steeds, that I too may obtain the deathless state."[25]

The direct reference to the king riding a horse in battle signals that horseback riding and cavalry warfare have increased in use and prestige, which is what we would expect of the inner Asian, horseback-riding, cavalry-using Kushans with whom Aśvaghoṣa is

[24] *Buddhacarita* 1972, 2008: Introduction.
[25] Ibid.: 5.75.

associated. Under these circumstances the great departure would have had a different valence in the first or second century CE than in *c.* 500 BCE, when it would have been in the nature of a warrior throwing dignity to the winds in order to make a hasty getaway.

As, according to this passage, the king himself appears in battle on horseback, we may suppose that the age of the great chariot warriors is at an end, at least in the Kushan realm, a territory half in the Indian northwest and half in Central Asia. For the appearance of the king on horseback implies the rising importance of cavalry warfare as well as the decline of chariot warfare. This evidence from the *Buddhacarita* is graphically confirmed by a headless stature of the great Kushan king Kaniṣka in horseback-riding dress: cutaway coat, loose trousers, felt boots, spurs (Fig. 3.3). This essentially cold-climate horseman's dress figured on Kuṣāṇa coins. It was imitated on early coins of the imperial Guptas as well, ruling from Pāṭaliputra—modern-day Patna in Bihar—far from

Fig. 3.3: Statue of the Kushan king Kaniṣka

the colder regions in which this kind of dress was appropriate. This evidence makes me think that when the Gupta emperor is referred to as "having no equal antagonist," the reference to chariots contained in the Sanskrit expression (*apratiratha*) must be taken metaphorically, not as a current reality. I conclude that the obsolescence of the chariot on the battlefield was under way, if not already an accomplished fact, by about the first century CE, following successful military incursions by several inner Asian mounted armies of Scythians (Skt. Śaka), Parthians (Skt. Pahlava), and Kushans.

What has made this point so obscure and difficult to secure by evidence is the enduring popularity of the epics, which colors all representations of battle in inscriptions, literature, figural representations, and the performing arts, perpetuating the prestige of the chariot long after it receded from the battlefield. As Gonda said of the wider scene of ancient civilizations, "in some cases nobility and almost everywhere divinity lag behind" the rise of cavalry. "Clinging to traditions they continued employing their wheeled vehicles for military, travelling, and representative purposes."[26] In India the valuation of the chariot seems to intensify, if anything, as we move from the Veda to the epic. As Hopkins notes, the Vedic gods rode two-horse-drawn chariots, except Indra, who had a four-horse chariot. And a blanket statement at the commencement of war in the *Mahābhārata* says that all chariots were drawn by four horses—although in the narrative of battle the chariots seem to be drawn only by a single pair of horses.[27] We are probably dealing with a further intensification of hyperbole indicative of boundless esteem for the chariot.

Taking the great dignity of the chariot as the leading aspect of the armies of Vedic times as our baseline, I ask what, then, did the introduction of the war elephant into this structure of valuation do in the formation of a new structure of valuation for *vāhanas*? What was the relation of the war chariot to the war elephant?

[26] Gonda 1965: 102.
[27] Hopkins 1889: 250–1.

One of the things we notice from the epics is that the famous named warriors are chariot fighters. Fighters riding elephants are mentioned, but they are often unnamed warriors; rarely are they kings. Duryodhana arrives at the battlefield on a lordly elephant, but when the action commences we find him fighting from a chariot.[28] In the *Arthaśāstra* the chariot and the elephant are equivalent. The soldier's prize for taking either is the same; and the king is advised to ride a chariot or elephant, or the force that is predominant in the composition of the army, or that with which he is most skilled.[29] The elephant is a royal conveyance, but the king uses other conveyances. Taken together, the ancient primacy of the war chariot leaves a strong impress upon the epics, and its prominence has to do with the setting of the story in a deeper past. The war elephant is also present, bearing kings or nameless fighters, but they are not equals of the great chariot warriors. In the *Arthaśāstra*, however, the privilege of the chariot has shifted toward an equality of chariots and elephants.

While the prestige of the chariot lingered very long, the addition of the elephant to the battlefield, and as a royal conveyance, appears to have been sudden, and the universalization of the war elephant in India proceeded apace. It produced a new way of "performing" kingship that was very durable. For example, when Bhārata hears of Rāma's banishment to the Central Indian forest at the behest of his mother Kaikeyī, he takes a fourfold army to the forest to beg Rāma to return. Rāma declines to go against his father's command, and Bhārata reluctantly agrees to rule as regent until Rāma's term of exile expires. As a sign of that role he places Rāma's sandals on elephant-back and returns to Ayodhyā.[30] The symbolism is immediately intelligible.

The performance of kingship from elephant-back—the association of the war elephant with kingship—gives the animal a symbolic power that spreads to other spheres of life, notably religion. Elephants suffuse Indian religions, and the royal character

[28] Ibid.: 205, 267n.
[29] *Arth.* 10.3.4–41, 45.
[30] *Rām.* 2.104.23.

of its symbolism is quite apparent. A famous example from Buddhist literature concerns an elephant named Nālāgiri, a tusker in musth, belonging to king Ajātaśatru of Magadha. The evil Devadatta, cousin and rival of the Buddha, persuades the king to let the elephant loose on the main street of the capital city to kill the Buddha. Devadatta has the elephant keepers ply Nālāgiri with toddy to further madden him, and then release him; but when the Buddha speaks to him he is suffused with love and bows down to him.[31] The logic of the story rests upon the concept of the war elephant, of its royal character, and the royal nature of the Buddha that the elephant acknowledges by its actions. The many Hindu temples today that keep an elephant to accept offerings and take part in processions of the deity, especially in South India, are among the most visible traces of this influence.

Of this kind is the annual procession of the Tooth Relic of the Buddha held in the highlands of Sri Lanka, in the seat of the last great kingdom of the island. The Tooth Relic was the paladin of Sri Lankan kingship, and the procession of it around the royal city, the Äsaḷa Perähara, perpetuates the royal processions of old described in the chronicle of the island, the *Mahāvaṃsa*. The kingship of the island was forced into the interior highland of Kandy by European powers (Portuguese, Dutch, English) occupying the rich coastal lowlands, but the royal procession of the relic survives even the extinction of the Kandyan kingship by the British in 1815. This celebration of kingship and its social order, in the analysis of H.L. Seneviratne, makes visible the departments of government, provinces, castes, deities of the temples (*devāle*) such as Śiva and Viṣṇu, the Buddhist *vihāra*, and the various units of the procession involving elephants, drummers, and dancers; it renders visible the magnificence of their patrons. At the head of the procession is the Officer of the Front, "riding an elephant and carrying a symbolic book that represented the *lēkham miṭi*, the state records of the lands of the kingdom," followed by the chief of the elephant stables, "riding an elephant and carrying a symbolic

[31] DPPN s.v. Nālāgiri.

goad (*aṅkuśa*), symbolic both of the power over the elephant, and of the department to which he belongs."[32] The Tooth Relic itself was borne on an elephant in a gold and silver sacred casket. Another example of the uses of the *rāja-vāhana* idea comes from the nineteenth-century Tamil country, when the last Tamil poets writing in the classical style were being patronized by zamindars and monasteries (*maṭha*). In one instance the publication of a new work of poetry was accomplished not only by the public reading aloud of the work for the first time, but also a procession in which the manuscript was borne around the temple square on elephant-back.[33]

Returning to the passage from Nearchus on the hierarchy of *vāhanas* in India, Strabo's quotation of Nearchus adds something different: "Nearchus says that a chariot drawn by elephants is considered a very great possession, and that they are drawn under yoke like camels; and that a woman is highly honoured if she receives an elephant as a gift from a lover. But this statement is not in agreement with that of the man who said that the horse and elephant were possessed by kings alone."[34] The first sentence gives new information about the lost Nearchus text on Indian *vāhanas* that is not contained in Arrian's version. The notion of a chariot drawn by elephants greatly appealed to the Romans: much later, we find representations of elephants under yoke drawing a vehicle, not in India but in connection with the Roman emperor Julian, signaling his victory over the Sassanians, who had used elephants against the Romans. We also find, at Pompei, a painting of the goddess Athena in a chariot drawn by four elephants under yoke.[35]

The second sentence of the passage is Strabo's own editorial comment, throwing doubt on the veracity of Greek writers on India because of their mutual contradictions. Strabo is much exercised by private vs royal ownership of horse and elephant

[32] Seneviratne 1978: 108.
[33] Ebeling 2010: 79.
[34] Strabo, *Geography* 15.1.43.
[35] Scullard 1974: pl. XX b, c.

in the Greek writers about India. He takes it as evidence that they were mostly liars. But in fact the two positions are not in contradiction, and the value of the observation is that Strabo put his finger upon something highly significant on which the Greek sources report reliably. The source that is supposed to have contradicted Nearchus is Megasthenes, who, in Strabo's summary, had said, "No private person is permitted to keep a horse or elephant. The possession of either is a royal privilege, and there are men to take care of them."[36] Nearchus was reporting on the situation of the Indus valley in the time of Alexander, while Megasthenes was reporting on the "easterners" (Prasioi, Prācyāḥ), that is to say the Mauryan empire whose capital was in the middle Ganga region, to which Megasthenes was sent as ambassador in the time of the Hellenistic successors to Alexander a few decades later. What we see is a tightening of the ownership of horses and elephants by the Mauryas as the policy of an ambitious kingdom, centralizing in this way the means of warfare with spectacular success. The strong interest of Indian kingship in elephants and horses gives kings an incentive to put limits upon private capture, trade, and ownership. This grows into a constant tendency, the expression of which ebbs and flows but is never entirely absent and is sometimes, as in the Mauryan case, carried to the highest degree, namely, royal monopoly.

Vyūha

Elephants have specific uses in war. This is what the *Arthaśāstra* says about the "works" (*karmāṇi*)—tasks or functions—of elephants:

> These are the tasks of the elephant corps: marching at the vanguard; making new roads, camping places and fords; repelling attacks; crossing and descending into water; holding the ground, marching forward, and descending; entering rugged and crowded places; setting and putting out fires; scoring a victory with a single army unit; reuniting broken ranks, breaking up unbroken ranks, reuniting

[36] Strabo, *Geography* 15.1.41.

> a broken formation; breaking an unbroken formation; providing protection in a calamity; charging forward; causing fear; terrorizing; demonstrating grandeur; gathering; dispatching; shattering parapets, doors, and turrets; and taking the treasury safely in and out.[37]

The functions of war elephants are many. The most dramatic of them are the breaking down of fortifications and sowing terror in enemy troops on the battlefield. There are in addition more prosaic but highly valuable functions, such as making roadways for the army, assisting in the crossing of rivers, and bearing the treasury.

These functions take place in the context of the army as a whole, and the *vyūha* or disposition of troops defines the place of the war elephant in relation to the other limbs. Armies encamping, marching to battle, and drawn up on the field of battle must be arranged in a certain order at each stage. An arrangement or array is called *vyūha*. The arrays have names and are drawn from a repertoire of arrays.

The *vyūha* is the most technical of the three named structures of use I have been examining in this chapter. *Vyūhas* figure prominently in the battlefield scenes of the *Mahābhārata*, and in the tenth book, on war, in the *Arthaśāstra*, as well as in later texts on kingship. But many perplexities of the texts make it difficult to understand how the *vyūha* really worked, and the stages of its development and spread. Some of the ambiguities stem from the poetic nature of the epic, and the cryptic, *sūtra* form of the great work on kingship; but the problem exists also because the term simply *is* technical and not easily made precise in words.

At the same time there is no mistaking the high importance these and other ancient sources attribute to the knowledge of *vyūhas*. This was strikingly demonstrated by Quaritch Wales (1952), whose pioneering work on the influence of the Indian model of kingship upon warfare in Southeast Asia gives drawings of *vyūhas* found in Java dating to about 1500 CE, and in Thailand from the nineteenth century. These show the cultivation of this

[37] *Arth.* 10.4.14.

branch of military science among the Indianizing kingdoms of Southeast Asia over a thousand years after the *Mahābhārata* and the *Arthaśāstra*.[38] They also show that the geographical and chronological reach of the *vyūha* as a structure of army order was very great, including the whole of India and perhaps many of the Indianizing kingdoms of Southeast Asia; and that the *vyūhas* continued to shape military practice for perhaps two millennia.

One would like to know more about both the geographic and chronological dimensions of this reach. Apart from the direct transmission of the knowledge of *vyūhas* from India to Southeast Asian kingdoms, warfare itself is a form of communication by which military practice is directly apprehended and spread across languages and cultures. One would like to know the relation, if any, of the Indian *vyūhas* to Persian military practice and to the lost Greek works on military tactics from the Hellenistic period; or, conversely, the influence of the latter upon the former. One would like to know whether the *vyūhas* continued in use in India in the times of the Turkish Sultanate and the Mughal empire. One would like to be able to identify *vyūhas* in ancient sculptural representations of war. There are more questions than there can be answers in the existing scholarship. For present purposes, however, a sketch of this important but elusive topic will suffice.

Both epics and the *Arthaśāstra* indicate the existence of older works on *vyūha* by Bṛhaspati and Uśanas, who are often named as the great authorities on the topic. Bṛhaspati and Uśanas (or Śukra) are the gurus of the gods (*devas*) and of the demons (*asuras*), respectively. The gods and demons use *vyūhas* in their own battles, which are thought of as models for human use. Indeed, in a passage in the *Mahābhārata* one side adopts a *vyūha* of the *devas*, and the other answers with a *vyūha* of the *asuras*; in another passage one side adopts a *vyūha* of Bṛhaspati and the other side answers with a *vyūha* of Uśanas.[39] It appears that books on warfare, including on the forming of *vyūhas*, did actually exist; and these included those

[38] See Chapter 7, Figs 7.7 and 7.8.

[39] *Mbh*. 3.269.5–6.

attributed to Bṛhaspati and Uśanas, which have since been lost.[40] The *Arthaśāstra* pays homage to Śukra (Uśanas) and Bṛhaspati at its start, as if they were divinities, but elsewhere speaks of texts, and of schools of Auśanasas and Barhaspatyas, that is, followers, respectively, of Uśanas and Bṛhaspati. Taken as a whole, the *Arthaśastra* treats both as divinities, and as the writers of texts at the center of whose work was knowledge of *vyūhas*.

Knowledge of *vyūhas* involves mastery of the various kinds of *vyūhas*, including which of the *vyūhas* is best suited to present circumstances, and how the army one has, with its strengths and deficiencies, is to be fitted into the chosen *vyūha*. The treatment of the topic is quite different in the *Mahābhārata* and the *Arthaśāstra*. The former gives us the poetry of war, and the tendency is to treat *vyūhas* as a rare and esoteric knowledge, the details of which therefore remain somewhat fuzzy and mysterious. Moreover the battle proper, the mêlée that takes place when the arrayed forces meet, is described rather as a series of duels between pairs of famous warriors rather than as the maneuvering of large bodies of fighters in relation to one another. The *Arthaśāstra* is straightforward and crisp in its treatment of *vyūhas*, without mystification, but also without the elaboration that someone coming fresh to the topic will need; the text needs a spoken commentary to flesh out its bare-bones outline.

In the *Mahābhārata* knowledge of *vyūhas* was a special study, distinct from the knowledge of weapons, riding, and fighting necessary for a warrior to know.[41] Such knowledge was rare and gave distinction. Possession of it was a qualification for battlefield leadership. It is treated as more than a technical matter, as a kind of mysterious knowledge that is the earthly reflection of divine models. Thus Bhīṣma, "skilled in *vyūhas*,"[42] says, when he is appointed to lead the Kaurava army:

> *senākarmaṇy abhijño 'smi* *vyūheṣu vividheṣu ca* |
> *karma kārayituṁ caiva* *bhṛ̥tān apy abhṛ̥tāṁs tathā* ||

[40] Hopkins 1889: 202–3.

[41] Ibid.: 203.

[42] *vyūhaviśāradaḥ*: *Mbh.* 6.77.11.

yātrāyāneṣu yuddheṣu labdhapraśamaneṣu ca |
bhṛśaṁ veda mahārāja yathā veda bṛhaspatiḥ ||
vyūhān api mahārambhān daivagāndharvamānuṣān |
tair ahaṁ mohayiṣyāmi pāṇḍavān vyetu te jvaraḥ ||

I am experienced in warfare and the various *vyūhas*, and I know how to direct soldier and nonsoldier alike to their tasks. In the ways of marching in convoys, waging battle, and neutralizing enemy fire I know as much, great king, as Bṛhaspati himself. I know all the *vyūhas* of gods, Gandharvas and men: with those I shall confound the Pāṇḍavas. Let your fears abate.[43]

In the description of the eighteen days of battle that make up the *Mahābhārata* war, each day begins with the choosing of a *vyūha* by one side, and of a counter-array or *prati-vyūha* by the other side, the choice of which is also part of the skill expected of a commander. Often they have specific names from the recognized repertoire: cart (*śakaṭa*), heron (*krauñca*), hawk (*śyena*), needle (*suci*), sea monster (*makara*), and so forth. The Kaurava's choice of the wheel (*cakra*) on the thirteenth day calls for the leadership of the youthful Abhimanyu, sixteen-year-old son of Arjuna, who alone knows how to penetrate it; unfortunately he has not learned how to get out of it and is killed in the attempt. But just as often the *vyūha* is unnamed, or given a vague descriptive name such as "huge" or "like the ocean," a *vyūha* "like a cloud" or a *vyūha* "unseen before."[44] Or it is said to be a *vyūha* of the gods or demons, or of Bṛhaspati, or of Uśanas. Furthermore, battle arrays are sometimes composites of two or three basic forms, such as the cart, lotus, and needle combination adopted by the Kauravas on the fourteenth day.[45] We cannot expect to recover the workings of *vyūhas* in real battles from materials such as these.

An essential part of the science of *vyūhas* is that once a particular array is taken up by one side (the larger force, normally), the other side chooses a counter-array (*prati-vyūha*) that will improve its chances. So one must know which *prati-vyūha* answers each *vyūha*. This of course depends upon many variables, including

[43] Ibid.: 5.162.8-10.
[44] Hopkins 1889: 208.
[45] Ibid.: 213.

which army is larger. One example from the *Mahābhārata* is clear enough: a larger force takes up the circle array, making its army an impenetrable mass; whereupon the smaller opposing army concentrates its force on a single point, and so takes the needle array.[46]

The logic of the *vyūha* doctrine becomes clearer in the *Arthaśāstra*'s tenth book, on war. On the march, the sea monster (*makara*) is the order of choice when expecting an attack from the front;[47] the cart (*śakaṭa*) when expecting an attack from the rear; the thunderbolt (*vajra*) if from the flanks; and "good-all-sides" (*sarvatobhadra*) when from all sides. The sea monster is two triangles joined at the apices, so presenting a wide base to attackers from the front (or perhaps simply an inverted triangle); the cart is a wedge, presenting a broad base to attackers from the rear; the thunderbolt comprises five staggered lines moving forward and therefore strong against a flank attack; and the name of the good-all-sides array speaks for itself.

Having chosen a suitable terrain for fighting,[48] the king should apportion his troops.[49] The parts of the *vyūha* are the wings (*pakṣa*), flanks (*kakṣa*), and center (literally, the chest, *urasya*), plus the reserve force (*pratigraha*). These parts are composed of units led by chariot, elephant, or horse, each with a complement of protecting forces. Three men fight in front of a horse, plus three footguards; fifteen in front and behind a chariot or an elephant, and also five horses. The king can then make a chariot formation of three-by-three rows of chariots in each of the two wings, two flanks, and the center, or 45 chariots in all, plus 225 horses and 675 foot soldiers. This is an even formation; an uneven formation would have different numbers in the wings, flanks, and center. A smaller force should be held in reserve to be inserted as needed. Similarly, a formation can be made up of units led by elephants or cavalry. The text then gives consideration to the placement of weaker and stronger troops in the formation.

[46] *Mbh.* 6.19.4.
[47] *Arth.* 10.2.9.
[48] Ibid.: 10.4.
[49] Ibid.: 10.5.

We then come to the overall shape of the formation.[50] The four primary *vyūhas* are staff (*daṇḍa*), snake (*bhoga*), circle (*maṇḍala*), and non-compact (*asaṃhata*). When wings, flanks, and center act evenly it is the staff; when they act unevenly it is the snake; when wings, flanks, and center join it is the circle; when they are not joined it is the non-compact. There follows a rapid and perplexing tour of the sub-varieties.

Each of the four primary types has several variations, giving thirty-three named types in all. Thus of the staff, when it breaks through with flanks, it is the cleaver (*pradara*); when it pulls back with wings and flanks, it is the buttresser (*dṛḍhka*); when it breaks through with the two wings, the irresistible (*asahya*); when the two wings are stationary and the center breaks through, the falcon (*śyena*); when these are carried out in the opposite way they become, respectively, the bow (*cāpa*), bow belly (*cāpakukṣi*), the fixed (*pratiṣṭha*), and the firmly fixed (*supratiṣṭha*). The one with wings like bows is the victor (*saṃjaya*); when it breaks through with the center it is the conqueror (*vijaya*); with wings like stout ears, the pillar-eared (*sthūṇakarṇa*); with double wing pillars, the wide conqueror (*viśālavijaya*); when wings are increased threefold, the army-faced (*camūmukha*); when the opposite, the fish-mouthed (*īṣāsya*). The staff in a straight line (going forward) is the needle (*śūcī*). Two staffs are the pincer (*valaya*); four, the invincible (*durjaya*).

The snake formation has either a snake motion (*sarpasārī*) or cow's urination (*gomutrika*). When the center has two divisions and the wings are in staff formation, it is the cart (*śakaṭa*); in the opposite case, the sea monster (*makara*). The cart interspersed with elephants, horses, and chariots is the flying-about (*pāripantaka*).

Of the circle formation, when it faces in all directions it is the good-all-sides (*sarvatobhadra*); with eight arrays it is the invincible (*durjaya*).

Of the non-compact formation, the thunderbolt (*vajra*) and the monitor lizard (*godha*) are forms in which five lines are joined to resemble the shape of their namesakes; when four arrays, the

[50] Ibid.: 10.6.

hearth (*uddhānaka*) or the crow's feet (*kākapadī*); when three, the half-moon (*ardhacandraka*) or crab-horned (*karkaṭakaśṛṅgī*).

When the center consists of chariot, flanks, of elephant, and rear of horse, it is the invulnerable (*ariṣṭa*); when foot, horse, chariot, and elephant are in formation one behind the other, it is the impregnable (*acala*).

In the final section of its tenth book the *Arthaśāstra* explains the choosing of a *prati-vyūha*: attack a cleaver with a buttresser; a buttresser with an irresistible; a falcon with a bow; a fixed with a firmly fixed; victor with a conqueror; a pillar-eared with a wide conqueror; a flying-about with a good-all-sides; and all *vyūhas* with the invincible. Of foot, horse, cavalry, and elephant forces he should use each latter one to attack a former one; and a deficient unit with a superabundant one.[51]

From the four types, the many sub-types, and the counter-types it is evident that the doctrine of the *vyūhas* in the *Arthaśāstra* has reached a certain fullness and is by no means in the first stage of development. It is somewhat surprising that in *Manu*, a text somewhat later than the *Arthaśāstra*, we meet only seven named *vyūhas*; whether it somehow preserves an earlier stage of development of the *vyūha* doctrine, as Hopkins thought, remains a question.[52] The number of different *vyūhas* in the *Mahābhārata* is impossible to determine for the reasons already given. It is difficult, therefore, to trace the development of the doctrine. All we can say at this stage is that it is fully developed in the early centuries of the Common Era, when the war elephant had been long a part of the universal norms of military practice in North India. The *vyūha* doctrine accompanied the war elephant to the Indianizing kingdoms of Southeast Asia; whether it also travelled westward we cannot begin to say.

[51] Ibid.: 10.6.42–4.

[52] Hopkins 1889: 194–5.

4

Elephant knowledge

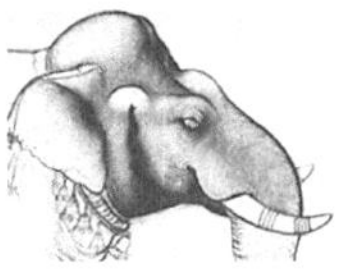

THE CAPTURE, TRAINING, DRIVING, AND maintenance of the war elephant depended upon a fund of knowledge on these matters as well as on the management and deployment of the animal for battle. Such knowledge was embodied in the staff of elephant establishments maintained by kings. The diffusion of the war elephant as an institution presupposes the spread of this knowledge, to understand which we need to discover how this body of information about elephants was formed, embodied, maintained, and transmitted from one generation to the next.

Our understanding of elephant knowledge will, however, be patchy and incomplete, for two reasons. In the first place, it was a complex formation. To maintain war elephants, their trainers had to acquire very specialized practical knowledge of many different aspects of elephants and their management. In the process of training them they had to accustom elephants to human presence, fire, the sounds of battle, new varieties of food, the language of commands, and so forth. In the second place, the written record of the ancient Indian past is the work of a privileged minority, largely religious specialists who stood at several removes of social distance from the mostly unlettered elephant men. Their writings were shaped by interests and perspectives different from those of the practical men from whom the substance of elephant lore derives. Sometimes, written elephant science cast itself free of practical knowledge and took the form of pure theoretical elaboration. For this reason, as a principle of method and interpretation of texts we must always estimate as best we may the distance between practical knowledge and formal, written knowledge.

In this chapter I will examine the practical knowledge about elephants embodied in the elephant staff of the king, and the formal, written elephant lore in Sanskrit texts in order to explore the relation of practical knowledge and elephant science. I will then take up the elephant knowledge contained in the two best sources, separated by over a thousand years: the Sanskrit text of the *Arthaśāstra*, and the Persian text of the *Ā'īn-i Akbarī*, both of which stand in close relation to practical knowledge. We will then be in a position to better analyze the processes by which the institution of the war elephant was diffused within India and beyond.

Practical knowledge

Getting and maintaining elephants requires a large staff. I will examine the staff in detail from the *Arthaśāstra* and the *Ā'īn* later in this chapter; for present purposes it will be useful to identify the crucial functions requiring specialized knowledge: the aforementioned capture, training, driving, and maintenance. The staff members assigned to these were the hunter, the trainer, the elephant driver or mahout, and the physician. These overlapped to some degree. The mahout, for example, was with the elephant most of the time and responsible for its maintenance, monitoring its health, altering its feed as appropriate to its condition, and treating minor ailments. Hunters and trainers could also be mahouts. The mahout almost always had an assistant to help him with his work and take over when he went on leave, and leaf-and-browse cutters who provided green fodder.

These specialized skills were learned by apprenticeship, so that lineages of teachers and pupils, often related as fathers and sons or uncles and nephews (we may suppose), extending more than a hundred generations shaped and transmitted the knowledge for the three thousand years of the war elephant's history, down to the present day. With the possible exception of the physician, this knowledge was transmitted by unlettered specialists without the aid of written works.

As we have seen, the *Mahābhārata*, which is centered upon the city of Hastināpura in the Doab or upper Ganges, indicates that elephant warriors and elephant drivers come mostly from peoples lying to the east, in an arc from the Himalayas in the north to the forests of South India: in short, from the elephant habitat of the monsoon forests. Such people are often identified with named ethnic groups or identified as *mlecchas* (foreigners/barbarians). It is entirely to be expected that elephant staff will have been found among the forest people of this forest-loving animal. This being so, forest people who became elephant hunters, trainers, and mahouts will have acquired positions in royal service and their positions will have been passed on to relatives, creating lineages of elephant specialists. Such lineages will have become part of the kingdom.

In the coming chapters I will give evidence showing that Indian hunters and trainers were acquired by Alexander and sought by his Hellenistic successors, and that Indian mahouts travelled with Indian elephants as far as the Seleucid kings of Syria and the Ptolemaic kings of Egypt—and possibly further. There is circumstantial evidence that North Indian mahouts transmitted their knowledge to locals in South India, and that the mahouts of India trained those in Sri Lanka and Southeast Asia. There is direct evidence that Southeast Asian mahouts accompanied diplomatic gifts of elephants by Southeast Asian kings to the emperor of China in Ming times. This shows that the unwritten knowledge of the mahout in particular, as also of the hunter and the trainer, is a crucial strategic asset for kings using war elephants, and that it was embodied in and spread by Indian mahouts, hunters, and trainers.

Even the word mahout seems to indicate the high strategic value of what is a subaltern position in the king's service. The English word mahout corresponds to Hindi *mahāvat*, which derives from Sanskrit *mahāmātra*.[1] The meaning of the word in Sanskrit is transparent: a person of great (*mahā*) measure (*mātra*). It indicates a royal official of high rank, a minister or counselor (*amātya* or *mantrin*). The inscriptions of Aśoka Maurya and the *Arthaśāstra* use the word *mahāmātra* for a high government official. It is surprising to find the elephant driver and the high royal official denoted by the same word. Mayrhofer remarks that there seems to be no unity between the two meanings.[2] Various other words for elephant keeper in Prakrit (*meṇṭha*, *miṇṭha*) and Pali (*hatthi-meṇḍa*) led him to suggest the possible influence of a non-Aryan word for elephant driver. Even if this is so, however, the elephant driver did eventually come to be called *mahāmātra*, a word transparently indicative of high importance, and this is the word for elephant driver in common use in both epics, the *Mahābhārata* and the *Rāmāyaṇa*, and in the law book of Manu. Other texts, notably the *Arthaśāstra*, have the word *hastipaka*, but mahout and its forebears seem to have dominated, as in the *Ā'īn-i Akbarī* (*mahāwāt*). Though the mahout was a lowly employee of the king, and virtually tied to the elephant in his keeping, it appears that his high value as an asset, as a military asset above all, was recognized through this word.

Due to the work of Piers Locke, Surendra Varma, and others there is beginning to be an ethnography of mahouts in the present day, which can, to some extent, be joined with the record of history. Some continuities are very striking, as when Nicolas Lainé shows that the Khamti of Assam train elephants with song and notes and that Megasthenes said the same of Mauryan India.[3] Lainé's work also shows the ways in which regional beliefs—of Southeast Asia in the case of Khamti practice—enter the practices of trainers as well, for example the notion that forest spirits residing in the hair of the elephant need to be exorcized by singeing their hair with a flaming torch. Because of the wide geographical spread of the

[1] Turner 1966: 572, s.v. 9950 *mahāmātra*.

[2] scheinen miteinander vereinbar zu sein: Mayrhofer 1986: 397.

[3] Lainé forthcoming. Aelian 12.44 says the Indians used a musical instrument to calm newly caught elephants.

institution of the war elephant there is bound to be a great deal of variation in what is essentially a vernacular tradition of practical knowledge. And it is certain to be difficult to reconstruct the history of this tradition, or family of traditions, because of its vernacular nature and its distance from the written record.[4]

Elephant science

In the *Mahābhārata* the education of three princes, Dhṛtarāṣṭra, Pāṇḍu, and Vidura, consists of the "Veda of the bow," horseback riding, fighting with clubs, sword and shield, elephant training (*gaja-śikṣā*), and the science of policy (*nītiśāstra*).[5] The last named has a written literature, but the others may have been skills learned by practice rather than from books. *Gaja-śikṣā*, in the context, probably means not the care and management of elephants but the special art of *fighting* from elephant-back, corresponding with the function of cavalry. Both involved riding bareback and fighting, and so the chief skill to be mastered was "keeping one's position."[6] Many passages referring to war elephants being well mounted by skilled riders confirm this interpretation.[7] In another passage the sage Nārada asks king Yudhiṣṭhira whether he has learned all the *sūtras*, those on elephants and those on horses and chariots.[8] *Sūtras* are concise rules to be memorized. They have a fixed form and therefore a literary aspect even if they are not written down, and learned by ear rather than eye.

All of this, and other passages to similar effect, have to do with the art and practice of war; not the capture, training, and management aspects of elephant lore, knowledge of which is in the hands of the elephant staff. Only the bits of interest to princes and warriors get discussed in the *Mahābhārata*. Of course, mahouts

[4] These two paragraphs draw upon an article on the deep history of mahouts: Trautmann forthcoming.

[5] *Mbh*. 1.102.17.

[6] Hopkins 1889: 266.

[7] For example, elephants which are *svārūḍhā yuddhakuśalaiḥ śikṣitair hastisādibhiḥ*: *Mbh*. 4.30.27.

[8] *Mbh*. 2.5.109.

too had to be skilled in fighting on elephant-back, as well as in the many other aspects of their care giving. And so we find in another passage that Kirāta (a forest people) mahouts (*mahāmātrāḥ*) are expert in the elephant art (*hastiśikṣāvidaḥ*).[9] The elephant lore referred to in the *Mahābhārata*, whether formal or purely practical, concerns the warrior who fights from the elephant, not the thousand details of capturing, training, driving, and maintaining an elephant for the king's use.

Nevertheless, there is a body of texts in Sanskrit that deals with elephants in this larger way. I will examine the relation of these works to the practical learning known to the king's elephant keepers. Although this body of texts is not large, only parts of it have been closely studied in modern times. This is unfortunate because so very many ancient Indian texts refer to elephants and presuppose a certain degree of acquaintance with elephant life, and of awareness of some details of elephant lore on the part of their lettered readers.

The earliest and best of them is the *Arthaśāstra*, which as noted is the earliest extant text on the science of kingship (*arthaśāstra*) and policy (*nītiśāstra*).[10] Successor works in this genre, such as the *Nītisāra* of Kāmandaka (*c.* 500–700 CE),[11] also speak of elephants but do not add a great deal to what the *Arthaśāstra* has to say on the topic. There are several later texts of more general scope that contain substantial amounts of elephant lore. They include the *Yaśastilaka* of Somadeva Suri (959–66); the *Mānasollāsa* of king Someśvara III Cālukya (1131); and the *Hariharacaturaṅga* of Godāvaramiśra, minister to Pratāparudradeva of the Gajapati kings of Orissa (sixteenth century).[12]

In all of these texts elephants are only a part of a larger subject matter, and the texts are datable. The specialized treatises of

[9] *Mbh.* 7.87.30.

[10] The *Arthaśāstra* eclipses and absorbs earlier works on the topic. I have already said much about it, with more to follow later in this chapter.

[11] Singh 2010: 32.

[12] To this list Edgerton (*ML*, Introduction: x) adds the *Bṛhatsaṃhitā* of Varāhamihira, a work on astrology, whose chapter 67 he considers (a bit generously) "a sort of miniature *gaja-śāstra*." Its date is 550 CE.

elephant lore form another class of texts and are undated. Franklin Edgerton's analysis and translation of one of these texts, the *Mātaṅgalīlā*, is an outstanding work of scholarship. He argues that elephant lore has a long antiquity, shown by its appearance in the *Arthaśāstra*, which is certainly true. In his view the specialized treatises on elephant lore come *after* the *Arthaśāstra*, being new formations in the developing literature of the conduct of the kingdom. This seems very likely. It is supported by the fact that the *Arthaśāstra* does not speak of an elephant science, which it would have had there been specialized treatises on elephants in its day; nor does it attribute elephant lore to holy personages of the deep past, as the surviving specialized treatises do.

Specialized Sanskrit treatises on elephant lore in print are:

Gajaśāstra (Elephant science) of Pālkāpya
Gajaśikṣā (Elephant training) of Nārada
Gajagrahaṇaprakāra (Exposition of the capture of elephants) of Nārāyaṇa Dīkṣita
Mātaṅgalīlā (The play of elephants) of Nīlakaṇṭha
Hastyāyurveda (Elephant life science) of Pālkāpya

For the *Gajaśāstra* we have two manuscripts, one in the Sarasvati Mahal Library at Thanjavur and the other in the library of the raja of Aundh, a small princely state in Maharashtra.[13] Both are evidently the same work but there are considerable differences: the first has 10 *prakaranas* and 754 verses, the second 19 *prakaranas* but only 551 verses; in both there are many irregular verses. The *Gajaśikṣā* and *Gajagrahaṇaprakāra* are both from single manuscripts in the Oriental Research Institute of the Sri Venkateswara University, Tirupati.[14] The *Gajaśikṣā*, a work of 9 *paṭalas* (the last of them incomplete) and 447 verses, has a commentary, *Vyakti*, of Umāpatyācārya. The *Gajagrahaṇaprakāra*,

[13] Both are published. The Thanjavur manuscript is edited by K.S. Subrahmanya Sastri, with Tamil translation, English paraphrase, and color illustrations; the Aundh manuscript is edited by Siddharth Yeshwant Wankankar and V.B. Mhaiskar, with substantial introduction, English translation, and illustrations.

[14] It is edited by Professor E.R. Sreekrishna Sarma.

a work of five *āśvāsas* and 881 verses in all, has no commentary. Both manuscripts are modern. The *Mātaṅgalīlā*, edited by T. Ganapati Sastri and translated by Edgerton, who compared it with the Thanjavur *Gajaśāstra* and the *Hastyāyurveda*, is the best studied of this group. It is a short work in ornate verses, containing 12 *paṭalas* and 253 verses. The *Hastyāyurveda* is a massive work of some 800 printed pages.[15] It is divided like other works of *āyurveda* into four major parts, Mahārogasthānam (18 *adhyāyas*), Kṣudrarogasthānam (72 *adhyāyas*), Śalyasthānam (34 *adhyāyas*), and Uttarasthānam (36 *adhyāyas*). No one has been tempted to translate it, and I do not know of scholarly analyses of it.

A late work of this kind, written in Assamese prose, is the *Hastividyārṇava* (Ocean of elephant-knowledge) of Sukumāra Barkāth, composed in the Śaka year 1656 (1734 CE) for the Ahom king Śiva Sinha and his queen Ambikā Devī, near the end of the period of the war elephant. The opening invocation mentions an earlier work called *Gajendracintāmani* (Wish-jewel of the Lord of Elephants) by one Śambhunātha, which the editor and translator, Pratap Chandra Choudhury, believes to have been a work in the Tai-Ahom language, of which the *Hastividyārṇava* is a recomposition in Assamese. At the same time, the Assamese work is fully within the tradition of the Sanskrit works of elephant science. It is abundantly illustrated. The manuscript has been published with an English translation.[16]

While the Sanskrit works of more general scope in which elephants are discussed are dated or datable, the specialized treatises are not; for the most part they are attributed to an immemorial past and a divine source. In this way practical knowledge of elephants has been appropriated by the literati from the staff of the king's elephant establishment and turned into the kind of knowledge over which the literati have authority. Paradoxically, the claim of great antiquity is in itself a sign that these texts are fairly recent,

[15] It is edited by Pandit Sivadatta.

[16] Lainé 2010 is a valuable study of it, putting the work in the context of the historical chronicles (*buranji*) of Assam.

and in any case more recent than the *Arthaśāstra,* which does not speak of elephant science or attribute knowledge of elephants to Pālakāpya or Nārada. Nevertheless it is worth examining this framing of elephant science as it has considerable scope and importance in the tradition.

The sage (*muni*) Pālakāpya is the nominal author of two of the texts, the *Gajaśāstra* and the *Hastyāyurveda*; and Nīlakaṇṭha, author of the *Mātaṅgalīlā*, attributes the substance of his work to Pālakāpya as well. Pālakāpya is supposed to have expounded elephant science to Romapāda, king of Aṅga in the middle Ganga valley, at the moment of first capture and taming of wild elephants. A fourth text, the *Gajaśikṣā*, is attributed to the sage Nārada and takes the form of a colloquy between Nārada and the god Indra, who, as we saw, rides the elephant Airāvata; unlike the topic of the same name in the *Mahābhārata*, it is not about the training of warriors riding elephants but the training of the elephants themselves. Nārada and Indra are well-known figures, and a colloquy between them is a literary form of a kind we may find in the Purāṇas—the compendia of history, mythology, and cosmology in the period of the Gupta empire and later, say from 320 CE onward. Unlike Nārada, who is well known in Purāṇa narratives and as the author of an important law book (among other texts), Pālakāpya is practically unknown outside the elephant science literature. The kingdom of Aṅga is associated with tamed elephants as early as the late Vedic period,[17] and a king Romapāda of that kingdom is an ally of prince Rāma in the *Rāmāyaṇa*. But the connection of this well-known king with this hitherto unknown sage appears to be a late formation. Some put Romapāda and Pālakāpya in the sixth century BCE, which is unlikely: that would have been the end of an independent Aṅga, which was absorbed by the growing power of its ambitious neighbor Magadha, under king Bimbisāra. Even if king Romapāda and the elephant-born sage Pālakāpya were real people, for which there is little evidence, the extant texts of elephant science are shown by their content

[17] As we have seen in Chapter 2.

to belong to a period after the *Arthaśāstra*, which was written much later.

The story of the sage Pālakāpya and king Romapāda casts the whole of elephant science into the terms of a Puranic story. In this narrative the chief causal mechanisms are the granting of boons (*vara*) or the infliction of curses (*śāpa*) by gods or Brahmin ascetics, and the mitigation of curses deemed too harsh (which, once uttered, cannot be rescinded) by assigning them a time limit (*anta*).

The story is as follows.[18] King Romapāda of Aṅga, ruling from his royal city of Campā, was troubled by reports that the crops of farmers were being destroyed by wild elephants. Sages who appeared in Campā by divine inspiration granted him the boon of being able to capture the elephants, which he did, subsequently giving the elephants to the sages. Pālakāpya, who lived constantly with the elephants and had learned their ways and attended to their needs with medicines and other means, was distressed when the elephants were captured during his temporary absence, and he wandered about in search of them. He came at last to Campā and king Romapāda, who showed him deference and hospitality, whereupon Pālakāpya told him the story of elephants and gave him knowledge of elephant science.

Formerly, he said, elephants could travel at will through the sky—and indeed, in the paintings with which the Thanjavur manuscript of the *Gajaśāstra* is illustrated these first elephants have wings. One day the elephants lit upon the branch of a large banyan tree in the Himalayas. The branch broke from their great weight and they fell upon the holy hermit Dīrghatapas (whose name means "severe austerities," implying his acquisition of extraordinary powers). He cursed them, whereby they could no longer fly and became the conveyances (*vāhana*) of human beings. He made an exception, however, for the elephants of the cardinal

[18] I follow Edgerton's translation of *ML*, and his notes on the versions of the story found in the Thanjavur manuscript of the *Gajaśāstra* and the *Hastyāyurveda*.

directions (*dig-gaja*), including the elephant of Indra, Airāvata. These latter petitioned the god Brahmā to relieve the distress of their cursed, earthbound kin who had fallen prey to disease, and he promised that a sage, fond of elephants and knowledgeable about medicine, would appear and cure them.

Pālakāpya was this sage, born of the beautiful Guṇavatī who had been cursed by the ascetic hermit Mataṅga to become an elephant—because he thought she had been sent by Indra to disturb his austerities and thus prevent him acquiring dangerous powers. Mataṅga mitigated the curse by declaring it should come to an end when she bore a son to the hermit Sāmagāyana. This came about, and Guṇavatī was restored to human form. The son, Pālakāpya, lived among the elephants and ministered to their medical needs, leaving them only to attend to his father in the hermitage three times a day, morning, noon, and evening—during one of which absences from the elephants the men of king Romapāda captured the animals.

The story goes on to detail the origin and character of the elephants of the quarters; the origins of the four types of elephants, noble (*bhadra*), slow (*manda*), deer (*mṛga*), and mixed (*miśra*); and etymologies of the many Sanskrit words for elephant. It then accounts for certain peculiarities of elephant physiology, showing how they came about from curses by the gods in response to elephant transgressions. By this means elephants' bodies, which were once otherwise and perhaps better, had assumed their present post-lapsarian shape. This way of explaining how things came to be as they are fixes upon certain physiological traits: inversion of the tongue (so shaped to facilitate drawing in large amounts of food); excessive internal fire (large appetite); lack of scrotum (internal testes); delight in dust, water, and mud; inability to fly, being earthbound, and serving as conveyances for men; loss of divinity; being attracted to their own dung and urine; and sweating internally. We can say that these peculiar features of the elephant body take the more familiar bodies of humans as the base from which they are identified as departures. Thus, elephants once sweated, but because the gods could not endure their offensive smell during their battle against the demons, the god Varuṇa turned their sweat inward so that it had henceforth to be expelled as a mist from their trunks. In fact, as we have seen, it is humans who are rare among mammals in having sweat glands over the greater part of their bodies.[19]

Thus elephant science ascribes authoritative statements about the origins and nature of elephants, elephant lore, and even the first capture of wild elephants to Brahmin sages and not to subaltern practitioners such as mahouts, trainers, and hunters—let alone to the forest people who shared their habitat with elephants. Nevertheless, as Edgerton argues, the elephant lore of Sanskrit texts shows a strong connection with practical knowledge and is by no means the learned imagining of literary types. On the contrary, the high degree of specialized knowledge that readers of these texts would have obtained is impressive. Edgerton gives a long glossary of specialized terms of elephant lore in the *Mātaṅgalīlā*, the meanings of which are not found in existing lexicons, neither in the ancient Sanskrit lexicons nor the modern scholarly ones.[20] His overall argument about the closeness of the elephant knowledge of the *Mātaṅgalīlā* to that of practitioners, except in places where well-known tropes of Sanskrit learning are evident, is convincing. It is much the same, one can add, in artistic renderings of elephants from ancient times to the present: Indian representations of elephants, almost all of them, show familiarity with live elephants, unlike, say, East Asian representations.

That said, there are ways in which the specialized treatises show a tendency toward the reinterpretation and theoretical elaboration of practical knowledge. A clear example is the explanation of the origin of the four castes of elephants in terms of the theory of the four world ages (*yugas*) that suffuses post-Vedic Sanskrit texts, and the three dispositions (*guṇas*), namely lightness (*sattva*), energy (*rajas*), and dullness (*tamas*), connected with the Sāṅkhya school of philosophy; both of these interpretive schemes fall within the

[19] As outlined in Chapter 1.
[20] *ML* 113–25.

expertise of the literate classes and would not have come from the elephant staff of the king. Edgerton notes that the *Hastyāyurveda* is the application to elephants of the doctrines of the medical treatment of humans. This is unsurprising, the intention being to indicate that it is an elaboration and application of the higher learning of literate classes to a domain otherwise in the care of unlettered practical knowledge. An example of such theoretical elaboration is the way in which the standard list of eight elephant forests found in the *Arthaśāstra* acquires a list of secondary forests (*upavanas*) in subsequent texts (*Gajaśāstra* 4). Another concerns the doctrine of twelve decades of an elephant's life.[21] In the *Mahābhārata* a sixty-year-old tusker is considered at the height of his powers, and I noted that this may have to do with the fact that tusks never stop growing. But the fact that the last set of molars is in place at sixty means that the elephant cannot last much longer than that age. To be sure, this fact was established by zoologists only in quite recent times, and earlier it would have been difficult to determine the true longevity of elephants in the wild. Nevertheless, it seems to me that the scheme of twelve decades in the specialized treatises is built upon the idea of six decades of increasing power and six of decline, and to derive from theorizing rather than observing. In support of this we find in the *Mātaṅgalīlā* that some of the names of the age-grades of elephants are without obvious etymologies in Sanskrit, and so probably derive from the "country" (*deśi*) terms of elephant handlers. Other names are transparent in Sanskrit, such as *yaudha*, "fighter." The decades from the sixth to the twelfth have no such special names and are simply numbered.[22] Finally, the elephant-science treatises show a multiplication of classifications of elephants from different points of view, some of which were surely derived from the intimate knowledge of handlers, with some of the others being

[21] This has been touched on in Chapter 2.

[22] The names of life stages in *ML* 5: *bāla* (first year), *puccuka* (2nd), *upasarpa* (3rd), *barbara* (4th), *kalabha* (5th), *naikārika* (6th), *śiśu* (7th), *majjana* (8th), *dantāruṇa* (9th), *vikka* (10th); *pota* (second stage [decade]), *javana* (3rd stage), *kalyāṇa* (4th stage), *yaudha* (5th stage).

artificial constructs by writers without practical knowledge of the matter.

To deepen our understanding of the logic of the war elephant institution I will examine the two especially valuable texts mentioned earlier, the *Arthaśāstra* and the *Ā'īn-i Akbarī* of Abu'l Fazl. These provide a cross-section, in some considerable detail, of the place of elephants in government practice at two periods separated from each other by about a thousand years, the former having been compiled around the first century CE and the latter in about 1590. Each text is by itself an exceptionally valuable source of information about monarchical government in its day, which is to say in ancient and early modern India, respectively. And each has much to say about the care, management, and deployment of war elephants. Bringing them together gives a sense of the body of knowledge about elephants that Indian kingdoms maintained.

The two are very different. The first is in Sanskrit, in the *sūtra* style of concise prose. This concision is sometimes carried to great lengths: it was a joke of ancient times that the maker of *sūtras* rejoices more in saving half a syllable than in the birth of a son. Because of this compression it is often difficult to make out the exact meaning of a given *sūtra*. The second text is in Persian of a rather expansive, not to say prolix, style, a much longer work in which the abundance of detail on a given topic offers difficulty of a different kind. The *Arthaśāstra* is a treatise of advice about the practice of kingship, taking as the object of that advice a hypothetical kingdom of middling size; the *Ā'īn-i Akbarī* describes a particular kingdom, that of the Mughal emperor Akbar, of very great size. The *Arthaśāstra* is squarely in the period in which the fourfold army ideal was fully in practice; the *Ā'īn* has, essentially, a threefold army of foot, horse, and elephant corps. What makes them alike, and useful for getting at the logic of the war elephant, is that each has a good deal to say about elephants as important assets of a well-run kingdom.

The *Arthaśāstra*

Because the *Arthaśāstra* purveys advice about how a hypothetical kingdom should be run, rather than describing an existing kingdom, the picture of government it gives is in a certain sense idealizing, but in a different way from the epics. The epics give us the poetry of kingship; the *Arthaśāstra* the prose. The *Rāmāyaṇa*, especially, presents us with paragons, of the prince (Rāma) and of the kingdom (Ayodhyā). The *Arthaśāstra* by contrast gives advice to a king whose kingdom may be *deficient* in some way, or be seized by this or that calamity needing remedy. The poetics of kingship in the epics tends toward the deliberate and open use of hyperbole, which has the advantage for us of making valuations evident. The *Arthaśāstra* on the other hand is always practical, drawing often on the knowledge of practitioners in a spirit of unflinching realism. It never resorts to hyperbole, giving instead what its author considers the best course of action for every situation in lived kingship.

A good example of this contrast is the very different ways of treating the condition of musth. In the poetry of kingship, as we have seen, war elephants always happen to be in musth, a tendency taken to its extreme in the description of the war elephants of Ayodhyā as being "always in musth," a sign of the most desired quality of the war elephant, his combativeness. In the *Arthaśāstra* musth is barely mentioned. Far from seeing musth as a desirable state, it is discussed in connection with the problems of dangerous levels of elephant aggression, embodied in the incorrigibly violent elephant (*vyāla*).[23] Here, musth is a problem of care and management.

In order to understand the place the *Arthaśāstra* accords to the war elephant in the overall structure of kingship it will help to take a short look at what we might call the itinerary of the text. The *Arthaśāstra* starts, in its first book, from the person of the king, his security in his own palace and family, his training, daily routine, and demeanor. Thereafter roughly half the remaining

[23] *Arth.* 2.32.8.

text addresses the internal administration of the kingdom in all its working parts, producing wealth, and maintaining good order. The other half deals with foreign relations, that is, diplomacy and war. The description of the administration deals with production that strengthens the elements of the kingdom; the overall tendency of the foreign relations part is to compare the assets of one's own kingdom with those of a foreign kingdom, choosing a course of action that will maximize the effects of one's relative strength and work around one's relative deficiencies. Elephants, being highly valuable assets, often figure in such calculations that lead to war or to diplomacy—which is to say war by other means. The overall movement of the text, then, is from the production of wealth and military strength to deployment and expenditure in war after careful comparative analysis of the strengths and weaknesses of one's own kingdom with that of the enemy. The war elephant is met with in both these parts of the itinerary.

The elephant forest

The portion of the *Arthaśāstra* dealing with internal administration opens in Book 2 with a tour of the hypothetical kingdom in terms of the economic zones into which the territory is divided. This gives us what we might call an ecology of the kingdom. First come a pair of chapters dealing,[24] respectively, with the settlement of the countryside into farming villages, and with the disposal of non-farming land into pastures and forests of several kinds—devoting the bulk of the chapter to elephant forests. These are followed by chapters on forts and the layout of the fortified city,[25] where the king resides, giving the point of view from which the preceding zones are viewed. Subsequent chapters give the duties of administrators connected with these areas and their different economic functions.

The ecology of kingship in this part of the *Arthaśāstra* follows its own order of priorities, leaving us in no doubt that the first

[24] Ibid.: 2.1–2.

[25] Ibid.: 2.3–4 and ff.

task of kingship is to establish villages of farmers who will till the land and pay taxes on the crops that are the principal means of revenue for the king and his government. Every other use of the landscape is secondary. Villages are to be augmented by luring foreign populations to come and settle, or by shifting the excess population into other parts of the kingdom. New farmers are to be favored by the king by providing them seeds, draft animals, and tax remissions for a period of time. Farming settlements are to be mostly of Śūdras, which is to say of cultivator-taxpayers, without superordinates such as landlords living off rents: in the ideal case no landed aristocracy should come between king and cultivator.

Pastures are marked as secondary to farms and farming villages in a number of ways: by being put in the chapter on the disposal of non-agricultural land (*bhūmichidra*, often called "waste," meaning land not cultivated);[26] in a passage stating that pastures are to be made in the land *between* farming villages;[27] and from the fact that the cowherd (*gopa*) is to live in the village,[28] not in the pastureland in which he works.[29] The pasture is already inhabited by troublesome occupants, namely dangerous wild animals and robbers.

Forests are put to several purposes, the first mentioned being wildernesses for study of the Veda and *soma* sacrifices by Brahmin ascetics. Next is an animal park for the king's pleasure, "a reserve with a single gate, protected by a moat and containing shrubs and bushes bearing tasty fruit, trees without thorns, shallow ponds, stocked with tame deer and other game, wild animals with their claws and fangs removed, and having male and female elephants and elephant cubs useful for hunting."[30]

[26] Ibid.: 2.2.

[27] Ibid.: 2.34.6.

[28] Olivelle, however, takes this term (literally "cow-protector") metaphorically, as "county supervisor," in series with the term before, the revenue officer (*sthānika*), and not in series with the following term, the elephant trainer. Either is possible.

[29] *Arth.* 2.1.7.

[30] Ibid.: 2.2.3.

Here, as later, elephants are not hunted but are used for hunting, as mounts for the king. There should also be an animal sanctuary in which all animals are welcomed as guests (*sarvātithimṛgam*) and protected.[31]

These formations bear a resemblance to the Iranian paradise, which is a walled animal park for the king. There is reason to believe that the walled royal reserve for game was propagated across Eurasia from Iran, spreading to Europe and Mongolia. The English word *paradise* comes from the Persian word meaning a park enclosed by a wall, via Greek accounts of the kings of Persia.[32] The Achaemenid empire of Persia, the largest up to its day (550–330 BCE) and extending to India (Sind, Gandhāra), must have influenced Indian kings in this matter, as in others, though it may be difficult to supply proof.

Forests are of two kinds, the materials forests (*dravya-vana*) for forest products, one for each kind of forest produce, with forest people settled in them; and elephant forests.

The elephant forest is the other pole of the by-now-familiar opposition of village and forest, the scene of the domestic and the wild. The elephant forest is to be established on the border of the kingdom, guarded by forest people (*aṭavi*). The overseer of the elephant forest and the elephant forest guards are to protect it. They are to kill anyone slaying an elephant; but someone bringing the ivory of an elephant that has perished naturally should be given a reward in coined money.[33] It is clear that the demand for ivory is to be satisfied from elephants already dead, not from killing them; and that killing them for any reason elicits the ultimate punishment.

The overseer of the elephant forest has a staff, of which the text mentions guards of the elephant forest, elephant keepers, foot chainers, border guards, forest rangers, and attendants. These, disguising their scent with the urine and dung of elephants and

[31] Ibid.: 2.2.4.
[32] Allsen 2006.
[33] *Arth*. 2.2.8–9.

concealing themselves with the branches of trees, should move with five or seven female elephant decoys to "find out the size of the elephant herds, by means of signs provided by sleeping places, footprints, dung and damage caused to riverbanks," and "keep a written record of elephants—those moving in herds, those moving alone, those driven from a herd, and the leaders of herds, as well as those that are dangerous, in musth, the youngster, and those released from captivity." They should capture elephants deemed excellent in the judgment of elephant trainers.[34]

Elephants are to be captured during the hot season, which is when they are more concentrated near the remaining sources of water and can be more easily seen because the deciduous trees have dropped most of their leaves. Twenty years is the ideal age for capture, and young animals, tuskless males (*makhnas*), diseased elephants, and females with young or suckling a baby are not to be captured.[35] This is a very important statement for it tells us that the capture is aimed at those most difficult to capture: large adults. As we shall see, the demographic profile of the king's elephants implied by this passage is very different from that of almost all other kinds of elephants in use, such as in timber operations, zoos, and circuses, in all of which the bias is toward females and the practice is to capture younger animals. This different demographic flows from the fact that the military use of elephants is paramount for Indian kings: "A king's victory is led by elephants. For elephants, with their enormous bodies and lethal onslaughts, can crush an enemy's troops, battle arrays, forts and military camps."[36]

Elephants and horses: the problem of supplies

In the ideal case a kingdom will have an elephant forest and will resort to it for war elephants and riding elephants, capturing wild

[34] Ibid.: 2.2.10–12.
[35] Ibid.: 2.31.8–10.
[36] Ibid.: 2.2.13–14.

adults aged twenty. But as we have seen,[37] the *Arthaśāstra* also speaks of eight regional elephant forests as a basis for a division into three classes of quality. In quality, and probably in quantity too, elephants are unevenly distributed across India because of the uneven distribution of their habitat, and kings disadvantaged by this factor are recommended to resort to other means for acquiring them. It is in this connection that the *Arthaśāstra* speaks of the comparative advantages of the Himalayan trade route and the southern route. The first supplies horses and elephants among other things; the second is the better, supplying elephants and a greater abundance of precious goods.[38] We must not suppose this is a free, price-making market. Kings are the main purchasers of horses and elephants; private ownership of either is restricted, and in the case of the Mauryas there was a royal monopoly, which was simply the limiting condition of a constant tendency of Indian kingship to treat horses and elephants as crucial military assets.

Elephants were also acquired in various kinds of king-to-king transactions. The *Arthaśāstra* does not give us a summary statement of the modes of acquisition. But it does give such a summary statement in respect of horses, so it will be useful at this point to return to the matter opened in Chapter 1 concerning the complementary distribution of horses and elephants in India, and the king's problems with securing their supply.

The overseer of horses, the *Arthaśāstra* tells us, should make a written record of the total number of horses, and the ways in which they have been acquired, of which the passage distinguishes seven: gift, purchase, taken in war, born in the herd, received in return for help (from an ally), pledged in a treaty, and borrowed for a limited time (again, from an ally). He is to record their pedigree, age, color, marks, class, and source, and report those defective, crippled, or sick.[39]

Thus horses circulated among kings in many ways that would also have pertained to elephants. Trade is only one of the modes

[37] In Chapter 1, Fig. 1.4.
[38] Ibid.: 7.12.22–4.
[39] Ibid.: 2.30.1.

of acquisition, but a crucial one as the best horses came from beyond India. Consequently, Indian kingdoms relied upon a long-distance trade in horses more or less throughout history. Horses, specially the better variety, came from only certain portions of the less forested, more arid, open, grassier landscapes of India and beyond, to the west and north; more particularly Central Asia, the native habitat of wild horses, and the great horse-breeding centers of Iran, Iraq, and Arabia. The specifics match up well with what we have seen in the epics, including the description of the horses of Ayodhyā. According to the *Arthaśāstra*, "the best come from Kāmboja (the northwest), Sindhu (Sind, the lower Indus valley), Āraṭṭa (in Punjab) and Vanāyu (Iran), the middling from Bāhlīka (Balkh or Bactria in northern Afghanistan), Pāpeya, Sauvīra and Titala; the rest are inferior."[40]

One of the enduring features of the history of kingship in India is that horses are both scarce and essential.[41] Most kingdoms not in the favored areas had to acquire them from afar at considerable cost. Thus the western and northern regions were privileged over the eastern and southern ones in respect of horses, and this greatly affected inter-kingdom relations. It helps account for the strong role of Central Asian armies in the formation of Indian kingdoms through conquest, of which there have been several. Major invasions of India from Central Asia, as noted, happened from time to time at intervals of several centuries: Śakas, Pahlavas and Kushans; Hūṇas; Turks; Mughals. The British Indian army was able to break out of the pattern of acquiring horses from Central Asia with the coming of cheap steam-powered transportation, turning New South Wales in Australia into a pastureland for the breeding of army horses, called Walers, for India.

But the king in the *Arthaśāstra* can also acquire horses through gift, war, an ally for help rendered, by treaty, and by borrowing (from an ally). Thus horses are assets of great interest to kings, and their circulation is governed largely by king-to-king interaction. They may also be bred in the stables, but the superiority of horses

[40] Ibid.: 2.30.29.

[41] Digby 1971; Trautmann 1982.

from the west and the north was never overtaken by country-bred horses.

Elephants on the other hand are a royal asset that is both essential and abundant, that is, native to India; and whose geography is complementary to that of horses. It seems likely that elephants circulated among kingdoms by the same instrumentalities as horses. Since the horse–elephant boundaries are contiguous in India, the two royal military assets are neighbours. The complementarity of elephants and horses in India is, as we have seen, the foundation of the ancient ideal of the fourfold army, and of the threefold army of the medieval and early modern periods.

Elephant stables and fodder

The fourfold army was a living institution in the *Arthaśāstra*, and there is no sign in it that the chariot was declining. The layout of roads, for example, makes provision for their use by various divisions. Thus ordinary roads are to be 4 *daṇḍas* wide (a *daṇḍa* is a staff), a royal highway of 8 *daṇḍas*, including the path in a battle array (*vyūha*); paths on irrigation works and in forests, 4 *daṇḍas*; paths for elephants and along fields, 2 *daṇḍas*; chariot paths, 2 *aratnis*; and so forth. Moreover, horses, elephants, chariots, and foot soldiers each have their overseer, whose duties are laid out in detail in the different chapters.

A significant part of the effort and expense of the kingdom was devoted to its livestock which, in the case of the military, consisted of elephants and horses for the fighting force, and bullocks for overland supply (as well as boats for supply by river), plus other draft animals, such as donkeys and camels, where they were available. Some of these had to be stabled in forts and the fortified capital city, and accordingly the *Arthaśāstra* gives directions for the making of stables, their staffing, and the provisioning of fodder.

A chapter is devoted to the overseer of elephants, who is in charge of the guarding of elephant forests and looking after stables, fodder for elephants of different classes, their work, harnesses, and other accoutrements, and the staff. He is to oversee the construction of a stable, with stalls for individual elephants containing tying post, plank flooring, and outlets for dung and urine. Provision is to be made for stabling war and riding elephants in the fort, and for elephants under training and rogue elephants outside the fort.[42] The daily routine allows for baths twice a day, followed by feeding. The overseer of elephants appears to supervise capture operations, the criteria of which have already been described, although the overseer of the elephant forest also seems to have a role.

Stabled animals need to have food brought to them, and, as we have seen, because they are working animals the energy expended has to be made up by fodder raised by farmers, or processed by workers to make it more concentrated and readily extractable. This more processed and human-like food comes from the storehouse or granary, which, therefore, has to issue foodstuff to the stables; the more natural part of the ration, which for elephants is grass and browse, is brought by grass cutters and leaf cutters attached to the stable.

In the routines of the granary it is laid out that the best of the milled *śāli* rice is to go to humans, the inferior part to animals. The amount of detail the *Arthaśāstra* gives is surprising.[43] The underlying principle is that the smaller the amount of rice obtained from milling a unit of paddy (rice in the husk) the higher the quality, as it is more thoroughly cleaned of the bran. Thus the lowest quality is 12 *āḍhakas* rice milled from 5 *droṇas* of *śāli* paddy, which is only suitable for a young elephant (*kalabha*), with higher qualities giving us a hierarchy of beings:

12 for a young elephant
11 for vicious elephants (*vyāla*)
10 for riding elephants
9 for war elephants
8 for foot soldiers
7 for chiefs
6 for queens and princes
5 for the king

[42] *Arth.* 2.31.2–4.
[43] *Arth.* 2.15.42.

Broken grains and bran are for the lowest-ranked humans and the lesser animals.

The overseer of the granary and those who draw on it have to know the rations for animals of different kinds. For example, the overseer of horses is to draw a month's ration from the granary for the horses in his care,[44] and the overseer of the granary must also know the ration. As individual animals vary by size, sex, and age, rations must vary accordingly, making the calculations complex. This complexity is met by formulating a few models, plus rules by which the model is to be reduced or increased to suit the needs of different classes of animals. In the case of elephants, the model food ration is given per cubit (*aratni*) of the animal's height, so that the calculation is one of simple multiplication. For horses the model ration is for the best type of horse, to be reduced by a quarter for the middling type, and another quarter for the lowest type. For bullocks the ration is as for horses, but with certain additions and subtractions.

This being so, there is a certain similarity of the food ration of bullocks, horses, and elephants. I leave aside the quantities, and how these may be stepped up or down for different classes of animals, to get at the substance of the ration. It has three structural parts: cultivated and processed food; the "invigorating drink" or *pratipānam* as a restorative (both these supplied from the granary); and the basic natural food of grass or browse.[45]

Bullock	**Horse**	**Elephant**
Ration		
oil-cake and broken grains	rice or barley; or *mudgu* or *māṣa* bean porridge	rice-grains
oil	fat	oil, ghee
rock salt	salt	salt
meat	meat	meat
yoghurt		

[44] Ibid.: 2.30.3.
[45] *Arth.* 2.29.43; 2.30.18; 2.31.13.

barley or māṣa bean porridge	juice or yoghurt	juice or yoghurt
Pratipānam		
milk or liquor, fat, sugar, ginger	liquor and sugar or milk	liquor or milk with sugar
Oil for the body		
oil for the nose	fat for the nose	oil for limbs and head
Natural fodder		
green fodder grass	green fodder grass	green fodder dry grass leaves of plants

To begin with, there is a core ration consisting of grains or beans, oil or fat, salt, meat, and yoghurt or juice for moistening the lumps. The most important of these and the largest in quantity is the grain ration, which is the most variable: for bullocks, oil-cakes or broken grains and bran; for horses, rice or *priyaṅgu*, or beans (*mudga* or *māṣa*), half-cooked; for elephants, rice grains. Next, the text also makes provision for an "invigorating drink" (*pratipānam*) which, for bullocks, consists of milk or liquor (*surā*) plus fat, sugar, and ginger; for horses and elephants, liquor and sugar, processed foods providing high energy. Then it gives an allowance of oil for the nose of the bullock, fat for the nose of the horse, or oil for the limbs and head of the elephant. All of this will have been supplied from the granary. Finally, the animals are given large quantities of more natural food: green fodder (*yavasa*) for bullocks and horses, grass and "leaves of plants" or browse ("without limit") for elephants, likely supplied by grass-and-leaf cutters attached to the stables.[46]

Included in the first part of the ration—the part that is issued by the granary for all three of these herbivorous animals—is the unexpected entry of meat (*maṃsa*). One of the translators of the

[46] See Bosworth 2002: 108 and fn. for information about rations in Hellenistic and modern sources.

Arthaśāstra, J.J. Meyer, struggling with this, proposed that the word indicates the "meat" of macerated fruits.[47] However, as Edgerton observes,[48] both the *Mātaṅgalīlā* and the *Hastyāyurveda* confirm that meat is prescribed for elephants,[49] mentioning the use of both meat and meat broth. Zimmerman's work on Ayurveda (1987) shows that meat and meat broth are often prescribed for humans, even for vegetarians, in cases of wasting illness. These items are believed to increase bulk under the exceptional circumstances of "distress" (*āpat*), by which taboos normally obtaining are suspended. Taking light from this, it seems we must understand that the meat in the *Arthaśāstra*'s rations for bullocks, horses, and elephants is indeed meat, intended for its restorative, strengthening power. I have heard that in recent times temple elephants in Kerala were fed small amounts of goat meat in balls of rice, with probably the same rationale.[50]

The elephant staff

The keeping of war and riding elephants entails a large establishment of government servants. As we have seen, in the elephant forest we have an overseer (*nāgavanādhyakṣa*) with staff divided among a fair number of special functions:

forest people	*aṭavi*
guard	*nāgavanapāla*
elephant keeper	*hastipaka*
foot chainer	*pādapāśika*
border guard	*saimika*
forest ranger	*vanacaraka*
attendant	*pārikarmika*[51]

[47] "Fruchtfleisch": *Arth.* 2.31.13, tran. Meyer, p. 218.

[48] *ML*, p. 26, n. 59.

[49] Ibid.: 11.25, 36; *Hastyāyurveda* iv, 15, 30, 87.

[50] Utthara Suvrathan (personal communication). Sukumar (2011: 231) confirms: "Strangely, the Malabar practice of feeding cooked goat's meat to elephants in poor condition seems to have continued in the Madras Presidency through the British period."

[51] *Arth.* 2.2.10.

In connection with the stables and the overseer of elephants (*hastya-dhyakṣa*) we find mention of these occupational specialties:

physician	*cikitsaka*
trainer	*anīkastha*
rider	*ārohaka*
driver	*adhoraṇa*
guard	*hastipa*
decorator	*upacārika*
cook	*vidhāpācaka*
fodder giver	*yāvasika*
foot chainer	*pādapāśika*
stall guard	*kuṭīrakṣa*
night attendant	*upaśāyika*[52]

This is a fairly complex division of labor, implying a large commitment of the kingdom's resource to maintain them and an internal hierarchy to coordinate efforts. The details are scarce but we can make out some. In the section on the stables, three of the staff are singled out from the others to receive a ration for themselves: the physician, stall guard, and cook, who are allocated boiled rice, fat, sugar, salt and, except for the physician, meat (Kangle surmises the physician may be of vegetarian caste). It appears that the lower ranks to these three are paid in food and wages, and docked for faulty work, namely, "keeping the stall unclean, not giving green fodder, making an elephant sleep on bare ground, striking it on an improper area, letting someone else ride on it, making it travel at an improper time or on unsuitable ground, taking it to water at a place that is not a ford, and letting it go into a thicket of trees."[53]

In the settlement of farming villages, the farmers themselves are to be mostly Śūdras, but provision is made for grants of land of two kinds, namely gifts to Brahmins (*brahmadeya*) for priests, preceptors, chaplains, and scholars learned in the Veda, which are heritable; and lifetime grants to government servants of a

52 Ibid.: 2.32.16.

53 Ibid.: 2.32.19.

high class,[54] among which are elephant trainers, physicians, horse trainers, and couriers. These, then, do not live in the forest or at the stables where they work, but in the village, indicating their normative, non-barbarian, non-tribal identity.

Where the lower-paid and lower-ranked staff is domiciled is not explained. But an important segment of the staff consists of forest dwellers who are called, simply, forest people (*aṭavi*), about whom the *Arthaśāstra* has a good deal to say. It is evident from its discussion of forest people that they were not simply the Other of Indian kingship, but had a more complex relation with kings. They represent both the furthest distance from the normative village farmer and an essential asset of the kingdom. To capture the complexity of the relation of forest people to the kingdom it will be necessary to examine it in some detail.

In the first place, forest people are to be used as guards of the elephant forest, and are to be settled in materials forests to guard them.[55] As we have seen, the elephant guards (who are from these forest people) are meant both to guard elephants against ivory hunters and also keep a running census of their numbers and types. Pastureland is to be patrolled by fowlers and hunters: "At the approach of robbers or enemies, they should sound an alarm with conches or drums, without letting themselves be caught either by climbing on to hills or trees or by using a swift conveyance (*vāhana*)."[56] Are these also forest people? Perhaps, but they are in any case also to report the movements of enemies and forest people (or possibly enemy forest people) by messenger pigeon or smoke signals.[57] Taken altogether, the evidence is that the king relies heavily upon forest people in his service to patrol forest and grazing land, which is to say the whole kingdom outside the farming village and the royal city.

In the second place, forest people are an essential element of the army. The types of troops are six: hereditary, hired, banded, allied,

[54] Ibid.: 2.1.7.
[55] Ibid.: 2.2.5.
[56] Ibid.: 2.34.10.
[57] Ibid.: 2.34.11.

alien, and forest troops.[58] In the course of things the *Arthaśāstra* makes it plain that the list is in order of decreasing reliability, with hereditary troops the most reliable and forest troops the least. Hereditary troops have the same feelings as the king and enjoy his regard for them; alien troops and forest troops do not have this sense of common identity, their only objective being plunder.[59] Forest troops are often joined with alien and treasonable troops as the sources of problems the king must attend to. In a fascinating passage, in which the author of the *Arthaśāstra* disagrees with the writers of previous *arthaśāstras*, forest tribes and highway robbers are compared:

> "Of highway robbers and forest people, highway robbers lurk under the cover of night, cause physical harm, are ever present, rob hundreds of thousands (in cash) and incite leading men to revolt, whereas, remaining far away and operating in frontier forests, forest tribes go about openly and in plain sight, and they plunder a single region," say the teachers.
>
> "No," says Kauṭilya. "Highway robbers rob (only) those who are heedless, are few in number and dull-witted, and are easy to recognize and apprehend, whereas, living in their own region and being numerous and brave, forest people fight in the open, plunder and destroy regions, and behave like kings."[60]

Thus, forest people have collective entities that are the equivalent of kingdoms and are formidable opponents.

Forest people are refractory and forest troops unreliable. But the difficulty of engaging forest troops is repaid by the special functions they perform. Among these are: as guides through the forest, when the enemy chooses terrain suited to them, when they are skilled in countering the mode of fighting of the enemy, when the enemy force is mostly forest troops, and when a small raid is to be repelled.[61] The king whose army is deficient is advised

[58] Ibid.: 9.2.1.
[59] Ibid.: 9.2.14, 19.
[60] Ibid.: 8.4.41–3.
[61] Ibid.: 9.2.7.

to recruit fighters from bands, robber bands, forest people, and barbarian (*mleccha*) tribes as well as secret agents capable of doing harm to enemies,[62] making it clear once again that forest people make among the least reliable troops. But in the ordinary case, all things being equal, the principle is that the king should take cognizance of the enemy troops and raise counter-troops accordingly, including forest troops to counter enemy forest troops.[63]

Difficult as it may be to raise and keep forest troops, and forest people for guarding materials forests, elephant forests, and pastureland, this is considered a necessary task for Indian kings.

Finally, for further information on the place of elephants and their human handlers in the overall structure of the kingdom, we look to what the *Arthaśāstra* says about the salaries of state servants.[64] This gives us a hierarchy in which elephant staff of various kinds are positioned. I give it as a list (omitting the highest ministerial levels):

8,000 *paṇas*	Heads of banded troops, **commandants of elephant, horse, and chariot corps**, and magistrates
4,000 *paṇas*	**Overseers of infantry, cavalry, chariot and elephant corps**, and **wardens** of materials and **elephant forests**
2,000 *paṇas*	Charioteers, **elephant trainers, physicians, horse trainers**, and carpenters, and the breeders of animals
1,000 *paṇas*	Diviners, soothsayers, astrologers, chroniclers, bards, and panegyrists; assistants to the chaplain; and all overseers
500 *paṇas*	Foot soldiers trained in the (fighting) arts, accountants, scribes, and the like
250 *paṇas*	Musicians and the makers of musical instruments
120 *paṇas*	Artisans and craftsmen

62 Ibid.: 7.14.27.

63 Ibid.: 9.2.25.

64 Ibid.: 5.3.

60 *paṇas*	Servants, helpers, attendants, **guards of quadrupeds** and bipeds, and foremen of laborers; also riders, bandits, and mountain diggers supervised by Āryas, as well as all attendants

In this pay scheme, military personnel are highly ranked, and so are the upper levels of the elephant staff. The highest paid in this list are the commandants in battle of the four limbs of the fourfold army; next to them, at half their pay, are the overseers of the four limbs, along with the warden of the elephant forests. The next lower step is occupied by the elephant trainer, physician, and horse trainer, the three ranks for whom the king is to give land in the village—an important sign of distinction. It is noticeable that the elephant trainer ranks very much higher than the mahouts and other staff who are at the lowest pay level, several steps below. The expertise of the trainer seems to be considered superior, and the *Arthaśāstra* singles him out as the one whose knowledge of the qualities of individual elephants is to govern the process of capture. On the whole the upper grades of the elephant staff are very well compensated.

Elephants in war

The production and maintenance of war elephants is easy to follow in the *Arthaśāstra* because it is a specialized operation. In warfare, on the other hand, elephants are parts of an ensemble that is complex to begin with, made more complicated by the contingency of relative numbers, terrain, season, and so forth. I have already recounted what the *Arthaśāstra* has to say on battle arrays,[65] as well as other ways in which elephants are deployed in combination with the three other kinds of troops. Here I will indicate a few additional things the text says about elephants in war.

First, as to seasons and landscapes. The king is advised to march to war with an army, of which the elephant division is the largest,

[65] In Chapter 3.

after the hot season is over, that is, from the onset of the monsoon into the cooler months. The theory that sustains this dictum is the idea of internal sweat, which becomes dangerous in the hot season: "For, elephants, sweating inside, become leprous. And not getting a plunge in water or a drink of water, they become blind through internal secretion."[66] Though the theory is wrong the dictum itself is right. Elephants will be the largest portion of the army when it traverses a region with plenty of water, or when it is raining; in the opposite case the army should consist mostly of donkeys, camels, and horses. Thus the complementarity of horses and elephants is again acknowledged and it conditions the composition of the force in relation to season and landscape.

Second, it is possible to single out the functions of elephants, their *karmāni* or actions, from the ensemble of the army.[67] These have already been cited, in the previous chapter, in the discussion of battle arrays: as we have seen, there are many functions during the march itself, as well as in camp, in addition to action on the field of battle and during the siege of forts.

Third, the modes of fighting for elephants can be isolated and named. The concision of the *sūtra* form makes the result somewhat abstract, but it compares closely the similarity and difference of functions for horses and elephants. Horses: "charging straight on; charging in a circular pattern; charging past; charging back; remaining attentive after dealing a crushing blow; pincer movement; zigzag movement; encirclement; scatterring; turning back to attack after a feigned flight;[68] protecting one's broken ranks along columns, in the front, on the two wings, and in the rear; and pursuing the broken ranks of the enemy." For elephants the modes of fighting are the same, minus scattering, but with the addition of "annihilation of the four divisions, whether they are combined

66 *Arth*. 45–7.

67 Ibid.: 10.4.14.

68 This maneuver, and others of this list, seem to reflect the Central Asian tactic of furious frontal attack and rapid retreat while firing the proverbial Parthian shot. The whole passage seems to assume a light cavalry with rapid movements, not the armored heavy cavalry of Iranian armies.

or separate; crushing the wings, flanks and breast; sudden assault; and attack on sleeping troops."[69]

In sum, the *Arthaśāstra* gives an unusually comprehensive view, however succinct its exposition, of the management of the elephant forest, the problem of elephant and horse supplies, the stabling and fodder of elephants, the functions and pay of the staff who attend them, and their deployment in war. It is exceptional for the realism of the picture it gives us, and shows many signs of having drawn information from living elephant specialists. The one prominent exception would be the doctrine of battle arrays, which certainly had prior writings upon which the author of the *Arthaśāstra* drew. In relation to what we know of those prior texts—from what is said about them in the *Arthaśāstra* itself and in the epics—the instructions on *vyūhas* in the *Arthaśāstra* seem to be the elaboration and further development of an earlier, simpler view.

The *Ā'īn-i Akbarī*

The *Ā'īn-i Akbarī* (Institutes of Akbar) is a remarkable text, a comprehensive account of emperor Akbar's government, composed at Akbar's behest by Abu'l Fazl, who had an army of assistants to enquire into all aspects of the government and record its rules and operations. It is the third part of a yet larger work, the *Akbarnama* (Chronicle of Akbar), the first two parts of which deal with the origins, genealogy, and succession to power of Akbar and the history of his reign. There is nothing quite like the *Ā'īn*, no pre-existing genre which it instantiates, and no succeeding text quite matches it. In addition, paintings were made by leading artists of the day to accompany the *Akbarnama*. The collection in the Victoria and Albert Museum, London, was made at the time the text was being composed, doubtless for Akbar himself.[70]

[69] *Arth.* 10.6.53–4.

[70] Some of these are reproduced in Figs 4.1–3.

Elephants figure prominently in the *Ā'īn-i Akbarī*, the reason being that Akbar took a deep interest in them. One hundred and one elephants were reserved for the king. Akbar himself took the place of the mahout, that is, he sat on the neck rather than at the shoulder or in a howdah behind a driver: "His Majesty, the royal rider of the plain of auspiciousness, mounts on every kind of elephants, from the first to the last class, making them, notwithstanding their almost supernatural strength, obedient to his command. His Majesty will put his foot on the tusks, and mount them, even when they are in the rutting season, and astonishes experienced people."[71] The danger of mounting an adult war elephant in musth cannot be overstated. Even making allowance for Abu'l Fazl's tendency to portray his king in the most flattering light, this picture of Akbar's pleasure in elephants and fearlessness in mounting an elephant in musth is abundantly attested. It appears vividly in Fig. 4.2, a pair of paintings making a double-page composition of an incident outside Agra Fort in 1561. They show Akbar riding on the neck of the royal elephant Hawa'i which was fighting the elephant Ran Bhaga. The latter turned to flee across a bridge of boats on the Yamuna river, which is shown to be collapsing under the weight of the elephants. It is striking to see the emperor as mahout, with bare feet and legs in the manner of a mahout. Later monarchs are often painted following Akbar's example by riding on the neck. Akbar's personal enthusiasm for elephants is also supported by a number of passages in which Abu'l Fazl speaks of the emperor having revised some part of the routines or administrative structures concerning elephants, and of having invented some bit of harness or some kind of ornamental trappings. The overall picture is one of active and continuous engagement by the king.

Abu'l Fazl expresses the connection of kingship with elephants, which his book takes as a premise, and the strategic value of their keepers: "Kings have always shown a great predilection for this animal, and done everything in their power to collect

[71] *Ā'īn* 47, Book 1.

a large number. Elephant-keepers are much esteemed, and a proper rank is assigned to such as have a special knowledge of the animal."[72]

In its estimate of the value of elephants, their use in war is at the fore. In the following passage, with which the chapter on the imperial elephant stables opens, horses are the units by which the elephant's value is reckoned:

> This wonderful animal is in bulk and strength like a mountain; and in courage and ferocity like a lion. It adds materially to the pomp of a king and to the success of a conqueror; and is of the greatest use for the army. Experienced men of Hindustan put the value of a good elephant equal to five hundred horse; and they believe, that when guided by a few bold men armed with matchlocks, such an elephant alone is worth double that number. In vehemence on one side, and submissiveness to the reins on the other, the elephant is like an Arab, whilst in point of obedience and attentiveness to even the slightest signs, it resembles an intelligent human being.[73]

Put in units of money rather than horses, the price of an elephant varies from a lakh (100,000) to a hundred rupees; while elephants worth 5,000 or 10,000 rupees are pretty common.[74] Under the care of an experienced keeper the value of an elephant will improve greatly, increasing as much as from 100 to 10,000 rupees.

In every way, the elephant plays a role in the government of Akbar similar to that in the hypothetical kingdom of the *Arthaśāstra*. This gives us confidence about the reality and long-term structural properties of the elephant in Indian kingship. Accordingly, much that the *Ā'īn* has to say about elephants is similar to the *Arthaśāstra* and need not be restated. I will, however, examine what the *Ā'īn* says on two subjects: the (Sanskrit) literature on elephant science existent at the time, and the details of elephant management. I shall also revert to the matter of horse and elephant supplies, on which the added detail of Mughal sources is especially helpful for our purposes.

72 *Ā'īn* 41.
73 Ibid.
74 Ibid.

Elephant science

Abu'l Fazl speaks of elephant science (*gajaśāstra*) by name, and in another passage says that the Hindus have written many treatises explaining the various tempers and diseases of elephants. He reproduces material from these "Hindu books" concerning the types of elephants (*bhadra*, *maṇḍa*, *mṛga*, *mīr)* and a classification by the three qualities or *guṇas* (*sattva*, *rajas*, *tamas*); the stages of gestation; the terminology for different age classes (*bāla*, *potha*, *vikka*, *kalabha*) which correspond with names that we meet in the *Mātaṅgalīlā*; the signs and seasons of musth; the elephants of the eight directions (*dig-gaja*) who are the progenitors of all earthly elephants; the division into eight classes named after the *devas*, *gandharvas*, Brahmins, Kṣatriyas, Śūdras, snakes, *piśācas*, and *rākṣasas*. It is perfectly clear that, by 1590 CE at the latest, specialized texts of elephant science were in existence and their contents were known to Abu'l Fazl.

How much the more theoretical elephant knowledge of Sanskrit texts, which Abu'l Fazl reproduces quite well, may have entered into Mughal practice is unclear. Perhaps it figured in judging the value of individual elephants through their "points,"—though Akbar's own classification shows no direct connection—and in the treatment of disease. But the long passage on *gajaśāstra* apart, valuable as it is in giving us a datable horizon for the development of the elephant science literature, the greater part of what the *Ā'īn* says about elephants comes from direct inspection of the structures of government for their care and management, and the practical knowledge of drivers, trainers, and supervisory staff.

Elephant management

Coming to the particulars of elephant management as depicted in the *Ā'īn*, the entire structure of its system rests upon an order of precedence among elephants arising from their place in the scheme of classification which, we are expressly told, was devised by Akbar. There are seven classes: *mast* (musth elephant), *shergir* (tiger seizing), *sādah* (plain), *majholah* (middlemost), *karha*, *phandurkiya*, and *mokal*. Each class is subdivided into large-sized, middle, and young, except the last, which contains ten subdivisions.

The grain ration is governed by the scheme of classes and sub-classes. For example, the daily ration of grain of the top group, musth elephants of the large size, is 2 *mans* 24 *sers*; that of the smallest, the *mokal* of the tenth sub-class, is 8 *sers*; and all others in between these extremes are stepped down from the next higher one by small gradations. Female elephants have a simpler classification, into four rather than seven ranks, with the same three subdivisions except for the last class which has nine subdivisions.

The classification system also governs the number and pay of the stable servants, and it is here that we first get a detailed picture of the staff assigned to a single elephant. The highest class, the musth elephant, has five and a half servants:

mahout, driver	*mahāwat*	200 *dams*[75] per month
assistant to the mahout	*bhoi*	110 *dams* per month
fodder giver	*meth*	4 dams daily on the march; otherwise 3½ *dams* daily

The mahout we have already met; but what is new here is the testimony that he usually has an assistant; and this assistant, here called *bhoi*, sits on the elephant's rump "and assists in battle and in quickening the speed of the animal" and often performs the duties of the mahout.[76] It is pretty clear from visual representations if not from ancient texts that the assistant to the mahout has been on the scene for a long time, perhaps from the start: the mahout not only needs a helper but also a substitute for times when he is unavailable. Thus what the *Ā'īn* gives us here is textual

[75] The *dam* is a copper coin that is the smallest whole denomination. It was convenient to reckon government accounts in this unit for greater accuracy, even though that made the numbers very large, rather than calculating in fractions of larger denominations. (Similar was the ancient Roman accounting by *sesterces*, also a small copper coin.)

[76] *Ā'īn* 44.

confirmation of ancient Indian practice, not a new function. The *meth* "fetches fodder, and assists in caparisoning the elephant."[77] The main duty is cutting grass and browse, but fetching the ration of cooked or parched grain may also be among his duties.

For the next lower class of elephant, *shergir*, the number and pay of the stable servants are stepped down: five servants in all, consisting of the mahout at 180 *dams*; the *bhoi* at 103 *dams*; and three *meths* with pay as before. These principles are carried through the whole classification, so that an order of precedence is made clear for superior stable servants as well as the elephants to which they are attached.

For warfare, elephants are formed into troops called *halqah*, of ten, twenty, or thirty elephants under the supervision of an officer called a *faujdār*. The pay of *faujdārs* depends upon the number of elephants in their troops.

This leads us to the complicated system of military ranks (*mansab*) and pay held by the army officers and administrators of the empire who were called rank-holders (*mansabdārs*). This system was denominated in horses, or rather horsemen. In it a commander of ten or twenty elephants was deemed equivalent to captains of one horse, called *ahadis*; a commander of a hundred, with several commanders under him, marks two horses; and some *faujdārs* of elephant troops were holders of *mansab* rank (*mansabdārs*). Akbar assigned several elephant troops to each of the high rank-holders and required the latter to maintain them.[78] It is the duty of the *faujdār* to "look after the condition and training of the elephants; he teaches them to be bold, and to stand firm in the face of fire, and at the noise of artillery; and he is responsible for their behavior in these respects."[79]

In addition to the military (*halqah*) elephants there was, as previously mentioned, a body of 101 elephants in the reserve (*khāsa*) of the king. For these latter the management scheme was somewhat different. The allowance of food was the same in quantity as for other elephants, but it was made more sumptuous

77 Ibid.
78 *Ā'īn* 44.
79 Ibid.

FIG. 4.1: ELEPHANT CAPTURE

from the *Akbarnama*

FIG. 4.2: AKBAR CROSSING A BRIDGE WITH MADDENED ELEPHANT
from the *Akbarnama*

اژمی اوبراین جسر براحده دهیدهکشتیهای جسرازان سپسی این دوکوه بیکرگاه درآب فرومیرفت

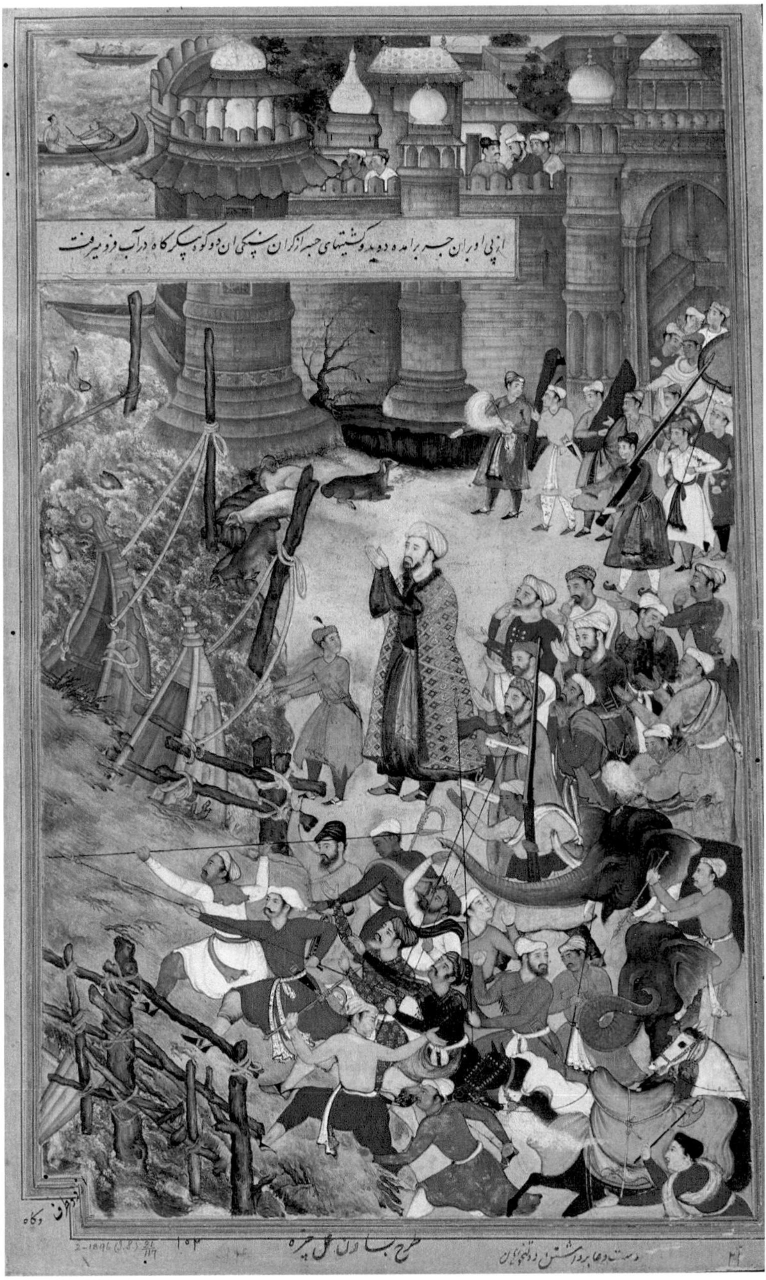

FIG. 4.2 (CONTINUED)

FIG. 4.3: CAPITULATION AFTER BATTLE
from the *Akbarnama*

with additions of sugar, ghee, cooked rice with chili, cloves, and other spices, and sugarcane in season. Since Akbar himself took the place of the mahout, the staff consisted of no ordinary mahouts but two or three *bhois* and four *meths*, at a suitable pay determined by the king.[80] The *bhois* of the king's reserve elephants got an additional month's pay whenever the king mounted the elephant they were assigned to, an honorarium which prefigures those given to mahouts after royal hunts in Nepal in recent times.[81] The royal elephants were also used for fighting one another in pairs for the entertainment of the king—or even with the participation of the king, as in the famous occasion depicted in Fig. 4.2. "Each elephant has his match appointed for fighting; some are always ready at the palace, and engage when the order is given"; on such occasions, too, the *bhois* were to receive a substantial honorarium.[82] Gifts to other staff are detailed, but so are fines for dereliction; for example, if a royal reserved elephant died its *bhois* were fined three months' wages.

For military men and the very large range of animals used by the army, complex provisions were made to muster them for visual inspection by the king, a few each day. Of royal elephants, ten were to be mustered on the first day of every solar month, and military elephants thereafter. The officer in charge of the elephants had to be ready to answer questions about the name (there are more than 5,000 elephants, each with a different name), how acquired, price, quantity of food, age, place of birth, season and duration of musth, when an elephant was made royal (*khāsa)*; its promotion in the *halqahs*; the time when its tusks were cut; how many times His Majesty mounted it; how many times it was brought for riding out; the time of last muster; the condition of the keepers; the name of the *amīr* in charge.[83] Newly acquired elephants were assigned a tentative rank by an experienced officer, and finally fixed by the king when he inspected them at the muster. The rank of royal elephants depended upon the number of times the king

[80] Ibid.: 46.
[81] Locke 2006: 80.
[82] *Ā'īn* 47.
[83] Ibid.: 78.

mounted them; of military elephants by their price. Elephants of rank-holding officers were assigned a rank by the king, and elephants of dealers were brought to the king, who fixed their rank and value.[84]

Elephants figure in the chapter on hunting,[85] but for live capture, not for killing (Fig. 4.1). Elephants, being ideal mounts for some kinds of hunting, are the means and not the objects of royal hunts. Four methods of live capture are given:

khedah	elephants driven by beaters and horsemen, then roped one by one
chor khedah	luring male elephants with a tame female
gād	driving elephants into a covered pit
bār	luring elephants into an area surrounded by a ditch and having one gate

Abu'l Fazl attributes to Akbar the invention of a fifth method, a drive on three sides that both pushes the elephants into an enclosure, and lures the males into it with tame females within. Fig. 4.1a shows Akbar on horseback inspecting a newly caught wild elephant during a royal hunt in Malwa, Central India.

The particulars of elephant capture and management found in Abu'l Fazl's invaluable record are fully in accord with traditional methods found in the *Arthaśāstra* over a thousand years earlier. The stability of practice is striking. There are, to be sure, no true steady states in historical time, and Akbar's army was quite different from that of Candragupta Maurya—for example in the absence of chariots and the very much larger cavalry. The elephant force, large as it was and prominent as it is in Mughal texts and paintings, may have been smaller than that of the Mauryas. But the continuities are more evident than the possible differences.

Horses and elephants

The Mughal empire ran on animal power to an impressive degree. Elephants, horses, camels, mules, and bullocks were held

[84] Ibid.
[85] Ibid.: 27.

in large numbers, and high-ranking military men (*mansabdārs*) were supposed to maintain substantial numbers of each. All these animals had a daily grain ration, so that the energy they brought to the work of the kingdom, especially its wars, came in significant part from agriculture. Put another way, a significant amount of the land was dedicated to supporting the animal power of the Mughal army, whether through pasture and forest, or cropland for raising fodder.

Horses, being crucial, were continually acquired from places to the west and north:

> Merchants bring to court good horses from ʻIrāq i ʻArab and ʻIrāq i ʻAjam, from Turkey, Turkestan, Badakhshān, Shirwān, Qirghiz, Tibet, Kashmir, and other countries. Droves after droves arrive from Tūrān [Central Asia] and Īrān, and there are now-a-days twelve thousand in the stables of His Majesty. And in like manner, as they are continually coming in, so there are others daily going out as presents, or for other purposes.[86]

The international horse trade was encouraged by the king, who established caravanserais of horse dealers who alongside their animals could find accommodation. The king's servants kept a roll of arriving horses; experts examined them and fixed their prices, denominated in gold coins called *mohur*. Values ran up to 500 *mohurs*, but most fell in the range of 10–30 *mohurs*.

Abu'l Fazl has praise for the breeders of horses in India. "Skillful, experienced men have paid much attention to the breeding of this sensible animal, many of whose habits resemble those of man; and after a short time Hindustan ranked higher in this respect than Arabia, whilst many Indian horses cannot be distinguished from Arabs or from ʻIrāqī breed." He says there are fine horses bred in every part of the country; but those of Cachh excel, being equal to Arabs. It is said that a long time ago an Arab ship was wrecked and driven to the shore of Cachh; and that it had seven choice horses, from which, according to the general belief, the breed of that country originated. In the Panjāb, horses called

[86] Ibid.: 49.

Sanūjī are bred resembling 'Irāqīs, and also in Agra and Ajmir, where they have the name of *pachwariyah.* In the Himalayas there are small but strong horses called Gūt, and in Bengal, near Kūch-Bahār, another breed called Tānghan, ranking between the Gūt and Turkish (Central Asian) horses, strong and powerful.[87]

Nevertheless, when it comes to the ranking of horses it is apparent that the models are Arabs, Persians, and Central Asian (Turkī) breeds, which is to say horses from beyond India, to the west and northwest. Thus the ranks, in order of decreasing value, are (1) *Arabs* (Arab bred or resembling them in gracefulness and prowess); (2) *Persian* horses (bred in Persia or resembling them in shape and bearing); (3) *Mujannas* (resembling Persian horses, and mostly Turkī, or Persian geldings); (4) horses imported from Tūrān (Turkī or Central Asians); (5) *Yābū* horses bred in India, the offspring of Turkī horses with an inferior breed; and the Indian-bred horses called (6, 7) *Tāzīs*, *Janglahs*, and *Tātūs*.[88]

The supply of horses and elephants was a crucial concern of the Mughal empire, both animals being essential for the army. Fig. 4.1a displays the Mughal army especially well. In it Akbar is again seated on the neck of his elephant in the position of the mahout. He is receiving the drums and standards captured from Abdullah Khān Uzbeg, governor of Malwa, in 1564. One sees both the armor of the elephant and that of the heavy cavalry, and other elements of the army.

In Chapter 1 I made use of Irfan Habib's invaluable atlas of the Mughal empire to establish the fundamental fact of army logistics for Indian kingship, the complementary distribution of horses and elephants, a structure of history from the invention of the war elephant, and the fourfold army in the late Vedic period through the period of Turkish and Mughal kings to the eighteenth century. I have also used Habib's Mughal material to establish a third point, between the first–second century *Arthaśāstra* and the Elephant Reserves of twenty-first-century India, to show that

[87] Ibid.: 49.

[88] *Ā'īn* 2, Book 2.

the tempo of retreat of wild elephants and their habitat was very slow till about 1800, and that it then dramatically increased. The present predicament of elephants in India is of very recent making. For thousands of years of the use of elephants by Indian kings the practice appears to have been more or less sustainable—a tentative conclusion I shall examine more closely in the last chapter.

The elephant-related matter of the *Ā'īn* is invaluable testimony for our purposes, in two ways. In the first place it establishes the long continuity, over the better part of two millennia, with the state of knowledge and practice that we can derive from the elephant-related content of the *Arthaśāstra*, which also gives us a datable cross-section of the content of the elephant science of its day. In the second place it enhances several details of what we know, notably in respect of the mahout's assistant, the different modes of capture, and issues of horse and elephant supplies.

The war elephant as an institution was widely extended in time and space, and sustained by a body of practices established from antiquity. For the most part this knowledge was embodied by its practitioners and transmitted by apprenticeship. Those who embodied it were the elephant hunter, trainer, driver, and physician. Of these, it appears clearly from the *Arthaśāstra* that the trainer had a high grade of pay, much higher than the mahout; the elephant trainer and physician resided in the village upon a grant of land made for life; and the physician may have been of higher, vegetarian caste.

At the same time, while practical knowledge was the foundation of the institution, Indians of all classes had some familiarity with living elephants. Sanskrit texts fed off this practical knowledge and its technicalities, including some of its jargon. Of the four main specialized forms of elephant staff, the physician certainly developed a written literature, if we may go by the 800-page manual of elephant medicine, the *Hastyāyurveda*. Even if it should prove to be a recent text, a work so extensive must have a longish trail of prior texts preceding it. For the rest of the literature of elephant science in Sanskrit, it appropriates the practical knowledge of the subaltern classes who formed the staff of the elephant establishment, framing it in the form of a descent from the gods and brahmanical sages through a series of incidents, parallel to the fall of elephants themselves from their former aerial and more resplendent forms. The enchantment of this body of knowledge cannot hide that much of it was made and transmitted by lineages of apprenticeship of practical men extending back literally thousands of years.

5

North India, South India, Sri Lanka

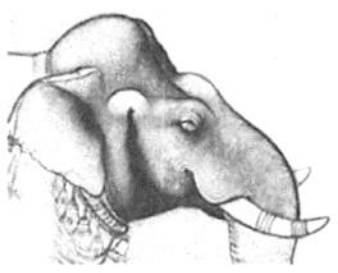

THE *PERPETUATION* OF THE WAR ELEPHANT as an institution depends, then, upon the embodied knowledge of practical specialists—the elephant hunter, trainer, driver, and physician—who have learned their trade through apprenticeship. The *spread* of the war elephant can occur when this embodied knowledge circulates through king-to-king relations of alliance and war. In this and the next two chapters I will trace that spread, first within India and South Asia more generally; then to the west of India as far as Carthage and Rome; and finally east to the Indianizing kingdoms of Southeast Asia. This diffusion is shown schematically in Fig. 5.1.

The rise of Magadha

The war elephant, I have argued, was invented sometime in the late Vedic period. By about 500 BCE the anti-Vedic religions, Buddhism and Jainism, had appeared. Their two founders, the Buddha (the Awakened) and the Mahāvīra (the Great Hero), were contemporaries, having been born in the middle Ganga valley—elephant country—at this period. The war elephant and the fourfold army are clearly visible in the canonical texts of Buddhism and Jainism, which is to say in their earliest writings. We cannot be sure that these canonical texts convey the conditions of that age accurately. However, since the evidence for late Vedic

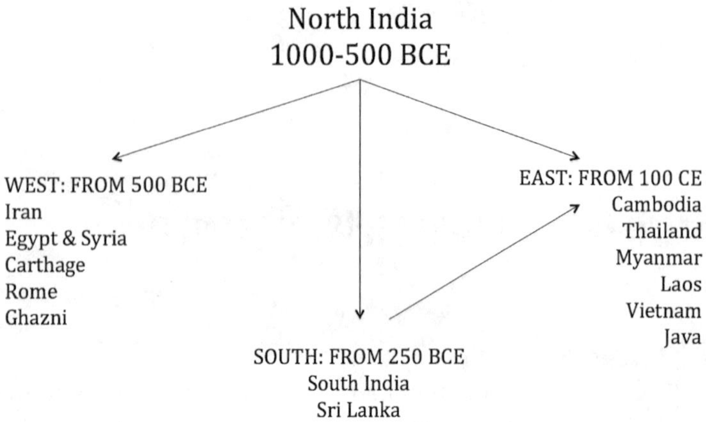

Fig. 5.1: Diffusion of the war elephant

invention of the war elephant is solid, we may accept that the war elephant and the fourfold army were established institutions in North India by the time the two new religions arose.

The outstanding political development over the following two centuries, 500–300 BCE, was intense interstate warfare among the principal polities, called the *mahājanapadas* in the sources, resulting in their unification under one of them, the kingdom of Magadha. This kingdom absorbed its neighbors and grew to a large empire encompassing nearly the whole of India. Looked at comparatively, this development was somewhat like that of China, namely, the interstate rivalry of the period called Warring States, followed by the forced unification of the states, first under Qin, then the Han, slightly later than the formation of the Mauryan empire. In India the interstate warfare was the classic period of the fourfold army, including the war elephant, and there is every reason to think that the control of horses and elephants was crucial to the outcome. I contend that one of the principal causes of Magadha's success in unifying northern India's warring states was its control of more and better war elephants than its rivals. Analysis of the list of the sixteen *mahājanapadas* shows this.

The political map of North India at the time of the Buddha and the Mahāvīra is captured in a stock list of the sixteen countries (*mahājanapadas*) in the Buddhist canon (see Fig. 5.2). They are territorial units but also ethnic ones, as their names are those of their people, in the plural. Thus, the kingdom of Magadha, which is one of them, is listed as "the Māgadhas," a people inhabiting a certain place. The antiquity and authenticity of the list is corroborated by the Jain canon, which has a similar list. Here is the Buddhist list, converted from names of peoples into names of countries, in the Sanskrit form.[1]

The sixteen *mahājanapadas*

1. Aṅga	9. Kuru
2. Magadha	10. Pañcāla
3. Kāśi	11. Matsya
4. Kosala	12. Śūrasena
5. Vṛji	13. Aśmaka
6. Malla	14. Avanti
7. Cedi	15. Gandhāra
8. Vatsa	16. Kamboja

The list, simple as it seems, is structured in certain ways. To begin with, its overall direction is from east to west, starting with Aṅga and Magadha in the middle Ganga valley and ending with Gandhāra and Kamboja in the Indus valley. That is, it moves from elephant country in the eastern part of North India to horse country in the west and northwest. Aṅga, as we know, is strongly associated with elephants, both in the late Vedic texts, in which the largest imaginable gift of elephants is attributed to its king, and the later texts of elephant science. These identify the first domestication of elephants with king Romapāda of Aṅga and

[1] *Dīgha nikāya* 2, p. 200; *Aṅguttara nikāya* 1, p. 213. *Mahāvastu* 1, p. 34 has the same list except that for the last two it gives Śibi and Daśārṇa. The Buddhist list is in Pali, but I have converted the names to their Sanskrit equivalents, which are used in the history books. A Jain list (in Ardha-Magadhi) occurs at *Bhagavatī sūtra* 15.1: Aṅga, Baṅga, Magaha, Malaya, Mālava, Accha, Vaccha, Koccha, Pāḍha, Lāḍha, Bajji, Moli, Kāsi, Kosala, Avāha, Sambhuttara.

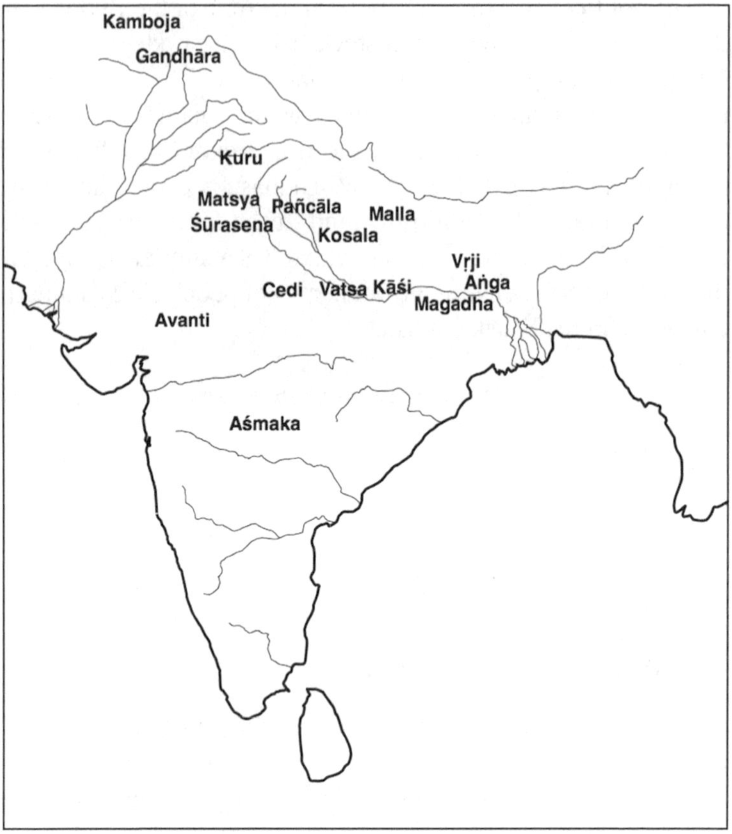

Fig. 5.2: Map of the sixteen *mahājanapadas*

ascribe elephant science to the sage Pālakāpya, who taught it to the king. Easterners in general are the elephant drivers and elephant fighters in the *Mahābhārata*. I infer from this that Magadha, because of its eastward position among the sixteen *mahājanapadas*, had an elephant advantage *vis-à-vis* its neighbors to the west of it, which is to say the following fourteen countries in the list. That is the first point.

Many of the *mahājanapadas* were kingdoms, but some were republics, such as Videha, a confederacy of tribes—within which the Mahāvīra, founder of Jainism, was born—and the Mallas. The

Śākyas, among whom the Buddha was born, also had a republican government, but it is not in the list, perhaps because of its small size or because it was absorbed by the larger and more powerful kingdom of Kosala. In the ensuing section I show that kingdoms were better able to amass war elephants than republics. This being so, the kingdom of Magadha had an advantage over the republics in its vicinity. This is the second point.

There is reason to think that the list of the sixteen *mahājanapadas* was a stereotypical one and did not exactly correspond with the political situation of the moment. Both the Buddha and the Mahāvīra met king Bimbisāra of Magadha, and his ambitious son and successor Ajātaśatru: we cannot reasonably doubt the historicity of these two kings. But by that time Magadha had annexed Aṅga, and prince Ajātaśatru was its governor. The incorporation into its domain of Aṅga, famous for its elephants, would have enhanced Magadha's advantage in this respect. Similarly, Kosala had absorbed Malla and Kāśī. This is the third point.

Finally, Magadha figures—with Kosala, Vatsa, and Avanti—in a short list of *mahājanapadas* in other passages of the Buddhist canon. These four countries evidently constituted the largest and most powerful of the sixteen in their day. Here again Magadha was in an advantageous position with respect to elephants, being the easternmost of the four. Thus, looked at in four different ways, the list of the sixteen *mahājanapadas* consistently shows Magadha very advantageously placed in relation to elephants.

According to representations of him in the Buddhist and Jain canons, Ajātaśatru was ruthless and ambitious. Despite his patronage of the Buddha and the Mahāvīra, the two canons do not fail to specify his sins. Impatient of his inheritance to the throne, he killed his father and made war with his neighbors to the north and the west, Videha and Kosala. Against Videha he was successful, as a result of which Magadha commanded the north and south banks of the middle Ganga. In a dispute with Kosala over an intervening territory of Kāśi, however, he was worsted, and according to the Buddhist canon captured alongside his foot soldiers, horses, chariots, and elephants—his fourfold army. Yet the king of Kosala released him and made peace. There is a passage in a later commentary attributing the victory of the Kosala king to his having overheard a conversation among Buddhist monks about which *vyūha* he should use to defeat Ajātaśatru. The Kosala king adopted the wagon array, the solution of the elder monk Dhanugahatissa, and was successful.[2]

Apart from Magadha's absorption of Aṅga and Videha in about 500 BCE, we do not know the steps by which it took over the remaining *mahājanapadas*. But the locations of the inscribed edicts of Aśoka, and the provinces of the Mauryan empire described therein, make it clear that by then the conquests of Magadha included all sixteen, reaching even far beyond into present-day Afghanistan and South India (Fig. 5.3).

In this history, kingship proved very expansive—much more so than the republics. The republics were by no means unwarlike; indeed they were considered the most formidable enemies and the most desirable allies by the *Arthaśāstra*.[3] They took territory and held slaves. But there seem to have been inherent limits to the extent to which they could or wished to absorb foreign peoples and territories. Videha is an example of growth by confederation of republics rather than conquest; perhaps that is the inherent tendency of this kind of polity. By contrast, the kingdoms of this period seem impelled to expand, and therefore to clash and absorb or be absorbed. Kingship being especially associated with war elephants and the fourfold army, as well as with the warfare and alliances of kings, we may suppose the model was rapidly adopted, making the fourfold army and its war elephants the ideal of a full force for an ambitious king.

It was a model that favored Magadha, with its access to the superior number and quality of elephants in the eastern forest, the Prācya-vana—always supposing it could also acquire horses. The war elephant and the fourfold army model that it made possible was the fuel for the inter-kingdom wars that eventuated in the empire

[2] Trautmann 1973: 162.
[3] *Arth.* 11.1.1.

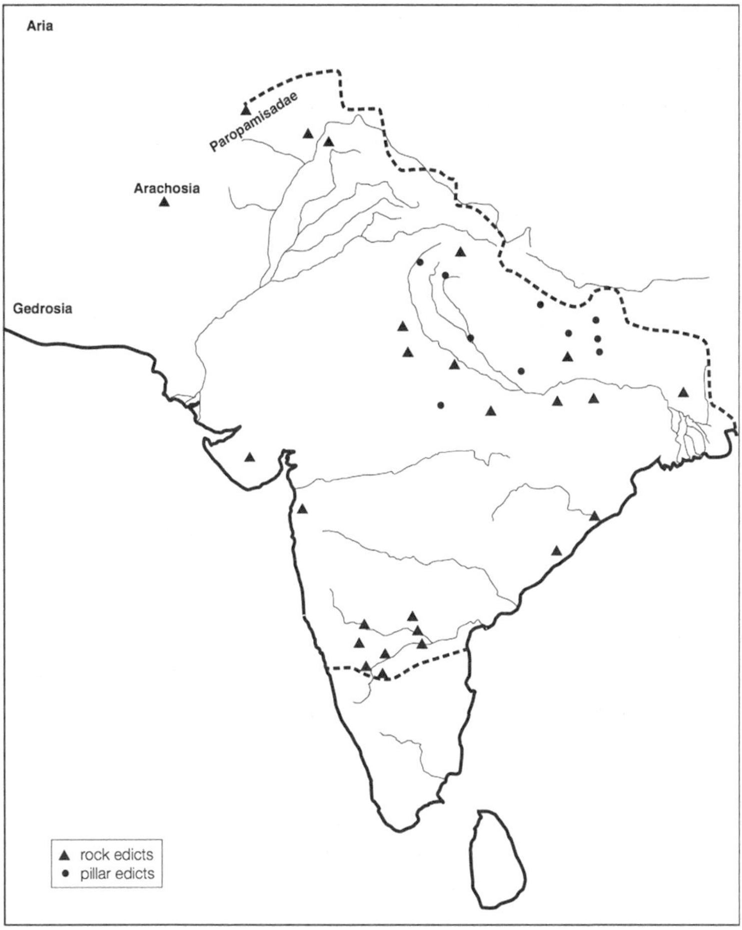

Fig. 5.3: Map of the Mauryan empire

formed by the Nandas and enlarged by the Mauryas. Historians have long discussed Magadha's success over other kingdoms and republics that it swallowed up, but the possible causes advanced have not included analysis of the army, the fundamental instrument of its power. I suggest that elephants played a key role. The war elephant and the superiority of the eastern region of North India in the supply of wild elephants, I propose, gave Magadha the edge over its competitors.

The Nandas and their contemporaries

The overall spread of Sanskrit-speaking peoples was eastward, from the valley of the Indus to the valley of the Ganga. The heartland of the Vedic religion was the Indus, the upper reaches of the Ganga valley, and the Doab of the Ganga and Yamuna rivers. Spiritually and ecologically it was identified with the land where the blackbuck or black antelope roams. The blackbuck loves open dry grassland and, as noted, alone among the many species of deer and antelope in India can graze in direct hot sunlight. It is *jāṅgala*, a creature of the dry grassland, as against the elephant, which is *ānūpa*, belonging to the wet landscape of the monsoon forest to the east.

Buddhism and Jainism, rivals to the Vedic religion, arose in the eastern edge of that expansion, in new lands with an elephant-friendly ecology on the periphery of Vedic territory. Consequently the view of the east and of easterners (Prācya) in the Vedic texts is unfavorable. For example, in the *Atharva Veda* a mantra to expel a fever wishes it away to the Māgadhas.[4] Because of this perspective, texts belonging to the tradition of the Veda take a jaundiced view of the rise of Magadha and the kings who ruled it, including those of the Nanda dynasty. This is especially so in the *Purāṇas*, brahmanical texts which represent the Nandas in unfavorable terms as low born, destroyers of the Vedic warrior class (*sarvakṣatrāntaka*), and the first within an evil age in which most kings will be Śūdras and unrighteous (*śūdraprāyās tv adharmikāḥ*). Evidently the kings of the region were regarded as upstarts, "new men" insufficiently attached to Brahmins and too receptive to the new religions. Nevertheless, the Nandas were called sole rulers (*ekarāṭ*) in the *Purāṇas*, kings who had brought all under their own rule.[5] We know this was not literally true: there were other kingdoms and republics in India independent of the Nandas, but it amounts to saying that they were rulers of an empire. Their capital was Pātaliputra, and other sources emphasize their

[4] *AV* 5.22.14.
[5] Pargiter 1913: 25, 69.

fabulous wealth, which was acquired by taxing everything—hides, resins, trees, stones, shops, and occupations.[6] The Nandas brought about a quantum leap in the level of taxation.

We have little reliable information on the Nandas and their rule. But, as it happens, it was during their reign that Alexander of Macedon brought his army across Iran into India. So the Alexander historians, writing in Greek and Latin, recorded some information about the military situation of India at the time, and this is invaluable for our inquiry. There are problems with these sources, to be sure, the principal one being that none of the Greek histories of the Nanda period are contemporary accounts, all having been written between three to five centuries later than the events of which they speak. But all of them draw upon earlier contemporary accounts by participants in Alexander's force, whose memoirs were lost because of the success of later histories of Alexander, being preserved only in these later works as fragments. To an extent, the contemporary accounts of Alexander can be reconstructed from these fragments, which are quoted or paraphrased in the accounts of these very Alexander historians—who used them and, by using, eclipsed them.

Alexander was in India briefly, 327–4 BCE, and the farthest east his army advanced was the Beas river in the Indus valley. He did not reach the Ganga valley or the Nandas. He wished to do so, as his aim was to find out whether, as he believed, the Ganga emptied into the world-encircling ocean, and he wanted to surpass the limits to which, according to tradition, Hercules and Dionysus had advanced in their eastward conquests. But his army, having reached the eastern edge of the Punjab at the Beas river, refused to go further. So he abandoned his advance toward the Ganga and led them down the Indus and back to Babylon.

Alexander certainly got information about the Nanda empire from his Indian allies in the Indian northwest. This information was recorded by his historians. The Nandas are not referred to by their dynastic name but by regional designations of peoples—the

[6] *Vaṃsatthappakāsini* 11.

Gangarides and Prasioi, that is, the people of the Ganga region and of the east (Skt. Prācya). This accords with the perspective from the Punjab. What concerns us is the military specifics: they had an army of 20,000 horses, 200,000 foot soldiers, 2,000 chariots, and 3,000 or 4,000 elephants.[7]

It is useful at this point to consider the variation of these numbers in the ancient sources:

	DIODORUS	CURTIUS	PLUTARCH	PLINY
Horse	20,000	20,000	80,000	30,000
Foot	200,000	200,000	200,000	600,000
Chariots	2,000	2,000	8,000	—
Elephants	3,000	4,000	6,000	9,000

It is very likely these numbers stem from a common source. Scholars of Alexander generally identify that source as Cleitarchus of Alexandria, who wrote a popular history of Alexander, now lost, but much relied upon by four later histories of Alexander—those of Diodorus, Curtius, Justin, and Plutarch; and Pliny, who deviates most from the others, will nevertheless have relied on the same source on the matter at hand. These authors constitute what is generally called the Vulgate tradition, meaning the popular version of the Alexander story stemming from Cleitarchus; and the Vulgate is contrasted with the much better history of Alexander written by Arrian, based on the narrative of Ptolemy, who was an eyewitness, and others. (Arrian does not give figures for the Nanda army.) In sum, the Alexander histories that survive fall into two distinct groups because of different sources that can be identified, at least in part. The assumption of a common source accounts for the family likeness of the figures in the table above. But it is their wild differences that are the real lesson of the table, and the consequent need for caution in accepting such figures.

These numbers are represented as having been the reason for the refusal by Alexander's men at the encampment along the Beas to advance further into India. That being the context,

[7] Diodorus 17.93; Curtius 9.2; Plutarch, "Life of Alexander," 62; Pliny 6.22.

writers will have had a motive for exaggerating the opposing Nanda forces to excuse the soldiers from the charge of cowardice. This is speculation, which serves the useful purpose of making us cautious; but it is not a fact, and the existence of a motive is not proof that it was acted upon. In any case, Alexander would certainly have sought out the best intelligence he could get on the countries of the Ganges from his Indian allies.[8]

The battlefield force of the Indian king whom the Alexander historians call Porus is smaller, but it is a substantial army on the *caturaṅga* plan.[9] The numbers given are 30,000 foot soldiers, 4,000 horses, 300 chariots, and 200 elephants.[10] Alexander's defeat of Porus on the banks of the Jhelum river (Hydaspes in the Greek sources) in the Indus valley was considered a great victory and described in detail by the Alexander historians; afterward, Alexander confirmed Porus in the rule of his own territory, and put him in charge of all his other conquered territories in India.

What is especially valuable for our investigation is that the Alexander historians explicitly distinguish Indian kingdoms from republics, naming the latter as independent Indian tribes, or self-ruling cities, or aristocracies, or democracies. This allows us to compare kingdoms with republics in their capacity to acquire and maintain war elephants.

Following the victory against Porus, the refusal of the army to continue eastward, and the turning southward down the Indus valley, the Alexander historians mention several of these republics and give figures for their military forces. In every case there is no mention of an elephant force, or at best of a small one. The Malloi and Oxydrakai were neighboring republics that combined to oppose Alexander; the force numbers list only foot, horse, and chariot, but not elephant.[11] When the Malloi sued for peace

[8] Bosworth 1996: 120.

[9] Evidently related to the Vedic name Puru, or perhaps the patronymic, Sanskrit *Paurava*, Prakrit *Poro*.

[10] Arrian, *History of Alexander* 6.15.4.

[11] Curtius 4: 90,000 foot soldiers, 10,000 horses; 900 chariots; Diodorus 17.87: 80,000 foot soldiers, 10,000 horses, 700 chariots.

their ambassadors brought gifts of horses and chariots with drivers, among other things, but not elephants. The Sabaracae or Sambustai, a democracy, had a force of 60,000 foot soldiers, 6,000 horses, and 500 chariots, no elephant force being mentioned.[12] It is possible, of course, that elephants were not as readily available in the southerly region of the Indus valley as in the northern. But Alexander received several gifts of elephants, almost all from kings who allied themselves with him. The Alexander historians, then, show that elephants are strongly associated with Indian kingship, and are rare or absent in republics.

One of the infrequent instances of war elephants associated with a republic concerns the Assakenoi, whom Alexander encountered before crossing the Indus into India proper. Their force was reported as 30,000 infantry, 20,000 cavalry, and 30 elephants. At Alexander's advance they took flight and released their elephants, and he took on Indian elephant hunters who recaptured them. It seems likely that the Indian republics did not reject elephant warfare but were less able to amass large numbers of the animal, as compared with the kingdoms. This is consistent with the hypothesis that the war elephant was an invention of Indian kingship.

Conversely, Alexander acquired elephants as gifts from kings, as offers of friendship or signs of capitulation, and as spoils of war. The king of Taxila (Skt. Takṣasilā) in the Punjab sent 25 elephants to seek his friendship; soon after, when Alexander crossed the Indus and reached Taxila, the king gave him a handsome gift of 200 talents of silver, 3,000 fattened oxen, 10,000 sheep, 30 elephants, and a feast for the army. King Abisares, seeing Alexander's success, sent his capitulation along with a gift of money and 40 elephants, but was careful not to show up in person. Somewhat after, he again sent elephants, some 30, but again made excuses for not showing up in person. After Alexander turned the army south and descended the Indus, king Mousikanos capitulated with "choice presents and all his elephants," and more elephants

[12] Curtius 8; Diodorus 17.102.

came as spoils of war from the storming of two cities of king Oxykenos.[13] This confirms the superior ability of kingdoms to acquire and maintain war elephants.

There is, however, one passage from the Greek sources, in Strabo, that directly contradicts this evidence. There are two traditions about what lay to the east of the Beas river where Alexander's army refused to advance. One of these I have already stated: the large force of the Nandas, under the denomination of Ganga dwellers and Easterners. The other tradition, which is found in Arrian, speaks of a republic and its elephant force: "On the other side of the Hyphasis [i.e. Beas river], so it was reported to Alexander, the country was fertile, the men good laborers of the soil and valiant warriors, who managed their own affairs in an orderly manner; most of them were under aristocracies, yet these made no demands other than reasonable. These people also had a number of elephants, a good many more than the other Indians, and these were, moreover, very large and courageous."[14] It is possible that both traditions are true, for republics could have lain immediately across the Beas river and the frontier of the Nandas further east. And it is consistent with what we know about elephant habitat in ancient times that eastward of the Beas there will have been elephants in greater number and superior size as well as energy. So far, then, there is no contradiction. But one ancient source—not an Alexander historian but the geographer Strabo—no doubt speaking of the same people, says, "They tell also of a kind of aristocratic order of government that was composed outright of five thousand counselors, each of whom furnishes the new commonwealth with an elephant."[15] This number, of 5,000 elephants in a republic, is the only passage in this body of literature that goes completely against my view that Indian kingdoms were far superior to republics in the matter of war elephants. Strabo offers it as an example of the way in

[13] Arrian, *History of Alexander* 6.15.6, 16.2.

[14] Arrian 5.25.

[15] Strabo, *Geography* 15.1.37. We do not know what Strabo's source for this was, and whether it is traceable to a member of Alexander's army.

which Greek writers, because of their ignorance and remoteness, magnify or make more marvelous the description of India on the far side of the Beas river; in other words he himself considered the number too large to believe.[16] In the next section I will argue that Strabo is *too* skeptical of the Greek writers on India and provide an instance of his being dead wrong. But in the present case he is right: no republic could maintain 5,000 war elephants, more than the number attributed to the Nandas, the most considerable regime of its time. It is neither credible nor consistent with what the Alexander historians say of other republics.

Elephants and the Mauryas

Megasthenes, in the entourage of Sibyrtius—satrap of Arachosia whose capital, Alexandria, is the present-day Kandahar in southern Afghanistan—was sent as ambassador to the court of the first Mauryan emperor, Candragupta. He wrote a most valuable account called, simply, *Indica*. Whether he was sent by Sibyrtius or by Seleucus is disputed—the latter was a general under Alexander who, during the scramble for power after his death made himself king of Syria, and eventually of all of Alexander's eastern conquests as far as the Punjab in India. But I leave that issue aside because it does not affect my inquiry.[17] The relevant fact is that Seleucus had made a treaty with Candragupta by which he acquired 500 elephants and ceded his eastern satrapies to the Mauryas, a matter to which we will return.

Megasthenes' *Indica* is especially interested in elephants and the army of the Mauryas and provides information very much to our purpose. But before we examine it I must say something about its difficulties and limitations. Ancient manuscripts are written on

[16] Ibid.

[17] C.E. Bosworth's "The historical setting of Megasthenes' Indica" (Bosworth 1996) is the most original article on Megasthenes in decades. It challenges the scholarly consensus that connects Megasthenes' embassy with Seleucus and the Seleucid–Mauryan entente. Bosworth connects it rather with the satrap Sibyrtius and puts it at an early date, before the Mauryan expansion into the Indus valley.

perishable materials, and before the making of multiple copies on paper by wood block printing—invented by the Chinese in the time of the Song dynasty—the survival of an ancient text depended upon an unbroken succession of handmade copies. Later books might eclipse earlier ones, whence they would cease to be copied; and this is what happened to the *Indica* of Megasthenes and the histories of Alexander by his contemporaries. All these books survive only in the fragments quoted by later books. The fragments can be reassembled, but there remain gaps for which we have no quotation in later surviving works, so there is always the question whether the fragment was accurately quoted; or, rather, how the original text of a fragment was altered by the purposes of the later text quoting it. It is well to keep this problem in mind.

The *Indica* of Megasthenes as reconstructed from its fragments opens with a glowing account of the fertility of India, allowing for two crops a year and, consequently, a large population. Because of it the elephants of India are larger and more abundant than those of Libya—which is to say Africa as known to the Greeks: "[India] produces an abundance of the largest elephants, supplying them with plentiful nourishment; because of this the animals greatly surpass in strength those produced in Libya. Thus many of them are captured by the Indians and trained for the contests of war, and it happens that they are especially effective in turning the balance toward victory."[18] As we shall see, the elephants of North Africa were at this time of the smaller race or species (*Loxodonta Africana cyclotis*) called forest elephants, which are indeed not as large as the Asian elephant. The ancient writers regularly affirm that the Asian elephant is the larger.[19]

Megasthenes gives an analysis of society and government in Candragupta's India which is valuable.[20] The social order was divided into seven groups which did not intermarry. This is a somewhat eccentric description of the caste system, which

[18] Megasthenes, fragment 4 (= Diod. 2.36.1).

[19] Details in Chapter 6.

[20] This discussion draws upon my earlier analysis of Megasthenes: Trautmann 1982.

consisted of the well-known four primary castes (*varṇa*) of priest (Brahmin), warrior (Kṣatriya), farmer or trader (Vaiśya), and serf (Śūdra), complicated by the introduction of additional functional divisions which do not correspond to social divisions represented in Indian sources. For our purposes the two most important castes in Megasthenes, and the first and second largest, are farmers and warriors.

What is so striking about the farmers in Megasthenes' depiction is that they do not go to war—they are a disarmed peasantry; and they and their land are inviolate, not to be disturbed by the soldiery. Here is Arrian's version of Megasthenes on this topic, with its arresting image of warriors killing one another while farmers peacefully go about their work: "The farmers . . . are the most numerous of the Indians. They have no military weapons and no involvement in matters of war, but they work the land and pay taxes to the kings and the cities that are autonomous. If war occurs between the Indians, it is illegal to attack the land of these workers or to devastate the land itself, and while some are making war and killing each other as opportunity serves, others nearby are quietly plowing or harvesting or pruning or reaping."[21] Both demilitarization of farmers and inviolability of cultivated land during warfare will have seemed striking differences to Greeks and Macedonians from the arrangements at home, where the army was the nation in arms and necessarily included farmers, and where destroying crops and orchards was a routine part of war. But if credible it would have been a great departure in India too, where a sea of farmers was the pool from which armies were drawn in every age. The disarming of the peasantry was likely a Mauryan innovation, one we do not find in the Vedic age, nor in later times when, to the contrary, the vast size of the peasant population and its cultivation of the military arts was a source of off-season employment.[22] For most of its history the great bulk of Indian armies was recruited from farmers.

[21] Megasthenes, fragment 19a (= Arrian, *Indica* 11.9–10).

[22] Gommans 2002; Gommans and Kolff 2001.

Equal and opposite to the disconnection of farmers from warfare is the disconnection of the warrior class from the land in Megasthenes' account. This may also have been a Mauryan innovation since it is so at odds with what obtains in all accounts of the old Vedic warrior class of the Kṣatriyas and their descendants in the accounts of the Alexander historians of the Indian northwest. That class was definitely wealthy, commanding farmland and subordinates, owning weapons and chariots and bringing them to battle. In Candragupta's kingdom the army was, it appears, entirely supported by wages paid by the state and had no farming estates to return to when war was over. The warrior class were not landowners. They were idle in peacetime and sufficiently well off to maintain servants of their own:

> The fifth class of Indians is the warriors, second to the farmers in number, who experience the greatest freedom and contentment. They are experienced only in the activities of warfare. Others make their weapons for them and provide for their horses, and others serve in the camps, caring for their horses and cleaning their weapons and driving the elephants, and also preparing and driving the chariots. When they must fight, they fight, but they are cheerful in peacetime, and are paid so much from the community that they easily support others.[23]

The army is huge. Megathenes says warriors are the second largest caste, second only to farmers, and gives the size of Candragupta's camp as 400,000. Taken altogether, we infer a large treasury and a vigorous system of taxation. It is entirely possible that elements of the Mauryan system were started by the Nandas. The latter had a reputation for enlarging the scope of taxation and their wealth to fantastic proportions. In the Vedic tradition they are said to have destroyed the Vedic warrior class, which, in the light of Megasthenes' testimony about Mauryan practice, may indicate a reliance on paid soldiers rather than a landed warrior class. Whatever the precedents of the Mauryan military system, nothing like it prevailed in the Indian states outside the growing empire of Candragupta.

[23] Megasthenes, fragment 19a (= Arrian, *Indica* 12.2–4).

I conclude from this that the centralization and enlargement of army power by these means were a large part of Candragupta's advantage in the expansion of his empire. This military advantage appears clearly in what Megasthenes says about Mauryan administration.

Megasthenes depicts the administration as having three main parts: country, city, and military administration, each directed by a board of five, and each with six functional divisions. The country/city distinction of civil administration corresponds well with what is found in Indian texts, administering the country having to do mainly with taxing farmers and herders and other rural producers, the city having to do with the regulation and taxation of markets, among other tasks. The military administration is, as we expect, divided among the parts of the fourfold army, plus divisions devoted to boats and oxen for the supply of the army. It is in this context that the all-important royal monopoly of arms, horses, and elephants is expounded. This rounds out the picture of the remarkable Mauryan military system: a disarmed farmer class whose function is to generate the bulk of taxation which pays for the army; a landless warrior class paid from the treasury; and a monopoly by the king of the ownership of elephants, horses, and arms. This system must have been the main engine of Mauryan expansion, and its unprecedented success would, in turn, have provoked emulation by kings who saw it. And that would in turn have worked as a powerful engine for the spread of the war elephant and the fourfold army.

Strabo, in his *Geography*, is critical of Greek writers on India, who, he claims, are mostly liars, including ambassadors such as Megasthenes. As we have seen, he believes descriptions of India beyond the Beas river—that is, the eastward limit which Alexander had reached—are given to exaggeration, and I have endorsed his doubt in one respect, namely, the 5,000 elephants attributed to the republic which lay immediately east of the encampment on the Beas. Yet on another matter Strabo is completely wrong, but his hyper-critical attitude toward his predecessors leads him unwittingly to put his finger on a highly significant fact.

Among the failings of the writers on India, he argues, is that they contradict one another: for Megasthenes spoke of a royal monopoly of horses and elephants, but this is contradicted by Nearchus, who had spoken of private ownership of them. As I have already indicated, this is wrong, but it is a telling error. Nearchus was a companion of Alexander, so his testimony relates to India within (west of) the Beas, the upper Indus valley, in which the private ownership of horses, elephants, and other means of conveyance was the norm. Megasthenes on the other hand was describing the situation in the heartland of the Mauryan empire, much further east, and somewhat later than Nearchus. Thus there is no contradiction, and Megasthenes is pointing to an innovation originating among easterners. Megasthenes shows us the unprecedented features of the Mauryan military machine that make its success in encompassing most of India intelligible. The war elephant is central to this success.

It is in keeping with this centrality, and with the fascination of Alexander and his companions and successors with the Indian war elephant, that Megasthenes gives a detailed explanation of the manner of their capture. Basically, the method is to use tame female elephants as bait, which shows that the aim was to capture large male tuskers suitable for battle, and not only to obtain elephants for work and to ride on. The method is to dig a large circular moat with a single wooden bridge, putting the female elephants within the moat. The wild elephants are not driven in during daytime, they find their own way in at night, drawn by the scent of the females. They go round the moat till they find the bridge and cross into the enclosure. Elephants that are too young or too old or diseased are released. The emphasis upon the capture of adult males is consistent with what the *Arthaśāstra* prescribes, and implies the same demographic profile of the royal herd of captive elephants—the dominance in it of adult males. Megasthenes describes the taming of newly captured elephants in some detail. They are allowed to become hungry and thirsty; their feet (hind feet, I imagine) are hobbled by brave skilled hunters; they are beaten by tame elephants till they fall over; a leather rope is put around the neck, and the skin of the neck cut with a knife so that they feel the noose when it is pulled. That is the stick; the carrot follows, consisting of singing with cymbals and drums to lull them to sleep, among other things.[24]

The spread of the Mauryan empire to nearly the whole of the Indian subcontinent completed the universalization within India of the *caturaṅgabala* ideal and the institution of the war elephant. Behind that spread was a machinery for the financing and staffing of the army, and a royal monopoly of the means of warfare. The unprecedented success of the Mauryan expansion would have been a powerful advertisement to other kings for adopting the war elephant and the fourfold army.

South India

South India is to this day richly endowed with monsoon forest, forest people, and wild elephants. The largest population of wild Asian elephants is in South India. It is not surprising therefore that the war elephant should have become part of the practice of kingship in the South.

We are fortunate that the conditions of kingship in ancient South India are captured in the classical literature of Tamil, in the body of works called the Sangam literature. The anthologies and epics comprising Sangam literature consist of courtly poetry patronized by the kings and chieftains of the Tamil country, selected and arranged by a *saṅgam* or collectivity of connoisseurs at the court of the Pāṇḍya king of Madurai in the first few centuries of the Common Era. It is essentially a heroic literature whose subject matter is the deeds and loves of kings and the warrior class.[25] It gives rich testimony of the presence of the war elephant and the fourfold army ideal in early South India.[26]

[24] Megasthenes, fragment 20a (= Arrian, *Indica* 13–15).

[25] Kailasapathy 1968.

[26] The pioneering work on elephants in the Sangam literature is *The elephant in the Tamil land* by E.S. Varadarajaiyer (1945), which is useful as a first overview.

What gives the literary world of this poetry special value to our theme is that it is based upon a division of the land into five ecological zones or landscapes. This is formulated in the poetics of the *Tolkappiyam*, a treatise on the grammar and poetics of the literature. Each of the five landscapes has its characteristic physical features, flora and fauna, and human social-economic forms of organization. By convention the five landscapes are named by their emblematic flower or tree:

Kuriñci (a red flower), the mountains
Mullai (jasmine), the pasture
Marutam (a tree bearing red flowers), the countryside
Neytal (a water flower), the seashore
Pālai (an evergreen), the wasteland, desert

Thus the mountains are the home of the *kuriñci* flower, of wild elephants, monkeys, and parrots, and of tribal people farming millet. *Mullai* is the scene of pastoralists herding their flocks; *marutam* of farming villages and wet rice agriculture; *neytal* of fisherfolk; and *pālai* of bandits who prey upon merchant caravans. This last is not so much a place as a time of year: the hot season, when the rising heat desiccates everything and the deciduous trees of the monsoon forest shed most of their leaves.

Günther-Dietz Sontheimer, scholar of nomadic pastoralists and their religions, remarked that, before the great deforestation of the last century or two, the different economic groups were more separate and their territories impinged and overlapped very little. He believed that the five landscapes of Sangam literature describe very well the ecological zones and economic patterns of South India and the Deccan, each of which, moreover, produced its own folk religion, its distinctive tribal gods which were eventually identified with the gods of high Hinduism in Sanskrit texts.[27]

These five landscapes are conventionally associated with different poetic situations, called *tiṇai*. Poetic types are two, *akam* and *puram*, indicating the interior world of love, and the outer

[27] Sontheimer 2004: 353–82.

public world of war and kingship, including royal hospitality to poets. The poetic situations of love poetry are lovers' meetings, furtive love, domestic love, love in separation, and elopement. Each is conventionally associated with one of the landscapes. Thus *kuriñci*, the mountainous region, is the setting for lovers' meetings, especially first love; the red *kuriñci* flower blossoms after twelve years, about the age at which a girl becomes sexually mature. A poem of love need only mention a wild elephant or other characteristic denizen of the *kuriñci* region to signal to the hearer that the theme is first love or a lovers' meeting. In this way the contents of the "interior landscape," as A.K. Ramanujan called it, function as exterior signs to indicate interior states.[28]

As we may expect, wild elephants are mostly mentioned in *akam* poems of *kuriñci*, as they are representative of that mountainous afforested landscape and no other. They are mentioned frequently. The people of this region are hunters and growers of millet. Elephants plunder their fields, causing much damage. It is a trope in this kind of poem for a young man of the kingdom to use the pretense that he has been hunting a wild elephant as the opening gambit of a conversation with a young woman he happens upon, asking if she has seen a wounded elephant pass by. Elephants, then, are hunted, and the tribal people of *kuriñci*, who are more or less equivalent to the forest people (*aṭavis*) of Sanskrit texts, kill and eat elephants when they can and sell their ivory. There seems to be no royal protection of wild elephants here, though of course we are dealing with poetic treatments that view these people from a distance, and as exotics, so we cannot rely on this.

While wild elephants appear in the poetry of *akam*, or love, tamed elephants mostly appear in poems of *puram*, or the heroic deeds of kings and chiefs. This heroic poetry has its situations or themes—cattle rustling, marching forth, siege, battle, victory—corresponding more or less to those of *akam*, but with its own emblematic flowers or plants.[29] The elements of the fourfold

[28] Ramanujan 1967.
[29] Ramanujan 1985: 251–7.

army are in full evidence here. A poem of *Puranāṉūru*,[30] one of the anthologies of *puram* poems, in an elegy for one Nampi Neṭuñceliyan by Pereyin Muruvalār, indicates the king was skilled in all four forms of fighting:

> He faced oncoming armies,
> looked on the backs of fleeing ones,
> galloped his horses faster than thought,
> drove chariots in the long city streets,
> rode tall and extraordinary elephants.

Battlefield descriptions, or of the dead after the battle is over, often indicate the four "legs" of the army. Elephants were far more plentiful in South India than horses, which had to be imported over long distances; nevertheless, chariots and cavalry are regularly indicated, directly or by abbreviation, along with foot soldiers (spearmen, for the most part) and elephants. Kings very often ride on elephants, in war and peace.

There is a definite pattern in the distribution of wild elephants and tamed war elephants in the Sangam literature. Wild elephants are found only in the mountainous landscape of *kuriñci*, among forest people. These people are in conflict with elephants over their crops, they cook and eat elephant meat and take ivory, but they do not capture and train elephants for their own use. Conversely, trained war elephants are associated strongly with kings—who will have used forest people to help them capture and train the animals. It is the same pattern as in the North, where the king's requirement of elephants means he must get the cooperation of forest people. We hear little in the Sangam poetry about how elephants were captured, there being only a few references to the pitfall method.

Besides the battlefield scenes of the *puram* poems, there is a substantial number of poems, in the genre called *pāṭān* or praise, extolling the king for his liberal provision of gifts to poets. Bards meeting at a crossroads will discuss kings whose hospitality they

[30] Ibid.: 171, no. 239.

have just enjoyed. According to one especially fine example, the poet says that the king gave him to eat till his teeth became blunt, like a plough in virgin soil.[31] Gift-giving is the other side of war-making; war accumulates wealth, which is then given away. And so the Tamil poetry of kingship, much as in the Sanskrit epics, displays both sides of the coin. Some kings are especially famous for their liberality and become the subject of poets who use striking visual images during displays of their ability with clever forms of hyperbole to indicate the king's generosity. Āy Aṇṭiran is one such king. In a poem by Muṭamōciyār, the king's stupendous liberality is implied by a description of his palace as stripped bare because of his generosity after the bards have sung and left; elephant posts are without elephants, and only wild peacocks strut around; the women of the palace have no jewelry, except only wedding jewels that cannot be given away; the palace is dimly lit, there being now little oil for the lamps; and yet the richly endowed palaces of other kings are no comparison with the empty palace of Āy.[32]

These poems are analogous to the *dānastutis*—praises of gifts by kings to poets—of the *Ṛgveda*.[33] But while the Ṛgvedic poems involve gifts of gold, slaves, cattle, horses, and chariots, they do not, as we have seen, include elephants. Only in the later Vedic texts, and the *Mahābhārata* and *Rāmāyaṇa* after the invention of the war elephant, does the elephant become the superlative royal gift. They are already so in the *puram* poems of the Sangam literature, in which the king gives the poet sumptuous new clothes to replace his worn-out ones, as well as food and drink, and sends him on his way bearing gifts of gold, or a chariot, or an elephant.

How did the institution of the war elephant, and conception of the fourfold army, take root in South India? We do not know the specifics of the propagation of these ideas and the techniques

[31] Nilakanta Sastri 1955: 74–5, citing *Porunarārrupaṭai*.

[32] *Puranānūru* 127 by Muṭamōciyār, in Ramanujan 1985: 151.

[33] Discussed in Chapter 2.

of putting them into practice. But they would have been made available to the kings of the South through the expansion there of the Mauryan empire. The inscriptions of the Mauryan king Aśoka are found in the South and indicate that he had diplomatic relations with the precedessors of those the Sangam poems call the three crowned kings of the Tamil country, Cōla, Pāṇṭiya, and Cēra. Aśoka refers to them by name (the Cēra as Keralaputra), these being the paramount kings, amid many other lesser ones.[34] Moreover, although the Sangam poetry is a unique formation whose homeland is South India, it shows a wider horizon of the imagination that encompasses the North. Thus, a king in these poems will be said to have conquered a realm reaching from the Himalayas to Kumari—Cape Comorin on the southern tip of India—and from sea to sea; another will have carved his dynastic crest upon the flank of the Himalayas; a third will have feasted the combatants of the *Mahābhārata* war. It is quite clear that the war elephant and its environing structures of use have taken root in South India through king-to-king communication in one form or another, and that the Mauryan empire is likely to have inspired its adoption there.

Sri Lanka

Evidence of the war elephant in Sri Lanka comes from a literature very different from that of South India. I have already alluded to the canon of Theravāda Buddhism of Sri Lanka, Myanmar, Thailand, and Cambodia, written in the Pali language (also, *nota bene*, called Magadhi), a North Indian language related to Sanskrit. As we have seen, the canonical Buddhist texts in Pali take the war elephant as an established institution in North India at the Buddha's time. The chronicle of Sri Lanka called the *Mahāvaṃsa* (Great Chronicle) is also written in Pali, by monks of the Mahāvihāra (Great Monastery). Because writers of the *Mahāvaṃsa* were monks, we cannot expect from it close descriptions of actual

[34] Aśokan inscriptions, 2nd Major Rock Edict.

battles. But it is very much a record of the kings of Sri Lanka and the Sinhala people, and their relation to the Buddhist order of monks, from the perspective of the Mahāvihāra. This being so, the *Mahāvaṃsa*, though a monastic production, has a fair amount to say about royal elephants and the fourfold army.

The chronicle does not give us an account of how the war elephant and its accompanying structures of practice were instituted in Sri Lanka: they are present, explicitly or tacitly, from the start. But there is no great mystery about how the Indian model of kingship and the war elephant reached Sri Lanka. First, the Sinhala language is one of the Indo-Aryan languages (a sub-family of Indo-European), that is, it is related to Pali, Sanskrit, and other languages of North India. The *Mahāvaṃsa* gives us a story about how the Sinhala people, under their king Vijaya, migrated from northern India to Sri Lanka. Although the account is somewhat mythological, the overall story—the establishment in Sri Lanka of a people speaking Sinhala, a language related to the Indo-Aryan languages of northern India—is certainly true. Second, Buddhism itself, originating in North India, was brought to Sri Lanka from India. In the *Mahāvaṃsa* account this happened in the time of the Mauryas, due to a son of Aśoka named Mahinda, a Buddhist monk who converted the king of Laṅkā and his followers. Buddhism will have brought with it ideas of Indian kingship, and in adopting Buddhism the kings of Sri Lanka will also have taken up the Indian model of kingship. And third, the kings of South India with whom the kings of Laṅkā often interacted were themselves influenced by the North Indian model of kingship: they had taken up the use of war elephants, chariots, and so forth. In sum, Indian kingship and its structures of practice will have reached Sri Lanka by various routes.

For example, in one of the first of the many passages mentioning elephants and horses, the king of Madhurā (Mathurai in South India) sends his daughter and the daughters of his ministers to be married to king Vijaya and his minsters. The procession is described: "When he had thus obtained many maidens and had given compensation to their families, he sent his daughter, bedecked with all her ornaments, and all that was needful for the journey, and all the maidens whom he had fitted out, according to their rank, elephants and horses and chariots, worthy of a king (*rājāhāraṃ ca hatthassarathaṃ*), and craftsmen and a thousand families of the eighteen guilds, entrusted with a letter to the conqueror Vijaya."[35]

Many instances of elephants and the fourfold army in the *Mahāvaṃsa* are found in descriptions of royal processions having to do with religious foundations or festivals. In such passages those describing the largeness of the procession, the multiplicity or completeness of its elements, and the sumptuousness of ornamentation (*alaṃkāra*) of the participants provide signs of the high honor conferred by the procession. For example, a procession of the king to honor the Mahāvihāra is described thus: the city and road to the monastery are adorned, and the king commands the drum to beat. The king leads the way on his chariot, followed by his ministers and the women of the harem, with chariots and carts, soldiers, elephants, and horses (*sayoggabalavāhana*), "in a mighty train,"[36] its fullness a visual sign of the high degree of honor being paid.[37]

When a shoot of the Tree of Enlightenment—under which the Buddha had received enlightenment—arrives, the fourfold army (*caturaṅgiṇī senā*), seven *yojanas* long and three *yojanas* wide, forms the procession led by the king and accompanied by a great body of monks.[38]

Yet another such procession, to receive relics of the Buddha, is described in similar terms: "[The king], glad at heart, well-versed in the duties of kings, arrayed in all his ornaments, surrounded on every side by all his dancing-women and his warriors in complete

[35] *MV* 7.55–7.

[36] The translator follows the explanation of the expression *sayoggabalavāhana* by the commentary: *ettha yoggaṃ ti rathasakaṭādi, balaṃ ti senā, vāhane ti hatthiassādi* (p. 111, n. 2), that is, *yogga* = chariots and carts, *bala* = army, *vāhana* = elephants, horses, and so forth.

[37] *MV* 15.188–90.

[38] Ibid.: 18.29.

armour, by a great body of troops, as well as by variously adorned elephants, horses and chariots (*hatthivājiratha-*), mounted his car of state that was drawn by four pure white Sindhu-horses and stood there, making the (sumptuously) adorned and beautiful elephant Kaṇḍula pace before him, holding a golden casket (to receive the relics) under a white parasol."[39] Such descriptions of processions organized to honor the religion and the order of monks, especially those of the Mahāvihāra, figure at especially important junctures in the history of the religion. Examples such as the foregoing occur frequently in the *Mahāvaṃsa*, and there is no point giving all of them as the ones at hand give the sense of the others as well. In all of them the high degree of honor is indicated by the completeness of the body making up the procession and the sumptuousness of ornaments. The fourfold army is a regular feature of this completeness, and of course elephants are an essential part, both of the completeness and of the sumptuousness of the procession.

Armies in the field are described using the same locutions. The army of king Duṭṭagāmaṇi comes "with chariots and carts, soldiers, horses and elephants,"[40] as in the reception of the Tree of Enlightenment; the same expression is used for the opposing king, Eḷāra the Damiḷa (Tamil). When his nephew takes the place of the fallen Eḷāra, Duṭṭagāmaṇi gives battle, mounted on his elephant Kaṇḍula, "with warriors mounted on elephants, horses and chariots, and with foot-soldiers in great numbers."[41] Elsewhere we read of "an army of four limbs."[42] This makes it clear that a neighboring passage mentioning men, horses, and elephants is to be interpreted as an abbreviated reference to the fourfold army: when Dappula brings from the mountain country a large host which surrounds the city with a large clamor, "With the neighing of the steeds, the trumpeting of the elephants, the rattle of the drums and their rhythmic sound, and the battle cries

[39] Ibid.: 31.36–9.

[40] *sayoggabalavāhano: MV* 25.1.

[41] *hatthassarathayodehi pattīhi ca anūnako*: ibid.: 25.81.

[42] *caturaṅginī senā*: ibid.: 48.122.

of the warriors the firmament was at that time near to bursting."[43] In this scene the fourfold army is rendered via sound, through the din it creates—a noise painting so to say—a trope of the classical literatures of India as well.

The fourfold army continues to appear on Sri Lankan battlefields long after we suppose chariots to have become obsolete, as late as the time of Gajabāhu (r. 1131–53).[44] Mānābharaṇa, king of Rohaṇa, has a fourfold army,[45] as does prince Mahinda in the time of king Parakkamabāhu I (r. 1153–86).[46]

The matter of the chariot is difficult to resolve. It ceased to be used on the battlefield in India some time after the Central Asian cavalry-based armies of the Kushans formed a conquest state in North India in the first century CE. But we know nothing about the times at which chariot warfare ceased in South India and Sri Lanka. Chariots appear frequently in early parts of the *Mahāvaṃsa*; one early king is regularly referred to by the epithet lord of chariots.[47] And, as we have seen, the notion of the fourfold army is used in periods so late that we can no longer be sure when other passages are indicating it by abbreviation or not. Abbreviation may take the form of mentioning elephants, horses, and men in the description of the army, leaving it unclear whether horses means cavalry and chariots; or it may take the form of mentioning chariots, horsemen, and elephant riders, leaving foot soldiers implicit; the first species of abbreviation is a problem when trying to track the chariot's demise. Even for times at which one must presume the battlefield chariot is no more, it pops up to take part in processions, perhaps in the character of a temple car—still today called a chariot, as we have seen. Even in the time of Parakkamabāhu, when the chariot surely disappeared from battle, and when, for example, the descriptions of battlefield booty include elephants and horses but not chariots, the four limbs of the

[43] Ibid.: 48.100.
[44] Ibid.: 70.217.
[45] Ibid.: 71.18.
[46] Ibid.: 72.198.
[47] *rathesabha*: ibid.: 15.11 and ff.

army nevertheless reappear in descriptions of his procession of the Tooth Relic of the Buddha. Here again we are given a noise picture of the kind we have already met:

> With the trumpeting of elephants and the neighing of horses, with the clatter of chariot wheels and the rattle of kettledrums; with the enrapturing tone of all the festive shell trumpets, with the roll of the great drums and the cries of victory of the bards; with the shouts of acclamation and loud clapping of hands and the jubilant cries (of the people) he filled the regions of the heavens with noise. The Monarch himself arrayed with all his ornaments, mounted his favourite, beautiful elephant which was hung with coverings of gold, and surrounded by many dignitaries, who rode their steeds, he went forth with great pomp from the splendid town, betook himself to the sacred Tooth Relic and to the glorious Bowl Relic, reverenced them in worthy fashion with hands folded on the brow, and while offering to them with his own hands sweet-smelling flowers he went on his way with both relics.[48]

Elsewhere in the long section on this great king we read directly of his having a fourfold army—e.g. the capital city has "incessant traffic of elephants, horses and chariots."[49] But as the institution of the war elephant continued long after the disappearance of the chariot from battle, the dating of its disappearance in Sri Lanka does not greatly affect the matter at hand.[50]

A subsidiary question is the degree to which the kings of Sri Lanka could supply themselves with horses. The *saindhava* or horse of Sindhu (Sind, the lower valley of the Indus) is mentioned more than once, in contexts that make it clear it is the best of horses. This is a very long way from home, and whether the humid tropics agreed with it is a question. At any rate, horses have a lifespan much shorter than elephants, so that if the kings of the island could not replace them by breeding them, a continual horse

[48] Ibid.: 74.221–7.

[49] Ibid.: 73.149.

[50] Geiger (1960: 155) is more skeptical about the *Mahāvaṃsa* evidence for elephants on the battlefield, without, however, giving strong grounds for his view.

trade from the northern pastures would have been needed. We do indeed hear of a horse-trade, or rather of a horse trader from the other coast, that is, South India, informing the Cola king of the vulnerabilities of the king of Sri Lanka.[51] One would like to know more about this trade. I am inclined to suppose horses were rare and valuable, liable to be reserved for the king and his army.

In the matter of elephants, on the other hand, Sri Lanka is very well endowed, and there is evidence that large male tuskers were sought by kings of India. There is a most interesting passage in the *Mahāvaṃsa* dealing with diplomatic relations of Parakkamabāhu I with Burma/Myanmar, here called Rāmañña.[52] The kings of Laṅkā and Rāmañña had long had good relations because of their common adherence to Theravāda Buddhism, sending one another envoys and presents. But somehow the king of Rāmañña "hearkened to the words of slanderers" against the envoys of Parakkamabāhu and deprived them of the maintenance usually given them. He put an end to the private trade in elephants with foreigners and, creating a royal monopoly, raised prices substantially. He also ended the practice of presenting an elephant to a vessel arriving with diplomatic gifts. Later, seizing such a ship with a diplomatic letter addressed to him—under the pretext that the letter had been sent to his enemy the king of Cambodia—he imprisoned the Lankan envoys in a fortress of the mountainous region, confiscating their money, their elephants, and their vessels, and putting them to hard labor. Further outrages ensued, including taking money and goods from envoys of Parakkamabāhu who had been sent to buy elephants, and giving them nothing in return. The king of Laṅkā sent a large expeditionary force by sea, captured the capital, and killed the king of Rāmañña. The people, in their fear of great retribution, sent a message to Parakkamabāhu saying they would render a tribute of elephants "in any amount" to avoid yet harsher conditions. Thereafter, numbers of elephants were sent and "they made anew with the Laṅkā Ruler who kept his treaties

[51] *MV* 55.13.
[52] Ibid.: 86.

faithfully, a pact of friendship."[53] We see here an international trade in elephants involving at least the Theravāda countries of Southeast Asia and Sri Lanka. At various junctures, the story involves different modalities: private traders, a royal monopoly of the trade with prices fixed by fiat, and exchange by way of giving and taking tribute. Such a trade is never truly free in the modern sense, being always closely involved with the royal interest in elephants. The modalities could change from purchase and sale to diplomatic exchange.

The last passage from the *Mahāvaṃsa* shows how transfers of elephants occurred in king-to-king relations, both of friendship and of war, sometimes directly, sometimes through royal envoys, sometimes through merchants, but governed always by the interests of kings.

Within South Asia the single-most important means for the spread of the war elephant was the kingdom of Magadha, and the empire that Magadha became under the Nandas and Mauryas. The success of its expansion did more than anything else to spread the ideal of the war elephant and the fourfold army. The testimony of Megasthenes goes to show that the Mauryas carried the tendencies toward centralization of power of the kings of Magadha to the highest pitch, separating farmers from warfare, separating warriors from the land, and monopolizing the means of warfare. Subsequent kings were unable to sustain these policies in full, although the tendencies they embody are often partially expressed. In the end it was difficult to keep the army separate from the ownership of agricultural land. It was always easiest to settle land revenues upon the officer class, and once so settled it was difficult to prevent the connection from becoming hereditary. And farmers themselves were so very substantial as a proportion of the whole population that they could never be wholly excluded from warfare. But in

[53] Ibid.: 76.75.

respect of elephants, and of horses, the tendency of kings to monopolize or at least control ownership often appears and can be considered a long-term tendency of Indian kingship.

We do not have direct evidence from ancient sources of the transfer of knowledge by elephant hunters, trainers, drivers, and physicians to local practitioners of these specializations. But the circumstantial evidence is substantial, and we have direct evidence in the Hellenistic sources, as we shall see in the next chapter. Specialists of this kind, often recruited from among forest people, speaking many different languages, did not spontaneously reinvent the war elephant and the body of knowledge by which its care and management were carried on through the ages, and in many different locales and cultures across a wide region of Eurasia. Above all the evidence is the content of that body of knowledge itself, the techniques of capture, training, care, and management, and such instruments of practice as the *aṅkuśa*.

Of the three structures of practice in which the war elephant finds a place—the fourfold army, the battle array, and the royal conveyance—the first and last are abundantly in evidence throughout the South Asia region; and of course war elephants continue to register in the sources long after the fourfold army gave way to a threefold one with the obsolescence of the chariot. The most technical of them, the battle array, leaves the fewest traces outside the Sanskrit epics and manuals such as the *Arthaśāstra*. But, as we shall see, it shows up vividly in Southeast Asia, at quite late dates, bespeaking a hidden history of long duration and wide geographic reach.

6

The Near East, North Africa, Europe

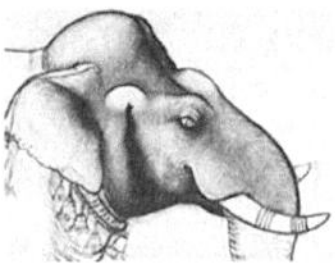

THE INSTITUTION OF THE WAR ELEPHANT IN South Asia expanded at first within the natural habitat of the wild Asian elephant. The war elephant, I have shown, was a crucial factor within a model of kingship and warfare developed in North India and then drawn upon by newly forming kingdoms in the orbit of the Mauryan empire. This model of kingship expanded—alongside Buddhism, Jainism, and Hinduism—ever further into an elephant-rich terrain, among polities receptive to new forms of kingship.

I now look westward to examine the amazing phenomenon of non-Indian kings taking up the war elephant, in terrains from which Asian elephants had long since become extinct and where there were no wild elephants or only wild African elephants. I have already indicated how costly it was to capture, train, and maintain the large male tuskers used for warfare. In regions to the west of India these costs escalated, but so did the rarity value of the war elephant. Accordingly, a diverse variety of kings in this region—Persian, Greek and Macedonian, Carthaginian, Roman, Ghaznavid Turk—thought it worth their while to go to extraordinary lengths to acquire war elephants and deny them to their enemies. As we shall see, the nub of the matter was access to the specialized knowledge and skills of Indian elephant men: hunters, trainers, drivers, and physicians. Traces of how this knowledge travelled to and was acquired by monarchs toward the west are scarce yet distinct in documents that record the conjuncture which brought about this unexpected arms race.

Scullard has mapped this development by locating battles and sieges in which elephants were used. In Fig. 6.1 I reproduce his map, to which I have added further battles and sieges, notably those among the Sassanians of Persia,[1] and the Ghaznavids of Central Asia.[2] All, except only the battle of the Jhelum in India, lie outside the habitat of wild Asian elephants and are shaped, therefore, by conditions of scarcity, great cost, and difficulty of acquiring new stock. The map shows seventy-two battles and sieges for which we have reliable records, over a period extending from 530 BCE to 1117 CE. If we had sufficient evidence, the map could be extended to cover South and Southeast Asia, where battles and sieges using war elephants would have been much more numerous. This, then, is the western periphery of the object of study. It extends entirely beyond the range of wild Asian elephants over a period of about 1600 years, made all the more impressive because of the extraordinary efforts it will have taken to supply and replenish the region with stocks of the animal.

Achaemenids and Assyrians

The Achaemenid empire of Persia (*c.* 550–330 BCE), the largest the world had seen to its time, must have been an inspiration for the formation of the Nanda and Maurya empires, even if there are few direct connections in surviving records, the evidence being circumstantial and thin. One such connection is the inclusion of a province of India called Gandāra (= Skt. Gandhāra) and of Hinduš (= Skt. Sindhu) in the empire of Darius I, as we know from his inscriptions and the account of Herodotus. There were Indian units in his army. In the reliefs at Persepolis there is a parade of different national types bringing tribute, and we could hope to find elephants there. Indians are among them, but not

[1] From Rance 2003.
[2] From Bosworth 1973, 1977.

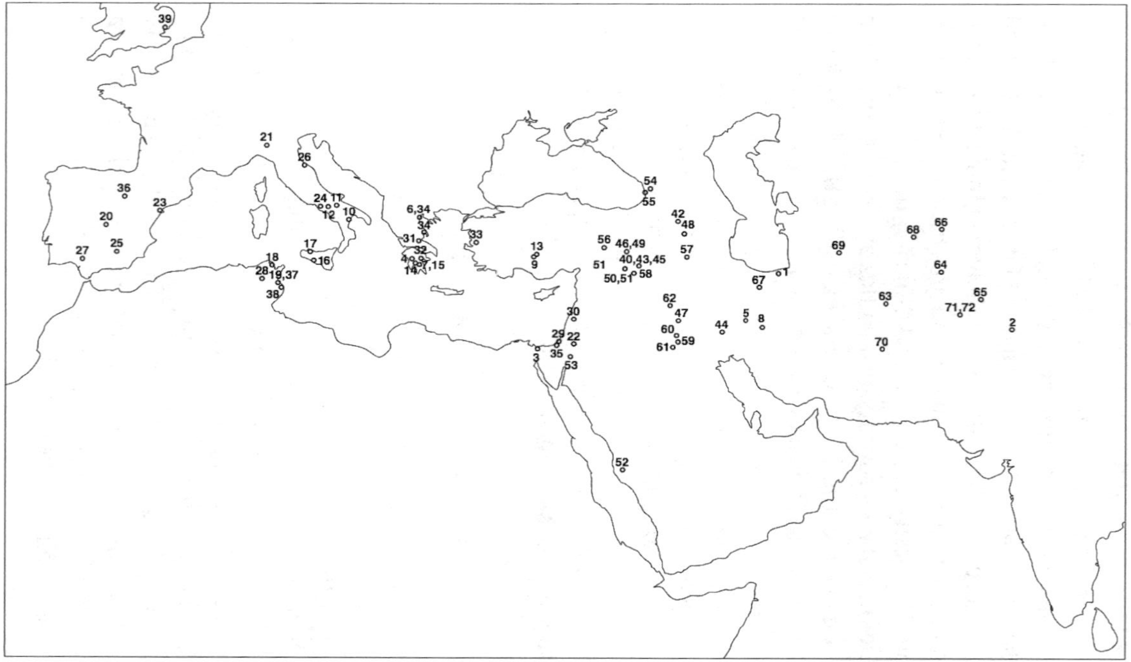

Fig. 6.1: Map of battles and sieges using elephants (in chronological order)

BCE: 1. Hyrcania 530; 2. Jhelum (Hydaspes) 326; 3. Pelusium 321; 4. Megalopolis 318; 5. Paraetacene 317; 6. Pydna (1) 316; 7. Argos (1) 316; 8. Gabiene 316; 9. Ipsus 301; 10. Heraclea 280; 11. Ausculum 279; 12. Beneventum

275; 13. Elephant victory 275; 14. Sparta 272; 15. Argos (2) 272; 16. Agrigentum 262; 17. Panormus 251; 18. Bagradas 239; 19. Utica (1) 238; 20. River Tagus 220; 21. Trebia 218; 22. Raphia 217; 23. Ibera 215; 24. Capua 212; 25. Baecula 208; 26. Metaurus 207; 27. Ilipa 206; 28. Zama 202; 29. Gaza 201; 30. Panium 200; 31. Cynoscephalae 197; 32. Thermopylae 192; 33. Magnesia 190; 34. Pydna (2) 168; 35. Beth Suron 164; 36. Numantia 153; 37. Utica (2) 46; 38. Thapsus 46.

CE: 39. Camulodunum 43; 40. Nisibis (1) 230; 41. Resaina 242; 42. Armenia 297; 43. Nisibis (2) 337; 44. Susa 350; 45. Nisibis (3) 350; 46. Amida (1) 359; 47. Zouma 363; 48. Avarayr 451; 49. Amida (2) 502; 50. Edessa (1) 503; 51. Edessa (2) 544; 52. Mecca 547; 53. Petra 550; 54. Archaeopolis 551; 55. Phasis 555; 56. Melitene 576; 57. Ganzak 591; 58. Arzamon 604; 59. Al-Qaraus 634; 60. Al-Buwayb 635; 61. Al-Qadisiyyah 637; 62. Samarra 977; 63. Khurasan 994; 64. Balkh 1008; 65. Nur and Qirat 1020; 66. Soghd 1025; 67. Ray 1033; 68. Caspian shore 1035; 69. Nasa 1035; 70. Taq 1051; 71. Ghazna 1116; 72. Shahrabad 1117.

elephants.[3] This is despite the fact that it was the time when the war elephant and the four-limbed army had become dominant as an ideal in northern India, and there was inter-state competition whereby Magadha—fortunately located in respect of the supply of elephants—began its progress toward becoming an empire that absorbed its rivals.

The impression of the Indian practice upon Achaemenid Persia, which had no wild elephants upon which to draw, was slight, but there are a few instances preserved in the fragmentary works of Ctesias of Cnidus, Greek physician to the great Achaemenid king Artaxerxes II during the years 415–398/7 BCE. Ctesias wrote accounts of Persia (the *Persika*) and India (the *Indika*). He was the first Greek, and indeed the first non-Indian we know of, to write about the Indian war elephant. Because of his writings Greeks became aware of the Indian war elephant long before Alexander encountered the living thing.[4] At Babylon Ctesias had seen with his own eyes an elephant overturn a palm tree at the command of its Indian mahout.[5] We must suppose both elephant and mahout came from India as a diplomatic gift or payment of tribute. As Nichols says in his commentary upon this passage, "It is likely the elephants Ctesias saw were gifts sent to the Persian king by the Indians. The fact that these elephants came with an Indian trainer shows that the Persians themselves had very little experience in keeping elephants and that the beasts were probably a curiosity for them as well."[6] Ctesias states that Indian kings use war elephants to lead the charge in battle, and to attack and tear down enemy walls when the king so orders, identifying both the main uses to which the Indian war elephant was put.[7] At the court of the king he saw Indian travelers from whom he will have obtained his information about elephants and other animals of India, and indeed all the material for his *Indika*, which was written without

[3] Sami 1954: 20, and plate facing p. 27.
[4] Ctesias 2008: 141; Goukowsky 1972: 474.
[5] Ctesias Fragment 45bα = Aelian 17.29.
[6] Ctesias 2008: 219.
[7] Ibid.

the inconvenience of actually travelling to India.[8] He says of the parrot, for example, that it can converse like a human in "Indian," implying that it was in the care of an Indian handler, but that it can be taught to converse in Greek.[9]

Ctesias records that Cyrus, founder of the empire, encountered the war elephants of Indian allies of the Derbikes of Hyrcania, south of the Caspian Sea. The Derbikes ambushed the Persian cavalry; Cyrus himself was wounded and killed by a javelin thrown by one of the Indians. The year would have been 530 BCE. "Cyrus campaigned against the Derbikes during the reign of Amoraios. By placing their elephants in ambush, the Derbikes repelled the Persian cavalry causing Cyrus himself to fall off his horse at which point an Indian—for the Indians were fighting alongside the Derbikes and supplied their elephants—hit Cyrus after he fell with a javelin below the hip to the bone inflicting a fatal wound . . ."[10] Thus elephants used in war came from India and required Indians to command them in this elephantless region, making both highly desired military assets.

A couple of centuries hence, the Alexander historians record, when Alexander of Macedon defeated him at Gaugamela (331 BCE), Darius III had an Indian contingent of fifteen elephants and others of his own,[11] much like the Derbikes who had incorporated Indians and their elephants in their forces. We could say, then, that Indians and their elephants were present at the creation under Cyrus, and the demise under Darius III, of the great Persian empire of the Achaemenids.

Ctesias' *Persika* starts with six books on the history of Assyria prior to the founding of the Persian empire. I have earlier reviewed the evidence of elephants in the cuneiform records of the Assyrians;[12] we have seen that the Assyrian kings hunted elephants, captured them for display, and took them as tribute before they

[8] Ibid.: 45.

[9] Ctesias, Fragment 45, from Aelian; Ctesias 2008: 45, n. 124.

[10] Ctesias = Aelian, Fragment 9; Ctesias 2008: 90.

[11] Arrian 3.8.8.

[12] In Chapter 2.

became locally extinct, but did not use them for war. Only after Alexander, in the Hellenistic kingdoms of his successors, are war elephants mentioned in cuneiform records. Before the cuneiform script had been deciphered in the nineteenth century, enabling the Assyrian inscriptions to be understood once more, Ctesias' six books in Greek on Assyrian history were what scholars had to rely on. In the nineteenth century, with the cuneiform records accessible, it became apparent that Ctesias' history of Assyria was entirely unreliable, indeed fanciful and wildly inaccurate. Nevertheless, what he says about war elephants in his narrative of the entirely imaginary Assyrian queen Semiramis going to war against Stabrobates, king of the Indians, otherwise unknown to history, is most telling.

Semiramis resolved to conquer the Indians because of the richness of their country:

> When she heard that the nation of the Indians was the greatest in the world and that they possessed the largest and most beautiful land, she resolved to launch a campaign into India where in those days Stabrobates reigned with countless soldiers and an incredible number of elephants, brilliantly adorned with terrifying instruments of war. India is a land of exceeding beauty divided by many rivers; there is water everywhere and it produces harvests twice each year. There is such an abundance of life's necessities that the natives are always provided with plentiful enjoyment. It is said that there has never been a famine or loss of crops in this country because of the good climate. It has an incredible number of elephants far surpassing those in Libya both in forcefulness and bodily strength. There is also an incredible supply of gold, silver, iron and bronze, and in addition to these, there is a large quantity of precious stones of all types as well as nearly everything pertinent to luxury and wealth.[13]

So elephants figure explicitly in this account of the fabulous wealth of India; they are a lure, but also a deterrent, for the Indian king had a large army, including a large body of war elephants, and he captured more wild elephants to train them for battle when he learned the army of Semiramis was approaching. To counter

[13] Ctesias, Fragment 1b = Diod. 2.16.

the elephants, Semiramis had 300,000 black oxen slaughtered and their skins sewn together to make fake elephants that were operated by men on camels over which the skins were draped. In the event, the Indian came to know the elephants were fake and routed the army of Semiramis.[14] We need not linger over the question whether Ctesias made up this story or found it readymade in some folktale about a time long past. What is striking is that it recognizes India as a land of wild elephants and captive elephants used in war; and the realm of the *Persika* is a land lacking elephants to counter the Indians' most distinctive force. In this respect the imaginary history of Semiramis and Strabobates takes place in a world resembling the real one of Ctesias' day.

That being so, for kings west of the Indus to take up the war elephant would have entailed importing them from India (or training up captive elephants from Africa). This happened very rapidly, and in the bright light of history, following the invasion of Alexander of Macedon.

Alexander

Alexander would have known something about elephants from his tutor Aristotle, who had written a good account of elephant physiology based in part on the works of Ctesias.[15] Possibly Alexander was familiar with Ctesias' *Persika*, with its imaginative account of Indian war elephants. At the battle of Gaugamela the quickness of the Macedonian attack appears to have prevented the Persians from properly deploying their elephants and those of their Indian allies, rendering them ineffective. This made an easy introduction to the actual Indian war elephant for Alexander, who seized the elephants of the enemy at Gaugamela, and doubtless their drivers and keepers as well. Throughout the rest of his campaign he was quick to acquire more of both as gifts from Indian allies and tribute from the defeated. He did not deploy

[14] Ctesias, Fragment 1b, Diod. 2.1–28; Ctesias 2008: 64–7.
[15] Scullard 1974: 37–52.

them in battle—perhaps because he did not have time to train his forces in their use—but there is good evidence that his experience of them was a means for him to work out defensive measures *against* war elephants; and this he put to good use during his time in India. However, while the historiography of Alexander tends to magnify his role in producing a mania for war elephants among his successors, he was seizing upon the practice of the Achaemenids, or at any rate of Darius III, which was to take up war elephants and their Indian drivers as a component of his army. According to a study by Bar-Kochva (1976), the army of the Seleucids who succeeded Alexander in the east had both special components of the Persian army of the time—Indian war elephants, and the famous scythed chariots with blades fixed to the hubs.

Elephants figure prominently in the histories of Alexander in India, as I have shown in the previous chapter. They play an important role in the battle formation of king Porus at the battle of the Jhelum—the most fully described and important battle of the Indian campaign—and feature in the great crisis of the expedition, the mutiny of Alexander's troops on the Beas, one reason for the crisis being the expectation that they would have to face numerous large and fierce elephants among the opposition further east. And about 200 elephants are mentioned among the diplomatic gifts and spoils of victory that Alexander collected and brought back with him to Babylon.[16]

Alexander was highly receptive to gifts of elephants and actively sought them as spoils of war. This is nicely illustrated by a passage in Arrian. As mentioned in the previous chapter, while marching to the Indus Alexander determined that Indians of the region, whom the Alexander historians call the Assakenoi, had fled. They had released their elephants to fend for themselves, grazing near the river. Alexander ordered local people to show him the way to the elephants. "Many Indians are hunters of elephants, and Alexander took pains to have them among his attendants, and at this time had

[16] The present-day Jhelum is, in the Alexander historians, the Hydaspes; the Beas is the Hyphasis. In this book I use the modern names.

their help in elephant hunts. Two of the beasts threw themselves over cliffs in the pursuit and perished; the rest were captured, permitted riders to mount them, and were put on the strength of the army."[17] Thus Alexander not only collected elephants, he also took on Indian elephant hunters prior to this incident. He had them, as well as mahouts, at hand when unexpectedly in need of them, meaning that he had acquired the knowledge and skill necessary to capture, train, and deploy war elephants, or at least the practical means to counter them in battle.

The battle of the Jhelum put this newly acquired elephant knowledge to use.[18] The forces of Alexander and Porus were encamped on opposite banks of the Jhelum, the latter's elephants making a direct crossing impossible. After many feints at a point further away, Alexander made a night crossing, some distance upriver, with a substantial force of cavalry and infantry, gaining the opposite bank by dawn. When Porus got wind of this he sent an advance guard of chariots, which however got stuck in the mud and was repulsed. He then drew up a force of 4,000 horse, 300 chariots, 200 elephants, and 30,000 foot soldiers. The *vyūha* he chose, as described by the Alexander historians, would have been, in Indian terms, some species of the staff (*daṇḍa*) array, with elephants to the fore stationed at intervals of 30 meters, the infantry behind, the cavalry and chariots in the wings. According to written battle orders captured after the defeat of Darius at Gaugamela, it appears the elephants were to have been stationed in the same way on that occasion as well, but had not been put in place when the battle began.[19] The similarity suggests the Persians had absorbed and put to use something of the Indian doctrine of battle arrays.

Alexander countered first by avoiding the enemy's strength, the elephants at the center, and relied on his own strong point, the cavalry, to break up the battle array of Porus and throw it into confusion. He massed his cavalry in three groups on his right, next

[17] Arrian 4.30.7–8.

[18] Scullard 1974: 66–71.

[19] Arrian, *History of Alexander* 3.11.3.

to the river. Archers disabled the opposing chariots and a furious cavalry attack drove the enemy wing of cavalry back and into the body of elephants and infantry, causing crowding and chaos. Porus' horses on the far wing came around behind the body of infantry in the center to reinforce the retreating opposite wing of cavalry. But it was pursued by a force of Macedonian horses which attacked it from the rear, so that the Indian cavalry was now crowded together and attacked from both sides. The Macedonian infantry then attacked the elephants with long spears (the *sarissa*), with the braver soldiers dashing in close and attacking the elephants' legs with swords and axes specially made for the purpose. The confusion in the opposing army spread and broke the battle order. Porus, on elephant-back, was captured; when Alexander asked him how he wished to be treated, he said, "As befits a king," whereupon Alexander installed him as governor of the region.[20] What is notable is the prior preparation Alexander made for infantry attacks against the elephants, and the making of special weapons for the purpose.

Elephants figure prominently in the grand crisis of this history—the mutiny of the army at the Beas river.[21] What lay to the east was more war elephants in large armies, principally of the Nandas, who lay in the path of Alexander's grand ambition to find the mouth of the Ganga. His men refused to advance so he turned his army south, down the Indus and through the desert of Gedrosia, back to Babylon, where he died an untimely death at the age of 32. The aftermath of this history was the rapid spread of the war elephant in western Asia, North Africa, and Europe. Alexander's interest in war elephants bore fruit *after* his death. The scramble for the succession among his companions created an arms-race dynamic that propagated the use of war elephants widely across the Hellenistic kingdoms of Asia and Africa, and beyond.

In that aftermath the Indian elephant and its mahout had enormous importance, practical and symbolic. At the very funeral

[20] Arrian 5.19.1–2; Plut. *Alexander* 60.15, 181e, 332e, 485b.
[21] See Chapter 5.

of Alexander, as described by Diodorus,[22] the hearse bore representations of horses and elephants; in particular, "Four long painted tablets exhibited the four arms of the imperial army: infantry, cavalry, navy, and elephants. The latter were no doubt Indian elephants, shown arrayed for war and carrying native mahouts in front and Macedonians fully armed behind them."[23]

Shortly after (320 BCE), Ptolemy issued a coin of Alexander wearing the scalp of an elephant, signifying his victories in India; the elephant become a metonym for India. The image is an evident fiction as the enormous head, trunk, and tusks of the elephant are shrunk down to a size fitting Alexander's head. The image alludes to another coin of Alexander showing, in a more realistic image, Herakles wearing the scalp of a lion. Many images of elephants followed in the coinage of Alexander's successors.[24]

Fig. 6.2: Coin of Alexander wearing an elephant scalp. Tetradrachm of Ptolemy I

Seleucus and Ptolemy

When Alexander died suddenly at Babylon his newly made empire was thrown into a crisis that unfolded over several decades before it settled into a more or less stable international order.[25] As

[22] Diod. 18.27.

[23] Troncoso 2013: 255.

[24] Ibid.: 256; Scullard 1974: Pl. XIII c.

[25] The date and time of Alexander's death—June 11, 323 BCE, about 4.00–5.00 p.m.—has been established by Depuydt 1997.

Alexander had made no provision for the succession, the question fell to the generals, governors of satrapies, and others. The struggle for power was a baffling sequence of short-term alliances among a dozen or so major players called the Successors (*diadochoi*), for whom the royal family of Alexander— consisting of a half-brother, Philip Arrhideus; mother Olympias; Persian queen Roxane; and son Alexander IV born after his father's death—were symbolic capital. Eventually the dozen major players were reduced to three: the kings of Syria, Egypt, and Macedonia. Syria and Egypt came under two of Alexander's generals: Seleucus, who had commanded the infantry that faced the elephants of Porus at the battle of the Jhelum; and Ptolemy, a commander of cavalry. Macedonia went to Antipater. Elephants played a prominent role in the wars of the successors and continued being used in the ensuing period, above all during the rivalry of the Seleucid kings of Syria with the Ptolemies of Egypt.

Pier Armandi, in his *Histoire militaire des éléphants* (1843), found that most aspects of the art of war among the ancients were well served by the scholarship of his day, but not the use of war elephants. This he considered an astonishing lacuna given that, for three centuries from Alexander to Caesar, there was scarcely a war among the countries surrounding the Mediterranean in which elephants did not have a great influence.[26] Manuals of tactics from Greek and Roman antiquity that had survived were written long after the military use of elephants had ended, and so had nothing to impart on that topic. Armandi therefore reconstructed those practices through analysis of the surviving descriptions of battles using elephants. Over a century later E.C. Scullard, a classicist, surveyed this territory anew; his *The elephant in the Greek and Roman world* (1974) has become the standard work. It is not a military history, but it includes descriptions of many battles using elephants, as well as non-military aspects of elephant use. Thanks to these two works and a few others we have a good understanding of the use of war elephants among the Macedonians,

[26] Armandi 1843: i.

Greeks, Romans, and Carthaginians. The entire process was set in motion by Alexander's interest in and collection of war elephants in India, and the fierce warfare over the succession, during which elephants proved valuable military assets, the more so because of their scarcity and the difficulties of acquiring them. War elephants were military gold.

Armandi's allusion to the Greek works on tactics is very apt, as we see from Philip Rance (2003), who has made a study of this body of work. Citing the sixth-century *De re strategica* by an anonymous writer (called by scholars Syrianus Magister), he says the four traditional branches of tactics were infantry, cavalry, chariots, and elephants; but in the surviving post-Hellenistic literature on tactics the last two were not discussed because even the special terminology was obsolete. Rance says it had become a commonplace of the surviving later works on tactics—from Asclepiodotus (*c.* 170–130 BCE) to Aelian (106–113 CE) and Arrian—to state that elephant and chariot warfare had become obsolete.[27] These surviving writings on tactics, which eclipsed earlier works that had discussed elephants and chariots, did not preserve even fragments from earlier writers on these topics because they would have been of no use to monarchs and army generals in their day. This is a great pity, for the older works will have had valuable information on elephant warfare.[28]

It is striking that the lost works on tactics recognized a fourfold division of forces which perfectly replicated the Indian ideal of the army as a four-legged beast (*caturaṅga*). This coincidence of Greek and Indian military theory has not been noted. How do we explain it? The four traditional branches of tactics must reflect the armies of the Hellenistic period, of which elephants had been a part—and chariots too. Although they had become obsolete in

[27] *Ars tactica*, written 138 CE.

[28] In addition to the works mentioned, Rance notes that the *Strategicon* of Maurice (*c.* 590s) does not mention elephants at all; and Vegetius' *Epitoma rei militaris* (late fourth century) explains briefly, in "a largely antiquarian chapter," how elephants and scythed chariots can be countered in battle: Rance 2003: 358–9.

Greece, they had remained in use, to some extent, in the Middle East, the old homeland of the chariot, as well as in India. The doctrine of the four branches corresponds well to the army of Seleucus in the analysis of Bar-Kochva (1976), for example. I believe that the four traditional branches of Greek works on tactics came about not by direct borrowing from the Indian doctrine of the *caturaṅga-bala*, but, just as happened in India, by the addition of the war elephant to a threefold army of infantry, cavalry, and chariots.

Battle descriptions show the great influence of the battle of the Jhelum and the manner in which Porus arranged his elephants at intervals in front of the infantry. In the battles of the Mediterranean peoples elephants were often deployed in this way, spaced out in front of the center or wings or both. They were deployed to scatter the infantry, cause terror in horses unused to their sight and smell, storm lines of fieldworks, dismantle entrenchments, and batter defensive walls during sieges. It was a trope of the literature that elephants could be maddened and become a danger to their own side.[29] There was much experimentation with defensive measures against war elephants, of which iron caltrops to immobilize or make them lame were quite effective, and counter-measures in the form of elephant armor.

There was also an important innovation in the shape of the "tower" or box (Gk. *thōrakion*) from which fighters on elephant-back had both protection and a solid platform from which to hurl their weapons. Paul Goukowsky (1972) has shown that this was a Hellenistic innovation, not a borrowing from the Indians who, as he rightly says, rode astraddle. This accords with what we have found in the epics, in which riding an elephant is a skill that warriors have to learn, distinct from the art of wielding weapons; and is represented so in sculpture at early sites such as Sanchi. On the Hellenistic side, Goukowsky drew attention to a coin, perhaps of Alexander himself, minted at Babylon, of which three have survived, celebrating the victory at the battle of the Jhelum.

[29] Rance 2003: 360.

It depicts Porus riding astraddle on an elephant, with a mahout on its neck holding an *aṅkuśa*, pursued by Alexander on horseback.[30] There is no howdah. The tower, then, was a Hellenistic invention unknown in India or Babylon in the time of Alexander, becoming evident in battles of the Hellenistic period after Alexander's death. Goukowsky dates the invention of the tower to the period 300–280 BCE and is inclined to attribute it to Pyrrhus or his engineers. Its purpose was to overcome the difficulty of warriors maintaining their balance when the elephant moved at speed—at a gallop as he says, though elephants do not truly gallop for they must at all times have three feet on the ground when moving.

Goukowsky's article is not known among Indianists, who have largely assumed the existence of the howdah from early times. Consequently, the problem of the invention of the howdah has gone unremarked, or is at best poorly addressed; and it will be a gain to state the problem clearly, even if I cannot solve it at this time.

Goukowsky believes that the Indians adapted the Hellenistic tower to their own needs as the modern howdah,[31] perhaps through the Seleucid satrapy of Bactria. But as he provides no evidence from contemporary Indian sources, his theory of such Indian adaptation of a Greek invention lacks evidence. And insofar as his interpretation rests upon the lack of elephant-riding skills among Greek and Macedonian fighters—such skills having in India been a specific part of military education—there seems no evident incentive for the Indians to have borrowed the Hellenistic tower. Moreover, the linguistic evidence not only does not support such a borrowing, it suggests an entirely different line of investigation.

The word howdah (Hindi *hauda*) is from Arabic *haudaj*, which implies a late formation, during or after the Muslim incursions in India. Moreover, the Arabic word referred originally to a platform on the back of a camel as a seat for the caliph or for a woman.[32] This implies not only a considerably later origin but

[30] Scullard 1974: pl. XIIIa, b.

[31] Goukowsky 1972: 492.

[32] Azfar Moin, personal communication; Yule 1968: 427; Wilson 1855: 203.

also a different function from the Greek tower. While the latter was a firm platform for warriors unskilled in riding bareback on an elephant, the howdah functions rather as a seat of honor for a person of high dignity.

The Indian evidence is little studied. Hopkins considers mention of the howdah in the epics as probably later additions; he elicits a passage in the *Mahābhārata* in which the howdah is mentioned under the name *vimāna*, but the passage in question is not found in the Critical Edition and is therefore likely to be more recent, as he proposes.[33] Moreover, I am unable to find support in the dictionaries for this meaning of *vimāna,* which from early times means the aerial chariot of a god—flying through the air, a veritable flying palace—a meaning which *does* appear in the epics in connection with the gods and Rāvaṇa, whose *vimāna* of seven stories was called *puṣpaka*, adorned with flowers.[34] What, then, is the Sanskrit word for howdah? Hopkins gives *varaṇḍaka* as the later word. This is confirmed by the dictionaries, but they give no textual citation outside the ancient lexicons.[35] Turner's *Comparative dictionary of Indo-Aryan* gives no reflexes of Sanskrit *vimāna* or *varaṇḍaka* in the meaning of howdah in modern languages.[36] Thus we have no references to howdahs in the epics, none in later Sanskrit literature referenced in the dictionaries, no reported reflexes of a Sanskrit word for howdah in modern Indian languages, and by contrast the use of a word of Arabic origin in Hindi and doubtless other languages. All of these

[33] "The great chiefs, princes, kings, mount elephants so rarely that we may be entitled to infer that the practice of a king's fighting from a great howdah (*vimāna*) on an elephant's back is later than the other methods of car-fighting, and that mention of it will be among the later additions. That was probably first customary in peaceful jaunts, and then extended to war; the latter must have been synchronous with the abdication of warrior prowess in the main; yet we find a few instances of elephants being ridden in war, notably by the Yavana prince . . . In vii.115.55 *vimāna* is howdah (later *varaṇḍaka*)." Hopkins 1889: 266–7 and 268, fn.

[34] Monier-Williams 1899; Böhtlingk and Roth 1855.

[35] Ibid.

[36] Turner 1966: 659, 11317 *varaṇḍa-*, 686, 11823 *vimāna*.

require further investigation, and it would be essential to survey visual representations of war elephants in Indian sculpture and painting through the centuries to fix the time of its advent.[37] For the present, I do not say that the howdah is an Arab or Muslim invention, only that it is likely to be an invention of the times at which Muslim armies made contact with India. As we will see,[38] the howdah is clearly present in the twelfth-century reliefs of the Khmer army at Angkor Wat, where it serves, indeed, as a seat of dignity for the king and his chieftains, not common warriors.

What we need to investigate is not the military use of elephants but the underlying logistics of their use. How did this three-century arms race acquire the elephants that fueled it? And how did it get the technical and practical knowledge of elephants that made it possible? Information on supplies of elephants and knowledge relating to their upkeep and use in war are both needed, and the war elephant embodies their unity. It will be useful to keep the questions of supply and knowledge separate.

In the first phase, the source of supply is clear. The herd of some 200 elephants that Alexander took to Babylon was seized and used in the wars of the Successors. In 317 BCE fresh stock in the amount of 120 elephants was brought into the succession struggle by Eudamus, the leading Macedonian official in the east, who murdered Porus and took all his elephants; Eudamus was called the elephant hegemon.[39] But the most spectacular addition to the stock came into the possession of Seleucus, who acquired 500 elephants from Candragupta of the Maurya dynasty; Candragupta had control of the more populous elephant forests of the east, the Prācya Vana of the *Arthaśāstra*. These elephants made Seleucus' fortune. The number given is so large that it has been challenged and requires close scrutiny.

[37] Geer 2008: 189–225 is a chapter on the Indian elephant in a survey of sculptural representations of Indian mammals. It is a useful starting point, but its survey of these materials does not advance knowledge of the howdah.

[38] In Chapter 7, Fig. 7.6.

[39] Heckel 2006: 120, citing Diod. 19.4.8, Plut., *Eumenes* 16.3; Bosworth 2002: 107.

Appian discussed the Syrian wars in his history of Rome. He said Antigonus declared himself king after the death of the last members of Alexander's family. Seleucus, Ptolemy, and others formed an alliance against Antigonus. Seleucus became master of all Syria from the Euphrates river to the sea, and inland Phrygia. Over time he also acquired Mesopotamia, Armenia, Seleucid Cappadocia, Persis, Parthia, Bactria, Arabia, Tapouria, Sogdia, Arachosia, Hircania, "and adjacent peoples that had been subdued by Alexander, as far as the river Indus," which meant that "the boundaries of his empire were the most extensive in Asia after that of Alexander." These vast territories abutted the growing empire of Candragupta Maurya. "The whole region from Phrygia to the Indus was subject to Seleucus. He crossed the Indus and waged war with Androcottus (Candragupta), king of the Indians, who dwelt on the banks of that stream, until they came to an understanding with each other and contracted a marriage relationship. Some of these exploits were performed before the death of Antigonus and some afterward."[40] Strabo specifies the terms of the treaty of peace with Candragupta: Seleucus ceded Arachosia, Gedrosia, Paropamisadae, and perhaps Aria, and Candragupta gave him 500 elephants.[41] This was before the death of Antigonus at the decisive battle of Ipsus, 301 BCE, because the 500 elephants were the means of Seleucus' success in that struggle. Early on in this context Seleucus was jokingly called Ruler of Elephants (*elephantarches*), as if to say he had more elephants than people under his rule.[42] His ownership of elephants was certainly the means by which he consolidated his rule over a very large population of humans.

Candragupta had overthrown the Nandas and taken over their empire, which in Alexander's time in India was confined to the east and did not reach the Indus valley. Appian's testimony implies that the westward expansion of Candragupta's empire now reached the Indus, and that Seleucus, on his eastward expansion—perhaps seeking to recapture Alexander's Indian

[40] Appian 11.55.
[41] Strabo 15.2.9.
[42] Plut., *Demetrius* 25.

possessions—came up against the Mauryan king, with whom he reached an accommodation which seems to have been to the advantage of both. Seleucus ceded a vast territory, comprising most of what is now Afghanistan, plus southern Pakistan: the region of present-day Kabul (Paropamisadae), Kandahar (Arachosia), and Herat (Aria); and the Makran coast of Pakistan in the province of Baluchistan (Gedrosia).[43] Seleucus, however, retained the satrapy of Bactria, which became the means of access to India for his successors. The largeness of the territory he ceded to Candragupta has provoked some scholarly doubts. Vincent Smith, who marshaled the sources for analysis, convincingly supported the veracity of the territorial cession.[44] The discovery in 1958 at Kandahar (also known in ancient times as Alexandria) of an inscription of Candragupta's grandson Aśoka, written in Greek and Aramaic, confirmed the accuracy of the ancient testimony.[45] In exchange for this large territorial concession Seleucus got a large body of elephants, which ensured the success of his growing power at the battle of Ipsus. Five hundred elephants is a great many, but the number is not impossible if we remember that the Mauryan homeland had the most numerous (and best quality), and that according to the account of Megasthenes the king held a monopoly of elephants.[46]

The Mauryans seem to have become from this time the regular suppliers of elephants to the Seleucids.[47] The other direct mention of Seleucid–Mauryan dealings in elephants comes a century later,

[43] See Fig. 5.3, the map of the Mauryan empire.

[44] Smith 1924: 158–60: "The extent of the cession of Ariāna by Seleukos Nikator to Chandragupta Maurya."

[45] Schlumberger, *et al.* 1958.

[46] Hartmut Scharfe (1971) argued that Candragupta capitulated to Seleucus, that the 500 elephants were in the nature of tribute, and that the four provinces were not ceded to him but put under his charge as satrap under Seleucus. The argument hinges upon the interpretation of the title *devānampiya* (usually taken to mean "beloved of the gods") by his grandson Aśoka, connecting it with a Hellenistic title, "friend of the kings." Scharfe is the first modern scholar, and so far the only one, to draw this conclusion. If it is true one wonders why the sources do not say it plainly.

[47] This paragraph draws upon Trautmann 1982.

in the period 212–205 BCE, which the Seleucid king Antiochus III spent asserting his authority over the eastern satrapies. During this time he concluded a peace with Demetrius, son of Euthydemus of Bactria, "accepting the elephants belonging to Euthydemus. He crossed the Caucasus and descended into India; renewed his friendship with Sophagasenus, the king of the Indians; received more elephants, until he had 150 altogether; and having once more provisioned his troops set out again personally with his army, leaving Androsthenes of Cyzicus the duty of taking home the treasure which this king had agreed to hand over to him."[48] Sophagasenus (= Subhagasena?) is not known from Indian sources, but as king of the Indians he is clearly a Mauryan emperor and not a petty raja.

It is unlikely that the Mauryan supply of elephants to the Seleucids was limited to these two occasions. For example, Antiochus III himself had had only 10 elephants when he faced Molon, rebellious governor of Media, in 221 BCE, but appeared at the battle of Raphia in 217 BCE with 102 elephants, and lost nearly all of them. Between the two dates he must have got more from India, as Polybius perhaps indicates when he says of the later period that Antiochus *renewed* his friendship with the Maurya. Earlier still, perhaps in 277 BCE, Antiochus I urgently sent to his satrap of Bactria for 20 elephants, which we can surmise were ultimately of Mauryan origin. Astronomical diaries from Babylonia record another such consignment of 20 elephants from the satrap of Bactria in the year 273 BCE.[49]

At least two ambassadors were sent by the Seleucids to the Mauryas,[50] Megasthenes to Candragutpa and Deimachus to his son Bindusāra. Both ambassadors wrote accounts of India, though only fragments remain. The Megasthenes fragments, as we have seen, are quite substantial, and show that his *Indika* paid great attention to the structure of the army, the royal monopoly of elephants, horses, and arms, and the method of capturing wild

[48] Polybius 11.34.

[49] Mentioned in the discussion of kings of Assyria, Chapter 2.

[50] Or the Seleucids and the satrap Sibyrtius: see Chapter 5, fn. 17.

elephants. The overall pattern, then, is of great interest on the part of the Seleucids in maintaining a supply of elephants from India through diplomatic relations with the Mauryas. In this they made good use of their satrapy of Bactria which, while it probably had no wild elephants of its own, was adjacent to India and more conducive for the passage of captive elephants to Babylon. The Bactrian satrapy eventually became an independent kingdom about the time that inner Asian Iranian nomads, the Parthians, made their inroads and took over Persia. The Parthians had only a limited interest in elephants. They interposed a barrier between the elephants of India and peoples to the west, especially the Seleucids, who depended upon them.

Ptolemy and Seleucus had been allies against Antigonus, but inevitably they became rivals once the common enemy was out of the picture. The object of rivalry was the rich southern coast of Syria, called Coele-Syria, over which they and their descendants fought. As the Seleucids had direct access to India through their satrapy of Bactria, the Ptolemies of Egypt were effectively denied access to Indian elephants, except those they acquired in battle. They were at a distinct disadvantage in their relations with the Seleucids, therefore, and in urgent need of a solution to the problem of supply. Ptolemy II Philadelphos, son and successor of the founder of the dynasty, is said to have sent an ambassador, Dionysus, to India. This would have been in the time of Bindusāra or, more likely, Aśoka. What would have been the objective of that embassy? Pliny states blandly that Dionysus was to write a description of the land.[51] But in the light of Ptolemy's drive to acquire and train African elephants I consider Casson's suggestion plausible, that Ptolemy, cut off from overland access to the elephants of India, would have sought hunters and trainers of elephants from there to help him establish his own operation,[52] much as Alexander in India had taken on Indian elephant hunters to round up the wandering elephants of the Assakenoi.

[51] Pliny 6.58; Casson 1993: 251.

[52] Casson 1993: 251.

The presence of Indian elephant men is evident in the documents. The most important datum is that it was Hellenistic usage to call the mahout, simply, "the Indian" (*Indos*); that is, "Indian" was given the specialized meaning of elephant driver. This usage is not found in the times of Alexander, since the Alexander historians use other terms. "The Indian" became a regular term for the mahout in the historians of the Hellenistic period following the death of Alexander. In Diodorus, Book 17, which gives the history of Alexander, we do not find "the Indian" used in this meaning, but we find it in Book 18, covering the Hellenistic period.[53] In some accounts of Hellenistic battles the elephant and its "Indian" alone constitute the military unit for pulling down fortifications or sowing terror among infantry. But more often we read in battlefield descriptions of the war elephant bearing two or three fighters—Macedonian or Greek—plus "the Indian." The dictionary of Hesychius defined *Indos* as "he who leads elephants from Aithiopia,"[54] indicating the Ptolemaic capture and training operation. Thus there is no doubt that Indian personnel were employed by the kings of this period.

This is a most telling fact, testifying that the Hellenistic kings acquired the knowledge essential for elephant handling by getting hold of Indian mahouts, and also hunters and perhaps others—though not elephant warriors, who were Macedonian or Greek. As we have seen, Goukowsky suggests that because such riders found it difficult to maintain their seat when the elephant was moving at speed, the tower was invented to give them a secure platform from which to fight.

As to the mahouts, the dictionary of Hesychius records two Greek reflexes of their equipment, one a word for the ever-present *aṅkuśa*, the other for *kandara*, another word for the same thing or something similar.[55] There are other Greek words from Indian

[53] Goukowsky 1972: 483.

[54] Goosens 1943: 52n.

[55] Gk. *angorpe*, a combination of *aṅku(śa)* and *orpe*, dialectical variant of *harpe*; and *gandara* (Goosens 1944).

languages that come from the military, such as an equivalent of Sanskrit *niveśana*, an army camp. The very word *mahāmātra* appears in a Greek plural, *mamatrai*; however, Hesychius does not define it as mahout, but as a general (*strategos*) among the Indians, perhaps something like a satrap, an office with civil and military aspects.[56] It is likely, as several scholars have averred, that locals were eventually trained to be mahouts, and that mahouts of other nationalities continued to be called Indians in a military though not ethnic sense. It would have been very difficult to establish a sufficient community of Indian mahouts to perpetuate itself, or to acquire fresh supplies of them so far from India. But we must suppose that Indian mahouts passed on their embodied knowledge to local apprentices, much as will have happened in India during the initial spread of the war elephant from its point of origin to other kingdoms in the subcontinent.

Ptolemy Philadelphos, then, set about capturing and training African elephants of Eritrea and Ethiopia and perhaps Lybia, with hunting stations formed along the coast of the Red Sea. About halfway down the coast they established Ptolemais of the Huntings (Ptolemais Theron) as a station from which the hunt set out. Elephants were brought here for shipment, ways having been found to convey elephants by boat up the Red Sea to the capital.[57]

Along this coast, according to Agatharcides, lived various tribal peoples he called Fish-eaters (Icthyphagoi), while inland were various others including the Elephant-eaters (Elephantophagoi). The different kinds of Elephant-eaters used different hunting methods, two of which seem, at a stretch, plausible: hamstringing

[56] Ibid. Earlier writers on Indian material in the dictionary of Hesychius, apparently unknown to Goosens, are Gray and Schuyler (1901), whose identifications are mostly wrong, and Lüders (1905), who identifies *mamatrai* with *mahāmātra*. Goosens' identifications are convincing, except for his tortured explanation of *pirissas*, a word for elephant in Hesychius, which Goosens identifies as a Prakrit form of *puruṣa* in the meaning of "male (elephant)." But it is probably connected with Akkadian *pīru*.

[57] Casson 1993; Burstein 2008.

with an ax and poisoned arrows. The third seems absurd, resting on a false idea about elephant physiology. Elephants, he says, like to sleep leaning against a tree because they have no joints in their legs and cannot get up if they happen to lie down. Such trees were partially sawn by hunters, so that when leaned against by elephants they snapped, the elephants fell and could not rise.[58] In the bestiaries of medieval Europe this story was a great favorite: it was put out that "nature hath given him no knees to bend," a belief that can be sustained only if one has never seen a live elephant.[59]

However that may be, there is a passage in Agatharcides that nicely expresses the difference between the regime of hunting elephants to eat them and hunting for war elephants: "Ptolemy king of Egypt ordered these [Elephant-eater] hunters by an edict to refrain from killing elephants, so that he himself might be able to have them alive; and he promised them great rewards for obedience. But not only could he not persuade them to obey, but they answered that they would not change their mode of subsistence for the whole kingdom of Egypt."[60] Ptolemy Philadelphos was attempting to impose a regime similar to the one we find in the *Arthaśāstra* concerning elephant forests—keeping wild elephants from being hunted for food or ivory so that they could be captured live and trained for war. Equally telling is

[58] Agatharcides 56.

[59] Carrington (1959) has much material on this amusing error, including this verse from John Donne (*Progress of the soul*, 39):

Natures great master-peece, an Elephant,
The onely harmlesse great thing: the giant
Of beasts; who thought, no more had gone, to make one wise
But to be just, and thankfull, loth to offend,
(Yet nature hath given him no knees to bend)
Himselfe he up-props, on himselfe relies,
And foe to none, suspects no enemies,
Still sleeping stood; vex't not his fantasie
Blacke dreames; like an unbent bow, carelessly
His sinewy Proboscis did remisly lie.

[60] Agatharcides 56.

the hunters' refusal to give up their way of life in exchange for rewards, even impossibly large ones: hunter-gatherers refusing the whole kingdom of Egypt—in a word, farming, kingship, civilization. The inner logic of this failed attempt to get forest people to stop hunting elephants for food jibes with the policy the *Arthaśāstra* recommends. Though the Ptolemies failed, because they could not enforce their wishes upon these forest people, the logic of the policy and its appearance in such distant places as India and Egypt confirm the hypothesis that the institution of the war elephant promotes a turning away from the ages-old hunting of wild elephants for food and ivory.

In spite of this lack of cooperation the hunting of elephants and training them for war went on. The Ptolemies almost certainly had the benefit of Indian mahouts in this process, and perhaps hunters and trainers too; they also appointed Greek officials to direct the operations. Furthermore, the inland kingdom of Meroe, above the fifth cataract of the Nile, which had wild elephants, captured and trained them for use, probably with the help of Indian mahouts. We have from Meroe a relief of one of their kings astride an elephant, riding bareback (Fig. 6.3). Very likely the Meroese culture of elephant-use reflects that of the Ptolemies, and it is tempting to

Fig. 6.3: Relief of elephant with king, Meroe

think they may have been a source of elephants and mahouts to them. Unfortunately, although the inscriptions of Meroe are in a known writing system, like the Etruscan inscriptions we cannot read them because we do not know the language in which they are written.[61]

Once the Ptolemies brought African elephants head-to-head with Asian ones in battles with the Seleucids, the differences between them became apparent. Contrary to what we expect, the Hellenistic sources regularly say that the Asian elephant was larger and stronger than the African. Polybius described the battle of Raphia, in the Fourth Syrian war, fought between Ptolemy V Philopater and Antiochus III in 217 BCE, to which Ptolemy brought 73 elephants and Antiochus 102. Polybius says:

> The way in which elephants fight is this. With the tusks firmly interlocked and entangled they push against each other with all their might, each trying to force the other to give ground, until the one who proves the strongest pushes aside the other's trunk, and then, when he has once made him turn, he gores him with his tusks as a bull does with his horns. Now most of Ptolemy's elephants were afraid to join battle, as is the habit of African elephants; for unable to stand the smell and the trumpeting of the Indian elephants, and terrified, I suppose, also by their great size and strength, they immediately run away from them before they get near them. This is what happened on the present occasion; and when Ptolemy's elephants were thus thrown into confusion and driven back on their own lines Ptolemy's Agema gave way under the pressure of the animals.[62]

The claim that Indian (or Asian) elephants are larger than the African was accepted through all antiquity, and into modern times. Toward the end of the nineteenth century, when Europeans became familiar with the very large African elephants of the sub-Saharan savanna, this came to be seen as erroneous. But as Gowers (1947, 1948) showed in a pair of classic articles, there are two types of African elephant, not one: the forest elephant and the savanna elephant. The former is indeed smaller than the Asian elephant

[61] Shinnie 1967.

[62] Polybius in Scullard 1974: 142–3.

while the latter is distinctly larger. There is good reason to think that the elephants of Eritrea, Ethiopia, and Sudan were of the forest type, as also the elephants of the foothills of the Atlas mountains, which the Carthaginians captured and trained, following the example of the Ptolemies of Egypt.[63]

In the passage quoted above we see that elephant-on-elephant warfare follows the manner of fighting among wild bull elephants, pushing head-to-head and trying to turn the flank of the opponent. The mahouts in this case are guiding elephants to do in human warfare what they would in the wild for their own, very different, purposes.

Carthaginians

Carthage, the Phoenician city-state near present-day Tunis, controlled a growing empire consisting of much of North Africa, Spain, Corsica, and a bit of Sicily. Rome controlled the Italian peninsula through a confederacy. The two growing powers were bound to clash, and after a titanic struggle for more than a century, i.e. the three Punic Wars of 264–146 BCE, Rome finally prevailed and extinguished its adversary.

Carthage had been using elephants in warfare before the conflict started, as early as 262 BCE. It had acquired and trained elephants from Numidia and Mauretania (modern Algeria and Morocco), which is to say the foot of the Atlas mountains. This population was likely to have been of forest African elephants, similar to

[63] Deraniyagala (1955: 28, citing *Spolia Zeylanica* 1948: 27 and pl. 10; Yalden, *et al.* 1986: 46) proposed a race of North African elephants, *Loxodonta africanus pharaoensis*, used by the Ptolemies and Carthaginians, that went extinct centuries ago. Brandt, *et al.* (2013) conducted a genetic study of the isolated population of elephants, numbering about a hundred, in Eritrea today. They conclude that the Eritrean elephants are like the savanna elephants and not like the forest elephants. They take the elephants of present-day Eritrea to be the same race of elephants the Ptolemies captured and trained two thousand years earlier, and claim to have refuted Gowers; but they do not give evidence of the supposed continuity. What is needed is to join genetics with the excavated remains of elephants of pre-dynastic Egypt (discussed in Chapter 2), and the historical sources.

those found south of the Sahara in the basin of the Congo, as I have said.[64] It is thought that the increasing warming and drying conditions following the end of the last ice age caused the Sahara to form and grow, leaving islands of forest elephants north of the desert, separated from the main body in the humid forests to the south.

We do not have much information about how the Carthaginians mastered the art of capturing and training wild elephants, but we may surmise that they followed the example of the Ptolemies and perhaps had their assistance. They must also have had the help of some Indian mahouts, also probably from Egypt. In any case the size and proficiency of the operation, as judged by its outcome, is impressive: "Having so decided they went about it on a generous scale: they had 50 or 60 [elephants] by 263 BC. After losing these to the Romans they had another 100 in 256, and 140 in 255. Whatever may be thought of the figure of 200 attributed to Asdrubel in Spain and of the stables allegedly for 300 elephants built in the walls of Carthage itself, the Carthaginians obviously, once they had adopted this new arm, decided to use it fully."[65] What is more, they somehow managed to transport substantial numbers of elephants by sea to Sicily and Spain, unprecedented in the distance traversed, a credit both to their navy and elephant handlers. As a result the Carthaginians were able to bring elephants to Spain and Italy for their wars against the Romans.

The most spectacular and best known of the Carthaginians' use of elephants was that of Hannibal at the outset of the Second Punic War. He brought thirty-seven elephants from Spain across the Rhone and over the Alps into Italy. Both terrains were exceedingly difficult. Hannibal prepared rafts to ferry the elephants across the Rhone, covering them with earth and using females to lure the males aboard; but the elephants panicked and fell into the river. Elephants, however, are good swimmers and got through. The crossing of the Alps was difficult both because of the terrain and

[64] Gowers 1947, 1948.
[65] Scullard 1974: 148.

the intense cold. Somehow Hannibal managed to get all thirty-seven over with his infantry and cavalry.

In one engagement described by Appian, Hannibal attacked the sleeping Roman soldiers of Fulvius in their camp, using elephants and mahouts alone, without mounted warriors.

> Then he ordered his Indians to mount their elephants and break into the camp of Fulvius through the open spaces, and over the piles of earth, in any way they could. He also directed a number of trumpeters and horn-blowers to follow at a short distance. When the Indians should be inside the entrenchments some of them were ordered to run around and raise a great tumult so that they might seem to be very numerous, while others, speaking Latin, should call out that Fulvius, the Roman general, ordered the evacuation of the camp and the seizure of the neighboring hill.[66]

Had it succeeded, the stratagem would have led the Romans into an ambush. We cannot know if these Latin-knowing elephant drivers called Indians were from India or not; possibly they were North African mahouts who learned the trade from Indian mahouts.

The elephants were instrumental in Hannibal's victory at Trebia, but numbers of them were killed by the enemy and others died of the cold. Gradually the herd grew smaller until only one remained, which Hannibal himself rode. The Romans under their general Fabius avoided battle and relied on ambush and small-scale guerrilla actions, so that the war became a drawn-out stalemate. Hannibal and his army remained in Italy for over sixteen years, 221–204 BCE. Reinforcements could not reach him, nor could he be defeated. He ravaged the countryside but was unable to take the cities, and the Romans, who were unable to expel him, avoided pitched battles and harried his forces. Finally they attacked his home city, Carthage, to draw him out of Italy, and at the battle of Zama near their capital the Carthaginians, under their greatest general, were defeated by the forces under Scipio (later titled "Africanus" for his victory). The Carthaginians had to accept the Roman terms, one of the clauses of the treaty of peace being

[66] Appian 7.7.41.

to surrender all their elephants and not capture and train more. Elephants were absent from the third and final Punic War, at the conclusion of which the Romans destroyed the city of Carthage.

The Carthaginian elephant most famous among the Romans was named Surus, proably meaning "the Syrian," though almost certainly an Indian elephant. He was immediately identifiable by his one broken tusk and was known for his energy in battle. He would have been acquired from Egypt and may have been the elephant upon which Hannibal rode during his Italian campaign.[67]

The Carthaginians showed enormous enterprise and organizational skill by implementing an elephant hunting and training operation, devising effective means of moving them by sea further than anyone hitherto, and deploying them in war.

Greeks and Romans

Pyrrhus (318–272 BCE), king of Epirus, a cousin of Alexander and connected by marriage to Macedon, Ptolemaic Egypt, and Syracuse in Sicily, is considered one of the great generals of antiquity. But he is also the original of the proverbial pyrrhic victory, a win so costly it is scarcely distinguishable from defeat. Pyrrhus typifies intemperate and overreaching ambition.

Epirus lay opposite the Greek settlements in southern Italy comprising Magna Graecia, which lay in the path of the expanding confederacy led by Rome. In 281 BCE Tarentum, one of the Greek cities there, appealed to Pyrrhus to lead their struggle against Rome, and in alliance with Macedon he formed an army for the purpose. This army had twenty elephants from Ptolemy II Philadelphos, which he used against the Romans to brilliant effect. He won costly victories at Herculaneum (280 BCE) and Asculum (279 BCE). The Greek cities of Sicily then appealed to him to free them from Carthage, and he accepted. But the struggle was long and his exactions to defray the expenses of war became so great

[67] Scullard 1974: 174–7; Sukumar 2011: 82.

that some of the Greek cities went over to the Carthaginians. Pyrrhus imposed a military dictatorship that proved deeply unpopular; but then Rome recruited fresh troops and enlarged its army, and Pyrrhus went to Italy to oppose the Roman expansion. After the battle of Beneventum (275 BCE) Pyrrhus was obliged to abandon Italy and return to Greece. He succeeded in wresting control of Macedon from Antigonas Gonatas; failed to place a pretender, Cleonymus, on the throne of Sparta; and died in a botched invasion of Argos, where he was intervening in a local conflict. His elephants panicked and blocked the narrow city streets of Argos, and Pyrrhus himself was killed when he was hit on the head by a tile thrown by a woman on a roof overlooking the street.[68]

Thanks to Pyrrhus the Romans were introduced to war elephants for the first time, which in some measure prepared them for the elephants of Carthage in the Punic Wars that followed. After their defeat at Herculaneum the Romans devised wagons with various devices to counter elephants, including an upright beam with transverse movable pole that had, at the end, tridents, spikes, or scythes with which to attack the animal from a safe distance. They did not prove very effective, but the Romans continued to devise counter-measures; repeated encounters took away the surprise and some of their terror.

Pyrrhus had had to get his 20 elephants and 25,000 men across to Italy, which at the Straits of Otranto, the narrowest point, was 40 miles. Scullard considers this possibly the longest sea journey of elephants to that time, the technical difficulties of which would have been formidable.[69] Not long after, the Ptolemies began transporting African elephants on the Red Sea. In the event, Pyrrhus' crossing encountered a storm and many had to swim ashore, but the army including the elephant corps was largely intact. In subsequent times the Carthaginians would undertake further feats of seaborne elephant transport, as we have seen.

[68] Scullard 1974: 101–19.
[69] Ibid.: 102–3.

Romans acquired captive elephants in battle during the Punic Wars and denied them to Carthage by sequestering their entire stock at the conclusion of the Second war. But they did not have reliable access to freshly caught elephants until, at the conclusion of the Third Punic War, Africa became a Roman province. Thereafter the Romans had African elephants from the source, in Numidia and Mauretania. It was only then that the Romans used them in battle, employing them to good effect in their expansion through the Hellenistic world against other elephant-using powers. They found that small numbers of elephants from their Numidian allies could be effective against barbarian nations that had not seen them before, notably the Celtiberians in Spain, and in southern Gaul, which became a Roman province (Provence, in France). There are testimonies of uncertain validity that elephants were used by Julius Caesar and Claudius to impress the natives in faraway Britain, though not as an instrument of war but as a royal mount, a *raja-vāhana*.[70] If the accounts are true they represent the farthest reach of the Indian model of kingship.

The last known Roman use of elephants in battle is by Julius Caesar, at Thapsus, 46 BCE, in his struggles against Pompey. Caesar, and Rome, acquired control of North Africa and soon extinguished the rule of the Hellenistic kings, Seleucid as well as Ptolemaic, who had used elephants against the Romans. To the east, the Parthians, Iranian-speaking nomads from Central Asia who had a horse-based army and were indifferent to war elephants, established their empire, replacing the Seleucids and coming up against the growing empire of Rome. The Parthians interposed a barrier between India and the Mediterranean world, bringing to a close the import of war elephants from India. Scullard says, "The Romans had fought their last battle with elephants for some 300 years."[71] After those three centuries the Roman empire faced the army of the Sassanians, successors to the Parthians, who resumed the use of war elephants in Iran, although the Romans, in their

[70] Ibid.: 194, 198–9.
[71] Ibid.: 197.

many wars with them, did not. The initial impetus for the arms race had been Asian elephants from India. These had advantaged Seleucus and others against the Ptolemies, who had countered them by developing methods of turning African elephants into elephants of war. Once the Romans finished them off they stopped using the war elephant and never took it up again.

Thus the Romans did not need war elephants in their struggles with enemies to the east, the Parthians, in the way that the Ptolemies had needed to capture and train African elephants to counter the Asian elephants of the Seleucids. Nevertheless, the Romans, having overtaken the source of African elephants and their specialized paraphernalia, were in a position to perpetuate an already formed complex. Instead they allowed it to die. Having done so, it would have been very difficult to restart it centuries later when they confronted Sassanian war elephants, even had they wanted to. It is worth asking why the Romans dismantled the machinery of the North African war elephant after mastering and utilizing it.

I can only say that the Romans seem to have been more enthusiastic about devising measures to play defense *against* the war elephant than to play offense *with* the war elephant. This attitude may account for the fact that they stopped using them at the very moment when they had the whole specialized complex in their hands, for they reached this consummation by the destruction of the elephant-using Carthaginians, Ptolemies, and Seleucids. It was well known to the Greeks and Romans as much as to the Indians that a war elephant was a two-edged sword: it could turn against and stampede the army of which it was a part. The measures to provoke such behavior were in themselves a military art, as were those such as elephant armor to prevent it. All users of war elephants had to have ways of dealing with this potential, defensively and offensively. The Romans seem to have fastened upon this weakness more than others, and to have been reluctant and skeptical users of the animal.

This attitude seems also to account for the fact that not only did the war elephant disappear from manuals of tactics after the

Roman empire expanded to North Africa and the Middle East, extinguishing the elephant-using Hellenistic kingdoms, but the newer manuals failed to convey any information about elephant tactics from the older manuals, except to say that the elephant force was obsolete. "Arrian, in his book on Tactics written in the time of Hadrian, says (22.6) that it was not worth while giving the units and commands of elephants with their names, since their use had long ceased."[72]

The Roman refusal of the war elephant, I suggest, was based upon a low estimate of its value. I further suggest that modern scholars of Greece and Rome have absorbed this Roman valuation. Not only did elephant warfare disappear from the manuals of tactics from the times of the Roman empire, but the Roman valuation was adopted by modern scholarship, accounting for the fact that Armandi and Scullard are virtually the only books on the subject in the last two hundred years.

The modern circus alludes in its name to the entertainments of the Roman Circus Maximus, in which elephants figured prominently. It is in this way, and not in war, that the Romans found a place for elephants in their world.

Sassanians

For Iran the history of elephant use is long but discontinuous. First there were the Achaemenids who, as we have seen from the record of Ctesias, had diplomatic relations with India involving the acquisition of exotic animals, including elephants, and in whose sphere we have a little evidence of the war elephant. Then, after Alexander's brief appearance, came the Seleucids, avid users of war elephants, whose supply chain of Asian elephants stretched across Iran. Then came the Parthians, Central Asian nomads speaking an Iranian language, who had little interest in the war elephant. Finally, the Sassanians, for whom there is abundant evidence of the use of war elephants, and of substantial friendly communications with Indian kings.

[72] Ibid.: 237.

The long-lived Parthian or Arsacid empire (247 BCE–224 CE) is interesting to us in two ways, both of them negative. The first is its role in stopping the flow of war elephants from India to the Middle East. It began by interdicting the Indian supplies of the Seleucids. The appearance of the Parthians coincided with the declaration of independence of the Bactrian satrapy from Seleucid control, from 250 BCE, by Diodotus I and Diodotus II. Bactria, as we noted, had been the Seleucids' conduit to the Indian supply, which was now doubly vulnerable—to its independent Bactrian Greek rulers and to their Parthian neighbors. In the longer run the Bactrian Greeks were shoved out of Bactria and were forced into India by the nomads, and became Hindu or Buddhist rulers of small kingdoms in the Punjab. The Parthians consolidated their control, which extended over much of what is now Iran and Afghanistan.

The second way in which the Parthians relate to our inquiry is their refusal of the institution of the war elephant. By this I mean that the Parthians were aware of war elephants and had the ability to get and maintain them, but chose not to. Parthian kings occasionally rode upon elephants and put images of elephants on some of their coins. They controlled parts of the Indian northwest, including Taxila, which had used war elephants since the time of Alexander and probably long before. Nevertheless, the Parthians did not use war elephants, preferring a style of warfare with Central Asian precedents centering upon cavalry. This is epitomized in their one legacy to the present day: the idea of the "Parthian shot," often naturalized into the "parting shot," that is, the shot of a mounted archer over the rump of his horse while retreating at speed, a decidedly Central Asian maneuver. However, the Parthian army combined Persian-style heavy cavalry of armored horses and riders, which the Greeks called cataphracts, with the more Central Asian-like light cavalry; and it was the former that served the place of elephants in battle.

With the Sassanians (224–651), however, the war elephant made a comeback in Iran. Elephants figured prominently in their wars against the Armenians, the Romans and, at the end, against the Arab Muslims, who finally conquered them. Elephants also figure prominently in the Sassanian royal hunt. These elephants will have come from India; it is not likely that there were wild elephants in any part of their territories. But those territories had expanded eastward till they touched India. Sassanians took in part of the ancient territory of the Kushans (Skt. Kuṣāṇa), whose vast empire was half in India and half in Central Asia. The Sassanian subordinates in the east were called Kushan-shahs, meaning rulers of the Kushans. There is abundant evidence of resumed diplomatic contact between Iran and India, which coincides with the Sassanians taking up the war elephant. At Ajanta in western India there is a painting of foreign diplomats, thought to be Persian, which is to say Sassanian. To the east of Iran,[73] al-Adli of Baghdad, in his treatise on chess, praised the Indians for three original contributions to the world: the game of chess, the animal fables of the *Kalila wa Dimna* collection (from the Sanskrit collection called *Pañcatantra*), and the place-notation of numbers using zero as a place-holder. These passed from India through Sassanian Persia to the Arabs on their way to worldwide spread. The Sassanians have left distinct traces of this movement, in a romance on the introduction of chess through diplomatic exchange between an Indian king Devaśarma and the Sassanian king, and the Pahlavi text of the *Kalila wa Dimna*. All this indicates a closer connection of India and Iran, and of greater king-to-king communication and exchange. With this diplomatic traffic, we must suppose, there was a flow of war elephants from the kings of India to the Sassanian kings of Iran. This is the larger context of Sassanian military use of elephants, which has been ably surveyed and analyzed by Philip Rance (2003) and Michael Charles (2007).[74]

The earliest records, concerning the first king, Ardashir I, and wars against the Armenians, are found in Armenian chronicles. These are doubtful, as it was a commonplace of the chronicles to depict the Persian enemy with large numbers of war elephants.

[73] As I have noted in Chapter 3.

[74] See Fig. 6.1 for the Sassanian battles and sieges using war elephants.

For this reason Rance believes it likely that Armenian battle accounts of Ardashir's time (the third century) were literary back-projections.[75] However, the trope itself is a significant datum, and in the well-attested instances of Sassanian use of war elephants, fourth to seventh centuries, there are several campaigns of the Sassanian kings using war elephants against the Armenians. These carry the use of war elephants in Asia far to the north of their habitat. The Armenians would have had no possibility of responding in kind, and the Persians, having gone to great expense to field these war elephants so far from the forests in which they had been captured, reaped the advantage, deploying them against opponents who could not match them. The Armenians would never before have even seen elephants, much like the Celtic-speaking peoples in what are present-day Spain, France, and England, against whom Rome used its elephants.

The Roman empire and the Persian empire, both in Parthian and Sassanian times, had a common frontier that was a site of war for over seven enturies. The Romans had given up the use of war elephants before the beginning of the Common Era, and the Parthians had not taken it up; but the Sassanians brought them to their wars with Rome, whose armies therefore had once again, centuries after, to confront them.

In Rance's analysis Sassanian elephants appear much more in sieges than in battles, as compared to the Hellenistic period. They are also often mentioned in road-making over rough terrain, and in baggage-hauling, and indeed in many other of the elephant functions indicated by the *Arthaśāstra*. They appear less in battle than in the earlier Greek and Latin accounts, and in India itself, at least in representations.

It is clear that the Sassanian kings began collecting elephants early in their reign and used them often in war. They also used them in the royal hunt, as we see in the Taq-i Bustan frieze (Fig. 6.4). In the richly depicted hunting scene elephants figure prominently. On the left-hand side, no less than twelve elephants,

[75] Rance 2003: 366–8.

Fig. 6.4: Sassanian royal hunt with elephants, Taq-i Bustan

in five sets, are shown driving wild boars toward the king, who shoots with bow and arrow from a boat in a lake, and another five elephants are shown below the king, also driving game. Each elephant is mounted by a mahout and his assistant, riding fore and aft of a rider of higher status, judging by his dress. The drive takes place in a large square space enclosed with a running tent-like wall of patterned fabric, raised on poles and secured to bushes with ropes. On the right side, outside the enclosure, the kill is field-dressed and borne away by elephants, five in all, these mounted only by the working men and not also the higher-status riders of the drive. No less than twenty-two elephants and their human attendants lend magnificence to this scene of royal hunting. It is a superb representation of the Sassanian theater of kingship. The magnificence was enhanced by the great cost of acquiring elephants and their keepers from India.

Elephants figured both in Sassanian representations and in those of their Roman adversaries. In a Sassanian relief at Bishapur III, Romans and Kushans appear before the Persian king, bearing gifts; those of the Kushan include two wild cats on leashes (perhaps tigers) and an elephant.[76] In this Sassanian representation the elephant is a sign of India; while in Roman representations the elephant, though certainly Indian in origin, functions as an emblem of Persia, as in a triumphal arch in Thessaloniki, Greece, celebrating the victory of the Roman emperor Galerius over the Persians at Satala (298 CE). In one panel,[77] Sassanian figures bearing gifts are accompanied by three elephants with mahouts and one large feline, which reproduces at one remove the gifts of the Kushans to the Sassanians at Bishapur (Fig. 6.5). In another representation, called the Barberini ivory, there is a central panel celebrating the victorious emperor Justinian with gift-bearing figures of Persians, the gifts including an elephant, a large tusk, and what looks to be a tiger—typical products of India employed as signs of Persia, as indeed they were for the Romans (Fig. 6.6).

The Sassanians used war elephants to the end of their reign, when they were overwhelmed by the armies of the early Islamic caliphate. Sassanian elephants figure in Tabari's accounts of the battles of al-Qarus (634 CE), al-Buwayb (635), and al-Qādisiyyah (637), by which the Sassanian empire was extinguished by the army of the Caliph.[78] An immediate effect of the success of Islam

[76] Canepa 2009: 73; unfortunately the image is too damaged to show here.

[77] Ibid.: 95.

[78] Rance 2003: 379.

Fig. 6.5: Persians bringing tribute, Arch of Galerius, Thessaloniki, Greece

was that the use of Indian war elephants in Iran came to an end. The first Muslim kingdom to take up the use of them was that of the Ghaznavids.

Ghaznavids

The peoples of Central Asia have, from time to time, formed conquest states that lay half in India and half in Afghanistan. The Parthians are an example. The Kushans of the first century CE, and the Hunas of the sixth century, are others. But it was the Ghaznavids (962–1186), Turkish rulers who established themselves in Ghazna, in Afghanistan, who used the treasure and the war elephants they acquired through their wars in India as resources against their Central Asian Turkish enemies. By this means they were able to deploy Indian war elephants far from their habitat against people who had never seen elephants and had no experience of countering them in battle, as did the Romans and

Fig. 6.6: Persians bringing tribute, Barberini ivory

the Sassanians before them. The Ghaznavids were the first Muslim kings to use elephants in battle in substantial numbers and to give them a definite place in their tactical theory.[79] They did so on a considerable scale.

The Ghaznavids sought out war elephants from India and took them in tribute or as spoils of war. C.E. Bosworth gives examples

[79] Bosworth 1973: 115.

of large numbers of elephants taken in war and recorded in the sources: 350 from Kanauj, 185 from Mahāban in 1018–19 CE and 580 from Rājā Ganda the following year. The Thanesar expedition of 1014–15 was undertaken because of the desire of sultan Mahmūd for the special breed of *śailāmani* elephants (evidently the mountain-going or *giri-cara* elephants of the Himalayas or Vindhyas, judging by the name, which means "of the mountains"); and "on another occasion the Sultan so coveted an elephant of proverbial excellence belonging to Chandar Rāy, ruler of Sharma, that he offered fifty ordinary ones in exchange."[80] The numbers of elephants in the Ghaznavid army, therefore, would have been substantial. Sultan Mahmūd reviewed 1,300 on one occasion, 1,679 on another. At the capital, Ghazna, the *pīlkhāna* or elephant stable had provision for 1,000, with a staff of Indians under an overseer of the elephant stable, *muqaddam-i pīlbānān*.[81]

Like the Mauryas long before and many Indian kings since, the tendency toward royal monopoly was fully in evidence among the Ghaznavids and other kings of the day: "The unpermitted use of elephants was tantamount to rebellion."[82] Elephants fell to the one-fifth share of the sultan when the spoils of war taken from Indian kingdoms were being parceled out. Elephants were royal gifts as well.

Elephants were used in war by the sultans of Ghazna from the beginning (Sebüktigin) to the end (Mas'ūd III) of the kingdom, and as far to the north as Khurasan and the Caspian Sea region (see Fig. 6.1). Bosworth says, "In India and the mountainous regions of Afghanistan, where stone for building was plentiful, the reduction of a fortified town or strong-point, rather than pitched battle, was often the crux of a campaign."[83] This may be the key to the pattern which Rance sees for the Sassanian military use of elephants, namely their greater prominence in sieges as against battles.

The Ghaznavid kingdom was replaced by a Turkish rival, the Ghurids. Their generals created a kingdom in India, the

80 Ibid.: 116.
81 Ibid.: 116–17.
82 Ibid.: 117.
83 Ibid.: 118.

Sultanate of Delhi, which dominated the North Indian scene for three centuries from 1208 CE, till they were displaced by the Mughals. The Turkish sultans, Central Asians by origin, like the Ghaznavids but ruling a territory in India containing wild elephants, incorporated elephants into their cavalry-based military, adopting the Indian military style in this respect, and transmitting its use forward to the Mughals, who ruled after them.[84]

Simon Digby's argument, that the Turks, once established as sultans of Delhi, owed their success to their ability to control the flow of elephants and horses in opposite directions across North India, was noted at the start of my book. This is nicely shown in a letter attributed to sultan Ghiyāth al-din Balban, in which he addresses his son Bughrā Khān when giving him the province of Bengal: "The Bengal ruler should continue to send presents, offerings and trustworthy and well-disposed emissaries to Dehli so that the Sultan of Dehli should not consider an expedition against the Kingdom of Lakhnavati [Bengal] the most urgent of matters. From time to time he should send a certain number of elephants to Delhi, which would have the consequence that the Sultan of Dehli would not close the road for horses [from the north-west on the Arabian Sea] to reach Bengal."[85]

The pattern is this: enthusiasm for shouldering the cost and trouble of acquiring, maintaining, and deploying elephants by some of the greatest generals of antiquity, such as Seleucus, Hannibal, and Pyrrhus. By contrast, lack of enthusiasm for war elephants on the part of the Romans, whose generals seem to have preferred playing defense when it came to elephants and offense with them only till they had conquered their elephant-using rivals—Hellenistic, Carthaginian, and Greek. Thereafter, they fronted an empire whose rulers, the Parthians, chose not to use elephants. Manuals of warfare and tactics dropped the elephant division from their

[84] Digby 1971.
[85] Ibid.: 68.

handbooks. The Sassanians resumed for centuries the Persian use of war elephants; elephants appear in Roman triumphs celebrating victories against the Persians, but not in their armies. Scullard says that "despite the uncertainty and despite the great expense and labour of feeding and transporting fodder, many states continued to employ them, while a hard-headed general like Seleucus thought that a large elephant-corps was worth more than control of North-west India."[86] But the Romans in the main took a different view. It is a *topos* of the classical sources that elephants can become a terrible danger to their own side if they panic. This seems to have been the dominant view for the Romans.

It seems to have been the dominant view of modern historians as well. Armandi tried to fill the lacuna in their work, but over a century later there is only one successor survey of the amazing fact that, from Alexander to Julius Caesar, elephants appeared in most of the great battles of antiquity, and in the armies of some of its greatest generals; and that they appeared again in the wars of the Sassanians and the Ghaznavids, far from the source of supply. Perhaps the Roman loss of interest, their low assessment of the cost/benefit ratio, is the reason that a historical phenomenon of great scope and duration has been largely orphaned by modern historical scholarship.

[86] Scullard 1974: 249.

7

Southeast Asia

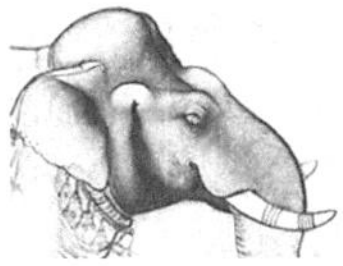

THE INDIAN INSTITUTION OF THE WAR elephant, then, spread west to lands that had no wild Asian elephants upon which to draw. In these new territories the practice meant importing trained elephants from India, or capturing and training North African elephants by using Indian techniques. The process began in the Achaemenid period, when part of India fell under Persian rule at about the time that elephant warfare had become a universal ideal for kings in northern India, *c.* 500 BCE. The use of war elephants to the west of India grew rapidly following Alexander and was perpetuated, long after elephant warfare had died out in Asia Minor and North Africa, by the Sassanians in Iran and the Ghaznavids in Central Asia. This was the development that Armandi recorded.

But there is another history of the war elephant beyond India—in Southeast Asia. Armandi knew of it only in its last stages because the early history of the Indianized kingdoms did not begin to be examined by Europeans until after his time, when the French, the Dutch, and the British imposed their rule over most of Southeast Asia. Scullard confined his survey to the Greek and Roman world. It is time to bring Southeast Asia into this history, especially for the comparative possibilities it affords, and subsequently China, which establishes the eastern limit of the phenomenon.

Here I complete that history by turning to Southeast Asia, especially continental Southeast Asia and the Indonesian island of Sumatra, where wild elephants were plentiful. Despite the natural advantage of wild elephant populations, however, Southeast Asians began to capture and train elephants for war much later than did the countries west of India, and many centuries after the invention of the war elephant in India. This late start is highly significant. War elephants are completely absent in the thousand-year span of the bronze age in Southeast Asia,[1] but they come into view as soon as *kingdoms* arise, about the first century CE. This supports my belief that the institution of the war elephant is strongly connected with kingship, that its very invention occurs under kingship. The appearance of the war elephant in Southeast Asia coincides with the rise of kingdoms and its use is found exclusively in kingdoms.

The kingdoms of Southeast Asia using elephants for war, moreover, were those that adopted *Indian* kingship as their model, as did neighboring kingdoms influenced by them. This is strong reason to think that the people of Southeast Asia did not spontaneously reinvent elephant warfare, but that the idea and techniques pertinent to the war elephant came from India. This compels me to take up the vexed issue of *Indianized states*, a disputed matter impossible to avoid given my argument about the Indian origin of elephant warfare.

États hindouisés, Indianized states, Indianizing kingdoms

Historians of Southeast Asia speak of *Indianized states*. The phrase comes from George Coedès and figures in the title of the English version of his history of this entity, *The Indianized states of Southeast Asia* (1968). Michael Vickery (2003), whose critique of Coedès is extensive and detailed, reminds us that in the French original it was *Hinduized* states (*états hindouisés*) (Coedès 1964), emphasizing the religious character of the phenomenon, and that

[1] Higham 1996.

it got secularized in translation. Coedès was the foremost historian of these early kingdoms of Southeast Asia, whose history was recovered by deciphering the Sanskrit inscriptions of Cambodia, from which a reliable chronology and dynastic succession of such states was derived. His book synthesizes the results of his work, as well as of other scholars in recovering the early history of Southeast Asia, and occupies a place of special authority in the field.

The referent for the category of Indianized states is always a *kingdom*, which moreover has certain defining attributes: its kings take names in Sanskrit and support religions from India; its monumental architecture in brick or stone is Indianate in style and Buddhist or Hindu in religion; and its inscriptions are written in the Brahmi script of India, in Sanskrit verse of the ornate courtly style called *kāvya*, praising the deeds of the king and recording grants of land to Hindu temples or Buddhist monasteries (to which are often added particulars in the local language).

Indeed, modified versions of the Brahmi script of India give the languages of Southeast Asia written form through kingdoms of this kind. Such kingdoms promoted Indian literary models and their expression in sculpture and dance, above all the *Mahābhārata* and *Rāmāyaṇa*, which have a strong presence in Southeast Asia to this day. The poetics of Indian kingship, then, is vividly present in Southeast Asian countries through the cultivation of the Indian epics, both in Sanskrit and in new versions of them written in Southeast Asian languages. The more technical aspects of kingship are conveyed through the *Arthaśāstra*, or, more likely, a successor text on kingship, the *Nītisāra* of Kāmandaka.[2] Above all, kingdoms of this kind show the war elephant and the Indian structures in which it is found: the fourfold army, the battle array, and the elephant as the conveyance of the king.

This, then, is the so-called Indianized state. To make such a historical formation intelligible it had to be decoded by means of Sanskritic learning and Sanskrit-based Orientalist analysis, which made possible the construction of a reliable chronology for

[2] Singh 2010.

the early kingdoms of Southeast Asia. This decoding took place largely under the colonial rule of the French in Indochina (present-day Vietnam, Laos, and Cambodia), the Dutch in Indonesia, and in part the British in Burma, Malaya, Singapore, and (during the Napoleonic wars) Java. Colonial rule gave European Orientalist scholarship the conditions under which the past of Southeast Asia could be made, quite literally, legible. It is consistent with this historical context that the great French Sanskritist Sylvain Lévi (1938) wrote of Indian culture in Southeast Asia under the rubric of "L'Inde civilisatrice," conceptualizing India's role as an earlier counterpart of France's self-justifying civilizing mission.

The scholarly outcome was a permanent gain, at least at the "skeletal" level of historical knowledge. Thanks to the scholarship that gave us the concept of the Indianized state, we have an invaluable framework of chronology, dynastic succession, and sequence of architectural styles. But the environing ideology and historical interpretations it fostered could not survive the rolling back of empires and the creation of an international regime of nation-states out of the colonial states in Southeast Asia following their independence after World War II. New interpretations of ancient history were needed. These came in answer to the excess of the "Indianized states" model, that is, the tendency to treat the Southeast Asian societies that were objects of Indianization as if this Indianization were written upon blank slates, passive recipients, or savages civilized from without. The counter-interpretations of the age of decolonization emphasized, rather, pre-existing indigenous cultural dispositions which conditioned the aspects of Indian civilization that were adopted by Southeast Asian kingdoms as well as the agency of Southeast Asians in the creation of their own kingdoms. Confronted by this new focus upon indigenism and agency, the power and "thickness" of Indianization waned in the historical writings of the new generation. At the extreme, Indianization was thinned out into a "veneer" atop the indigenous cultural base.[3] In the project of Michael Vickery on

[3] Vickery 1998; Higham 2002: 294, citing Vickery but taking a middle course.

early Cambodian states, reading the Khmer portions of the royal inscriptions gives access to non-elite classes and their culture; other scholars, focusing on elites, read Indianization against the grain, positing indigenous beliefs that selected certain parts of the Indian repertoire to dress them up with.

Veneerism is the interpretive inversion of *blank-slateism*; it is the proper excess of the indigenism thesis. Victor Lieberman has written the best analysis of the historiography on this question.[4] He distinguishes two approaches, "externalist" and "autonomous," depending upon whether the underlying tendency is to stress external agency provoking change in Southeast Asia, or the agency of Southeast Asians which is deemed autonomous. He argues that the currently favored autonomous histories, embracing indigenism, can be unhistorical in another way, positing a changeless Southeast Asian culture beneath the veneer of Indianization. He proposes a middle way, a more processual conception. Lieberman—to put his long and nuanced analysis all too briefly—stresses the sustained movement of Southeast Asian states toward *integration* in response to both external and indigenous dynamics.

To better express the processual nature of the object of study, following Lieberman's example, it may help to revise the terminology.

It is well to be clear that the kind of state we are talking about, the adopter of the Indian model of kingship, is specifically and exclusively the *kingdom* and not states of all kinds. "Kingdom" should replace "state" in the received formula because it is more concrete and cannot leave the impression that any kind of state can take up Indianization. It also reminds us that at the core of the process are not only the religions of India but the Indian model of kingship. This is the more appropriate when talking of war elephants, of course, as it is in kingdoms that war elephants play such a significant role.

Indianized kingdoms, then, rather than Indianized states. But the critics of the concept are quite right to point out that the agents of this Indianization were the kings of Southeast Asia, and not, or not

[4] Lieberman 2003: 1, 6–66.

only, Indian agents of the spread of Indian religion and kingship. This self-Indianization aspect, and the processual nature of the phenomenon, I suggest, can be better expressed by changing the concept on the front end as well: *Indianizing* kingdoms rather than Indianized ones. That is the terminology I will use in what follows.

It is worth observing at the outset that there is a great similarity between peninsular India and Sri Lanka on the one hand, and Southeast Asia on the other, in the adoption of models of Indian kingship and the religions associated with their kingdoms. More particularly, the spread of the institution of the war elephant within Southeast Asia is, in its broad processual features, very like its spread within South Asia itself. That process is very different from the processes by which the institution of the war elephant spread to the elephantless kingdoms west of India—the Greek and Roman world of Scullard's book.

Indianizing kingdoms and elephants

It is a paradox of the Indianizing kingdoms that much of the best information about the earliest of them comes from Chinese sources, not Indian. These kingdoms had continuing diplomatic relations with China, though India was the major source of their religions (Hinduism and Mahāyāna Buddhism) and models of royal practice. The Southeast Asian kings took Sanskrit names, and their monumental architecture bears Sanskrit inscriptions. India was a constant referent in the world of these royal inscriptions. One inscription says that the Cambodian king's fame had spread as far as Kāñcīpuram in South India,[5] another that the king has conquered the earth as far as the Indus valley.[6] On the other hand Indian sources speak of Southeast Asia as the land of gold (*suvarṇabhūmi*), or the golden continent (*suvarṇadvīpa*), but

[5] K 725, verse 4, IC 1: 8. "K" numbers refer to the general list of inscriptions of Cambodia, "IC" in eight volumes (K = Khmer; there are also inscriptions with "C" numbers for the kingdom of Champa).

[6] K 254, verse 3, IC 3: 182.

beyond such general references offer precious little about the Southeast Asian kings and kingdoms. We are obliged to rely on Chinese diplomatic reports, and the inscriptions in Sanskrit and indigenous languages of the kingdoms themselves.

The earliest of the Indianizing kingdoms, beginning perhaps in the first century CE, is Funan, stretching over contemporary southern Cambodia as well as Vietnam in the Southeast Asian mainland, in the delta of the Mekong river.[7] Funan bears a Chinese-sounding name because we know of it through Chinese sources, though the word may be a reflex of Khmer *phnom*, mountain or hill, as in the name of the present-day capital of Cambodia, Phnom Penh. One source signals its Indianizing character in saying the kingdom was founded by a Brahmin named Kauṇḍinya who married a princess of that country, daughter of a *nāga*—a cobra, or dragon. But the report is very much later than the time of which it speaks and may be a foundational charter formed much after the fact. We get inscriptions of the kings themselves, which are in Sanskrit, again much later than the first century CE starting point that the genealogies imply. Nevertheless, the date seems to correspond with the archaeological indications of enlarged settlements in the delta of the Mekong about that time. The era of the Indianizing kingdoms lasted a long time, 1,500 years or more, with after-effects that continue to this day.

The invaluable written record and body of monuments of the Indianizing kingdoms are supplemented by an increasingly rich archaeological record of the kingdoms themselves, and of their prehistory in the Southeast Asian bronze age. From this we begin to possess materials by which to better understand the conditions under which pre-state societies adopted aspects of Indian kingship, leading to the formation of the Indianizing kingdoms.

We do not have a clear idea of how an Indian model of kingship came to be adopted by nascent Southeast Asian kingdoms, but

[7] For this important but somewhat shadowy state, the starting point of the Indianizing kingdom phenomenon, the standard treatment is that of Coedès 1968; the classic work is Pelliot 1903; Vickery 2003 is an excellent recent treatment, skeptical of early Indianizing; Khoo ed. 2003 reports on recent archaeology.

we know a good deal about the conditions under which kingship itself arose. The production of bronze and copper artifacts and the cultivation of rice were the two main precursors of the rise of kingdoms. The first had—according to Higham (1996), whose synthesis of the bronze age of Southeast Asia is invaluable—reached the Southeast Asian mainland by about 2500 BCE, the second by about 1500 BCE.

Copper and tin are both available in mainland Southeast Asia, and the production of bronze or copper artifacts began early, the arts of smelting and casting perhaps absorbed from north China, where bronze was widely used. The quality of bronze production in Southeast Asia rose to a very high pitch in the making of bronze drums or gongs. These are called Dongsonian, named after the site Dong Son in northern Vietnam where they were first excavated, and datable to an interval that Higham puts at 600 BCE to 100 CE. They may be the beginnings of the distinctive music tradition of Southeast Asia, which used gongs and xylophones, as in the ensembles of Indonesia called *gamelan*, so distinctive of the region and so different from the music of India and China. The drums are finely made, cast from clay molds by the lost wax method and decorated with images of nature and social life, including warfare. Examining the corpus of bronze drums of Southeast Asia as a whole, I have found a useful clue about the rise of elephant warfare in the region.

Heger (1902) published the first systematic study of 165 metal drums, and Parmentier (1918) another, by which time the corpus of known drums had grown to 188; by the time of Goloubew (1929), Dong Son had been excavated and his survey could contextualize the bronze drums in relation to metal artifacts and other remains.[8] Examining the illustrations of drums in these publications I find many representations of animals, especially birds of various kinds, fish, and deer, but only one instance of an elephant, which is clearly wild because it is in the company of other wild animals.[9]

[8] Higham 1996: 26–8.

[9] Heger 1902: 2, Tafel VI, Trommel von Saleier.

Scenes of human activity, both at peace and war, are many, but none show horses and elephants. Scenes of warfare show feathered warriors on foot or in boats, bearing spears or clubs and shields. Some are depicted in a naturalistic style, but many in a style so highly mannered as to be at once beautiful and almost impossible to decode. Thus the body of works reviewed in the early surveys of bronze drums shows a style of warfare completely lacking in horses and elephants. This corroborates my argument that war elephants in Southeast Asia begin with the advent of Indianizing kingdoms.

However, a number of finely decorated bronze drums have been found in Indonesia, the objects, evidently, of a long-ranging maritime trade with the mainland. These have been given names by their owners, and one of them, a drum called Makalamau from the island of Sangean east of Sumbawa in the Lesser Sundas (but now lodged in the National Museum of Indonesia), gives abundant evidence of elephants, as seen in Figs 7.1–2.[10] Of twenty panels on the band at the bottom of the body of the drum, one has been destroyed. But eleven of the remaining nineteen have elephant representations, one of them with a man on its back, and another with a man climbing onto its neck by grasping the ears and climbing the trunk. This is a mode of mounting characteristic of Indian mahouts and may still be seen today, requiring the active cooperation of the elephant, which, by implication, has been trained in the Indian manner. There are also panels of horses, one with a man holding the bridle and a saddle or blanket on the back of the horse, another with a mounted warrior, another of a horse eating from a manger. The manufacture and decoration of the drum are Dongsonian and it will have been made in mainland Southeast Asia, perhaps Vietnam itself, reaching Indonesia via trade. Two factors point to this drum belonging to a late date in the development of such drums: first, the rarity of elephant representations and complete absence of tamed elephants mounted by humans in the earlier surveys of drums; second, the great distance

[10] Heine-Geldern 1947; Taylor and Aragon 1991.

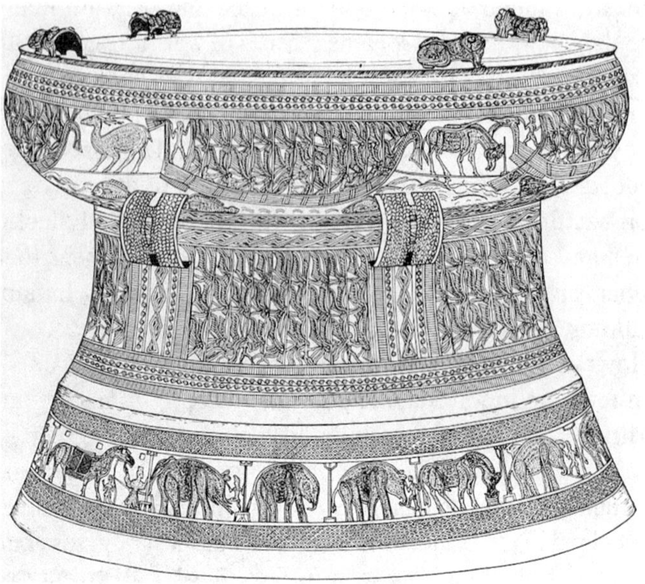

Fig. 7.1: The drum called Makalamau

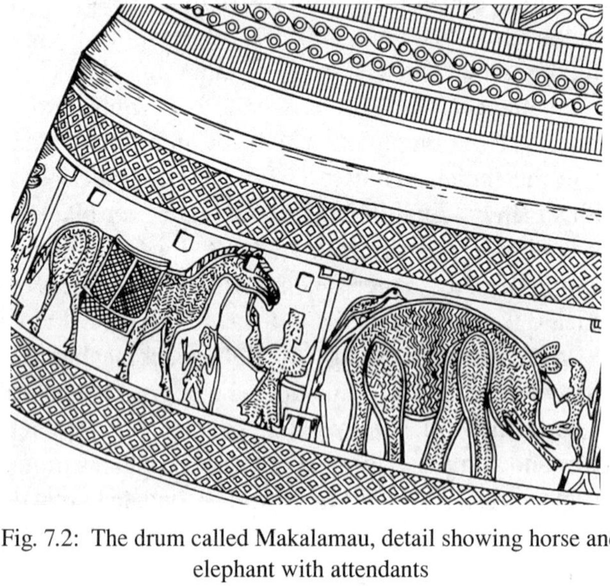

Fig. 7.2: The drum called Makalamau, detail showing horse and elephant with attendants

of this drum from the place of its production on the Southeast Asian mainland. Both imply that its time horizon is after the onset of the Indianizing kingdoms of the mainland, well after the time of Funan and other such early kingdoms and proto-kingdoms.

Like the making of objects in bronze, rice cultivation seems an early precursor of the rise of kingdoms in Southeast Asia. The cultivation of rice seems to have had its beginnings in south China, in the middle and eastern regions of the Yangzi river. It spread southward to the Southeast Asian mainland, largely along the coast. (At this period south China was not yet Han Chinese and its inhabitants spoke other languages.) Rice cultivation profoundly altered the human landscape of the region. Before its introduction, Southeast Asia was settled by foragers who lived inland; after its introduction the coastal areas where river valleys run to the sea were settled and the population quickly grew, especially along the Red river, Chao Phraya, and Mekong rivers and their deltas. Rice cultivation brought with it sedentary communities of farmers which agglomerated into larger communities through their chiefs.

Into this setting came, from the first century BCE or even somewhat earlier, a maritime international trade which connected India and Rome to the west with China to the east, passing through the early rice-cultivating societies of present-day southern Cambodia and Vietnam. This was, of necessity, a trade in luxuries, for only luxuries could bear the very high costs of transport across large distances. As such, it was closely connected with the emergence of kingship—because kingship requires a hierarchy of statuses with the king at the top—and of which sumptuous goods, which are expensive because of their rarity or exotic origin, are the visible signs. Southeast Asia, specifically the region around the Mekong delta, benefited from this international luxury trade and participated in it, acquiring the kinds of goods which were also resources for building kingship. The process corresponds with that in Tamil-speaking South India, where we find Mediterranean wine, red coral, and gold coins consolidating the kingship of Colas, Pāṇḍyas, and Ceras.

This, then, was the context in which Indianizing kingdoms arose, beginning in the valley of the Mekong in what are now Cambodia and southern Vietnam. Having discussed the king, I come now to the elephant.

In the present day, wild elephants are found in mainland Southeast Asia, in Myanmar, Thailand, Malaysia, Laos, Cambodia, and Vietnam, in decreasing order of numbers. In island Southeast Asia they are found only in the western parts of Indonesia, where they have long existed on the island of Sumatra, and also in Kalimantan on the island of Borneo, to which, however, they were imported in historic times by elephant-using kings. Both the mainland and much of the island world of Southeast Asia were elephant habitat for a very long time before the arrival of humans. Because much of the island world sits on the Sunda Shelf in shallow seas, during periods of worldwide cooling, when seawaters were bound up in polar icecaps and the sea level fell, islands and mainland became connected. The elephant population was divided and reunited by the rise and fall of the sea level in the deeper past and was widely diffused in the region when humans arrived. Elephants continued to be scattered so in Southeast Asia for ages before the rise of kingship, without ever being put to use in warfare. If humans hunted them, we have little evidence of it. By and large, elephants appear in the historical record only under the Indianizing kingdoms, from Funan of the first century CE onward, not earlier.

The Indian epics in Southeast Asia

Ideals of kingship emanating from India were sustained in Southeast Asia by the extraordinary popularity of the *Mahābhārata* and *Rāmāyaṇa* there. The epics of India are living presences in Southeast Asia, materials for creative retelling and performance in many different artistic media. A quick overview of this phenomenon will position us to estimate the degree to which the *poetry* of Indian kingship informed the *practice* of kingship in Southeast Asia. I will limit discussion to the literary expression of the epics in Southeast Asia, first in inscriptions and then in publicly recited texts.

The Sanskrit inscriptions of Cambodia draw upon the Indian epics and the *Purāṇas* for their imagery, much like the inscriptions of India. Most of them are records of endowments made to religious institutions, Hindu or Buddhist, and open with an invocation of the gods and a eulogy (*praśasti*) of the reigning king: his heroic qualities are extolled and compared favorably to those of the gods or past heroes. Thus king Rājendravarman is "like Arjuna in battle" in an inscription of *c.* 952–61 CE,[11] while in another the enemy king of Campā is likened to Rāma's antagonist Rāvaṇa.[12] An ancestral king, also named Rājendravarman, who reigned from 44 CE is said to have conquered in the four directions guarded by Indra, whereas Arjuna conquered only a single region, the north, on the occasion of the royal consecration (*rājasūya*) of his older brother Yudhiṣṭhira.[13] In another inscription the poet compares the king favorably to Viṣṇu and Rāma, the first having killed an individual of low birth (the *daitya* Bāṇa, perhaps) with the aid of the king of the birds (Garuḍa); the second (having killed Rāvaṇa) with the help of the king of the monkeys (Sugrīva); while the Khmer king killed the enemy, a person of high birth, with his own arm, fighting alone, in unequal battle.[14]

Elephants figure often in these eulogies, and occasionally in the list of gifts to the religious institution on whose monument the inscription is fixed. Thus, in an inscription of Indravarman of 881,

[11] *yo 'rjunako yudhi*, K 70, verse 71, IC 2: 59.

[12] *śrījayaindravarmmā cāmpeśvaro rāvaṇavat*, K 485, verse 68, IC 2: 169.

[13] *jitvaikavīro diśam indraguptāṃ* |
yo dakṣiṇān dehabhṛtān didīpe |
prācetasīñ cetasi sottarāñ ca |
na rājasūyāya tu jiṣṇur ekām ||
K 807, verse 30, IC 1: 80. The allusion is to *Mbh.* 2.23–9, Digvijaya-parvan.

[14] *vijātim āśritya hariḥ khadgendraṃ*
rāmaḥ kapīndrañ ca ripūn mamardda |
svavāhum ājau viṣame sujātim
ajāraroṣas tu ya ekavīraḥ ||
K 218, verse 9, IC 3: 47.

elephants with attendants (*dviradendrās sagaṇikā*) are part of the foundational gift.[15] Another inscription, of Jayavarman V dating to 676, refers in the Khmer portion to a gift of the chief of the elephants of the king (*sāmantagajapati*), and to king Jayavarman III as having come in the past to the forest tract near the village to capture an elephant.[16] Consistent with the pattern we see in the *Mahābhārata*, elephants are rare, superlative royal gifts. And they are used, above all, in war. Reverting to the description of the first Rājendravarman, we read, "Accompanied by his soldiers massed in one place with troops of elephants and horses, as by a celestial army eager to see combat, he advances eager to vanquish the enemy."[17] This implies that the army of the king was fourfold, of the kind in the epics and the *Arthaśāstra*, where elephants are a component within the larger structure.

Inscriptions, however, are unique texts in unique locations, and their being written in Sanskrit means they can have been read, if they were read at all, by the very few who had studied the language. The epics were recited daily in some temples and much studied by those who had learned Sanskrit, but again the social reach of such recitations and study will have been short. But these socially narrow practices were a kind of base for the far more consequential and socially thick spread of the epics through their emplacement in the languages of Southeast Asia. The Brahmi script, in which the Indian epics and the Sanskrit inscriptions were written, afforded a medium through which written literatures in the languages of Southeast Asia could be created, and the Indian epics afforded the main subject matter of the earliest and most widely known works.

The literature of Java is an outstanding example.[18] The language called Kawi (from Sanskrit *kavi*, poet) is a highly refined and exalted register of Old Javanese, studded with Sanskrit loanwords. Kawi literature has a large body of epic works called *kakawin*

[15] K 310, verse 38, IC 1: 22.
[16] K 140, verse 3, IC 6: 14.
[17] K 807, verse 72, IC 1: 85.
[18] I rely here on the comprehensive survey of Zoetmulder (1974).

(from Sankrit *kāvya*, courtly poetry). These poems are written in the elaborate meters of Sanskrit *kāvya*, with names like "crest-jewel of spring" (*vasantatilakā*) and "tiger's play" (*śardūlivikrīḍita*), the same meters in which the Sanskrit inscriptions of Cambodia and of India are written, but here used in an unrelated language. There is a *Kakawin Ramayana*, telling the *Rāmāyaṇa* story, and a *Kakawin Bharatayuddha,* telling the *Mahābhārata* story, and many more, such as *Kakawin Arjunawiwaha* (the marriage of Arjuna) and *Kakawin Arjunawijaya* (the conquests of Arjuna). Arjuna is a favorite character of this literature; he is considered a paragon of refinement and heroism.

The *Kakawin Bharatayuddha*, a poem of some 700 verses written in 1157, retells the story of the great epic and is replete with references to the fourfold army, using Sanskrit loanwords for horse (Kawi *aswa*, Skt. *aśva*), chariot (K. *rata*, Skt. *ratha*), and elephant (K. *gaja*, Skt. *gaja*). The battle arrays and counter-arrays (*vyūha* and *prati-vyūha*) are a prominent part of this retelling.

Thomas Stamford Raffles, governor of Java during the Napoleonic interlude, when the British took over the Dutch holdings in Indonesia, 1811–14, gave the first account of this work in English, a very extensive one which includes a translation and paraphrase of the whole, made with the help of Javanese scholars.[19] What is so striking about this text is that the cities and countries of India in the poem are identified with cities and kingdoms of the islands of Java and Madura, so that the Indian story is entirely emplaced in the geography familiar to its hearers—the Indonesianization of an Indian story. Raffles was impressed by "how deeply rooted is the belief that the scene of this poem was in Java."[20] The scene of the *Rāmāyaṇa*, on the other hand, was not believed to have been in Java, but there was an impression that Hanuman, after the death of Rāvaṇa, fled to Java and took refuge on a particular hill called Kandali Sada. This is the place in the

[19] Raffles 1965 [1817]: 410–68. Supomo (1993) gives the text in roman and full translation, with a study of its Indian sources.

[20] Ibid.: 412.

Rāmāyaṇa where Hanuman performed austerities, and "such is the superstition of the neighbourhood that they never perform any part of the story of the Rāmāyana in the vicinity, lest Hanuman should pelt them with stones."[21]

The performance of these Kawi-language tellings of the epics of India, now thoroughly made at home in Java, is done through these poems. It is made vivid through the theater (*wayang*) of various kinds, especially the shadow puppet theater (*wayang kulit*), which continues to this day, and also the dance drama of the courts. The shadow puppet theater, especially, is the means by which this essentially courtly literature has suffused the culture of Java as well as Bali and other Indonesian islands. Until fairly recently every village had its puppet master (*dalang*) and gamelan orchestra for performances on special occasions. The diffusion of the court culture of the Indianizing kingdom from top to bottom of the social system reminds one of the wide social circulation of classical literature and opera in Italy, where a bus driver may very well be able to sing an aria of Italian opera or recite Dante's *Inferno* from memory. In this way, while an Indianizing courtly literature deeply penetrated the social scale and was emplaced in the Indonesian landscape, it also acquired a contemporaneity through performance in which the time of the story and the time of the presentation and other times in between were collapsed in the telling. In a performance I saw, by a troupe from Surakarta, performed at the University of Michigan, the army of the king was depicted by a puppet showing horses, elephants, foot soldiers, cannon, and the flag of present-day Indonesia; while the chariot of Arjuna was a puppet of an eighteenth-century Dutch-style coach, not a military vehicle at all, on which Arjuna nevertheless fought as the great chariot warrior he is.[22]

In the literatures of mainland Southeast Asia both epics are represented, but the *Rāmāyaṇa* has an especially large presence. In Cambodia there is the Khmer-language *Reamker* (Rāma's fame);

[21] Ibid.

[22] "Kresna duta" performed by the Indonesian Institute of the Arts, Surakarta, *dalang* Jaka Riyanto, University of Michigan, September 24, 2011.

in Thai the *Ramakien* (Story of Rāma); in Malay the *Hikayat Seri Rama* (chronicle of Śrī Rāma); in Lao *Phra Lak Phra Lam* (lord Lakṣmana and lord Rāma); in Burmese the *Yana Zatdaw* (drama of Rāma). These are not simple translations of the Sanskrit *Rāmāyaṇa*—the *Rāmāyaṇa* of Valmīki composed in India—but retellings of the story which contain much new material, of both narrative and poetic ornamentation.[23] Here again, as in Indonesia, the works of literature are also the basis of paintings, dance drama in the courtly style, and shadow puppet theater. They are very popular and by no means confined to a small elite at the king's court.

Because of these many retellings the epics are not single texts but a field of variation. In a classic article, F. Martini (1938) showed the existence of differences between the Rāma story in the *Rāmāyaṇa* of Valmīki and the Cambodian text of the *Reamker*, and that the bas-reliefs at Angkor Wat depicting scenes from the life of Rāma were drawn not from the Sanskrit but from the Khmer version, giving evidence of its existence and influence at the time.

Southeast Asian literatures have made the *Mahābhārata* and *Rāmāyaṇa* living presences to this day. In Indonesia, for example, the leading characters of the epics are widely known and used as references by which to describe the character and personality of living people.[24] The popular reach of the epics in Southeast Asia continued unhindered by the spread of Theravāda Buddhism in Burma, Thailand, Cambodia, and Laos, and Islam in Malaysia and Indonesia.

The pattern is similar in India itself, where every regional language has its own version of the epic stories, such as the *Rāmcaritamānas* of Tulsi Das in Hindi, and Kamban's *Rāmāyaṇa* in Tamil, and performances of them such as the Rāmlīlā dance-drama based on the work of Tulsi Das. In recent times both epics were turned into multi-episode television serials which had, I

[23] Raghavan 1975; Richman ed. 1991; Srinivasa Iyengar ed. 1983.

[24] Alton Becker, personal communication.

venture to think, the largest viewership of a television program anywhere in the world up to that time—80 million, according to Paula Richman (1991); not to speak of movie versions, virtually from the beginning of cinema in India, of a kind called "mythologicals,"[25] and comic books.

In the face of this phenomenon—the capacity of the Indian epics to generate a large body of interrelated literatures in unrelated languages—it is patently inadequate to speak of a veneer of Indian culture in Southeast Asia. Much more satisfactory is the formulation of Sheldon Pollock (2006), who speaks of a Sanskrit *cosmopolis* created by literature. In this sphere Sanskrit serves as a standard that authorizes other literatures, or, more exactly, it creates literatures in other languages by determining what literature is.

Through the epics the Indian model of kingship was performed and made appealing and popular, at the same time as it was retold, changed, and emplaced in the local landscape.

Armies cosmic and earthly

Thus the war elephant suffuses the imaginary of the Indianizing kingdoms of Southeast Asia, along with the larger structures of which the war elephant is an element among others: the fourfold army, the royal conveyance, the battle array—*caturaṅga*, *rājavāhana*, *vyūha*. Let us see if we can discern what actual practice might have been. This is not a straightforward task, because the sources so thoroughly emplace the epic story and its narratives of war in the Southeast Asian landscape, and collapse the time of the epic with time present, that the actualities of practice become hard to make out through this highly colored optic.

An example from Java may serve to get a sense of the distance between the poetry of kingship and its practice. Java has not had wild elephants in recent times and must have been supplied by captives from Sumatra. Thus, when we read the *Nāgarakṛtāgama*,

[25] Baskaran 1981.

a Kawi-language *kakawin* of 1365 written in praise of king Hayam Wuruk of Majapahit, we find elaborate poetic celebrations of royal tours, of which the pattern of the telling sustains the intent but not the practice of the Indian pattern. Thus the king, the queens, and the leading grandees of the kingdom are borne by palanquin, and their baggage trains are of oxcarts, the number of which indicates the rank of the person to whom they are attached. Horses and elephants are mentioned, but only briefly and without particulars, so that I infer they are brought in to add color and magnificence to the word picture but are not, truly, a significant working part of the machinery of the royal progress.[26] While the war elephant suffuses the Kawi literature and its theatrical performances, it probably played a small role in practice.

When we turn to Cambodia, on the other hand, where wild elephants were readily available, the picture is very different.

On the practice of warfare in Southeast Asia we have two surveys. H.B. Quaritch Wales wrote the pioneering work, *Ancient South-East Asian warfare* (1952), which, making allowance for the externalist perspective of its time, remains very useful. And Michael Charney's *Southeast Asian warfare, 1300–1900* (2004) is an excellent overview of the later period. Both are immensely valuable for the study of war elephants and the context of their use in Southeast Asia.

However, for present purposes it will be helpful to follow the more specialized study of Michel Jacq-Hergoualc'h, *The armies of Angkor: military structure and weaponry of the Khmers* (in French, 1979; English tran. 2007). This important work confines itself to the close study of Cambodian armies as depicted in bas-reliefs at only three sites, and as a matter of method does not examine the depiction of divine or mythological armies. The first of the three sites is Angkor Wat, the monument of Sūryavarman II (*r.* 1113–50) with exquisite reliefs of armies and battles around its long perimeter wall. The second is the Bayon of Jayavarman VII (*r.* 1181–1218), whose outer wall contains some battle

[26] Pigeaud and Prapantja 1960.

scenes. The third site is Banteay Chmar, also of Jayavarman VII. Here the wall on which the reliefs were carved has collapsed at several places, and what remains is often difficult to get close to because the approach is strewn with large blocks of fallen wall. Restoration work may once again make it available for study, but for the present one must rely on photographs made by General de Beylié in 1913 and kept in the Musée Guimet in Paris. The magnificent reliefs of Angkor Wat and the Bayon are well restored and may be studied directly. They have been photographed many times, which facilitates the kind of close scrutiny and comparison of the different representations which Jacq-Hergoualc'h's work accomplishes. Since his study was published, excellent color photographs, by Jan Poncar and his associates, of the Angkor perimeter wall and some of the Bayon have been published.[27]

Both Quaritch Wales and Jacq-Hergoualc'h focus attention on the representation of the armies of the Cambodian kings in these reliefs and have little to say about the battle scenes involving gods and demons, and those from the epics. But for our purposes it is useful to see divine armies, those of the epics and present-day ones, together for the sake of comparison, so that we get the measure of the distance that separates the actual armies of Angkor from the ideals one finds in the myths of the *Purāṇas* and legends of the epics. The Angkor Wat reliefs, which consist of battles and armies of all these kinds, are especially helpful. Let us take a rapid tour of them.

The normal direction in which to walk around an Indian monument is the sunwise or clockwise direction, considered auspicious, keeping the object to your right. The reliefs of Angkor Wat seem to follow a program, which begins with the creation, and moves to various battles of the gods, to scenes from the *Rāmāyaṇa* and *Mahābhārata*, to king Sūryavarman and the Cambodian army, to the judgment of souls and their fate in heaven and hell. The oddity is that this apparent program runs in the inauspicious counterclockwise direction. Long ago Jean Przyluski argued

[27] Poncar and le Bonheur 1995; Poncar and Maxwell 2006.

this was because it was a monument to king Sūryavarman II, who was deified after his death, as indicated by his deification name Paramaviṣṇuloka in inscriptions at the site; that it is a tomb or at any rate a memorial to the dead, and therefore to be circumambulated in the counterclockwise direction appropriate for funeral rites. Whatever the reason, the broadly chronological progression from creation to the past, the present, and the next life does lead us to view the reliefs in this direction.

Creation is depicted on the west wall, right side, through the churning of the ocean of milk, a wonderful representation of the gods (*devas*) and demons (*asuras*) pulling on opposite ends of the snake Vāsukī, coiled around a pillar—the centerpiece of a churner—held in place by Viṣṇu; above are heavenly dancers (*apsaras*) and below, fish, crocodiles, and the tortoise on whose carapace the pillar rests. At either end of the snake and the gods and demons pulling on it stand their armies. The gods (Fig. 7.3) are recognizable because they wear the Khmer headdress; the demons (Fig. 7.4) wear an exotic headdress, perhaps that of the Chams. Both these divine armies have foot soldiers bearing spears, elephants with drivers and *aṅkuśas*, armed noblemen in howdahs, and chariots drawn by horses. We do not see cavalry as such, but I take the representation of elephants, horses, and men to be the visual equivalent of the verbal shorthand descriptions of the fourfold army we have met before. The chariots are, here and elsewhere, constructed very like the Cambodian oxcart, as Groslier has shown.[28]

The succeeding three panels show cosmic armies looking very like the fourfold armies of the epic stories, with some enhancements. Moving to the right side of the west wall we see the battle of Prāgjyotiṣa, in which Kṛṣṇa battles Nāraka, and around the corner (north gallery, right side), the battle of Śonitapura in which Kṛṣṇa defeats the demon Bāṇa, with inscriptions stating that they were left unfinished, and completed much later, by another king, in 1546–64. In these depictions of the armies in the full fury

[28] Groslier 1921: 98, fig. 61; Jacq-Hergoualc'h 2007: 158.

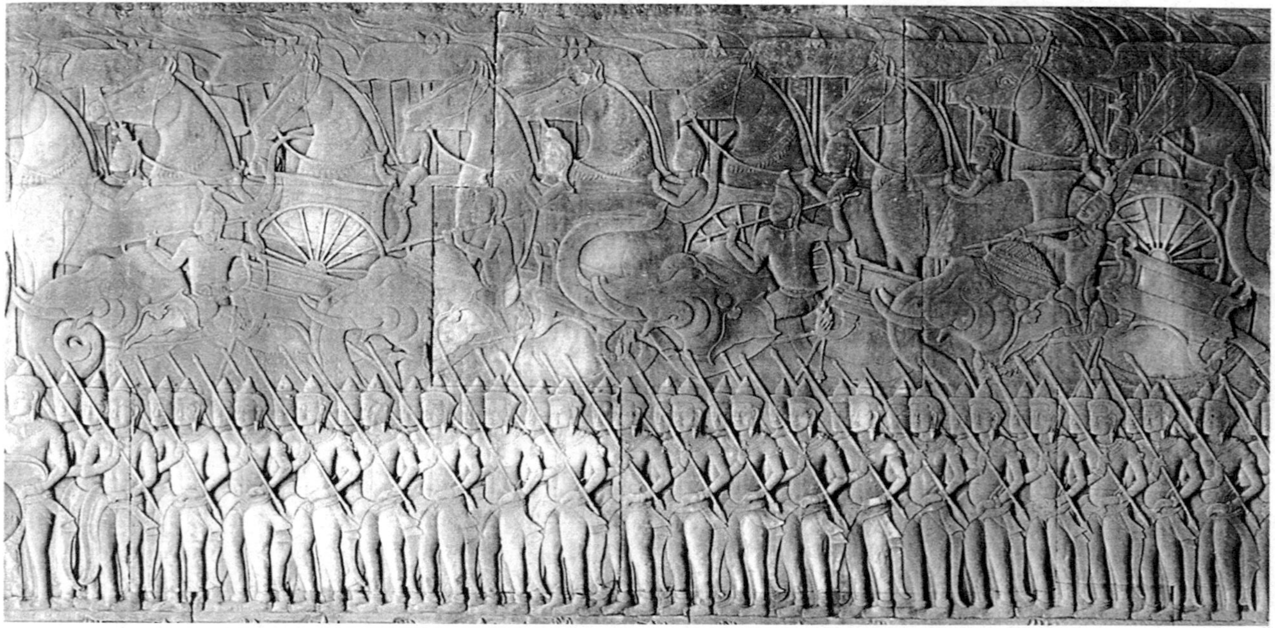

Fig. 7.3: Army of the gods. Angkor Wat, twelfth century

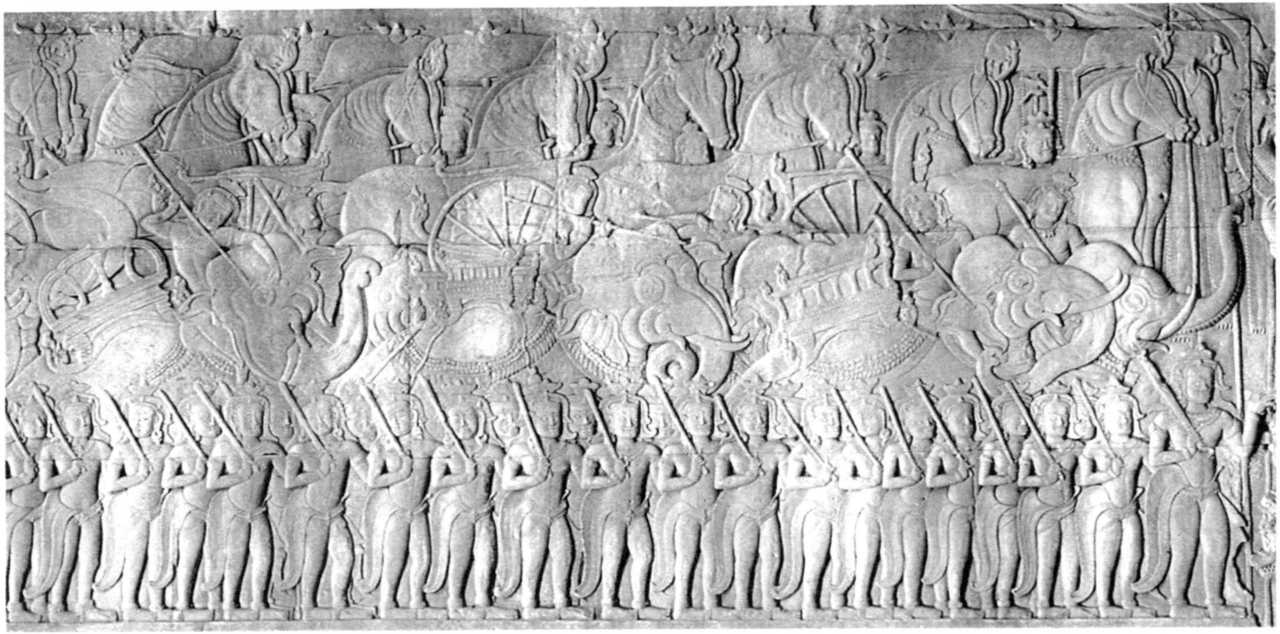

Fig. 7.4: Army of the demons, Angkor Wat, twelfth century

of battle, all elements of the fourfold army are in evidence. High-class warriors fight atop both chariots and elephants, as indicated by umbrellas, a sign of status. A consequence of the greater power of divine and monstrous opponents is representational enchancement, such as a chariot pulled by a lion, or spear-bearing warriors mounted on peacocks, or the god Agni riding a rhinoceros. On the remaining panel (north gallery, right side) is the Tarakamaya war, in which Viṣṇu defeats the demon Kalanemi, showing more enhancements of the fourfold-army model.

The eastern gallery is devoted to battle scenes from the two epics, panels showing scenes of the *Rāmāyaṇa* on the left and the *Mahābhārata* on the right. The first depicts the battle of Laṅkā, which, as I have said before, is an unequal one because Rāma is in exile and his army consists of monkeys, albeit superhumanly strong ones, while the enemy has a large fourfold army. Rāvaṇa, with his ten heads, many arms, and chariot pulled by a pair of lions is opposed by Rāma firing flights of arrows. The second depicts the battle in which Yudhiṣṭhira, leader of the Pāṇḍavas, kills Śalya, leader of the Kauravas. The overall scene is one of two armies whose leading warriors are chariot fighters, a very human scene with a minimum of enhancements to the fourfold army, in which chariots are at the forefront.

From the time of the epics in those panels we come to the near present in the next panel, on the south gallery, left side, showing the Cambodian king and his army. First we see king Sūryavarman II on his throne, surrounded by his officials and attendants; an inscription in Khmer says, "His supreme majesty, Lord Paramaviṣṇu-loka, staying on Mount Śivapāda and commanding the army to descend."[29] Further to the right we see the army on the march, in the plains. It largely consists of foot soldiers carrying spears, and grandees on the howdahs of elephants with drivers on their necks. These are the great men of the kingdom, their high rank indicated by umbrellas held over them—very long-handled umbrellas held by attendants on the ground. They are, moreover, particular, named

[29] Poncar and Maxwell 2006: 183.

persons with titles, indicated by short Khmer inscriptions. Many of them, rulers of specified provinces, have Sanskrit personal names such as Vīrasiṅghavarman and Dhanañjaya. The elephant riders are precariously perched in their howdahs, one foot in and the other out, reminiscent of the dance and the poetic trope in the *Mahābhārata* of warriors advancing to battle "as if dancing" (*nṛtyan iva*). The king is borne on an elephant in the center of the army, as indicated by his crown, with a similar adornment on the head of his elephant, preceded, according to the inscription, by his priest, the *rājahotṛ*. The van is led by one Pamañ, a non-Sanskrit name meaning "hunter," whose followers are called Syāṃ Kuk, or Siamese. As the name of their leader indicates, these are forest people, distinguished from Khmer warriors by their different hairstyle and irregular ranks. They appear to be scouting the way through the forest. The army has only a few horses, no chariots. The next and final panel, on the right side of the southern gallery, shows the judgment of the dead by king Yama.

Quaritch Wales and Jacq-Hergoualc'h, in spite of differing perspectives, agree that the historic Khmer armies had no chariots in battle, even though the armies of the gods and demons and epic heroes did; and that horses were rare and cavalry negligible. In India itself chariots had disappeared from the battlefield about the first century CE, in Kushan times;[30] they lingered in literature and artistic representations of the epics, but in forms that tended to become less like the actual battlefield chariot of the past—such as chariots with four wheels instead of two. As a result, the idea of the fourfold army was an ideal attached to the armies of the legendary past in India, as in Angkor. It is consistent with the absence of chariots in Cambodia that the Sanskrit inscriptions of Cambodian kings, while often praising the warlike qualities of kings by comparing them with epic heroes, do not speak of chariots, nor call the king a great chariot warrior (*mahāratha*).

I suggest that the unremarked disappearance of the ideal of the great chariot warrior (still present, of course, in representations

[30] As shown in Chapter 3.

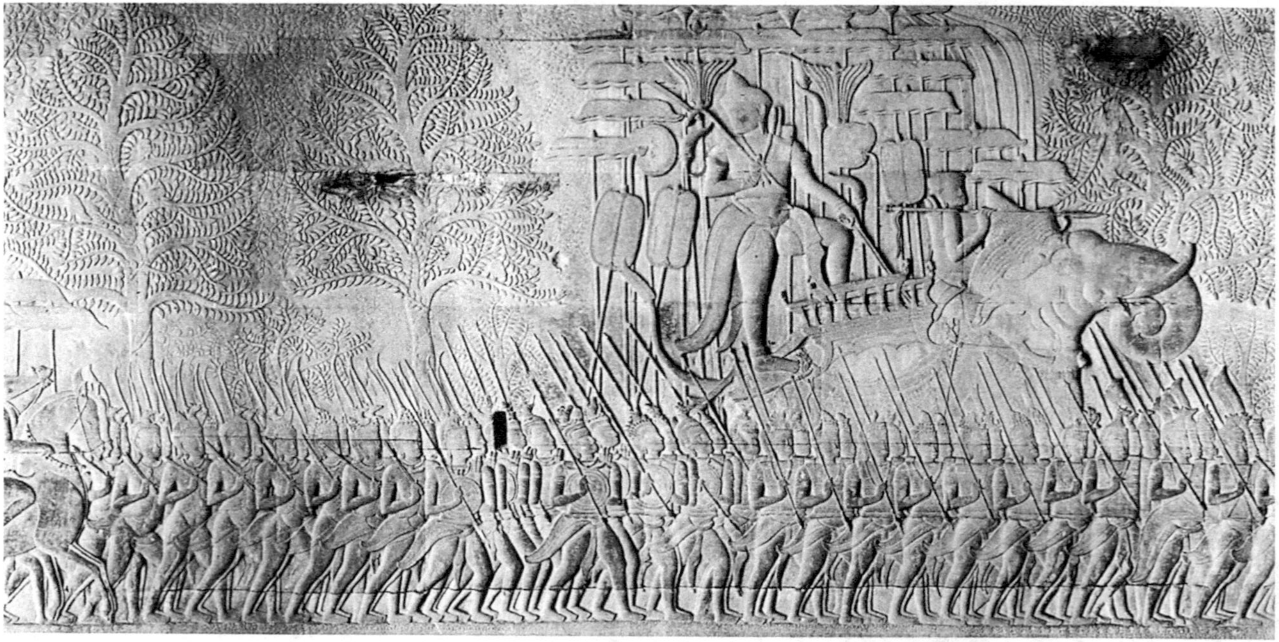

Fig. 7.5: Army of king Sūryavarman II, Angkor Wat, twelfth century

of epic heroes) has another effect. We have seen in analysis of the *Mahābhārata* that, given the preeminence of the chariot-warrior ideal, elephants tend to be associated with easterners, barbarians, and forest people; they are mounted by elephant fighters of lower rank, and only occasionally by kings. In the case of Sūryavarman's army at Angkor Wat, it is made abundantly clear visually, by means of umbrellas and other signs of rank, as well as via the brief label inscriptions in Khmer, that individual grandees of the kingdom are armed elephant fighters (Fig. 7.6). In India the departure of the chariot from the battlefield because of the rise of Central Asian-style cavalry exalted the status of the war elephant. In Southeast Asia the environment made chariots impractical and elephants abundantly available to the high-born. We do not see common fighters on the shoulders of elephants in these scenes of Khmer armies at Angkor Wat, the Bayon, and Banteay Chmar.

Fig. 7.6: War elephant with Cambodian nobleman bearing a battle-ax Angkor Wat

Jacq-Hergoualc'h tends to minimize Indian influence and sharply separate the Indianizing representations of Cambodian kingdoms from the actual practice of their armies. His work is a valuable corrective. One sees, for example, that the weaponry of the army is eclectic and by no means wholly Indianizing, as shown by the Khmer battle-ax (*phkā'k*), traceable to the prehistoric period, and the distinctive Chinese double-crossbow; both of them connected with war elephants. His analysis of the mahout and *aṅkuśa*, silently assumed to be Indian in origin, is the more valuable as it goes against his skepticism about the extent of Indian influence. The mahout sits on the neck of the elephant, cross-legged or with legs on either side, holding, often, a buckler for defense and invariably an *aṅkuśa*. While the mahouts in the Angkor reliefs have hair arranged in uniform fashion, those of the Bayon and Banteay Chmar are more various. Some of them are Cham or Cham-inspired; and indeed the Chams—at different periods allies and antagonists of the Khmer kings—were also avid users of the war elephant and seem to have been known as especially good mahouts, having been so used by the Khmer army.

How did the Indian institution of the war elephant spread to these Indianizing kingdoms?

We have seen that, in relation to the Indian war elephant in the Hellenistic kingdoms, the written evidence comes from the Alexander historians in Greek and Latin, not from Indian writings, which are rich in the poetry of war and the prose of elephant management but poor in contemporary accounts of battle. From the available sources, however, we can confidently say that the main mechanism for the transfer of war elephants and knowledge of how to use them came about principally through king-to-king transactions of royal gift exchange, battlefield capture, extraction of tribute, and the like. Even if the elephant driver, the mahout, and his *aṅkuśa* is invisible in—to take the most striking example—the exchange of 500 elephants for large eastern satrapies between Candragupta Maurya and Seleucus, we know from what follows that mahouts were part of the transaction because they and their successors become visible in the sequel, being named "the Indian" and depicted in sculpture with the unmistakably Indian two-pointed hook.

Is this the pattern that connects the war elephant of Southeast Asian kingdoms with India? Probably not. The Seleucids had no wild elephants, elephant forests, or forest people familiar with wild elephants in their kingdom when they took up the war elephant, though the Ptolemies and the Carthaginians were somewhat better placed in such matters on account of their access to the wild forest race of African elephants. The Southeast Asian kings, on the other hand, had abundant wild elephants, forests, and forest people, so they could have spontaneously reinvented the war elephant. But several circumstances suggest why this did not happen. There was, first, the long connection of trade between Southeast Asia and India; second, the rise of the luxury trade involving Rome, India, Southeast Asia, and China, and its probable role in quickening the nascent kingdoms in the very region—southern Cambodia and Vietnam—where they first arose; and third, the drawing of these kingdoms upon India for writing systems, religions, and techniques of kingship. Given all these, the appearance of the war elephant in the new kingdoms cannot have been uninfluenced by the Indian model. A sure sign of influence is the *aṅkuśa*, which we find here. In all these ways the Southeast Asian kingdoms were like the kingdoms of South India and Sri Lanka, and different from peoples to the west of India who took up the war elephant.

These considerations are reasons to think that the knowledge of Indian (possibly South Indian) hunters, trainers, mahouts, and physicians was transmitted to Southeast Asia, but not the elephants themselves, and to surmise that the means of transmission were king-to-king transactions, which we saw at work elsewhere in the diffusion of the war elephant. In the many debates among historians of the means by which Indian forms were transmitted to Southeast Asia, such mechanisms are surprisingly absent. Indian *invasion* has been proposed and discredited long ago. *Trade*, especially the international luxury trade, is certainly a part of the picture. Direct "Hinduization" by *brahmins* from India has been a favorite. But diplomatic and other connections between Southeast Asian kings and those of India has not been part of the discussion, for the good reason that there is almost no direct evidence of it; by contrast, in the Chinese records there is abundant evidence of diplomatic and military transactions between the Southeast kings and China. It is symptomatic of the nature of the evidence that our sole early record of royal emissaries from India at the kingdom of Funan is from the ambassador of China, who was there at the same time. Evidently there *were* such connections between Southeast Asian and Indian kingdoms, however intermittent and discontinuous. It would not have taken much to plant the institution of the war elephant in conditions so favorable and so receptive. It would have been a further instance of the same process that brought the war elephant to South India and Sri Lanka.

Is there an alternative possibility? Southeast Asia had an abundance of wild elephants and forest people with knowledge of them. The Shan and their linguistic cousins seem especially associated with keeping elephants in historic times, as do several other groups. But the archaeological record does not show capture and training of wild elephants before the rise of kingship any where in the world, while in Southeast Asia such domestication is positively associated with the first kingdoms. The adoption by these kingdoms of an Indianizing style, the ubiquity of war elephants, and the two-pronged hook of Indian type among them make it impossible to believe that the institution of the war elephant was invented a second time.

The apogee, end, and afterlife of the Indic model

"No animal was more closely identified with kingship in Southeast Asia than the elephant."[31] The many kingdoms that followed the collapse of Angkor—on the mainland and on the islands of Sumatra and Java—used elephants in battle and as the conveyance

[31] Charney 2004: 132.

of kings. Horses were all very well, but in the hierarchy of mounts the elephant was supreme. Among Burmese and Malayans, nobles of the highest rank rode elephants, those of lesser rank rode horses, and the lowest ranked went by Shanks' pony. In Aceh, on Sumatra, the king alone had the power to grant his nobility the privilege of being conveyed by elephant.[32] Among Buddhist kingdoms the white elephant had an immense value, as had the white elephant of Indra, Airāvata, at Angkor, in a three-headed form indicating his extraordinary nature; and the feminine form of the name attaches to the Irawaddy river. Virtually all the peoples who formed kingdoms used elephants in this way: Burmese, Siamese, Mon, Khmer, Cham, Malay, Achenese, Javanese, as is richly documented in their royal chronicles and confirmed by Portuguese, Dutch, and English accounts of the early modern period. Even a cursory examination of these chronicles shows a picture very like that of the *Mahāvaṃsa* in Sri Lanka, of the constant use of elephants in war, and the fame of certain named elephants who excelled in war. Kings often participated in the capture of wild elephants, by driving them into a stockade or by luring males with tamed females, as in India.

The apogee of the war elephant in Southeast Asia developed within the Indian doctrine of the battle array or *vyūha*, which is definitely in evidence in Southeast Asia, as Quaritch Wales was the first to observe. The *vyūha* is mentioned as such in at least one of the early Khmer inscriptions in Sanskrit: "Having shattered the enemy army which had protected itself by the circle array, he became as Garuḍa, in the region of Mahendra, in his desire of seizing the ambrosia of victory."[33] It is possible that mention of Garuḍa implies a counter-array to the circle array, as an array called Garuḍa is known, and as we shall shortly see.

The *Bhāratayuddha* of Java, in the Kawi language, retold the *Mahābhārata* story, taking special care to mention the *vyūhas*

[32] Ibid.: 168, 135.

[33] *vibhidya śātravaṃ vyūham yo viśac cakrarakṣitam* |
garudmān iva āhendrañ jayāmṛtajighṛkṣayā ||
K 806, verse 150, IC 1: 93.

and *prativyūhas* or counter-arrays taken by the opposing sides. It is surprising, nevertheless, to find in Raffles a drawing of the *makara* array employed by the army of Mataram as late as 1500 (Fig. 7.7).[34] A *makara* is a kind of sea monster resembling a crocodile; here it has evolved into what looks more like a crayfish. The numbered figures on Raffles' illustration indicate the forces of the different commanders. Quaritch Wales gives Siamese diagrams of *vyūhas* called Garuḍa, hawk (*śyena*), buffalo (*mahiṣa*), sea monster (*makara*), lion (*siṅha*), lotus (*padma*), circle (*cakra*), demon (*preta*), powerful (*krodha*), sun (*sūrya*), and thousand-rayed (*sahasrāṅgśu*), all Sanskrit names, most found in the *Mahābhārata* and the *Arthaśāstra*.[35] King Naresuan was said to have used the lotus array in 1592, when he encamped, during a war with the Burmese.[36] Burmese armies are reported to have used the lotus, wheel, cart, bull, scorpion, cloud, and other arrays from Pali Buddhist and Sanskrit sources.[37] While the drawings of arrays in Raffles and Quaritch Wales are quite late, there can be no doubt that they have a long tradition of use in Southeast Asia behind them.

The Indic doctrine of battle arrays may be hidden in European accounts of Southeast Asian armies drawn up for battle. Charney suggests La Loubère did not know such models were operative when he described the battlefield formation of the Siamese army in the late seventeenth century:

> They range themselves in three lines, each of which is composed of three great square battalions; and the King, or the General whom he names in his absence, stands in the Middle Battalion, which he composes of the best Troops, for the security of his Person. Every particular Captain of a Battalion keeps himself also in the midst of the Battalion which he commands; and if the nine battalions are too big they are each divided into nine less, with the same symmetry as the whole body of the army.[38]

[34] Raffles 1965 [1817]; in Wales 1952: 198–9 and Charney 2004: 7.
[35] Wales 1952: 200–6.
[36] Ibid.: 74.
[37] Charney 2004: 8.
[38] Quoted in ibid.: 73.

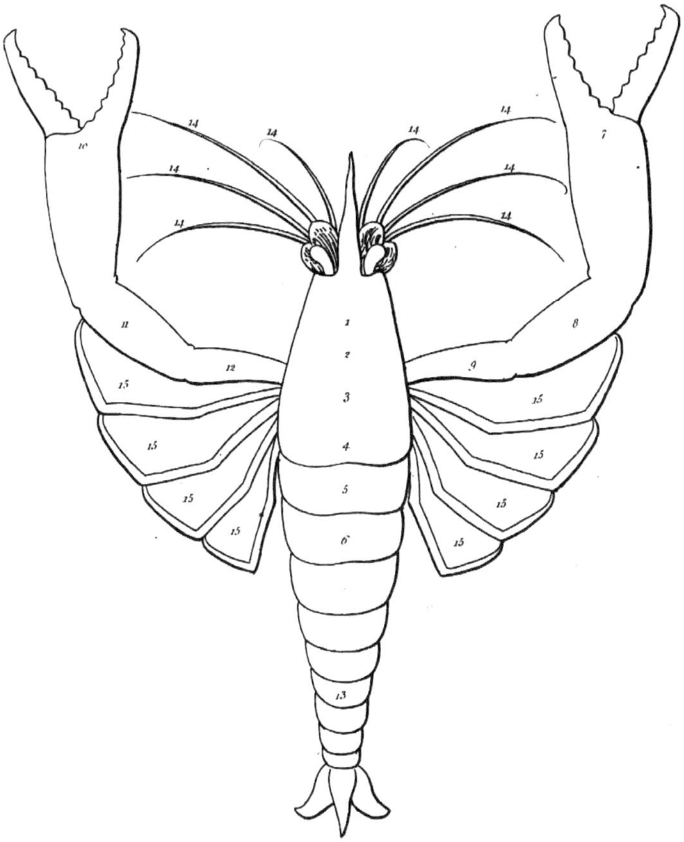

Fig. 7.7: *Makara-vyūha* from the kingdom of Mataram, Java, *c.* 1500 CE

1. Mantris; **2.** senāpati; **3.** princes and relatives of the sovereign; **4.** the sovereign; **5.** Pangiran Adepati (heir apparent); **6.** Pini Sepuh, elders of rank; **7.** Bupati Bumi; **8.** Wadana teng'en; **9.** mantris of the sovereign; **10.** Bupati Mancha nagara; **11.** Wadana Kiwa; **12.** Magtri Katang gung; **13.** Majegan; **14.** Prajurit (troops of the senāpati); **15.** Prajurit (guards of the sovereign and heir apparent).

Here the structure of practice in which the war elephant serves as an element is hidden in plain sight.

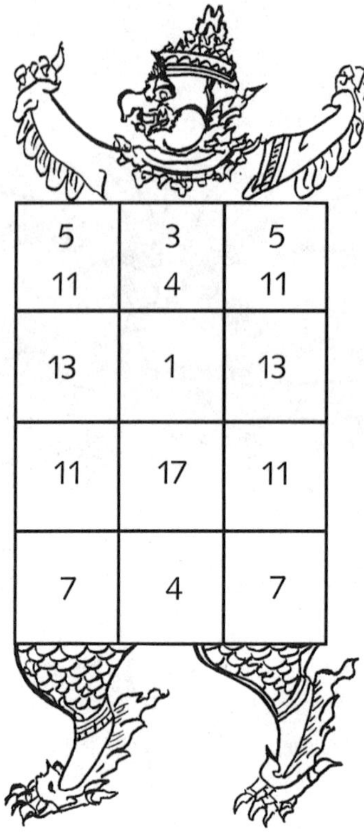

Fig. 7.8A

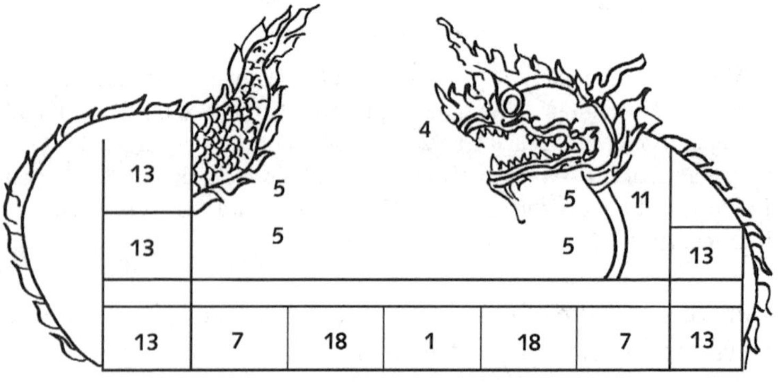

Fig. 7.8B

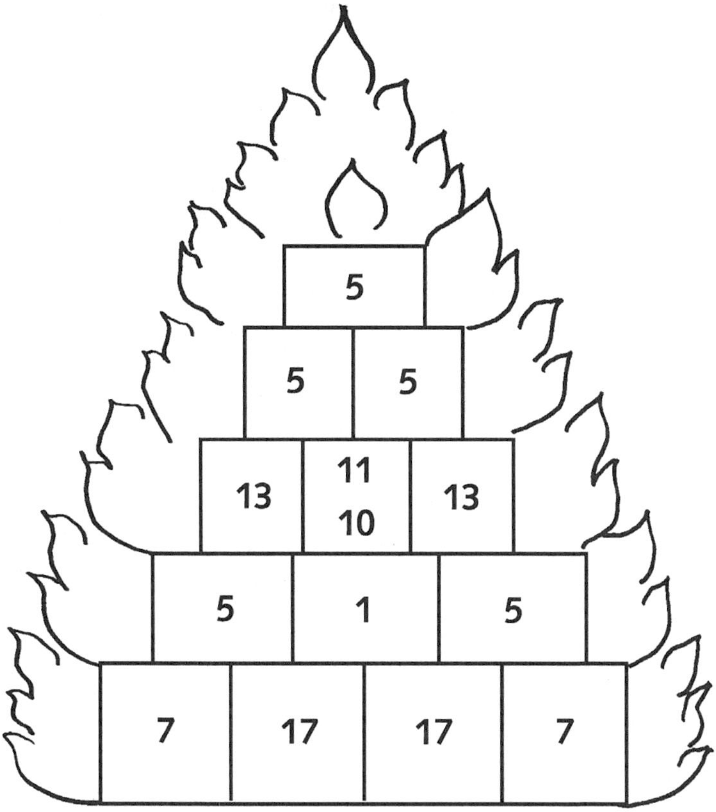

Fig. 7.8C

Fig. 7.8A–C: Diagrams of *vyūhas* from a Siamese manuscript

A. Garuḍa; B. sea-monster (*makara*); C. lotus (*padma*), "said to have been used by King Naresuan in AD 1592."

1. Commander-in-chief; 2. main army; 3. foot guards; 4. golden lance and shield bearers; 5. infantry, weapons unspecified; 6. infantry with bows, crossbows, firearms (handguns or muskets), spears and swords; 7. infantry with spears; 8. infantry with spears and swords; 9. infantry with shields and swords; 10. archers; 11. cavalry; 12. cavalry with swords; 13. elephants; 14. elephant lancers; 15. vanguard; 16. rearguard; 17. reserves; 18. firearms, probably cannon; 19. cannon; 20. *ratha*, here carts (not in these diagrams).

Gunpowder is often said to have put an end to the war elephant, but that is not exactly so. Early on in the gunpowder age—early in the Mughal period, and in the period of the Turkish sultans before them—it was found that elephants could be trained to withstand the sound and smell of gunfire. Musketeers would fight from atop elephants. What is more, small cannon called *gaj-nal* could be mounted on the backs of elephants and used in battle; there are records of them being used as late as 1720. Such elephants carried two men and two guns.[39] Guns of this kind were used both in India and Southeast Asia.

As cannon and musketry grew in power and increased in accuracy the elephant became ever more vulnerable. Elephant armor had to be increased, and the howdah had to have metal plating. Such an armored howdah was called *ʻimāri*, anglicized to *amhara.* The practice of mounting the commander on an elephant so that he could see and be seen became a liability in a period of the increasing use of firepower. "Nādir Shāh wondered at this Indian habit of mounting the general on an elephant: 'What strange practice is this that the rulers of Hind have adopted? In the day of battle they ride on an elephant, and make themselves into a target for everybody!'"[40]

Finally, in the eighteenth century, elephants disappeared from the battle line in India. The latest date I have been able to find for the use of elephants in battle comes from Cambodia, in 1833. That, according to the account in Khmer of a Buddhist monk, the Venerable Pich, was the year in which a Siamese army marched through Cambodia to invade Dai Viet (Vietnam) with "a multitude of enormous elephants." Siamese troops mounted on elephants and horses attacked a force of 1,500 Khmers, killing many and taking numerous captives. It was, perhaps, the last battlefield deployment of the war elephant.[41] Although elephants continued to serve

[39] Irvine 1903: 176.

[40] Ibid.: 177.

[41] Kiernan 2008: 207, 211–13. I am grateful to John Whitmore for drawing my attention to this source.

armies by hauling heavy guns and baggage, and even war material on the Ho Chi Minh trail as recently as the Vietnam War, due to gunpowder—a means of warfare that originated in China—the war elephant properly so-called was no more.

8

Drawing the balance, looking ahead

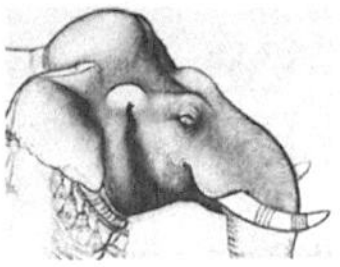

THE INSTITUTION OF THE WAR ELEPHANT has come to an end, although parts of the built-up web of practices that sustained it continue, organized by a different logic. We cannot examine it as one would a living system and can only reconstruct it as best we can from its surviving remains. On the other hand we can see it, imperfectly to be sure, as a completed whole, and in its full extent.

Having surveyed the object in its entirety, I will now put it in comparative perspective, first by resuming the examination of China, land of elephants but not of the war elephant; and second by examining the different logic of what came after the age of the war elephant, namely that of the timber elephant. The aim of these comparisons will be to clarify, by contrast, the institution of the war elephant so far as I have been able to reconstruct it. Finally, I will examine the prospects for elephants under the regime of the nation-state.

China

Some idea of the war elephant in India will have been known in China through Buddhist missionaries and their scriptures, and the Chinese Buddhist monks who travelled to India to acquire copies of holy writings. As to direct knowledge, the border between Southeast Asia and China is the limit of the eastward spread of the war elephant as an institution. There was continuous diplomatic activity between the Indianizing kingdoms of Southeast Asia and China, in the course of which many trained elephants and their mahouts were sent to China as tribute. The Chinese were repeatedly brought face-to-face with the war elephant, through diplomacy and also in battle. The absence of the war elephant in China is, as I noted, the result of a deliberate choice, the refusal of an institution of which the Chinese had good knowledge. Fortunately for us the Chinese have left a rich record of their past through which we can trace the relation of its kings and people with elephants, and its relations with elephant-using peoples in Southeast Asia.

In Chapter 2 I examined the cases Wen Huanran elicited for the period before 500 BCE, the time by which the war elephant had become universal in North India as part of a full fourfold army. I concluded that while there is some evidence for elephant capture and taming, it is rare and exceptional, and elephants were not regularly used in war. Here I will examine the entire 7,000-year period in Wen Huanran's writings, beginning with the map by which he shows the retreat of wild elephants (Figs 1.1–2).

Wen's map was developed out of ninety data points from many regions of China, representing finds of elephant remains or textual references to live elephants or both. From the chronological patterning of these data points he interpolated boundary lines representing the northernmost limit of wild elephant distribution at a given date; lines on the map indicating the northern boundary of wild elephant populations give snapshots of the distribution at different periods, and the lines taken together give a moving picture of the consistent southward retreat of wild elephants over the whole course of Chinese civilization and its written record, till today, when but a few hundreds are left in pockets of Yunnan, along the border with Myanmar. Wen mentions a count of 168 elephants in Yunnan, and a later estimate showing they had increased to about 400 after having been classified as a Level One nationally protected animal.[1]

[1] Wen 1995.

How to interpret the retreat of the elephants? We need to return to our starting point, the arguments of Wen Huanran and Mark Elvin.

As we have seen, Wen argued that climate was the prime cause, reinforced by human action (forest clearance for agriculture, ivory hunting). In his view, the evolution of the Asian elephant has given it attributes that make it an especially sensitive indicator of changes in its environment. Being highly specialized—in its size, the elongation of its trunk, and the structure of its teeth—its requirements of warmth, sunlight, water, and food are high whereas its ability to adapt to environmental changes is low. The overall direction of climate change in China over the past 7,000 years or more has been from warm to cold, according to Wen, although within that trend there have been shorter periods of reversal. The climate pattern matches the southward shift of the northern limit of wild elephant range, which at times went back and forth due to minor reversals of the overall trend. Writing from a natural history perspective over a fairly long period of time, in Wen's analysis climate comes to the fore as a cause of elephant retreat in China. But, secondary to climate change, he identifies human activities causing environmental damage that put the elephant in its present endangered condition. The wanton capture and killing of elephants in the historical period (that is, the span of Chinese civilization) has been calamitous.

Elvin, as noted, accepts Wen's argument and the special status of the wild elephant as the equivalent of the miner's canary for environmental history. He pays due respect to climate change but attributes more to environmental degradation by humans. In his narrative elephants function as a symptom of such degradation. This is brought out at the beginning, after which they fade from the narrative and the book turns to the human agents of the general distress of wildlife in China, the elephant being emblematic of this.

How exactly we should draw the balance between climate and human agency in accounting for the well-attested fact of the retreat of the elephants in China I am not qualified to say. I take it as established that both are at work. But we can use the history of the war elephant to shed further light on the subject. It can explain the contrast between India and Southeast Asia, where wild elephants persist, and China, in which they have largely retreated.

Such a comparison can begin by examining the interactions between the Indianizing kingdoms of Southeast Asia and the empire of China in relation to elephants. We have a valuable resource in the *Ming Shi-lu*, an extraordinary daily chronicle of the Ming dynasty (1368–1644), some 40,000 pages long. Geoff Wade has extracted and translated passages having to do with Southeast Asia and put them online.[2] Of these, sixty-seven have to do with elephants, spanning nearly the whole period of the Ming.

The first of these entries is dramatic. It records that a king of Annam (i.e. northern Vietnam) named Chen Shu-ming sent an envoy to the Ming emperor, offering an elephant as tribute; but as the king of Annam to have previously sent an embassy had a different name, questions were asked and it emerged that the present king had caused the former one to commit suicide and sent tribute in the hope that the emperor would recognize him as the legitimate successor. The Chinese refused the tribute.[3]

Embassies bearing tribute to the Chinese emperor came from Annam, Champa, Cambodia, Siam, and Java. These are Indianizing kingdoms, except for Annam, which is generally considered to have been more oriented toward the Chinese model of kingship, for it was under Chinese rule during several longish periods up to 1000. In spite of this the Chinese records show clearly that Annam, as one of the kingdoms immediately adjacent to the Indianizing kingdoms, regularly followed their practice in using war elephants. Diplomatic gifts or tribute that the kings of Annam sent to the Chinese emperor often consisted of elephants.

Elephant drivers are mentioned several times in the records of the diplomatic missions of Southeast Asian kings to China;

[2] Ming Shi-lu 2005.

[3] Ibid.: March 13, 1372.

sometimes they are mentioned among recipients of gifts made by the Chinese to the embassy and its king when tribute has been accepted. An embassy from Champa may serve as an example. It is full of particulars about the gifts given and the relative rank of the recipients. At the very end of this long recital we meet elephant drivers, who are given gifts, along with soldiers, at the lowest rank of the personnel who make up the embassy:

> Bao Bu-ling-shi-na-ri-wu, the son of A-da-a-zhe, the king of the country of Champa, who had been sent with others by his father, came to Court and offered congratulations on the Emperor's birthday. He presented 54 elephants, elephant tusks, rhinoceros horn, pepper, ebony, laka-wood and floral silk cloth, and offered as tribute to the Heir Apparent elephant tusks and other products. It was Imperially commanded: that headwear and a belt as well as suits of clothing made from patterned fine silk interwoven with gold thread be conferred upon the king of the country; that 200 liang of gold, 1,000 liang of silver, two suits of clothing made from blue silk gauze interwoven with gold thread, two suits of clothing made from red silk gauze interwoven with gold thread, two suits made from blue fine silk embroidered with gold thread and two suits made from red fine silk be conferred upon the king's son Bao Bu-ling-shi-na-ri-wu; and that two suits of clothing made from blue silk gauze interwoven with gold thread, two suits made from red silk gauze and two suits each of clothing made from red and green patterned fine silks, six bolts of fine silks and 150 liang of silver be conferred upon the king's grandson Bao-gui Shi-li-ban. Paper money, silk gauzes, fine silks and clothing, as appropriate, were conferred upon the deputy envoy, the chiefs and and the interpreters. In addition, clothing was conferred upon the 150 elephant attendants and soldiers.[4]

Elephant drivers are sometimes mentioned as having been transferred with the tribute of elephants. On one occasion tribal allies of the Ming in Yunnan were made elephant drivers in the Ming military, an honor under the circumstances, but in other circumstances Chinese officials were reduced to the rank of elephant drivers, which shows their low status in Chinese eyes. Elephant drivers register, faintly but distinctly, in these records.

[4] Ibid.: September 24, 1386.

Ming forces had often to confront war elephants on the battlefield in Yunnan, in the hands of what are called "bandits," who were *yi*, non-Han people, the approximate equivalent of Indian "forest people." We should not take the minimizing talk of bandits in the Ming records at face value. For example, the Bai-yi insurgent Si Lun-fa raised a force reckoned at 300,000 men and over 100 elephants; this is an enormous force, doubtless exaggerated, but one that cuts right against the minimizing language of banditry. In this and some other cases the insurgent forces of Yunnan in the Ming period are kingdoms, like the elephant-using Indianizing kingdoms of contemporary Southeast Asia. We may take them as the furthest extension of the war elephant into East Asia.

In one engagement of this war, a Ming force of 30,000 cavalry confronted the Bai-yi army of 10,000 men with many elephants, 30 of them in the vanguard, their chieftains riding elephants like the chieftains of Sūryavarman II in the Angkor Wat reliefs of his army. The Chinese neutralized the elephants of the enemy with volleys from guns and arrows shot by some kind of mechanism. Each elephant had armor and bore a howdah on its back; bamboo tubes hung on the two sides containing short lances. The Chinese force managed to kill more than half the elephants, and 37 were taken alive.[5] The imperial forces were ordered to offer the remaining insurgents surrender terms: paying for the costs of the war, and a tribute of 500 elephants, 30,000 buffaloes, and 300 elephant attendants.[6] The consequence was the setting up of state farms for elephants under the Trained-Elephant Guard, sending home all Bai-yi elephant handlers, and the dispatch to the capital of the captured elephants under their handlers from Champa. The record explains: "Previously, a Trained-Elephant Guard was established with the special function of capturing elephants. When the Xi-ping Marquis Mu Ying destroyed the Bai-yi and captured these people, he sent them to this guard for employment. At his time, it was closed down and they were sent home."[7] This is the

[5] Ibid.: May 6, 1388.
[6] Ibid.: May 25, 1388.
[7] Ibid.: August 6, 1388.

closest the Chinese came to training elephants for their own use in this Ming period source. It is significant that they had to rely on mahouts of the *yi* people of Yunnan and Champa for this. About the same time, the Indianizing kingdom of Cambodia sent an embassy offering a tribute of 28 elephants, 34 elephant handlers, and 45 slaves; and the non-Indianizing kingdom of Annam a tribute of 4 elephants and 3 elephant handlers.[8]

Thus the Chinese emperors appear to have been pleased to receive elephants, doubtless for display and possibly for conveyance, along with those capable of handling them, but only briefly and episodically got into the business of capturing and training them, and then only for battling the "bandits" who used them. And they were pleased to receive elephant tusks in tribute. It is evident that by Ming times the Chinese sources of ivory, and the wild elephants it came from, were largely confined to Yunnan and the kingdoms of Southeast Asia.

These Ming sources—from a time when the use of elephants on the battlefields by Indianizing kingdoms of Southeast Asia was in full force, and by kingdoms of India as well—establish clearly that the boundary between Southeast Asia and China was the limit beyond which the institution of the war elephant did not extend, even when the Chinese directly experienced elephants in battle. Choices made much earlier by Chinese kings in the style of warfare, when elephants roamed China more or less throughout, excluded the war elephant.[9]

Why?—we may ask. When so many non-Indian people adopted the war elephant—Persians, Greeks and Macedonians of the Hellenistic period, Carthaginians, Romans (briefly), Ghaznavids

[8] Ibid.: October 15, 1388; January 10, 1389.

[9] The absence of war elephants is confirmed by a collection of papers on Chinese ways of warfare published decades ago (Kierman and Fairbank eds 1974), and a recent collection on military culture in imperial China (Di Cosmo ed. 2009), as well as the aforementioned non-mention of elephants in the ancient Chinese art of war literature. Di Cosmo (2002) brings out very clearly the strong orientation of Chinese military development toward the problem of nomadic cavalry from Inner Asia.

and Turks, some Southeast Asians—why did the Chinese not do so? What is the reason for the India–China difference in this respect?

The land ethic in India and China

We have seen that the *Arthaśāstra* prescribed death for those killing wild elephants, and that Indian kings mostly captured them for use and did not kill them for sport. It is worth saying again that this was not out of a sentiment favoring wildlife, but purely for reasons of state, or king-centered self-interest of the most direct kind. The interest in protecting elephants in the wild cannot have been entirely effective. We cannot measure how effective it was. But China provides evidence for the effect of the *absence* of conservation measures. While Indian kings tended to protect wild elephants even against the interest of their farmers, in China kings tended to clear forests of large wild animals including, above all, elephants, to make forest land safe for humans, and for conversion to farmland.

In Elvin's analysis *interest* is the key to human action: it leads to the maximization of agriculture and the degradation of the environment, of which the elephant's retreat is the emblem. But "interest" itself needs examination, for it is by no means a simple found object to be picked up and used as a tool as if it had been made for us. "Interest" in this argument is economic, that which is imperatively needed and therefore trumps philosophy, religion, ethics—in a word, interest is the pre-cultural core of being pertaining to universal human needs proceeding from the nature of the human body. This being so, what constitutes interest will be immediately evident; and once Elvin has demonstrated the toothlessness of philosophy and the like in conserving the environment, interest is revealed to be the engine of its degradation.

I do not agree with this view. In the first place, interest is not a self-evident term. It is relative both to long-enduring features of the human body and more recent historical formations, such as kingship and plow agriculture, which are not eternal but have a definite starting point in time and a course of development thereafter. Which is to say, interest itself is subject to historical contingencies and change. In the second place, interest is always plural in any human endeavor, so that to advance one's interests is always also to draw a compromise among them from many possible compromises. Maximizing interests also always involves compromise: every real-world king or farmer is always juggling competing interests and as a consequence making choices. Such choice-making is always highly constrained by circumstances but never wholly dictated by them. And, once made, a choice may settle into a durable pattern of similar future choices.

With this as starting point, we must say that the pattern of land-use among a given human group is not the outcome of interest alone but a pattern of relations among interests. The patterning of actual choices that have become settled choices—the collective, historical patterns of long (but not everlasting) duration—we may call a *land ethic,* adapting a phrase from Aldo Leopold for present purposes.

It is fitting to turn to the great conservationist at this point, for Aldo Leopold, by example and exhortation, called for an environmental history, or a history of human effects upon the landscape, to complement and qualify the historian's grand narrative of progress. All historians now writing in this sub-field of the discipline are in a tradition that springs from Leopold. He also called, in a famous essay on "The land ethic," for an ethical relation to the land on the part of landowners; for a tempering of economic and personal interests because of their often dire environmental consequences; and beyond that, promoting a sense of community between humans and all other species.[10] In this appeal the land ethic is a unitary thing, treated as a transhistorical

[10] The essay comes at the end of *A sand county almanac* (1949) published just after Leopold's untimely death (reprinted in Leopold 2013). Worster (1994: 284) considers "The land ethic" a seminal text: "More than any other piece of writing, this work signaled the arrival of the Age of Ecology; indeed, it would come to be regarded as the single most concise expression of the new environmental philosophy."

entity that tempers economic interest. An environmental history built on such a foundation, however, is likely to be one in which the outcome, in gross, is already known before the data are examined; it is likely to be a story of environmental degradation that marches with the story of economic progress as its darker self, its shadow.

An environmental history *not* given by forces deemed unchanging will pose itself a greater risk. It will posit that patterns of land use are the settled effects of *choices* among interests that are *plural*, making the concept of land ethic typical of specific human groups for particular, though perhaps very long, periods of history, whose qualities and outcomes are not already known. It is at the same time an ethical or moral entity, as Leopold intended; it is a sense of how land *should* be used; but it is simultaneously the particular ethic of a specific human group. This can be a tool with which to explain, or more deeply describe, the difference between India and China as the difference between two quite different land ethics.

On such an understanding we may ask: what is the land ethic of Indian kingship? It is evident how large a role animals—cattle, buffaloes, sheep, goats, horses, elephants, and camels—play in Indian kingdoms for food, draft, transport, and the military. In the matter of domestication, India before the Veda, i.e. India of the Indus civilization, can be thought of, according to Possehl (2002), as a part of the Middle East: wheat, barley, cattle, sheep, and goats are native to it, and they may have been domesticated independently. Thereafter came the horse of Central Asia; then the wetland—*anūpa*—domesticates: rice, water buffalo, chicken (from the red jungle fowl of the northeast), elephant. The domestication of the elephant was only the final addition to an established and growing pattern that impressed its own logic on the landscape—a specific land ethic.

We can give detail to the picture by taking light from the *Arthaśāstra*'s chapters on the settlement of the countryside.[11] The countryside is to be divided up into economic and ecological zones

[11] *Arth.* 2.1–2; Trautmann 2012: 86–105.

of farming villages, pastures, trade routes, timber forests, elephant forests, and mines; all connected with the city, which is the seat of kingship, by relations of economic exchange and taxation. In this version of the ideal kingdom and its ecology, the primacy and normativity of agricultural villages is evident. But pastoralism as a specialized way of life is clearly formed, and pastureland is interdigitated with farming villages, assigning the land in between villages to grazing animals. This land may be endangered by wild animals and robbers, and the cowherd may be given residential land in the village. The picture of a juxtaposition of pastoralists and agriculturists on land as shown in the *Arthaśāstra* (here greatly abbreviated) is corroborated by the ethnography of pastoralists in present-day India, where animals often graze the stubble and simultaneously fertilize the farmer's field after harvest. Pastoralism also occupies forests, and pastoralists shade into forest people, at least in the view from above. Thus, pastoralist castes in the Peninsula may be called various kinds of Kurumbas, while forest people will be called Jenu Kurumbas, whose name indicates the wild honey they collect; forest people (from the perspective of the normative farming village) being another kind of pastoralist, so to say. Elephant men are drawn from forest people called Kurumbas, among others. In this scenario, domestic animals may be kept and stall-fed or grazed by farmers living in villages; but they may also be herded in larger numbers by specialist lineages of pastoralists in proximity to farmers and connected with them by relations of economic exchange. The forest may be grazed by their herds and turned into a parkland or a scrub jungle. The picture is not of deforestation as such, but of forest degradation. As we have seen, this is not necessarily a bad thing for elephants, who are fond of bamboo and other products of grazing by animals domesticated and wild. Within this pattern the elephant does not have quite the emblematic significance for the environmental history of India that it has for China; if anything, forest degradation helps elephant numbers.

That the land ethic of Chinese kings is very different from this, we have already begun to see. The clearing of dangerous animals from forests is the king's special duty under that ethic, and extending cropland is the other. Pastoralism as a specialized way of life is largely separated from farming geographically. The high degree of separation is captured by Tregear when he speaks of the two economies, the pastoralist of the northwest, and the agriculturist of the plains of the great river valleys, the two economic zones being divided from one another by the Great Wall;[12] although we could as well say that it brings them together, since the complementarity of the two economies invites relations of exchange between them. Pastureland for horses, sheep, and goats abounds among the non-Han peoples of the northwest, while the farmlands of the heartland had precious little land dedicated to pasture. Farming and pastoralism were "two ways of life," mutually exclusive and hostile to one another.[13] Horses, sheep, and goats were (and are) largely the business of non-Han peoples beyond the Wall.

In that respect it will be to our purpose to examine the two economies in relation to the pattern of domestication that, in India, was the larger context of elephant capture and training. In ancient China one finds reference to "five crops" and "six livestock species" in descriptions of completeness and abundance. The six species are horse, cow, sheep/goat, pig, dog, and chicken. Jing, *et al.* (2008) give earliest dates for these domestic animals from archaeological remains:

dog	10,500–9700	BP (before present)
pig	8200–7000	BP
cow	4500–4200	BP
sheep/goat	4400	BP
horse	3300–3050	BP
chicken	3300–3050	BP

There are many similarities with and differences from the Indian pattern, but I will comment only on a few that seem especially telling. Jing, *et al.* identify five subspecies of pigs in China, from

[12] Tregear 1966: 51–8.

[13] Ibid.

every region of China proper, north and south, including Taiwan.[14] These subspecies are ancestral to the many breeds of domestic pigs of China recorded by Epstein,[15] who says there are over a hundred different breeds and varieties. There are many ancient burials containing skeletons of sacrificed pigs. This contrasts strongly with India, where the pig was known from Vedic times but is little mentioned in the ancient literature and came to be regarded as unclean by upper-caste Hindus and Muslims in India. In China, sheep, goats, and horses appear in the valley of the Yellow river quite suddenly and considerably later than the oldest domesticates, the dog and pig, and are strongly associated with the drier and grassier or afforested lands of the second economy beyond the Wall.

To be sure, there were and are domestic animals in the vast agrarian zone within the Wall, for food, draft, and transport. Draft animals in the form of cattle, water buffaloes (in the south), and donkeys are needed on farms for plowing and transport, and their numbers are significant. Chickens and pigs are more numerous on farms, along with ducks and other animals needing no pasture. The agricultural land of the great river valleys, as shown in a classic study of the early twentieth century,[16] is lightly stocked compared to other countries (China: 2 crop hectares per animal; Denmark: 0.4 hectare), certainly lighter than India, for which the recurring complaint is of overgrazing by cattle and goats. One great cause of this difference is the huge place of milk and milk products in India, and limited amount of dairy for most of the heartland of China till recent times. But there are other causes, too. The burden of transportation in the Chinese plain was borne, to a remarkable degree, by humans, using the wheelbarrow, carrying-pole, or backpack, and comparatively less by animals, even though human transport is the most expensive form, per ton-mile, as we shall see later in this chapter. Wheeled vehicles were used less, pack

[14] Jing, *et al.* 2008: 88, Table 3.2.
[15] Epstein 1971: 69–93 and plates 90–133.
[16] Buck 1982: 218–26.

animals and humans more. India by contrast is from the time of the Indus civilization a land of oxcarts, and until recently the movements of great armies were accompanied by a second army of oxcarts carrying provisions. On the other hand a great amount of collective labor was expended on canals in China, with canal and river transportation becoming highly developed. Finally, many forests in China have been gradually turned into cropland.

The role of animal power in the military of China was also different from that of India. The environment afforded the possibility of a fourfold army like India's, in that horse and elephant habitat came together, but it did not develop. The war elephant, if it was experimented with in the early period, did not take hold, and in later times when it was directly encountered the Chinese refused it. As to horses, the Warring States period (451–221 BCE) of continuous internecine strife began as a scene in which great men were chariot warriors, as in the Indian epics, and had a culture of war that held ritual, divination of outcomes by oracle bones, and an aristocratic moral code in high esteem. The introduction of cavalry can be precisely dated to 307 BCE, for which moment we have the record of king Wuling of the state of Zhao persuading his ministers, against considerable opposition, to adopt a cavalry of Inner Asian style, that is, of mounted archers. It was a specific point of contention that such a cavalry involved adopting also the dress of Inner Asia (as it did in India, following the Kushan model), which would offend propriety and be hateful to the people of the kingdom. Wuling however overcame the objections, and Chinese cavalry on Inner Asian lines was launched.[17] At the end of the Warring States period the kingdoms were unified by Qin, in 221 BCE; and the famous entombed terracotta army of the unifier, Qin Shihuang, is an army containing both chariots and cavalry horses as well as masses of foot soldiers.[18] A more pragmatic attitude to war began to replace the aristocratic, ritualized, moralizing one of the earlier age, and the literati began to lose interest in

[17] Di Cosmo 2002: 134–8.
[18] Luo 1983; Chang 1996; Portal and Kinoshita eds 2007.

the military, possibly because of its increasing association with the land of nomadism. As in India and everywhere else, chariots finally ceased to be used on the battlefield.

Nicola Di Cosmo asserts that Wuling's adoption of cavalry had been not only defensive, to keep nomads at bay, but also offensive, against his non-nomad neighbors. Nevertheless, because the source of supply remained in the north, there developed what Kierman calls "two more or less opposite modes of fighting." He says: "One was a direct acceptance of the main external adversary's style of war (barbarian clothing and horse-borne soldiery, with the development of the stirrup a just-possible later extension of the sequence). The other, more appropriate to the city-and-agriculture base of Chinese civilization, was the development of highly organized infantry tactics, and weapons adapted to them."[19]

This twoness of military modes answered to the very different relations of Chinese kingship to the north and to the south. Southern China, in spite of its difference in climate and landscape, flora and fauna, languages and peoples, seems always to have afforded a field into which Chinese civilization might readily expand, even if it was altered in doing so. But, as so memorably described by Owen Lattimore (1951), whose classic work is essentially the cultural history of that second, pastoral economy beyond the Wall, the relations of Chinese kingship with the peoples of inner Asia were highly fraught, needing as it did a cavalry-based army to defend against its horse-rich inner Asian enemies, one in which border peoples inevitably played a large role. At the same time agrarian China also needed relations of exchange by which the second economy could supply the lack of the first.

According to Chang Chun-shu the word for elephant appears on the bamboo slips of the Central Asian frontier of China, on two records, one of them referring to carts drawn by elephants.[20] Such bamboo slips, found at several sites, constitute a valuable collection of early government documents, but the elephant notices are on only two of some 30,000 such records that have

[19] Kierman 1974: 63.
[20] Chang 2007: 2, 147.

been recovered. It was the elephant's misfortune to feel at home in the land that liked agriculture, and that nurtured a civilization whose land ethic tended to minimize pasture and forest. This is the pattern that sent elephant numbers into such a steep decline everywhere except in a few pockets of Yunnan. Thus the *why* of the Indian adoption (indeed, the invention) of the war elephant, and the Chinese refusal of it, touches very early decisions and the different land ethics they generated. It has to do with something deep and stubborn.

To a degree the large difference in the land ethics of India and China persists. But, as we have already seen, China today has its own environmental movement for the protection of wildlife, including the elephant, centering on Yunnan.[21] India, too, has undergone rapid changes in government policy and public opinion in respect of elephants and other wildlife. We should not treat the long-enduring land ethic of either as a kind of unchangeable doom. In both regions the existing land ethic is under rapid revision.

In Elvin's analysis of the Chinese pattern of land use economic self-interest is a given—perhaps of human nature, or of a specific form of socio-economic organization (agriculture, kingship). The simple directness and materialism of the term is pleasing for the clarity it affords but is otherwise deficient. Royal interest is not self-evident and its content is defined by the choices made; or rather, the *pattern* of *interests*, which defines royal interests very differently in the two civilizations. We need the larger context in which the war elephant was adopted or refused. The larger context is, in the first place, the more general pattern of animal domestication in India and China; and in the second place a more general outlook upon how land should be used, both together resulting in starkly differing outcomes for the elephant.

The age of the war elephant

The war elephant was the dominant form of elephant use in India and elsewhere for nearly three millennia. The ideal form of the

[21] Hathaway 2013.

war elephant (adult male tusker, aggressive in spirit, subject to vigorous musth) identifies the desirable points of elephants for capture, the targets of the capture operation itself, and, by extension, the population profile of captive elephants. As we shall shortly see, capture operations and population profiles for other kinds of the animal—timber elephants, zoo elephants, circus elephants—change greatly after the demise of the war elephant.

The war elephant finds its highest value in the battle or the siege. These are comparatively rare events. We have seen that elephants have other military functions on the march and in the encampment. Outside warfare, elephants serve as large, visible stores of value, so that even in a peaceable procession they signal the military potential of the kingdom. Thus, analysis should not draw a sharp boundary between the functions of elephants that are military on the one hand and "ceremonial" on the other. The institution of the war elephant dominates both.

In the age of the war elephant, as the chronicles of Sri Lanka show so abundantly, the public procession in its highest form is the fourfold army, with its war elephants, on the march. Therefore the war elephant ideal pervades this form, even when the procession honors a religious relic or has some other religious purpose—even in the present-day procession of the Tooth Relic, long after the demise of Sinhalese kingship. This illustrates the work of the war elephant as a model for other functions. In terms of religion, again, the divinized elephant appears first as the mount of Indra, the king of the gods and their war leader, which indexes the invention and normalization of the war elephant; Gaṇeśa, elephant-headed son of Śiva and remover of obstacles, emerges only much later.[22] There is every indication that forms and meanings flow from the war elephant to other functions of elephants, and *from* kingship *to* religion, not the other way around. As a corollary, by focusing upon the war elephant we examine the thing itself, and not its secondary effects; we approach the heart of the matter.

Now that the details have been placed in evidence, we need to return to the thesis they are meant to sustain. My hypothesis

[22] Getty 1992 [1936]; Courtright 1985.

has been that the institution of the war elephant promoted the persistence of the elephant in India, and more generally in South and Southeast Asia. This is not a claim about ideas of non-violence, or nature reverence, or divinity, at least not in the first instance, but about royal interest.

It is not a claim that Indian kingship was essentially "green." We have only to think of the royal hunt, in which large numbers of animals other than elephants were driven and killed, to see this. The Taq-i Bustan frieze (Fig. 6.4), in which men on elephants drive wild boars in the royal hunt, is emblematic; so is the section of the *Ā'īn* where we find elephants hunted only for capture and training, unlike the other animals discussed. Eventually, in India, the meat of "useful" animals, including elephants, is considered forbidden, as al-Bīrūnī recorded in the twelfth century.[23] The logic of the prohibition on beef perhaps extended to horses, camels, elephants, and others considered useful to man. The *Arthaśāstra* prescribes death for the killers of elephants. In general, the strong royal interest in elephants extends to matters of ownership, of which the Mauryan policy, with its royal monopoly of the ownership of horses, elephants, and arms, is the extreme case. The tendency of royal interest and its logic are perfectly clear; the only question is how effective it was. As a beginning it is important to observe that in India royal interest not only aimed to protect elephants, but that in doing so it acted against the age-old practice of hunting elephants for food and ivory, the pattern of the prehistoric period before kingship; and at the same time it reversed the tendency of the kings of the early civilizations to use elephants in ways that directly decreased their numbers. The remaining problem is to measure the effectiveness of Indian royal practice.

Indian kingship, when compared to the republic—the competing political form of the period—appears to have been better able to amass resources for large projects combining and coordinating specialized workers and their different kinds of knowledge. The capture and training of wild elephants draws upon this superior ability. The sheer scale and complexity of capturing and training

[23] al-Bīrūnī 560; Sukumar 2011: 148, 182.

the most difficult elephants make me believe Indian kingship is the locus of invention of the war elephant, and conversely to doubt that it gradually emerged from the practices of forest people.[24]

Kingship puts increasing demands upon the environment. The attraction elephants held for early kings in many countries, in the form of large-scale royal hunts, capture and display, and tribute-taking, is documented. Alongside forest clearance to extend agriculture, royal interest in the animal increases the pressure upon wild elephant populations; for example, the local extinction of the Syrian elephant may be due to royal hunts. But the invention of the war elephant in India reversed such tendencies. Again, it is not just that the institution has a positive effect upon wild elephant numbers, but that it also reverses the direction of earlier royal interest.

What makes the hypothesis counterintuitive is the evident fact that the capture of wild elephants for war in India will have reduced their number. Moreover, since captive war elephants did not reproduce themselves, stock replenishment was by further captures. This put a pressure of unknown magnitude upon the size of the wild elephant population. In addition to the local demand for war elephants, a great part of the demand in countries west of India was supplied by India, beginning with those 500 elephants sent by Candragupta Maurya to Seleucus, the effect of which will have been to reduce wild elephant numbers in India. Moreover, the capture of wild African elephants by the Ptolemies and Carthaginians did not have the beneficial effects upon local populations of African elephants that I suggest as likely for India, and for that matter in South and Southeast Asia together. Local extinction, indeed, was the sequel of the Ptolemaic elephant capture machinery in Africa, regardless of whether capture was the main cause or only subsidiary. But, as we have seen, even though they failed, the Ptolemies at least attempted to create a regime of wild elephant protection among the elephant-eating

[24] Bishop (1921) argued that Shan or Tai speakers of ancient China and Southeast Asia held elephants not for war but for religious purposes.

forest people by offering subsidies not to kill elephants. It did not succeed because political management in the hinterland of Ptolemaic Egypt was incomplete; its kings were neither able to control the region of wild elephant habitat continuously nor for sufficiently long duration—the converse of the situation in South and Southeast Asia.

Capturing elephants in the wild certainly increases the pressure on their population; but Indian kings also reduced pressure by protecting wild populations from being hunted for food by forest people and others, even as it reversed the direction of earlier royal practices. On balance, the net effect of these practices on elephant populations in South and Southeast Asia was positive. One has only to look to the retreat of the elephant in China to get a sense of how significant this reversal has been in South and Southeast Asia under kingship on the Indian model. In Southeast Asia there is the added factor of a human population density very much lower than that of India and China—perhaps a mere 10 per cent of the latter—which will have contributed to a larger elephant population independently of the effect of the institution of the war elephant.

Population geography of elephants is another consideration that tests the hypothesis. We have seen the map of former and present distributions of Asian elephants (Fig. 1.3). We should expect the furthest extremes of the area to be the most thinly populated and the center the most thickly populated. Local extinction can be expected to have begun at the extremes, namely Syria and China, leaving the center, which is to say South and Southeast Asia, with the largest wild populations. And that has been the case. The reason, then, for the persistence of the elephant in South and Southeast Asia would be because it lies in the center of the species geography.

Undoubtedly this is true, in gross. But when we come to particulars, the effect I have been trying to document becomes evident, by comparison. The case of China is the most telling. The consideration in question explains the retreat of the elephant from the northern China extreme of its distribution well enough; but not at all from southern China, whose monsoon forests, in which elephants flourish, are similar to those of South and Southeast Asia. Southern China is dotted with place-names indicating the former abundance and normativity of wild elephants. Bishop gives examples of place-names associating elephants with the south.[25] The great Qin unifier of China, Shihuang, named the far southern part of his empire the "Commandery of the elephants." Under the Han, northern Guangxi was known as "The district of the elephants." There is a "Great" and "Little elephant pass" in Sichuan, "Elephant neck" in Yunnan, and "Elephant hill" near Guangdong, all in southern China. Elephants were deliberately cleared out by the actions of Chinese kings, imposing upon southern China the pattern of the north. The Chinese refusal of the war elephant did not save wild elephants; quite the contrary, it caused the inexorable retreat of elephants.

The overall difficulty of confirming the hypothesis I have proposed is that, while it is possible to elucidate the *logic* of policy choices and institutions and their *direction*, it is difficult to attach *quantities* to the tendencies in question. The best we can do is reason backward from effects to causes, inferring intensities from outcomes. Here the *Arthaśāstra* on the one hand (Fig. 1.4) and the *Ā'īn* and allied Mughal sources (Fig. 1.6) on the other come to our aid, showing that the elephant range remained much the same over nearly two millennia of the period of the war elephant, while the ETF Report (Fig. 1.5) shows that the range shrank and numbers crashed after about 1800 when, with the coming of British rule to much of India, sport hunting of elephants was introduced, human numbers began to soar under the colonial peace, and the land ethic radically changed.

The brief reign of the timber elephant

Although the age of the war elephant came to an end in the nineteenth century, there is something to be gained by carrying the story forward over the last two centuries. In the first place, it

[25] Ibid.: 304–5.

gives us a point of comparison with the war elephant, enabling us to see in what way the later structures of use differed, among timber elephants above all, and also in modern zoos and circuses. In the second place, a substantial literature on the capture, training, management, and medical care of elephants in English was produced in the last two centuries, which is to say after the demise of the war elephant and during the ascendancy of the timber elephant.[26] This literature is helpful in interpreting ancient and medieval sources, but to use it intelligently and critically for the study of the deeper past we need to understand the transformed conditions of elephant use out of which it came.

Following the demise of the war elephant, the timber elephant came to the fore. Kings continued to maintain state elephants for public processions and as mounts for hunting parties; temples maintained elephants for religious festivals; the army used them for baggage and hauling large guns, especially over rugged terrain; they continued to be of use in large building projects; and they were sought by foreigners for zoos and the modern revival of the ancient Roman circus. Above all, they were used for timber operations. Elephants had long been used for extracting timber. But in the nineteenth century there was a sharp rise in the local and international demand for tropical hardwoods, due mainly to the railroads, which needed an enormous number of ties or sleepers; and steamships, which needed hardwood decks. The result was a rapid increase in the use of elephants for the extraction of timber from the forests native to them. The timber elephant came to be the dominant type in South and Southeast Asia. The age of the timber elephant was comparatively brief, about two centuries, and it has come to an end recently in most countries, except Myanmar, where it continues in full force under an entity of the state, the Myanma Timber Enterprise.

The timber elephant of colonial Burma and independent Myanmar is an especially good case for our purposes because

[26] Tennent 1867; Sanderson 1893; Evans 1910; Milroy 1922; Ferrier 1947; Hepburn n.d.

of its early start and comparatively long duration; because of the large numbers of elephants employed both by large private companies such as the Bombah Burmah Trading Corporation and by the forestry department of the state; and because it generated a useful literature. Three works are especially helpful here. G.H. Evans, *Elephants and their diseases: a treatise on elephants* (1910, many editions), coming out of British Burma, gives a lot of information about conditions of capture, sale, and use in the early twentieth century, as well as information about medical care, both the traditional healing methods of the elephant keepers and the European methods of their employers. The memoir of Toke Gale, *Burmese timber elephant* (1974), written in retirement after twenty-eight years of work with timber elephants, 1938–66, begins with the author graduating from Rangoon University and joining a British timber company as a forest assistant. He works through World War II (and the Japanese occupation of Burma), then serves as a forest manager under the State Timber Board, and later as a Deputy Director of Forests. The book is especially useful because the author, from a family prominent in government service and coming from the royal capital of Mandalay, has consulted older works on elephants and often has telling comparisons of current practice with how things were under the Burmese kings, that is, in the age of the war elephant. Finally, Khyne U Mar has written a PhD thesis, "The demography and life history strategies of timber elephants in Myanmar" (2007).[27] She has drawn upon the "studbook" of 8,006 elephants captured between 1910 and 2000,[28] of which the information on 5,292 was complete enough to be included in the study group. These works, and others,[29] comprise a good record of the timber elephant of Burma/Myanmar.

At the outset, we find that the general context has greatly altered. Elephants were freely owned by private persons in the

[27] The PhD was at University College London; see also Khyne U Mar 2002.

[28] Khyne U Mar 2007: 58.

[29] Especially Williams 1950 which, in addition to giving a first-hand account of timber-elephant management in Burma, tells the story of an escape by elephant from Japanese-occupied Burma in World War II.

early twentieth century, and as freely bought and sold in market conditions not subject to the gravitational force of kingship; indeed, Burmese kingship had been extinguished by the British. Elephants were valuable assets for making money in the international timber trade, especially the trade in teak for the decks of ships, now driven by steam generated by coal. Shans, Karens, and other non-Burmans captured, trained, and used elephants for riding and other purposes, both as prestige goods held by chiefs in large numbers, in the manner of kings, and for sale. Elephant rustling was commonplace, especially along the border with Siam/Thailand; and a stolen elephant taken across the border and sold in Siam might be stolen again and resold in Burma.[30]

This pattern of smuggling is in part a result of the fact that timber elephants are at work in the forest, among forest people. It is also a result of the practice of the timber industry to set the elephants free at night, with perhaps a drag chain or loose hobbles so that it will not wander far while feeding in the forest. At first light or even before, the mahout (*oozie* in Burmese) sets out to find his elephant and returns to camp for breakfast, harnessing up and going off to work for the day. The practice of night release greatly eases the cost of feeding which, for elephants kept in stables, will mean employing two cutters of grass and browse for each elephant,[31] plus the transport, by elephant, of the fodder. Night release, moreover, gives opportunities for sexual encounters between tamed elephants, or between tamed and wild ones. A working female may therefore become pregnant and give birth and, after a short interval, return to work with a baby at her heel, running alongside and suckling when it can.

Under this practice some elephants are born in captivity; but because of the heavy work effort females have a longer interval between births, so that the sluggish reproductive rate of wild elephants (gestation of about twenty months; single births, very rarely twins; substantial interval between pregnancies) is slowed even more. For this reason the population of tamed elephants

[30] Evans 1910: 13–14.
[31] Tennent 1867: 175 n. 1, for Ceylon.

cannot replace itself with births to tamed elephants. The working stock has always had to be replenished by the capture of wild elephants. Currently, however, efforts are being made to end wild capture and make the domestic stock self-reproducing.

The work of the timber elephant is very demanding and has several entailments. The workday is eight hours with a rest at midday and access to shade and water. As we have seen, Evans makes it clear that the wild elephant spends almost all its waking hours eating in order to replace the energy expended by grazing and moving about to find its food. Timber work removes eating time and adds an expenditure of energy, resulting in an imbalance which has to be restored by a supplement of food cooked or otherwise processed to give a higher level of accessible energy. Energizing concoctions (comparable to the *pratipānam* or invigorating drink for draft animals in the *Arthaśāstra*), including treats of salt and tamarind, have to be given. The working season is about 160 to 180 days per year, with two months of rest, sometime in November–December, and in the hottest season before the monsoon rains, March-April-May, which is the period when most conceptions take place. Even with all efforts to ensure that elephants are not overworked and sufficiently rested, Toke Gale believes that vital statistics show the heaviness of work taking a toll upon them. But the numbers he gives do not bear this out and show, to the contrary, that mortality is highest in the youngest and oldest age groups, that is, age groups within which there is little or no work.[32] Accidental death and heart failure are the risks to which timber elephants are exposed when in harness. When we examine mortality month by month, it appears to be greater during

[32] The figures for 714 deaths of timber elephants over 16 years are: age 9 and under (78 deaths); 10–17 (27); 18–35 (185); 36–54 (222); 55–70 (202). Toke Gale concludes that the bulk of deaths occur during the working years, ages 18–54 (1974: 78–9). The difficulty is that the age groups are not of uniform duration. When we correct for that by computing deaths per year for each age group we get what we expect, high yearly mortality in the youngest group, lowest in the next group, and increasing mortality in every subsequent group: age 9 and younger (8.6 deaths per year), 10–17 (3.4), 18–35 (10.3), 36–54 (11.7), 55–70 (12.7).

the hottest and coldest months, the very seasons at which they are given extended rest.[33] Taken together, and somewhat contrary to our author, it is unclear whether the stress of work contributes to mortality. Khyne U Mar lists "major risk factors" contributing to the mortality pattern as malnutrition, heat stress, lack of quality forage in summer, musth, capture, taming, and work-related stress, and of these she considers stress of capture the greatest.[34]

The timber-elephant business relies on a number of bodily "points" in distinguishing among elephants for quality, some of them inherited from the highly developed systems of points in use in the age of kings, which is to say the age of the war elephant. The conformation of the spine, seen in profile, falls into five types.[35] The most suitable for a timber elephant is "the back that hangs down like the bough of a banana tree. Others are the straight flat back; the one shaped like the back of a pig; the back resembling a fresh-water herring; and the one that appears broken and curves sharply backwards. Ancient Burmese writers held that an elephant having a back with several humps like a bull would bring poverty to its owner."[36]

The tusks of male elephants fall into a number of classes.[37] Elephants with two intact tusks are *swe-zone* or "tuskers"; with one long tusk, *tai*, with one short tusk, *tan*; with no tusk, *haing* (the Indian *makhna*). "To compensate for their lack of tusks, the haings have much better developed trunks, and can definitely lift heavier teak logs than tuskers, and appear to be more inclined to be ill-tempered." Pairs of tusks fall in several groups such as the *thabeik-pike*, "like the hands of a Buddhist monk carrying his begging-bowl."[38]

The timber business has its own way of assessing these inherited schemes of bodily points, of which the most notable concerns the tusks of male elephants. For while tusks are of use

[33] Toke Gale 1974: 79–80.

[34] Khyne U Mar 2007: 90.

[35] Pictured in Toke Gale 1974: 10.

[36] Ibid.: 11.

[37] Pictured in ibid.: 14.

[38] Ibid.: 15.

in shifting heavy logs, they can be a danger to keepers and other elephants, so that the regular practice was "tipping," sawing off the tip of the tusk every two or three years, well ahead of the pulp cavity (which would cause nerve damage and expose the tusk to infection), to limit the damage of fights. Indeed, the whole drift of timber work was to keep elephant aggression at a minimum, quite the opposite of the culture of the war elephant. Musth is a problem to be managed, not a virtue, as it is in the ancient Indian epics.

This principle shows clearly in the actualities of elephant capture.

There are five modes of capture in the Burma of Toke Gale's book: *kheddah* or *kyone*, essentially a trap into which wild elephants are driven; *mela-shikar* or *kyaw-hpan*, capture by leather lasso; the decoy method, using a female to lure a tusker; the pitfall; and immobilization. Pitfalls were used during World War II under the Japanese occupation, but not before or since. In 1968 immobilization by darting with etorphine hydrochloride was introduced and has since become the method of choice as having a low incidence of death.[39] I will describe these methods to get at the resulting demography of timber elephants and its difference from the demography of war elephants. I will examine the *kheddah* system in some detail.

Kheddah or *kyone* was widely used in British India as well as Burma. A Y-shaped structure is built of very large tree trunks affixed firmly at close intervals in deep holes to make a funnel leading to the stockade at its base, which is just wide enough to hold a group of elephants (five to ten) in single file without room to turn around. The mouth of this stockade has a sliding door made of tree trunks, suspended ten meters in the air by a rope running to the back of the cage. When beaters have moved wild elephants into the cage, the leader of the hunt cuts the rope with a sword-like large knife (a *daw*), and the gate crashes down, burying its sharpened points into the earth and thus closing the stockade. Captives are removed from the stockade as quickly as possible to minimize

[39] Toke Gale 1974: 85–106; Khyne U Mar 2007: 31.

danger to elephants and the men who will look after them. "For every moment that the captives are in the narrow confines of the stockade, they struggle furiously to free themselves by dashing their foreheads, or pressing with all their might their hind legs against the posts that form two walls or railings of the enclosure. And every time they do this, elephanteers spear their foreheads or their legs to prevent them from breaking the posts down."[40] At the same time, certain kinds of elephants are freed or killed:

> Very old animals, or cows heavy with calf, are set free. It so happens that sometimes a tusker is among the captives, and, if he is likely to endanger the lives of others in the stockade in his desperate bid for freedom, a .450 rifle is judiciously employed at close range, and the animal is painlessly destroyed. The other animals in the funnel eventually find their way back to the jungle, their nerves somewhat shattered, but physically none the worse for their experience except a few torn ears, bruised trunks and foreheads and a few damaged toenails.[41]

The elephants are led out from the stockade one at a time, by means of an exit gate, to an individual cage or crush where they are held until their fury has worn off and they become ready to receive training—a difficult process, which may take some days, and which achieves its ends by inducing hunger and deprivation of sleep. Drives take place in the cooler months from December through February, and there may be three in a season; 7,000 elephants are said to have been caught by this method in the seventeen years from 1910–11 to 1926–7.[42]

A significant number of elephants die or are released as unsuitable due to old age, poor condition, or advanced stage of pregnancy; Toke Gale puts the rate at 12.4 per cent of captured elephants for all these causes over the period 1945–6 to 1966–7.[43] Khyne U Mar puts the mortality rate for *kheddah* capture much

[40] Toke Gale 1974: 95.
[41] Ibid.
[42] Ibid.: 97.
[43] Ibid.

higher, at 30.1.[44] Capture and breaking is certainly very hard on elephants. And the elephant hunters are exposed to mortal danger, too. Evans gives the annual post-capture mortality of captive elephants in Burma at 10 to 20 per cent for his period, *c.* 1910, more in line with Toke Gale's figure, though whether it is based upon actual counts or is an educated guess does not appear. Possibly the incidence declined with better inoculation for anthrax and surrus, the leading causes of death among tamed elephants.[45]

We now come to the all-important matter of the demographic profile resulting from this method. Gale gives us the heights of 2,556 elephants captured over eighteen years, which makes a very telling profile of the results of the *kheddah* system. The age structure of the result is what we would like to know, but it is not directly knowable, and height is a good surrogate for it.

Height	Percentage
3'0"–3'11"	4
4'0"–4'11"	13
5'0–5'11"	26
6'0"–6'11"	25
7'0"–7'11"	26
8'0"–8'11"	5
9'0" and up	1

The results of the *kheddah* system and the choices made by those who direct the hunts are evident. It is a wholesale system, capturing whole herds of elephants in all age grades. But as herds usually consist of mothers and their children, and adult males lead solitary lives outside herds, the usual composition of captive groups, we may surmise, is adult females and immature elephants of both sexes; it is an unexpected and unwanted accident if a tusker is captured in the stockade, and he may be shot, as we have seen. The policy of selection is to release old, infirm, or pregnant elephants, from which we infer that adult females and their

[44] Khyne U Mar 2007: 30.
[45] Evans 1910: 30.

young progeny are kept. The height chart confirms the pattern: a substantial number of elephants, even ones as small as three feet at shoulder, are young, even very young; and very few are large adults, that is, adult males. This population profile is conducive to timber work, and very different from the one needed for the work of the war elephant.

The other, less used methods of capture can be described more briefly.

The lasso method, *mela-shikar* or *kyaw-hpan,* involves capturing elephants by a very long rope of braided leather. Hunters on the backs of tame elephants move in among wild elephants and slip a noose over the trunk, pulling it over the head. They follow the lassoed wild elephant, which takes off and does not stop until exhausted. Other hunters slip a noose on a hind leg and make it fast to a nearby tree. This method is still used in Thailand, by forest people speaking a Khmer language.[46] Single capture means fewer captives, but it does not need as large a body of men, as does *kheddah*, the preparations for which require a large workforce. And of course it does its selection of captives before the fact. For the most part the captives are young, smaller than the adult elephant used to capture them, and the method is not suited to capturing adults.[47] It is associated with the remote northern regions of Myanmar, and the training methods, involving folk songs, are similar to those described by Nicolas Lainé (forthcoming) for forest people of northeast India, who capture immature elephants and prepare them for training with lullabies.

Finally, there is the decoy method, using a tame female to lure a wild male. This is especially suited to capturing elephants for war; as Toke Gale says, "In old Burma, this method was practiced essentially for the purpose of acquiring elephants of war"; it is the method recorded by Megasthenes as used by the Mauryans two thousand years ago. It is worth quoting Toke Gale's description of the preliminaries:

[46] Pittaya, *et al.* 2002.
[47] Khyne U Mar 2007: 33.

> The Burmese kings would detail a team of scouts to observe the movements of wild herds in the forest. When a handsome tusker was located, the team would at once inform the Sin-wun Sit-ke—the Commissioner of Royal Elephants—who would in turn check up on the reports personally, and then submit his findings to the king. After the king had studied the reports in detail, he would dispatch special artists and experts on elephants into the forest. The artists would make detailed drawings of the outstanding anatomical points in the elephants, and these drawings, together with the statements from the experts, were later put up to the king. When the king was satisfied that the description and likeness of the wild tusker conformed to the good characteristics of a royal elephant, nine to fifteen teams of elephanteers, under the Auk-a-wun, were assigned the herculean task of capturing him.[48]

Here we see that the method of capture is suited to the ideal of the war elephant: a large male tusker, who would be solitary and not suited to capture by *kheddah*, sexually active and therefore amenable to following a tame female into captivity. It was little used in the timber industry.

Of the five ways of securing elephants, the pit method was used only during World War II, under Japanese occupation. It is regarded as a primitive expedient and as far too likely to result in the death of the elephant. The decoy method was not suited to the demographics that the timber industry sought. *Kheddah* was the main method, and *mela-shikar* a secondary one, but both were banned by the Myanmar government in 1985 because of the high rate of elephant mortality, in favor of the new method—immobilization by dart gun.

The overall outcome of these practices is a demography that reflects the needs of the industry, very different from the age of the war elephant in which the adult male tusker was the leading type. The sex ratio in the timber industry showed a distinct preference for females. Thus in Khyne U Mar's large study group 3,313 captive-born elephants showed a balanced sex ratio (1,527 male, 1,562 female); but among 2,161 wild-caught elephants the

48 Toke Gale 1974: 104.

ratio had nearly twice as many females as male (766 male, 1,395 female). The gender statistics of the timber elephant of Myanmar show about 60 per cent female and 40 per cent male overall.[49] Zoo holdings of elephant in recent times are similarly biased toward females: of 1,087 elephants in 354 zoos, 18 per cent (200) are male, 82 per cent (887) female.[50] In the circus the bias toward the more tractable females is very pronounced, if we may judge from a record of the elephant herd of the Ringling Brothers Circus, 1968–78, which shows all females but one for most years.[51]

The era of the timber elephant has been formally ended by government action in India, Laos, and Thailand, because of a combination of international conservation and animal welfare advocacy on the one hand, and a need to protect severely reduced forests on the other. In Myanmar the timber elephant continues, and remains, as Richard Lair has said, a living museum of the great age of the timber elephant.[52] It cannot continue unchanged. Old methods of capture have been replaced by immobilization, and every effort is being made to promote the reproduction of tame elephants and end the capture of wild ones in deference to international sentiment against capture.[53] It seems unlikely that even this can continue indefinitely. Everywhere, machines using fossil fuels are replacing the timber elephant.

The elephant and the nation-state

On February 3, 1862, as the American Civil War raged, Abraham Lincoln sent a letter to Rama IV, King Mongut of Siam. He thanked him for letters sent the year previous (February 14, 1861), and gifts accompanying them: "a sword of costly materials and exquisite workmanship; a photographic likeness of Your Majesty and of Your Majesty's beloved daughter; and also two elephants'

[49] Khyne U Mar 2007: 58, 62.
[50] Clubb and Mason 2002: 26, Table 3.
[51] Sabu 1979.
[52] Lair 1997: 101.
[53] Khyne U Mar 2007.

tusks of length and magnitude such as indicate that they could have belonged only to an animal which was a native of Siam." But he politely declined the king's offer of a breeding stock of elephants to be set loose in the forests of the South:

> I appreciate most highly Your Majesty's tender of good offices in forwarding to this Government a stock from which a supply of elephants might be raised on our own soil. This Government would not hesitate to avail itself of so generous an offer if the object were one which could be made practically useful in the present condition of the United States.
>
> Our political jurisdiction, however, does not reach a latitude so low as to favor the multiplication of the elephant, and steam on land, as well as on water, has been our best and most efficient agent of transportation in internal commerce.[54]

The forests of the South were not then in the control of the United States, they were held by the Confederate States that had seceded, giving Lincoln a reason to decline the offer.

King Mongut's letter bears a three-headed image of Airāvata, the elephant of Indra, king of the gods, a figure much loved by rulers of the Indianized kingdoms of Southeast Asia.[55] He meant to benefit the people of the young nation-state with a valuable source of animal power. It was not an outlandish proposal; Americans depended greatly upon animal power, and, as Mongut pointed out in his letter, they had tried importing camels for communications across the drylands of the American Southwest (the experiment had not taken). But they depended increasingly upon steam and other forms of power and transport whose energy came from fossil fuels. The American Civil War already had a somewhat industrial aspect, with large shipments of men and material delivered to the battlefield by rail and steamship. Animal power was on its way out. Moreover, although it did not seem so in 1862, when kingship was ascendant and republics almost non-existent, the nation-state was to become the norm. Ours is a world with ever-fewer kings,

[54] Lincoln 1953: 125–6.

[55] Photo and transcription in Young 2005: 20, 184–5. The letter itself is in the National Archives and Records Administration, College Park, Maryland.

without war elephants, in which animal power of all kinds is, we may say, on its last legs. Thus the technological-economic force of steam power, and the political form of the nation-state, have combined to reshape the landscape for elephants.

To bring this study to the present, I need to say a few words about both transitions: from animal power to steam power, and from kingship to nation-state. I need also to show the changes to the land ethic that follow from global movements for conservation and animal welfare, and the continuing dangers which put the persistence of the elephants in doubt.

The story of the advance of steam power is known well enough, but the economic result of the new technology is not so well known despite being a central fact of our times: transport became, suddenly, very cheap, because of fossil fuels generating steam power. This is well illustrated from early-twentieth-century China, where Buck compiled statistics on the rural economy of the 1930s, a time when man-powered transport was commonplace, animal power had limited scope, and steam power was on its way up. Skinner has drawn the following comparative figures from the statistics compiled by Buck. The dollar cost of transporting a ton of goods one mile was, junk 21¢, animal-drawn cart 40¢, wheelbarrow 63¢, pack donkey 71¢, runner with carrying-pole $1.39. As we should expect, water transport was cheapest and human transport the most expensive, while animal power, represented in the sole form of donkey transport, lay in between. But the cost of transport per ton-mile was very much lower by the new means of transportation: steamboat 8¢, railroad 9¢.[56] The cost advantage of the new technology was enormous, so it was bound to displace animal power and human power so long as the cost of the new forms of energy remained low, as it has till now. In such circumstances, elephant power was bound to decline, along with bullock power, donkey power, camel power, and the like, with a substantial reduction of cropland and pasturage devoted to the needs of working animals.

[56] Skinner n.d.: 213, n. 116; Buck 1937: 346–7, Tables 4 and 5.

Turning to the political transition from kingship to the nation-state in the lands of the Asian elephant, South and Southeast Asia, the salient fact is that it began under the intrusion of European powers forming their Asian empires. In this process some of the Indianizing kingdoms of the region were simply brought to an end. The kingdom of Ceylon, having retreated to the highlands of Kandy when the coastal regions were taken, first by the Portuguese and then by the Dutch, was extinguished by the British when they took over in 1815. The British ended the Burmese kingdom in 1885; Bao Dai of Vietnam abdicated in 1945 and his kingdom came to an end; the Lao kingdom was ended by the Pathet Lao in 1975; the kingdom of Nepal was ended by the parliament of Nepal as recently as 2008.

In British India the story is more complex. Kingship, at least that of the Indian princes who allied themselves with the British, was perpetuated, with real but reduced powers. The Indian princes continued their rule over two-fifths of the territory of India, while the British ruled the remaining (more heavily populated) three-fifths directly. Defeated powers were pensioned off; or their kingship was extinguished, as with the Mughal dynast following the insurrection of 1857. After the partition of British India in 1947 the nation-states of India and Pakistan ended the territorial powers of the princes and commuted their former income into privy purses paid by the state. In 1974 the Republic of India put an end to the privy purses by amendment to its constitution. This finally ended the legal powers of Indian kingship.

Its effects upon captive elephants was dramatic. The Indian kingdoms that had survived British rule could no longer afford to keep elephants. They emptied their stables, giving ownership to their keepers, who were also let go.[57] Most of the elephants of kings became itinerant working elephants, earning the keep of their keepers by being rented out for work or for ceremonial occasions: weddings, birthdays, temple festivals, advertising, begging. (In Kerala, however, owning elephants to be hired out

[57] I am grateful to Surendra Varma for this point.

for temple festivals has become a vanity project of the well-to-do in the post-royal era.) For all intents and purposes 1974 marks the end in India of the relationship of kings with elephants.

Kingdoms remain in Bhutan, Thailand, Cambodia, and the sultanates of Malaysia and Java. New kingdoms are not coming into existence. The culture of elephant use invented by Indian kingdoms more than three thousand years ago is fading, lingering only in history, literature, and the arts.

The winding-up of British India and the formation of the new nation-states of India and Pakistan began a tidal wave of newly independent nations from shrinking European empires, in Asia, Africa, and the Caribbean, turning both imperial rulers and the ruled into self-contained nation-states, and making the nation-state form normative for the world. Wild elephants have become wards of the nation-state. They depend upon the will and effectiveness of nation-states to protect them, in national forests and parks. The shrinking numbers of privately owned domestic elephants are monitored and regulated ever more closely by the state.

Possible futures

The persistence of the elephant is much in doubt. About the prospects of the African elephant there is little reason for optimism, given the sharp increase in demand from East Asia for ivory; civil wars and insurgencies yielding well-armed private armies in need of funds; simple poaching for food or for ivory; and states that are unequal to the task of countering all these. The population of Asian elephants is much smaller, but its prospects are somewhat better, though there are many causes for concern. To make out possible futures for the Asian elephant, it is well to begin by examining the forces making for its retreat and persistence in recent times.

As we have seen through the mapping of wild elephants at different ages from the beginning of the Common Era (i.e. in the *Arthaśāstra*) to about 1800, that is, for the last two millennia of the age of the war elephant, the retreat of wild elephants in India was fairly limited, a pattern very different from the sharp and continuous decline in China documented by Wen Huanran. On the other hand the decline of elephant numbers in India was greatest in the period after 1800, coinciding with the spread of British rule.

What were the causes of this accelerated retreat? Sport hunting by Europeans was a major cause. While the hunting of elephants for sport, for food, or for ivory was known from ancient documents such as the *Rāmāyaṇa* and the Tamil Sangam poetry dealing with forest people of the mountainous region, the instances of such mentions are few. For the most part wild elephants were protected; the purpose of hunting elephants was to capture them live and use them for war or in hunting, to drive game and as perches from which to shoot. This pattern changed with the coming of British rule to India, Ceylon, Burma, and Malaya. The British brought European sport hunting, taxidermy, trophy records, and a flood of hunting literature to record its accomplishments.[58] Individual hunters in the nineteenth century killed, in some cases, hundreds of elephants; and in one, over a thousand. Colonial rule combined with the growing firepower of rifles to take a toll upon the wild elephant population that was without precedent, in addition to the capture of elephants for work. The umbrella stand made from the foot of an elephant is a symbolic relic of that colonial moment and the trivial ends for which elephants were deprived of life.

An engraved scene celebrating the killing of an elephant by the Prince of Wales may serve as an emblem of the period (Fig. 8.1). It comes from a hunt organized for him in Ceylon, in the course of a trip to India, the memorial of an admirer in a published diary of the prince's tour.[59] The scale of the effort to guarantee the desired result was immense; some 1,200 to 1,500 men had been engaged as beaters. The prince took his place in a stand on a high rock at 9:00 a.m. and did not get his kill till the late afternoon. The elephants—a group of three females led by an old tusker, and another of seven females—did not cooperate, and all efforts

[58] Lahiri-Choudhury 1999; Rangarajan 2001; Hughes 2013.
[59] Russell 1877.

Fig. 8.1: The Prince of Wales shoots an elephant in Ceylon, 1876

to force the elephants in the desired direction having failed, the beaters were instructed to set fires and to shoot into the rear ends of the elephants. The prince shot a few elephants without killing them before he got his kill. The carcass, pictured here, "was not that of the redoubtable tusker"; in other words, he had killed a female. He "climbed upon the mountain of flesh," modeling an iconic picture in the heroic mode, and then cut off the tail, "according to custom."[60]

In addition to sport hunting, other causes of Asian elephant decline derive from a single root, beginning in the colonial period and continuing in the period after independence: the rapid growth of human population and consequent demands upon the landscape. The human population of the earth has grown over the last two centuries from a billion to seven billion. In India the retreat of the elephants has accelerated with that of population growth from the nineteenth century, made possible by the colonial peace. Human population growth entailed the expansion of human habitat and agriculture, including livestock, encroaching on elephant habitat and dividing it into islands, isolating elephant populations from one another. In India, pastureland and forest have been somewhat preserved for millennia, but both are subject to the grazing of a large stock of domestic animals and wild grazing animals; these pressures have grown tremendously in the last two centuries, and the greatly increased degradation of forests is the result.

A system of state forests and national parks was constructed in the colonial period to protect forests from such pressures. Following German and French models, forests were emptied of human settlements. The burden of that protection, therefore, was borne by the forest people whose settlements were cleared from the forest to its periphery, and whose customary rights of hunting and gathering were curtailed or commuted.[61] More recently, in accord with the views of the international conservation community, elephant capture for timber operations has been ended. Private

[60] Ibid.: 254.
[61] Guha & Gadgil 1989.

ownership of elephants continues but is increasingly hedged with laws and curtailed by declining elephant numbers. The overall tendency is toward the end of domestication and the protection of wild elephants in forests and parks from which human settlements have been removed.

The present situation is complex. Forces making for the persistence of elephants include the global movements for conservation and animal welfare, hostile to the domestication of elephants and their use in timber operations. Powerful forces are at work for the preservation of elephants in forests from which resident humans have been removed. The finance has often been generated by eco-tourism. Conversely, two forces threaten the persistence of Asian elephants in India: the international ivory trade, and human–elephant conflict.

Europe and the Americas used to impose a heavy annual demand upon African elephants for their ivory, which was made into piano keys, billiard balls, and luxury items. But other materials have taken their place, and this trade has largely come to an end. India has, via the Wildlife Protection Act of 1986 and a ban on the import of ivory from Africa in 1991, stopped its ages-old tradition of ivory-carving.[62] But a large and growing demand from East Asia, and the price spike it has caused, have increased poaching. This is destroying wild elephant populations in Africa and it has led to an upsurge of male tusker poaching in India and Southeast Asia. This has even led one criminal to saw off the tusk of a museum specimen in Paris.[63] If the price continues to rise, every object of ivory will become more vulnerable to theft.

Ivory poaching in India (and also a new elephant meat trade in some parts) has grown rapidly in the 1990s, employing a range of weapons from poisoned arrows and spears to muzzle-loading rifles (some of them home-made) to semi-automatic weapons.[64] The problem cannot be solved once and for all, but it can be managed by good surveillance and police action.

[62] Menon, *et al.* 1997: 2.

[63] March 31, 2013; website of The Telegraph News.

[64] Menon, Sukumar, and Kumar 1997.

Human–elephant conflict, however, is bound to rise with the increase in human population and, ironically, from the very success of measures for the protection of wild elephants—in the degree to which they bring about an increase of elephant population. This is a structural fact of central significance, for it means that the management of the problem is ever more difficult.

Human–elephant conflict has a long history. Its central locus is crop-raiding by elephants, especially adult males; it largely rises, therefore, with the beginnings of agriculture. The story of first domestication and the formulation of elephant science by the sage Pālakāpya is emblematic, as these come about, according to the story, because elephants are destroying crops in the kingdom of Aṅga during the reign of Romapāda.[65] As long as there has been farming, there has been the problem of protecting crops from wild animals, especially the adult male elephant. Harassment can provoke elephants to rampage, endangering both elephants and farmers.

As we have seen, the report of the Elephant Task Force of 2007 gives the scale of the problem in round numbers: an annual death toll of 100 elephants and 400 humans. Some of those elephant deaths are accidents, such as being hit by a train or truck, or electrocution by touching a transmission line. Some of the human deaths are of mahouts killed by their own elephants, but many come out of the raiding of crops and the ongoing low-level warfare between farmers and elephants. Crop-raiding bulls will often have small-arms bullets (.12 and .22 caliber) in their hide from skirmishes with farmers. Every day of the year one or two deaths, human or elephant or both, are prominently reported in the news, making the conflict visible even to people in cities.

These pressures will continue to grow with the gradual enforced demise of domestication. The end of the timber elephant exacerbates the problem most dramatically in Thailand, where half the timber elephants and their mahouts were thrown out of work suddenly by legislation banning logging. They became begging elephants in the cities, their conditions much worse than in timber

[65] As summarized in Chapter 4.

camps with the practice of night-time release into the forest.[66] Elephant holdings of circuses and zoos are declining too, due to the activism of the international animal welfare community. Popular opinion likely would not allow a policy of culling wild elephants in order to keep numbers at a given level. Other means will have to be found to take care of the increase of elephant population, or conflict will increase. Such means will perhaps look somewhat like zoos, but with larger grounds—more like wildlife parks. Models already exist in refuges for rescued elephants. Refuges of the future, perhaps, will resemble those in the *Arthaśāstra*.

Kingship, once the normative mode of political organization in India as in much of the world, is now nearly finished, never to return; and with it the institution of the war elephant. But it has left a legacy which, in India and Southeast Asia, is the persistence of the elephant relative to its decline overall. It is because of the institution of the war elephant that wild Asian elephants have survived at all, into the age of the nation-state. And more generally, the commitment to the grazing domesticates—cattle, sheep, and goats—for the last 5,000 years and continuing strong today in India, has helped preserve the forest and its wild creatures, although compromising it and at the worst degrading it into scrubland.

Judging from the increase of wild elephant numbers in India recently, it appears that the nation-state can secure the future of elephants—if it is committed and able to put its policies into action. The main challenge, paradoxically, will be finding ways of coping with the results of its success, since success in elephant protection increases the incidence of elephant–human conflict. But the greater problem all along has been the increase of *human* numbers: our ruinous success as a species. We need to find ways to secure our own future, and in doing so, that of our fellow creatures.

[66] Baker and Kashio eds 2002: 4.

Bibliography

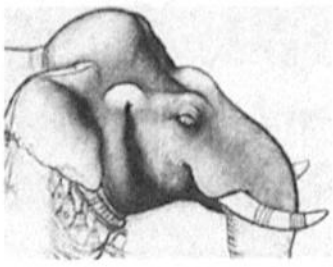

Ancient and medieval sources

Aelian = Aelian, *De natura animalium*

Aelian 1958. *On the characteristics of animals*. A.F. Scholfield, tran. Loeb Classical Library, nos 446, 448, and 449. Cambridge: Harvard University Press.

Agatharcides

Agatharcides 1989. *On the Erythraean Sea*. Stanley M. Burstein, tran. Works issued by the Hakluyt Society, 2nd ser., no. 172. London: Hakluyt Society.

Ā'īn-i Akbarī

Abū al-Fażl ibn Mubārak 1993. *The Ā'īn-i Akbarī: a gazetteer and administrative manual of Akbar's empire and part history of India*. Calcutta: The Asiatic Society.

Ait. Br. = Aitareya Brāhmaṇa

Keith, Arthur Berriedale 1920. *Rigveda Brahmanas: the Aitareya and Kauṣītaki Brāhmaṇas of the Rigveda*. 1st ed. Cambridge, Mass.: Harvard University Press.

al-Bīrūnī

Bīrūnī, Muḥammad ibn Aḥmad 1910. *Alberuni's India. An account of the religion, philosophy, literature, geography, chronology, astronomy, customs, laws and astrology of India about A.D. 1030*. An English ed. London: K. Paul, Trench, Trübner & Co., Ltd.

Aṅguttaranikāya

The Anguttara-Nikâya 1955–61, 6 vols. Richard Morris, ed. London: Published for the Pali Text Society by Luzac.

Annals of Aššur-dān II

Weidner, Ernst F. 1926. Die Annalen des Königs Aššurdân II. von Assyrien. *Archiv für Orientforschung* III: 151–61.

Appian

Appian 1912–13. *Appian's Roman history*. Horace White, tran. The Loeb Classical Library, 2-5. London: W. Heinemann; Cambridge, Mass.: Harvard University Press.

Arrian

Arrian [History of Alexander and Indica] 1976, 2 vols. P.A. Brunt, ed. and tran. Loeb Classical Library, 236, 269. Cambridge, Mass.: Harvard University Press.

Arth. = *Arthaśāstra*

Kauṭilya 1969. *The Kauṭilīya Arthaśāstra*. 2nd ed. R.P. Kangle. University of Bombay Studies: Sanskrit, Prakrit, and Pali, nos 1–2. Bombay: University of Bombay.

Kauṭilya 2013. *King, governance, and law in ancient India: Kauṭilya's Arthaśāstra*. Patrick Olivelle, tran. New York: Oxford University Press.

Kauṭilya 1926 *Das altindische Buch vom Welt- und Staatsleben: das Arthaçāstra des Kauṭilya*. J.J. Meyer, tran. Leipzig: O. Harrassowitz.

Aśokan inscriptions

Hultzsch, E., ed. 1969. *Inscriptions of Aśoka*. New edition. Corpus inscriptionum Indicarum, vol. 1. Delhi: Indological Book House.

Assyrian dictionary

Assyrian dictionary, ed. Ignace J. Gelb, vol. 12, 2005: 418–20, s.v. pīru A. The Oriental Institute, University of Chicago.

Atharvaveda

AV = Whitney, William Dwight, ed. and tran. 1905. *Atharva-Veda-Samhita*. Harvard Oriental Series, vol. VII–VIII. Cambridge, Mass.: Harvard University Press.

Buddhacarita

Aśvaghoṣa 1972. *Buddhacarita*. E.H. Johnston, ed. *The Buddhacarita; or, Acts of the Buddha. Complete Sanskrit text with English translation*. Delhi: Motilal Banarsidass.

Aśvaghoṣa 2008. *Buddhacarita. Life of the Buddha by Aśvaghoṣa*. Patrick Olivelle, tran. Clay Sanskrit Library, 33. New York: New York University Press: JJC Foundation.

Ctesias

Nichols, Andrew 2008. The complete fragments of Ctesias of Cnidus: translation and commentary with an introduction. PhD, University of Florida.

Cūlavaṃsa. See *Mahāvaṃsa*.

Curtius

Curtius Rufus, Quintus 1971. *Quintus Curtius*. Loeb Classical Library. London: W. Heinemann; Cambridge, Mass.: Harvard University Press.

Dīghanikāya

The Dīgha-nikāya 1890. T.W. Rhys Davids, J. Estlin Carpenter, eds. London: Pub. for the Pali Text Society, by H. Frowde.

Diod. = Diodorus

Diodorus 1961. *Diodorus of Sicily*. Charles Henry Oldfather, tran. Loeb Classical Library, 279, 303, 340, 375, 384, 389–90, 399, 409, 423. Cambridge, Mass.: Harvard University Press; London: W. Heinemann.

DPPN = *Dictionary of Pali proper names*.

G.P. Malalasekera 1960. *Dictionary of Pali proper names*. London: Published for the Pali Text Society by Luzac & Co.

Gajagrahaṇaprakāra

Gajagrahaṇaprakāra of Nārāyaṇa Dīkṣita, ed. E.R. Sreekrishna Sarma. S.V.U.O. Journal, Texts and Studies, offprint no. 1. Tirupati: Sri Venkateswara University Oriental Research Institute, 1968.

Gajaśāstra

Pālakāpya 1958. *Gaja Śāstram of Pālakāpya Muni*, ed. and Tamil tran. K.S. Subrahmanya Sastri and English summary by S. Gopalan. Saraswati Mahal Series No. 76. Tanjore: T.M.S.S.M. Library.

Pālakāpya 2006. *Maharsi Palakapya's Gajasastram*, with the Sanskrit commentary, Bhavasandarsini of Anantakrisnabhattaraka. Eds Siddharth Yeshwant Wankankar and V.B. Mhaiskar. Delhi: Bharatiya Kala Prakashan.

Gajaśikṣā

Gajaśikṣā by Nāradamuni, with the commentary Vyakti of Umāpatyācārya, ed. E.R. Shreekrishna Sharma. S.V.U.O. Journal vol. 18—Texts and Studies—offprint no. 5. Tirupati: Sri Venkateswara University Oriental Research Institute, 1975.

Gupta inscriptions

Fleet, John Faithful 1888. *Inscriptions of the early Gupta kings and their successors*. Corpus inscriptionum indicarum, v. 3. Calcutta: Printed by the Superintendent of Government Printing, India.

Hariharacaturaṅga

Godāvaramiśra 1950. *Hariharacaturangam (Godavaramisra pranitam)*, ed. S.K. Ramanatha Sastri. Madras Government Oriental Series no. XVII. Madras: Government Oriental Manuscript Library, 1950.

Harṣacarita

Bāṇa 1897. *The Harṣa-carita of Bāṇa*. Edward B. Cowell and Frederick William Thomas, tran. London: Royal Asiatic Society.

Hastividyārṇava

Sukumar Barkath 1976. *Hastividyārṇava*, ed. and tran. Pratap Chandra Choudhury. Gauhati: Publication Board, Assam.

Hastyāyurveda

Pālakāpya 1984. *The Hastyāyurveda by Pālakāpya Muni*, ed. Paṇḍita Śivadatta. Ānandāśrama Sanskrita Series no. 26. Poona: Ānandāśrama Press.

IC = *Inscriptions du Cambodge*

Cœdès, George 1937–66. *Inscriptions du Cambodge*, 8 vols. Collection de textes et documents sur l'Indochine. Hanoi and Paris: École française d'Extrême-Orient.

Lüshi Chunqiu

Lü Buwei 2000. *The annals of Lü Buwei*. John Knoblock and Jeffrey Riegel, tran. Stanford, Calif.: Stanford University Press.

Macc. = *Maccabees 1*

Maccabees 1936. *Maccabaeorum liber I*. Werner Kappler, ed. Septuaginta: Vetus Testamentum Graecum, 9/I. Göttingen: Vandenhoeck & Ruprecht.

Mbh. = *Mahābhārata*

Mahābhārata: critical edition 1933–71. V.S. Sukthankar, ed. Poona: Bhandarkar Oriental Research Institute.

MV = *Mahāvaṃsa*

Mahāvaṃsa 1958. *The Mahavamsa*. Wilhelm Geiger, ed. London: Published for the Pali Text Society by Luzac.

Mahāvaṃsa 1958. *The Mahavamsa*. Wilhelm Geiger, tran. London: Published for the Pali Text Society by Luzac.

Geiger, Wilhelm, ed. 1980 [1925, 1927]. *Cūlavaṃsa*. 2 vols reprinted as one. London: Pali Text Society.

Geiger, Wilhelm, and Christian Mabel (Duff) Rickmers, trans. 1929. *Cūlavaṃsa, being the more recent part of the Mahāvaṃsa*. London and Colombo: Pali Text Society.

Mahāvastu

Mahāvastu 1882. *Le Mahâvastu; texte sanscrit publié pour la première fois et accompagné d'introductions et d'un commentaire.* E. Senart, ed. Paris: Société asiatique.

Mahāvastu 1949. *The Mahāvastu.* John James Jones, tran. Sacred Books of the Buddhists, v. 16, 18–19. London: Luzac.

Manu

Manu 2005. *Manu's code of law: a critical edition and translation of the Mānava-Dharmaśāstra.* Patrick Olivelle, ed. and tran. New York: Oxford University Press.

Megasthenes

Brill's new Jacoby (Brill online reference works), BNJ 715, tran. Duane W. Roller.

Mencius

Mencius 1932. *Mencius.* Leonard Arthur Lyall tran. London: Longman, Green.

Ming Shi-lu

Wade, Geoff 2005. *Southeast Asia in the Ming Shi-lu.* http://www.epress.nus.edu.sg/msl/.

ML = *Mātaṅgalīlā*

Nīlakaṇṭha 1910. *The Mātaṅgalīlā of Nīlakaṇṭha,* ed. T. Gaṇapati Śāstrī. Trivandrum Sanskrit Series, no. X. Trivandrum: Government of HH the Maharajah of Travancore.

Nīlakaṇṭha 1931. *The elephant-lore of the Hindus; the elephant-sport (Matanga-lila) of Nilakantha.* Mātangalīlā. Franklin Edgerton, tran. New Haven: Yale University Press.

Nearchus

Brill's new Jacoby (Brill online reference works). BNJ 133. Michael Whitby tran.

Pliny

Pliny 1961. *Natural history.* H. Rackham and W.H.S. Jones, tran. Loeb Classical Library, 330, 352–3, 370–1, 392–4, 418–19. Cambridge, Mass.: Harvard University Press.

Plut. = Plutarch

Plutarch 1982. *Plutarch's Lives* (lives of Alexander, Eumenes, and Demetrius). Bernadotte Perrin, tran. Rev. Loeb Classical Library, 46–7, 65, 80, 87, 98–103. Cambridge, Mass.: Harvard University Press; London: W. Heinemann.

Polybius

Polybius 2010. *The histories*. W.R. Paton, tran. Rev. Loeb Classical Library, 128, 137, 160, 161. Cambridge, Mass.: Harvard University Press.

Purāṇas

Pargiter, F.E. 1962. *The Purāṇa text of the dynasties of the Kali age; with introd. and notes*. 2nd ed. Varanasi: Chowkhamba Sanskrit Series Office.

Rām. = *Rāmāyaṇa*

The Vālmīki-Rāmāyaṇa: critical edition 1960–75. G.H. Bhatt and U.P. Shah, eds. Baroda: Oriental Institute.

RIMA = The royal inscriptions of Mesopotamia

RIMA 1. Grayson, Albert Kirk 1987. *Assyrian rulers of the third and second millennia BC (to 1115 BC)*. The royal inscriptions of Mesopotamia, v. 1. Toronto and Buffalo: University of Toronto Press.

RIMA 2. Grayson, Albert Kirk 1991. *Assyrian rulers of the early first millennium BC*. The royal inscriptions of Mesopotamia, v. 2–3. Toronto: University of Toronto Press.

RV = *Ṛg Veda*

Ṛg Veda 1966. *Ṛgveda-saṃhitā*. F. Max Müller, ed. 1st Indian ed.

Sachs-Hunger

Sachs, Abraham, and Hermann Hunger 1996. *Astronomical diaries and related texts from Babylonia*. Denkschriften / Österreichische Akademie der Wissenschaften. Philosophisch-Historische Klasse, <247., 299., 346.> Bd. Wien: Verlag der Österreichischen Akademie der Wissenschaften.

Śatapatha Brāhmaṇa

Śatapatha Brāhmaṇa 1983. *The Śatapatha Brāhmaṇa in the Kāṇvīya recension*. W. Caland and Raghu Vira, eds. Delhi: Motilal Banarsidass.

Selby

Selby, Martha Ann 2003. *The circle of six seasons: a selection from old Tamil, Prakrit and Sanskrit poetry*. New Delhi: Penguin.

Strabo, *Geography*

Strabo 1966. *The geography of Strabo*. Horace Leonard Jones and John Robert Sitlington Sterrett, tran. Loeb Classical Library, 49–50, 182, 196, 211, 223, 241, 267. Cambridge, Mass.: Harvard University Press.

Twenty-four stories of filial piety

Er shi si xiao comp. Guo Jujing. *The Chinese repository* 6.3 1837: 130–1.

Vaṃsatthappakāsiṇī

Vaṃsatthappakāsiṇī 1935. *Vaṃsatthappakāsinī: commentary on the Mahāvaṃsa*. G.P. Malalasekera, ed. London: Pali Text Society.

Vaṃsatthappakāsiṇī 1977. *Vaṃsatthappakāsinī: commentary on the Mahāvaṃsa*. G.P. Malalasekera, tran. London: Pali Text Society.

Vedic Index

Macdonell, Arthur Anthony, and Arthur Berriedale Keith 1912. *Vedic index of names and subjects*. Indian Texts Series. London: J. Murray, for the Government of India.

Xuanzang

Xuanzang 1957. *Si-yu-ki. Buddhist records of the Western world.* Samuel Beal, tran. New ed. Calcutta: Susil Gupta.

Zuo zhuan (The Zuo commentary on the Chunqiu annals)

The Ch'un Ts'ew with the Tso Chuen, James Legge, tran. 2nd ed. (The Chinese classics, vol. 5) 1991. Taipei: SMC Publishing.

Modern sources

Allsen, Thomas T. 2006. *The royal hunt in Eurasian history*. Encounters with Asia. Philadelphia: University of Pennsylvania Press.

Alvarez, L.W., W. Alvarez, F. Asaro, and H.V. Michel 1980. Extraterrestrial cause for the Cretaceous-Tertiary extinction. *Science* 208: 1095–1108.

Anthony, David W. 2008. *The horse, the wheel, and language: how Bronze-Age riders from the Eurasian steppes shaped the modern world.* Princeton, N.J.; Woodstock: Princeton University Press.

Armandi, Pier Damiano 1843. *Histoire militaire des éléphants*. Paris: D'Amyot.

Baines, John 2013. Celebration in the landscape: a hunting party under Amenemhat II. In *High culture and experience in ancient Egypt*, pp. 187–234. Sheffield, South Yorkshire; Bristol, CT: Equinox.

——— forthcoming. La tombe thébaine d'Amenemhab. In *Les biographies de l'Egypte ancienne*.

Baker, Iljas, and Masakazu Kashio, eds. 2002. *Giants on our hands: proceedings of the international workshop on the domesticated Asian elephant*. Bangkok: FAO Regional Office for Asia and the Pacific.

Bar-Kochva, Bezalel 1976. *The Seleucid army: organization and tactics in the great campaigns*. Cambridge Classical Studies. Cambridge; New York: Cambridge University Press.

Baskaran, S. Theodore 1981. *The message bearers: the nationalist politics and the entertainment media in South India, 1880–1945*. 1st ed. Madras: Cre-A.

Bhakari, S.K. 1981. *Indian warfare: an appraisal of strategy and tactics of war in early medieval period*. New Delhi: Munshiram Manoharlal.

Bishop, Carl W. 1921. The elephant and its ivory in ancient China. *Journal of the American Oriental Society* 41: 290–306.

Bock-Raming, Andreas 1996. Mānasollāsa 5, 560–623: ein bisher unbeachtet gebliebener Text zum indischen Schachspiel, übersetzt, kommentiert und interpretiert. *Indo-Iranian journal* 39: 1–40.

Böhtlingk, Otto von, and Rudolf von Roth 1855. *Sanskrit-wörterbuch herausgegeben von der Kaiserlichen akademie der wissenschaften*. St Petersburg: Buchdr. der K. Akademie der wissenschaften.

Bosworth, A.B. 1983. The Indian satrapies under Alexander the Great. *Antichthon* 17: 37–46.

——— 1996. The historical setting of Megasthenes' Indica. *Classical philology* 91 (2): 113–27.

——— 2002. *The legacy of Alexander: politics, warfare, and propaganda under the successors*. Oxford; New York: Oxford University Press.

Bosworth, C.E. 1965. Military organisation under the Būyids of Persia and Iraq. *Oriens* 18/19: 143–67.

——— 1968. The armies of the Saffārids. *Bulletin of the School of Oriental and African Studies, University of London* 31: 534–54.

——— 1973. *The Ghaznavids; their empire in Afghanistan and eastern Iran, 994–1040*. 2nd ed. Beirut: Librairie du Liban.

——— 1977. *The later Ghaznavids: splendour and decay: the dynasty in Afghanistan and northern India, 1040–1186*. Persian Studies Series, no. 7. New York: Columbia University Press.

Brandt, Adam L., Yohannes Hagos, Yohannes Yacob, *et al.* 2013. The elephants of Gash-Barka, Eritrea: nuclear and mitochondrial genetic patterns. *Journal of heredity*: est078.

Buck, John Lossing 1937. *Land utilization in China: statistics*. Nanking: University of Nanking; Chicago: University of Chicago Press.

Burstein, Stanley M. 2008. Elephants for Ptolemy II: Ptolemaic policy in Nubia in the third century BC. In *Ptolemy II Philadelphus and his world*, ed. Paul McKechnie and Philippe Guillaume, pp. 135–47. Leiden; Boston: Brill.

Canepa, Matthew P. 2009. *The two eyes of the Earth: art and ritual of kingship between Rome and Sasanian Iran*. Transformation of the Classical Heritage, 45. Berkeley: University of California Press.

Carrington, Richard 1959. *Elephants; a short account of their natural history evolution and influence on mankind*. New York: Basic Books.

Casson, Lionel 1993. Ptolemy II and the hunting of African elephants. *Transactions of the American Philological Association* 123: 247–60.

Chakravarti, Prithwis Chandra 1972. *The art of war in ancient India*. 1st ed. Delhi: Oriental Publishers.

Champion, Harry George, and Shiam Kishore Seth 1968. *A revised survey of the forest types of India*. Delhi: Manager of Publications.

Chang Chun-shu 2007. *The rise of the Chinese Empire*, 2 vols. Ann Arbor: University of Michigan Press.

Chang, Wen-li 1996. *The Qin terracotta army: treasures of Lintong*. London: Wappingers' Falls, NY: Scala Books; Cultural Relics Publishing House; distributed by Antique Collector's Club.

Charles, Michael B. 2007. The rise of the Sassanian elephant corps: elephants and the later Roman empire. *Iranica antiqua* 42: 301–46.

Charney, Michael W. 2004. *Southeast Asian warfare, 1300–1900*. Handbook of Oriental Studies; South-East Asia, Section 3. v. 16. Leiden: Brill.

Chowta, Prajna 2010. *Elephant code book*. Bangalore: Asian Nature Conservation Foundation.

Clubb, Ros, and Georgia Mason 2002. A review of the welfare of zoo elephants in Europe: a report commissioned by the RSPCA. Royal Society for the Prevention of Cruelty to Animals.

Coedès, George 1948. *Les états hindouisés d'Indochine et d'Indonésie*. Paris: Boccard.

——— 1968. *The Indianized States of Southeast Asia*. Honolulu: East-West Center Press.

Coomaraswamy, A.K. 1942. Horse-riding in the Ṛgveda and Artharva-veda. *Journal of the American Oriental Society* 62: 139–40.

Date, Govind Tryambak 1929. *The art of war in ancient India*. London: Oxford University Press.

Davies, Cuthbert Collin 1959. *An historical atlas of the Indian peninsula*. 2nd ed. Madras, New York: Oxford University Press.

Davies, Norman de Garis 1973. *The tomb of Rekh-mi-Rē′ at Thebes*. New York: Arno Press.

Deloche, Jean 1986. *Le cheval et son harnachement dans l'art indien*. Lausanne: Caracole.

——— 1988. *Military technology in Hoysaḷa sculpture: twelfth and thirteenth century*. New Delhi: Sitaram Bhartia Institute of Scientific Research.

——— 1990. *Horses and riding equipment in Indian art*. English ed. Madras: Indian Heritage Trust.

——— 2007. *Studies on fortification in India*. Collection indologie, 104. Pondicherry; Paris: Institut français de Pondichéry; École française d'Extrême-Orient.

Depuydt, Leo 1997. The time of death of Alexander the Great: 11 June 323 B.C. (–322), *ca*. 4:00–5:00 PM. *Die Welt des Orients* Bd. 28: 117–35.

Deraniyagala, P.E.P. 1955. *Some extinct elephants, their relatives, and the two living species*. Colombo: Printed at the Govt. Press.

Di Cosmo, Nicola 2002. *Ancient China and its enemies: the rise of nomadic power in East Asian history*. Cambridge, UK; New York: Cambridge University Press.

———, ed. 2009. *Military culture in imperial China*. Cambridge, Mass.: Harvard University Press.

Digby, Simon 1971. *War-horse and elephant in the Dehli Sultanate: a study of military supplies*. Oxford: Orient Monographs.

Dikshitar, V.R. Ramachandra 1987. *War in ancient India*. Delhi: Motilal Banarsidass.

Dobby, Ernest Henry George 1961. *Monsoon Asia*. Chicago: Quadrangle Books.

Ebeling, Sascha 2010. *Colonizing the realm of words: the transformation of Tamil literature in nineteenth-century South India*. SUNY Series in Hindu Studies. Albany: State University of New York Press.

Epstein, H. 1971. *Domestic animals of China*. New York: Africana Pub. Corp.

Eisenberg, John F., George M. McKay, and M.R. Jainudeen 1971. Reproductive behavior of the Asiatic elephant (Elephas maximus maximus L.). *Behaviour* 38 (3/4): 193–225.

Elvin, Mark 2004. *The retreat of the elephants: an environmental history of China*. New Haven: Yale University Press.

Erdosy, George 1988. *Urbanisation in early historic India*. BAR International Series, 430. Oxford, England: B.A.R.

ETF Report. Elephant Task Force, and Mahesh Rangarajan 2010. Gajah: securing the future for elephants in India. The report of the Elephant Task Force, Ministry of Environment and Forests, August 31, 2010. Ministry of Environment and Forests, Government of India.

Evans, G.H. 1910. *Elephants and their diseases: a treatise on elephants*. Rangoon: Superintendent, Government Printing, Burma.

Fairhead, James, and Melissa Leach 1996. *Misreading the African landscape: society and ecology in a forest–savanna mosaic*. African Studies Series, 90. Cambridge and New York: Cambridge University Press.

Feeley-Harnik, Gillian 1999. "Communities of blood": the natural history of kinship in nineteenth-century America. *Comparative studies in society and history* 41 (2): 215–62.

Ferrier, A.J. 1947. *Care and management of elephants in Burma*. N.p.: Williams, Lea & Co.

Finkel, Irving L., ed. 2007. *Ancient board games in perspective: papers from the 1990 British Museum colloquium, with additional contributions*. London: British Museum Press.

Fisher, Daniel C. 1987. Mastodont procurement by Paleoindians of the Great Lakes region: hunting or scavenging? In *The evolution of human hunting*, ed. Matthew H. Nitecki and Doris V. Nitecki, pp. 309–421. New York: Plenum Press.

——— 2008. Taphonomy and paleobiology of the Hyde Park mastodon. In *Mastodon paleobiology, taphonomy, and paleoenvironment in the late Pleistocene of New York State: Studies on the Hyde Park, Chemung, and North Java sites*, ed. Warren D. Allmon and Peter L. Nester, pp. 197–290. Palaeontographica americana, 61.

——— 2009. Paleobiology and extinction of proboscideans in the Great Lakes region of North America. In *American megafaunal extinctions at the end of the Pleistocene*, ed. G. Haynes, pp. 55–75. New York: Springer Science + Business Media.

Frankfort, Henri 1936. *Progress of the work of the Oriental Institute in Iraq, 1934–35*. Chicago: University of Chicago Press.

Friedman, Renée F. 2004. Elephants at Hierakonpolis. In *Egypt at its origins: studies in memory of Barbara Adams*, pp. 131–68. Orientalia Lovaniensia analecta, 138. Leuven, Paris, Dodley, MA: Peeters.

Fukai, Shinji, Jiro Sugiyama, Keizo Kimata, Katsumi Tanabe 1983. *Tōkyō Daigaku Iraku Iran Iseki Chōsadan hōkokusho*, Report 19: Taq-i Bustan III, photogrammetric elevations.

Gadgil, Madhav, and Ramachandra Guha 1993. *This fissured land: an ecological history of India*. Berkeley: University of California Press.

Geer, Alexandra Anna Enrica van der 2008. *Animals in stone: Indian mammals sculptured through time*. Handbuch der Orientalistik. Zweite Abteilung, Indien, Abt. 2, Bd. 21. Leiden; Boston: Brill.

Geiger, Wilhelm 1960. *Culture of Ceylon in mediaeval times*. Wiesbaden: O. Harrassowitz.

Getty, Alice 1992 [1936]. *Gaṇeśa: a monograph on the elephant-faced god*. New Delhi: Munshiram Manoharlal.

Goloubew, Victor. 1929. L'âge du bronze au Tonkin et dans le Nord-Annam. *Bulletin de l'Ecole française d'Extrême-Orient* 29 (1): 1–46.

Gommans, Jos J.L. 2002. *Mughal warfare: Indian frontiers and highroads to empire, 1500–1700*. Warfare and History. London; New York: Routledge.

——— and D.H.A. Kolff, eds. 2001. *Warfare and weaponry in South Asia, 1000–1800*. Oxford in India Readings. New Delhi; New York: Oxford University Press.

Gonda, J. 1965. The absense of vāhanas in the Veda and their occurrence in Hindu art and literature. In J. Gonda, *Change and continuity in Indian religion*, pp. 71–114. The Hague: Mouton.

——— 1989. *The Indra hymns of the Ṛgveda*. Orientalia Rheno-traiectina, v. 36. Leiden; New York: Brill.

Goossens, Roger 1943. Gloses indiennes dans le lexique d'Hesychius. *L'antiquité classique* 12: 47–55.

Goukowsky, Paul 1972. Le roi Pôros, son éléphant et quelques autres. *Bulletin de correspondance hellénique* 96 (1): 473–502.

Gowers, William 1947. The African elephant in warfare. *African affairs* 46 (182 [Jan.]): 42–9.

——— 1948. African elephants and ancient authors. *African affairs* 47 (188 [July]): 173–80.

Gray, Louis H., and Montgomery Schuyler 1901. Indian glosses in the lexicon of Hesychios. *The American journal of philology* 22 (2): 195–202.

Gröning, Karl, and Martin Saller 1999. *Elephants: a cultural and natural history*. Cologne: Konemann.

Groslier, George 1921. *Recherches sur les Cambodgiens d'après les textes et les monuments depuis les premiers siècles de notre ère*. Paris: A. Challamel.

Grove, Richard, Vinita Damodaran, and Satpal Sangwan, eds. 1998. *Nature and the Orient: the environmental history of South and Southeast Asia*. Studies in Social Ecology and Environmental History. Delhi, New York: Oxford University Press.

Guha, Ramachandra, and Madhav Gadgil 1989. State forestry and social conflict in British India. *Past and present* (123): 141–77.

Habib, Irfan 1982. *An atlas of the Mughal Empire: political and economic maps with detailed notes, bibliography and index*. Delhi; New York: Oxford University Press.

Hathaway, Michael J. 2013. *Environmental winds: making the global in southwest China*. Berkeley, Los Angeles, London: University of California Press.

Hecht, S.B., K.D. Morrison, and C. Padoch, eds. 2014. *The social lives of forests: past, present, and future of woodland resurgence*. University of Chicago Press.

Heckel, Waldemar 2006. *Who's who in the age of Alexander the Great: prosopography of Alexander's empire*. Malden, MA; Oxford: Blackwell.

Heesterman, J.C. 1957. *The ancient Indian royal consecration: the Rājasūya described according to the Yajus texts and annotated.* The Hague: Mouton.

Heger, Franz 1902. *Alte metalltrommeln aus Südost-Asien*, 2 vols. Leipzig: K.W. Heirsemann.

Heine-Geldern, Robert 1947. The drum named Makalamau. *India antiqua*, Special Issue: 167–79.

Hepburn, William n.d. *Elephants, care and treatment*. Typescript. "This book has been compiled from notes left by the late William Hepburn, Veterinary Surgeon to the B.B.T.C., and is the result of many years' study by him of elephants in their domestic state." Robert L. Parkinson Library and Research Center, Circus World Museum, Baraboo, Wisconsin.

Higham, Charles 1989. *The archaeology of mainland Southeast Asia: from 10,000 B.C. to the fall of Angkor*. Cambridge World Archeology. Cambridge; New York: Cambridge University Press.

——— 1996. *The bronze age of Southeast Asia*. Cambridge World Archaeology. Cambridge; New York: Cambridge University Press.

——— 2002. *Early cultures of mainland Southeast Asia*. Bangkok: London: River; Thames & Hudson.

Hopkins, Edward Washburn 1889. *The social and military position of the ruling caste in ancient India, as represented by the Sanskrit epic*. New Haven, Conn: Tuttle, Morehouse and Taylor.

Houlihan, Patrick F. 1996. *The animal world of the pharaohs*. London, New York: Thames and Hudson.

Hughes, Julie E. 2013. *Animal kingdoms: hunting, the environment, and power in the Indian princely states*. Ranikhet: Permanent Black; and Cambridge, Massachusetts and London: Harvard University Press.

Irvine, William 1903. *The army of the Indian Moghuls: its organization and administration*. London: Luzac & Co.

Jacq-Hergoualc'h, Michel 1979. *L'Armament et l'organisation de l'armée khmère aux XIIe et XIIIe siècles, d'après les bas-reliefs d'Angkor Vat, du Bàyon et de Banteay Chmar*. Musée Guimet, Collection recherches et documents d'art et d'archéologie, 12. Paris: Presses Universitaires de France.

——— 2007. *The armies of Angkor: military structure and weaponry of the Khmers*. 1st English ed. Bibliotheca Asiatica. Bangkok, Thailand: Orchid Press.

Jing Yuan, Han Jian-Lin, and Roger Blench 2008. Livestock in ancient China: an archaeozoological perspective. In *Past migrations in East Asia: matching archaeology, linguistics and genetics*, ed. Alicia Sanchez-Mazas, Roger Blench, Malcolm D. Ross, Ilia Peiros, and Marie Lin, pp. 84–104. London and New York: Routledge.

Kailasapathy, K. 1968. *Tamil heroic poetry*. Oxford: Clarendon Press.

Keith, Arthur Berriedale1925. *The religion and philosophy of the Veda and Upanishads*. Cambridge, Mass.: Harvard University Press; London: H. Milford, Oxford University Press.

Kenoyer, Jonathan M. 1998. *Ancient cities of the Indus Valley Civilization*. 1st ed. Karachi: Islamabad: Oxford University Press; American Institute of Pakistan Studies.

Khoo, James C.M. 2003. *Art & archaeology of Fu Nan: pre-Khmer kingdom of the Lower Mekong Valley*. Bangkok: Orchid Press; Singapore: Southeast Asian Ceramic Society.

Khyne U Mar 2002. The studbook of timber elephants of Myanmar with special reference to survivorship analysis. In Iljas Baker and Masakazu Kashio, eds. 2002. *Giants on our hands: proceedings of the international workshop on the domesticated Asian elephant*, pp. 195–211. Bangkok: FAO Regional Office for Asia and the Pacific.

——— 2007. The demography and life history strategies of timber elephants in Myanmar. PhD thesis, University College London.

Kierman, Frank Algerton, and John King Fairbank, eds. 1974. *Chinese ways in warfare*. Harvard East Asian Series, v. 74. Cambridge, Mass.: Harvard University Press.

Kosambi, D.D. 1956. *An introduction to the study of Indian history*. Bombay: Popular Book Depot.

——— 1965. *The culture and civilization of ancient India in historical outline*. London: Routledge and Paul.

Lahiri-Choudhury, Dhriti K. 1999. *The great Indian elephant book: an anthology of writings on elephants in the raj*. New Delhi; New York: Oxford University Press.

Lainé, Nicolas 2010. Les éléphants sous la cour ahom (XIIIe-XIXe s.). *Athropozoologica* 45.2: 7–25.

——— forthcoming. Pratiques vocales et dressage animal. Les mélodies huchées des Khamtis à leurs elephants. In Bénard N., Poulet C. ed., *Chant pensé, chant vécu, temps chanté: Formes, usages et représentations des pratiques vocales.* Rosières-en-Haye: Éditions Camion Blanc.

Lair, Richard C. 1997. *Gone astray: the care and management of the Asian elephant in domesticity*. RAP publication, 1997/16. Bangkok, Thailand: FAO Regional Office for Asia and the Pacific.

Lal, Makkhan 1984. *Settlement history and rise of civilization in Ganga–Yamuna doab, from 1500 B.C. to 300 A.D.* New Delhi, India: B.R. Pub. Corp.; Distributed by D.K. Publishers' Distributors.

Lattimore, Owen 1937. Origins of the Great Wall of China: a frontier concept in theory and practice. *Geographical review* 27 (4): 529–49.

——— 1951. *Inner Asian frontiers of China*. 2nd ed. American Geographical Society [of New York] Research Series, no. 21. Irvington-on-Hudson, N.Y., New York: Capitol Pub. Co., American Geographical Society.

Laufer, Berthold 1925. *Ivory in China*. Anthropology, Leaflet 21. Chicago: Field Museum of Natural History.

Legrain, Leon 1946. Horseback riding in the third millennium B.C. *University Museum Bulletin, University of Pennsylvania* 11.4: 27–33.

Leopold, Aldo 2013. *A sand county almanac & other writings on ecology & conservation*. Library of America, 238. New York: Library of America.

Lévi, Sylvain 1938. *L'Inde civilisatrice; aperçu historique*. Publications de l'Institut de civilisation indienne. Paris: Librairie d'Amérique et d'Orient, A. Maisonneuve.

Li Chi 1977. *Anyang*. Seattle: University of Washington Press.

Lieberman, Victor B. 2003. *Strange parallels: Southeast Asia in global context, c. 800–1830*, vol. 1. Studies in Comparative World History. New York: Cambridge University Press.

Lincoln, Abraham 1953. *Collected works*. Roy Prentice Basler, ed. New Brunswick, N.J.: Rutgers University Press.

Locke, Piers 2006. History, practice, identity: an institutional ethnography of elephant handlers in Chitwan, Nepal. PhD thesis, University of Canterbury.

Lüders, Heinrich 1905. Eine indische glosse des Hesychios. *Zeitschrift für vergleichende Sprachforschung auf dem Gebiete der Indogermanischen Sprachen* 38 (3): 433–4.

Luo, Zhongmin, ed. 1983. *Qin Shihuang ling bing ma yong*. Di 1 ban. Beijing: Wen wu chu ban she: Xin hua shu dian Beijing fa xing suo fa xing.

Mackay, Ernest John Henry 1937. *Further excavations at Mohenjo-daro, being an official account of archaeological excavations at Mohenjo-daro carried out by the government of India between the years 1927 and 1931*. Delhi: Manager of Publications.

MacPhee, R.D.E., ed. 1999. *Extinctions in near time: causes, contexts, and consequences*. Advances in Vertebrate Paleobiology. New York: Kluwer Academic/Plenum Publishers.

Mahadevan, Iravatham 1977. *The Indus script: texts, concordance, and tables*. Memoirs—Archaeological Survey of India, no. 77. New Delhi: Archaeological Survey of India.

Mark, Michael 2007. The beginnings of chess. In *Ancient board games in perspective*, ed. Irving L. Finkel, pp. 138–57. London: British Museum Press.

Marshall, John Hubert 1951. *Taxila, an illustrated account of archaeological excavations carried out at Taxila under the orders of the Government of India between the years 1913 and 1934*. Cambridge: University Press.

——— 1973. *Mohenjo-daro and the Indus civilization; being an official account of archaeological excavations at Mohenjo-daro carried out by the Government of India between the years 1922 and 1927*. Delhi: Indological Book House.

Martin, Paul S. 2005. *Twilight of the mammoths: ice age extinctions and the rewilding of America*. Organisms and Environments, 8. Berkeley: University of California Press.

———, and Richard G. Klein, eds. 1984. *Quaternary extinctions: a prehistoric revolution*. Tucson, Ariz.: University of Arizona Press.

Martini, François1938. En marge du Rāmayāna cambodgien. *Bulletin de l'Ecole française d'Extrême-Orient*. Tome 38: 285–95.

Mayrhofer, Manfred 1986. *Etymologisches Wörterbuch des Altindoarischen*. Indogermanische Bibliothek. Heidelberg: C. Winter.

Menon, Vivek 2009. *Mammals of India*. Princeton Field Guides. Princeton: Princeton University Press.

———, R. Sukumar, and Ashok Kumar 1997. *A god in distress: threats of poaching and the ivory trade to the Asian elephant in India*. Technical report / Asian Elephant Conservation Centre, no. 3. Bangalore: Asian Elephant Conservation Centre, Indian Institute of Science.

Michel, Ernst 1952. Ein neuentdecter Annalen-Text Salmanassars III. *Die Welt des Orients*, Bd. 1, H. 6: 454–75.

Milroy, A.J.W. 1922. *A short treatise on the management of elephants*. Shillong: Government Press, Assam.

Monier-Williams, Monier 1899. *A Sanskrit–English dictionary etymologically and philologically arranged with special reference to cognate Indo-European languages*. New ed. Oxford: The Clarendon Press.

Morrison, Kathleen D. forthcoming. Opening up the pre-colonial: primeval forests, baseline thinking, and other archives in environmental history. In *Shifting ground: people, animals, and mobility in India's environmental history*, ed. M. Rangarajan and K. Sivaramakrishnan. New Delhi: Oxford University Press.

Mukherjee, Radhakamal 1938. *The regional balance of man: an ecological theory of population*. Madras: University of Madras.

Murray, Harold James Ruthven 1913. *A history of chess*. Oxford: Clarendon Press.

Nilakanta Sastri, K.A. 1955. *The Cōḷas*. 2d ed. rev. Madras University Historical Series, no. 9. Madras: University of Madras.

Nowak, Ronald M. 1999. *Walker's mammals of the world*. 6th ed. Baltimore: Johns Hopkins University Press.

OEAE 2001. *The Oxford encyclopedia of ancient Egypt*, 3 vols. New York: Oxford University Press.

Oki, Morihiro, and Shōji Itō 1991. *Genshi Bukkyō bijutsu zuten / Ancient Buddhist sites of Sānchi & Barhut / photograph Morihiro Oki; text Shōji Itō*. Tōkyō: Yūzankaku.

Parmentier, Henri. 1918. Anciens tambours de bronze. *Bulletin de l'Ecole française d'Extrême-Orient* 18: 1–30.

Patel, Manilal 1961. *The dānastutis of the Ṛg-Veda*. Vallabh Vidyanagar, India.

Pelliot, Paul 1903. Le Fou-nan. *Bulletin de l'Ecole française d'Extrême-Orient*, Tome 3: 248–303.

Pigeaud, Theodore G. Th., and Prapantja 1960. *Java in the 14th century: a study in cultural history: the Nāgara-Kĕrtāgama by Rakawi Prapañca of Majapahit, 1365 A.D.* Koninklijk Instituut voor Taal-, Land- en Volkenkunde. Translation Series 4. The Hague: M. Nijhoff.

Pittaya, Homkrailas, Rōtčhanaphrưk Prawit, and Hǣng Prathēt Thai Kānthǭngthīeo 2002. *Ta Klang: the elephant valley of Mool River Basin*. Bangkok: Tourism Authority of Thailand.

Pollock, Sheldon I. 2006. *The language of the gods in the world of men: Sanskrit, culture, and power in premodern India*. Berkeley: University of California Press.

Portal, Jane, and Hiromi Kinoshita, eds. 2007. *The first emperor: China's terracotta army*. London: British Museum.

Poncar, Jaroslav, and Albert Le Bonheur 1995. *Of gods, kings, and men: bas-reliefs of Angkor Wat and Bayon*. London: Serindia Publications.

Poncar, Jaroslav, and T.S. Maxwell 2006. *Of gods, kings, and men: the reliefs of Angkor Wat*. Chiang Mai, Thailand: Silkworm Books.

Poole, Joyce H. 1987. Rutting behavior in African elephants: the phenomenon of musth. *Behaviour* 102 (3/4): 283–316.

Possehl, Gregory L. 2002. *The Indus civilization: a contemporary perspective*. Walnut Creek, CA: AltaMira Press.

Puri, Gopal Singh 1960. *Indian forest ecology: a comprehensive survey of vegetation and its environment in the Indian subcontinent*. 1st ed. New Delhi: Oxford Book & Stationery Co.

Raffles, Thomas Stamford 1965 [1817]. *The history of Java*, 2 vols. Oxford in Asia. Historical Reprints. Kuala Lumpur, New York: Oxford University Press.

Raghavan, V. 1975. *The Ramayana in Greater India*. 1st ed. Rao Bahadur Kamalashankar Pranshankar Trivedi Memorial Lectures, 1973. Surat: South Gujarat University.

Ramanujan, A.K. 1967. *The interior landscape; love poems from a classical Tamil anthology*. UNESCO Collection of Representative Works. Bloomington: Indiana University Press.

——— 1985. *Poems of love and war: from the eight anthologies and the ten long poems of classical Tamil*. Translations from the Oriental Classics. New York: Columbia University Press.

Rance, Philip 2003. Elephants in warfare in late antiquity. *Acta Ant. Hung.* 43: 355–84.

Rangarajan, Mahesh 2001. *India's wildlife history: an introduction*. Delhi: Permanent Black in association with Ranthambhore Foundation: Distributed by Orient Longman.

———, and K. Sivaramakrishnan, eds. 2012. *India's environmental history*. Ranikhet: Permanent Black.

Reid, Anthony 1995. Humans and forests in pre-colonial Southeast Asia. *Environment and history* 1 (1): 93–110.

Richman, Paula, ed. 1991. *Many Rāmāyaṇas: the diversity of a narrative tradition in South Asia*. Berkeley: University of California Press.

Roy, Kaushik, ed. 2010. *Warfare, state, and society in South Asia, 500 BCE–2005 CE*. New Delhi: Viva Books.

——— 2011. *Warfare and politics in South Asia from ancient to modern times*. New Delhi: Manohar Publishers & Distributors.

Russell, William Howard 1877. *The Prince of Wales' tour: a diary in India; with some account of the visits of His Royal Highness to the courts of Greece, Egypt, Spain and Portugal*. New York: R. Worthington.

Sabu 1979. *Mustn't forget*. Niagara Falls, NY: the author. Ringling elephant history. Robert L. Parkinson Library and Research Center, Circus World Museum, Baraboo, Wisconsin.

Sami, Ali 1954. *Persepolis (Takht-i-Jamshid)*. Shiraz: Musavi Print Office.

Sanderson, G.P. 1893. *Thirteen years among the wild beasts of India: their haunts and habits from personal observations; with an account of the modes of capturing and taming elephants.* 5th ed. London: W.H. Allen.

Sanft, Charles 2010. Environment and law in early imperial China (third century BCE–first century CE): Qin and Han statutes concerning natural resources. *Environmental history* 15: 701–21.

Schachermeyr, Fritz 1966. Alexander und die Ganges-Länder. In G.T. Griffith, *Alexander the great: the main problems*. Cambridge: Heffer; New York: Barnes & Noble.

Schafer, Edward H. 1957. War elephants in ancient and medieval China. *Oriens* 10 (2): 289–91.

Schaller, George B. 1967. *The deer and the tiger; a study of wildlife in India*. Chicago: University of Chicago Press.

Scharfe, Hartmut 1971. The Maurya dynasty and the Seleucids. *Zeitschrift für vergleichende Sprachforschung* 85 (2): 211–25.

Schlumberger, D., L. Robert, A. Dupont-Sommer, and E. Benveniste 1958. Un bilingue gréco-araméenne d'Asoka. *Journal asiatique* 246: 1–48.

Scullard, H.H. 1974. *The elephant in the Greek and Roman world. Aspects of Greek and Roman life.* Ithaca, NY; London: Thames and Hudson.

Semenov, Grigori L. 2007. Board games in Central Asia and Iran. In *Ancient board games in perspective*, ed. Irving L. Finkel, pp. 169–76. London: British Museum Press.

Sen, Chitrabhanu 2005. *The Mahabharata, a social study*. 1st ed. Calcutta: Sanskrit Pustak Bhandar.

Seneviratne, H.L. 1978. *Rituals of the Kandyan state*. Cambridge Studies in Social Anthropology, 22. Cambridge; New York: Cambridge University Press.

Sharma, S., M. Joachimski, M. Sharma, H.J. Tobschall, I.B. Singh, M.S. Chauhan, and G. Morgenroth 2004. Lateglacial and Holocene environmental changes in Ganga plain, Northern India. *Quaternary Science Reviews* 23 (1–2): 145–59.

Sharma, S., M.M. Joachimski, H.J. Tobschall, I.B. Singh, C. Sharma, and M.S. Chauhan 2006. Correlative evidences of monsoon variability, vegetation change and human inhabitation in Sanai lake deposit: Ganga plain, India. *Current science* 90 (7): 973–8.

Sherwin-White, Susan M., and Amelie Kuhrt 1993. *From Samarkhand to Sardis: a new approach to the Seleucid Empire*. London: Duckworth.

Shinnie, P.L. 1967. *Meroe; a civilization of the Sudan*. Ancient peoples and places, v. 55. New York: F.A. Praeger.

Shoshani, Jeheskel, and John F. Eisenberg 1982. Elephas maximus. *Mammalian species* 182: 1–8.

Singh, Sarva Daman 1963. The elephant and the Aryans. *Journal of the Royal Asiatic Society of Great Britain and Ireland*.

——— 1965. *Ancient Indian warfare with special reference to the Vedic period*. Leiden: E.J. Brill.

Singh, Upinder 2010. Politics, violence and war in Kāmandaka's *Nītisāra*. *Indian economic and social history review* 47 (1): 29–62.

Skinner, G. William n.d. *Marketing and social structure in rural China*. Tucson: Association for Asian Studies. Reprinted from *The Journal of Asian Studies* 1964–5.

Smith, T.M., and Robert Leo Smith 2009. *Elements of ecology*. 7th ed. San Francisco, CA: Pearson Benjamin Cummings.

Smith, Vincent Arthur 1924. *The early history of India from 600 B.C. to the Muhammadan conquest*. 4th ed. Oxford: Clarendon Press.

Soar, Micaela 2007. Board games and backgammon in ancient Indian sculpture. In *Ancient board games in perspective*, ed. Irving L. Finkel, pp. 177–231. London: British Museum Press.

Sontheimer, Günther-Dietz 2004. *Essays on religion, literature and law*. New Delhi: Indira Gandhi National Centre for the Arts and Manohar Publishers.

Sparreboom, M. 1985. *Chariots in the Veda*. Memoirs of the Kern Institute, no. 3. Leiden: E.J. Brill.

Spate, O.H.K., and A.T.A. Learmonth 1967. *India and Pakistan: a general and regional geography*. 3rd ed. revised and completely reset. London: Methuen.

Srinivasa Iyengar, K.R., ed. 1983. *Asian variations in Ramayana: papers presented at the International Seminar on "Variations in Ramayana in Asia: Their Cultural, Social, and Anthropological Significance", New Delhi, January 1981*. New Delhi: Sahitya Akademi.

Stebbing, Edward Percy 1922. *The forests of India*. London: J. Lane.

Sukumar, R. 1989. *The Asian elephant: ecology and management*. Cambridge Studies in Applied Ecology and Resource Management. Cambridge; New York: Cambridge University Press.

——— 2011. *The story of Asia's elephants*. Mumbai: Marg.

Supomo, S. 1993. *Bhāratayuddha: an old Javanese poem and its Indian sources*. Śata-piṭaka Series, 373. New Delhi: International Academy of Indian Culture and Aditya Prakashan.

Surovell, Todd, Nicole Waguespack, P. Jeffrey Brantingham, and George C. Frison 2005. Global archaeological evidence for proboscidean overkill. In *Proceedings of the National Academy of Sciences of the United States of America*, vol. 102, no. 17 (April 26), pp. 6231–36.

Taylor, Paul Michael and Lorraine V. Aragon 1991. *Beyond the Java Sea: art of Indonesia's outer islands*. Washington, D.C.: New York: National Museum of Natural History, Smithsonian Institution; H.N. Abrams.

Tennent, James Emerson 1867. *The wild elephant and the method of capturing and taming it in Ceylon*. London: Longman, Green.

Toke Gale, U 1974. *Burmese timber elephant*. Rangoon, Burma: Trade Corp.

Trautmann, Thomas R. 1971. *Kauṭilya and the Arthaśāstra; a statistical investigation of the authorship and evolution of the text*. Leiden: Brill.

——— 1973. Consanguineous marriage in Pali literature. *Journal of the American Oriental Society* 93: 158–80.

——— 1982. Elephants and the Mauryans. In *India: history and thought. Essays in honour of A.L. Basham*, ed. S.N. Mukherjee, pp. 254–81. Calcutta: Subarnarekha. Reprinted in Trautmann, *The clash of chronologies: ancient India in the modern world* (New Delhi: Yoda, 2009), pp. 229–54, and in *India's environmental history*, ed. Mahesh Rangarajan and K. Sivaramakrishnan (New Delhi: Permanent Black, 2012), pp. 152–81.

——— 2009. *The clash of chronologies: ancient India in the modern world*. New Perspectives on Indian Pasts. New Delhi: Yoda Press.

——— 2012. *Arthashastra: the science of wealth*. New Delhi: Allen Lane.

——— forthcoming. Toward a deep history of mahouts. *Rethinking human-elephant relations in South Asia*, Piers Locke, ed. New Delhi: Oxford University Press.

Tregear, T. R. 1966. *A geography of China*. Chicago: Aldine Pub. Co.

Troncoso, Victor Alonso 2013. The Diadochi and the zoology of king-ship: the elephants. In *After Alexander: the time of the Diadochi (323–281 BC)*, ed. Victor Alonso Toncoso and Edward M. Anson (Oxford and Oakville: Oxbow Books), pp. 254–70.

Tucker, Richard P. 2011. *A forest history of India*. New Delhi; Thousand Oaks: Sage.

Turner, R.L. 1966. *A comparative dictionary of the Indo-Aryan languages*. London; New York: Oxford University Press.

Uno, Kevin T., Jay Quade, Daniel C. Fisher, George Wittemyer, Ian Douglas-Hamilton, Samuel Andanje, Patrick Omondi, Moses Litoroh, and Thure E. Cerling 2013. Bomb-curve radiocarbon measurement of recent biologic tissues and applications to wildlife forensics and stable isotope (paleo)ecology. *Proceedings of the National Academy of Sciences*, doi/10.1073/pnas.1302226110: 1–6.

Varadarajaiyer, E.S. 1945. *The elephant in the Tamil land*. Annamalai

University Tamil Series, 8. Annamalainagar: Annamalai University.

Varma, Surendra 2013. Gentle giants on the move. *Sanctuary Asia* (October).

——— 2014. *Captive elephants in India: ecology, management and welfare*. Compassion Unlimited Plus Action (CUPA) and Asian Nature Conservation Foundation (ANCF), Bangalore, India.

Varma, Surendra, P. Anur Reddy, S.R. Sujata, Suparna Ganguly, and Rajendra Hasbhavi 2008. *Captive elephants of Karnataka: an investigation into population status, management and welfare significance*. Elephants in Captivity: CUPA/ANCF Technical Report, no. 3. Bangalore: Compassion Unlimited Plus Action (CUPA) and Asian Nature Conservation Foundation (ANCF).

Varma, Surendra, P. Anur Reddy, S.R. Sujata, Suparna Ganguly, and Rajendra Hasbhavi 2009. *Captive elephants of Andaman Islands: an investigation into the population status, management and welfare significance*. Elephants in Captivity: CUPA/ANCF Technical Report, no. 11. Bangalore: Compassion Unlimited Plus Action (CUPA) and Asian Nature Conservation Foundation (ANCF).

Varma, Surendra, S.R. Sujata, N. Kalaivanan, T. Rajamanickam, M.C. Sathyanarayana, R. Thirumurugan, S. Thangaraj Panneerselvam, N.S. Manoharan, V. Shankaralingam, D. Boominathan and N. Mahanraj 2008. *Captive elephants of Tamil Nadu: an investigation into the status, management and welfare significance*. Elephants in Captivity: CUPA/ANCF Technical Report, no. 5. Bangalore: Compassion Unlimited Plus Action (CUPA) and Asian Nature Conservation Foundation (ANCF).

Varma, Surendra, Suparna Ganguly, S.R. Sujata, and Sandeep K. Jain 2008. *Wandering elephants of Punjab: an investigation of the population status, management and welfare significance*. Elephants in Captivity: CUPA/ANCF Technical Report, no. 2. Bangalore: Compassion Unlimited Plus Action (CUPA) and Asian Nature Conservation Foundation (ANCF).

Varma, Surendra, George Verghese, David Abraham, S.R. Sujata, and Rajendra Hasbhavi 2009. *Captive elephants of Andaman Islands: an investigation into the population status, management and welfare significance*. Elephants in Captivity: CUPA/ANCF Technical Report no. 11. Bangalore: Compassion Unlimited Plus Action (CUPA) and Asian Nature Conservation Foundation (ANCF).

Vickery, Michael 1998. *Society, economics, and politics in pre-Angkor Cambodia: the 7th–8th centuries*. Tokyo, Japan: The Centre for East Asian Cultural Studies for UNESCO, The Toyo Bunko.

——— 2003. Funan revisited: deconstructing the ancients. *Bulletin de l'Ecole française d'Extrême-Orient* 90–1: 101–43.

Wales, H.G. Quaritch 1952. *Ancient South-East Asian warfare*. London: B. Quaritch.

Wen Huanran 1995. *Zhongguo li shi shi qi zhi wu yu dong wu bian qian yan jiu*. Wen Rongsheng, ed. First ed. Chongqing: Chongqing chubanshe (*The shifts of plants and animals in China during the historical period*. Chongqing: Chongqing Publishing). The portions dealing with elephants, translated for me by Charles Sanft, are:

Chapter 15, pp. 185–201. Wen Huanran, Jiang Yingliang, He Yeheng, and Gao Yaoting. Initial research on Chinese wild elephants in the historical period.

Chapter 16, pp. 203–9. Wen Huanran, ed. Wen Rongsheng. Reexamining the distribution of wild elephants in China during the historical period.

Chapter 17, pp. 211–19. Wen Huanran, ed. Wen Rongsheng. Reexamining the shifts in the wild elephant's range during the historical period in China.

Wheeler, Robert Eric Mortimer 1968. *Early India and Pakistan: to Ashoka*. Rev. ed. Ancient peoples and places, v. 12. New York: Praeger.

Wink, André 1997. Kings, slaves and elephants. Ch. 3 in *Al-Hind: the making of the Indo-Islamic world*, vol. 2: The Slave Kings and the Islamic conquest, 11th–13th centuries, pp. 79–110. Leiden, New York, Köln: Brill.

Wiseman, D.J. 1952. A new stela of Aššur-naṣir-pal II. *Iraq* 14 (1): 24–44.

Williams, James Howard 1950. *Elephant Bill*. 1st American ed. Garden City, NY: Doubleday.

Wilson, H.H. 1855. *A glossary of judicial and revenue terms: and of useful words occurring in official documents relating to the administration of the government of British India, from the Arabic, Persian, Hindustání, Sanskrit, Hindí, Bengálí, Uriya, Maráthi, Guzaráthí, Telegu, Karnáta, Tamil, Malayálam, and other languages*. London: W.H. Allen and Co.

Woodbury, Angus Munn 1954. *Principles of general ecology*. New York: McGraw Hill.

Woolley, Leonard, and Max Mallowan 1976. *Ur excavations,* vol. VII*: The old Babylonian period*, ed. T.C. Mitchell. British Museum Publications.

Worster, Donald 1994. *Nature's economy: a history of ecological ideas*. 2nd ed. Studies in environment and history. Cambridge [England]; New York: Cambridge University Press.

Wrangham, Richard W. 2009. *Catching fire: how cooking made us human*. New York: Basic Books.

Yalden, D.W., M.J. Largen, and D. Kock 1986. Catalogue of the mammals of Ethiopia. 6. Perissodactyla, Proboscidea, Huyracoidea, Lagomorpha, Tululidentata, Sirena and Cetacea. *Monitore zoologico italiano/ Italian journal of zoology* N.S. supplemento 21: 33–103.

Young, Dwight 2005. *Dear Mr. President: letters to the Oval Office from the files of the National Archives*. Washington, D.C.: National Geographic.

Yule, Henry 1968. *Hobson-Jobson; a glossary of colloquial Anglo-Indian words and phrases, and of kindred terms, etymological, historical, geographical and discursive*. 2nd ed. Delhi: Munshiram Manoharlal.

Zheng, Dekun 1982. *Studies in Chinese archaeology*. Studies Series / Institute of Chinese Studies, Centre for Chinese Archaeology and Art, 3. Hong Kong: Chinese University Press.

Zimmermann, Francis 1987. *The jungle and the aroma of meats: an ecological theme in Hindu medicine*. Comparative Studies of Health Systems and Medical Care. Berkeley: University of California Press.

Zoetmulder, P.J. 1974. *Kalangwan: a survey of old Javanese literature*. Koninklijk Instituut voor Taal-, Land- en Volkenkunde. Translation Series, 16. The Hague: Martinus Nijhoff.

Index

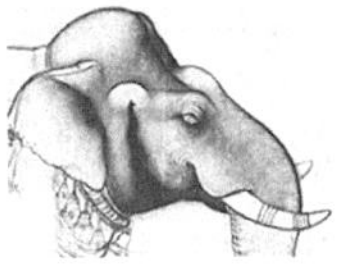